Santa Clara
County
Free Library

REFERENCE

 5816

Western Frontiersmen Series
VIII

KIRBY BENEDICT
From a tintype in the family album of the judge's grandniece,
Cora Benedict Page of Kent, Connecticut.

KIRBY BENEDICT
Frontier Federal Judge

An account of legal and judicial development
in the Southwest, 1853-1874, with special
reference to the Indian, slavery, social
and political affairs, journalism, and
a chapter on circuit riding with
Abraham Lincoln in Illinois

by
AURORA HUNT

Author of *The Army of the Pacific,* and
James H. Carleton, Frontier Dragoon

THE ARTHUR H. CLARK COMPANY
Glendale, California
1961

Contents

PREFACE 11

THE YOUNG BARRISTER 15

A FLEDGLING POLITICIAN 25

CIRCUIT RIDERS IN ILLINOIS 33

A FEDERAL JUDGE IN NEW MEXICO 49

CHIEF JUSTICE 69

DUE PROCESS OF LAW IN THE INDIAN PUEBLOS . . 89

PEONAGE AND SLAVERY 107

THE SUPREME COURT DECISIONS OF JUDGE BENEDICT . 121

REVISION AND CODIFICATION OF NEW MEXICO LAWS . 129

WASHINGTON CORRESPONDENCE 133

CIVIC AND SOCIAL AFFAIRS 173

LOSS OF OFFICE AND PRESTIGE 183

NEW VENTURES FOLLOW DISBARMENT 191

THE JUDGE BECOMES A JOURNALIST 207

BEFORE THE TRIBUNALS OF MAN AND GOD . . . 221

APPENDIX: BENEDICT'S SUPREME COURT DECISIONS . 235

BIBLIOGRAPHY 247

INDEX 259

Illustrations

Portrait of Kirby Benedict . . . . *Frontispiece*

Saint Andrews Episcopal Church, Kent, Connecticut   19

Courthouse at Paris, Illinois 37

The Stolen Portrait of San José 95

Land Grant to Acoma Pueblo, 1689 96

Air-view of Acoma Pueblo 97

View in Pueblo Acoma 97

Laguna Pueblo 98

Letter to Lincoln, June 2, 1861 147

Burro Loads of Wood 148

Bird's-eye View of Santa Fe 197

Masthead of the New Mexico Union . . . 215

Map of New Mexico Territory, 1855 257

Preface

The blossom cannot tell what becomes of its perfume and no
man can tell what becomes of his influence that rolls away from
him on its mission. The onward sweep of time rapidly winds
the shroud of oblivion around most of our frontier lawyers so it
becomes a duty to preserve their names and deeds for posterity.
No class of men was more influential than the lawyers when the
United States acquired possession of New Mexico. They were
by no means a common order of men either in character or public
service.

Thus wrote Kirby Benedict while editor and proprietor of the *Santa Fe Weekly Union* in 1873. Previously
he lived in Illinois where he served as probate judge of
Macon County, and was a member of the house of
representatives of the state legislature. As a practicing
attorney he rode the Eighth Judicial Circuit with young
Abraham Lincoln, Stephen A. Douglas, David Davis,
and other prominent lawyers.

While in New Mexico he held the office of United
States associate justice for one term and chief justice
for two terms. In his Concord carriage he traveled
hundreds of miles between the county courthouses to
weigh the evidence presented, explain the difference
between the laws of Mexico and the United States,
carefully instruct the jurors, and insist upon correct
translation from English and Spanish. Then when the
verdict was rendered, he pronounced sentence accord-

ing to the laws in force at that period although his New England conscience may have revolted against some of them.

Many of the old district court records have been destroyed by fire; some have been misplaced but there may be others that eventually will be discovered. Those still extant are deposited in the archives of the various county courthouses but each county does not always possess its own records. They are reposing on some top shelf or in the basement of a neighboring county courthouse. However, enough remain to portray the services of these early lawyers, especially Kirby Benedict who was a descendant of one of the early colonial families.

Across the nation, from Connecticut to California is a multitude of persons, too numerous to name individually, to whom I am greatly indebted for research assistance on this work. To them I extend my sincere thanks.

Judge Benedict's grandniece, Mrs. Cora Benedict Page, and Miss Elizabeth Hopson, both of Kent, Connecticut, have been able to furnish details about the Benedict family. Translations of Spanish documents and papers have been made by Peter Ortega, B. J. Whitten, and H. B. Moxley. The National Archives, Washington, has furnished microfilms of over three hundred pages of manuscript documents.

For the Illinois period of Kirby Benedict's life, much help has been rendered by persons at the Chicago Historical Society, Illinois State Historical Library, public libraries at Decatur and Tuscola, the Masonic Grand Lodge, and Prairie Lodge no. 77 at Paris, Illinois, the office of the Illinois Supreme Court, and Russell J. Crossman of the Tuscola National Bank.

The public library at Sunbury, Ohio, and D. C. Hoover of the Sunbury Savings and Loan Company have helpfully contributed, as has Mr. Paul Downing of New York, who supplied information about Judge Benedict's Concord coach.

In New Mexico special commendation is due, for help and hospitable cooperation, to the staffs and personnel of the Museum of New Mexico, the State Law Library, The Kit Carson House, Masonic Grand Lodge at Albuquerque, and Montezuma Lodge no. 1, the University of New Mexico Library, Las Cruces Public Library, the district courts of the counties of Santa Fe, Valencia, and Doña Ana, and to the office of the State Corporation Commissioner. Judge Luis Armijo of Las Vegas, and Jennie Avery of Santa Fe provided valuable assistance.

Helpful aid was given by those at the Arizona Pioneers' Historical Society, the Arizona Department of Library and Archives, and the Fisk Public Library of Natchez, Mississippi. It is difficult to express adequate appreciation for continued assistance from the staffs of the Huntington Library, the Public Library and the County Law Library of Los Angeles, the Bancroft Library, and Whittier College Library.

And lastly I highly commend and sincerely appreciate the many hours of efficient work by my secretary, Miss Mary Thibadeau, and the help of Helen E. Moore, reader and critic.

The Young Barrister

Kirby Benedict, associate of Abraham Lincoln in Illinois and later federal judge in New Mexico, was born in Kent, Connecticut, on November 23, 1810. He was the youngest of eight children of John and Chloe Benedict.[1]

His boyhood passed uneventfully in the quiet village on the banks of the Housatonic. There were fish to be caught in the river as it rippled its summer waters and winter cataracts through the valley that lay green and serene between the bordering hills. Chestnuts ripened in the fall when the maple trees flashed their splendor and Mount Algo offered her gentle slopes for young legs to climb.

The elementary schools of Kent provided ample opportunities for young Kirby as they were in session nearly the entire year. Male instructors were employed during the winter, but in the summer the women assumed that duty while the men harvested the wheat, rye, Indian corn, flax, and buckwheat or repaired the chestnut rail fences and the bridges that had been damaged by the winter storms.

Among the early remembrances of Kirby, was the arrival of long-awaited letters from his oldest brother Benjamin and sister Maria who had joined the Con-

---

[1] Benjamin, born in 1790; Stephen, 1792; John, 1795; Delilah, 1799; Maria, 1800; Grandison, 1804; Germon, 1806; and Kirby, 1810.

necticut pioneers in the great western surge to the old
Northwest. Benjamin was twenty years older than
Kirby and by the year 1822, he was married and owned
land near Delaware, Ohio.

The migration of the first Benedict family began
generations previous in France. Subsequent moves were
to Germany, Holland, and England. Thomas,[2] the
progenitor of the family in America, was born in Not-
tingham, England, in 1617 and when he reached his
twenty-first birthday, he sailed for America.

Soon after the arrival of Thomas Benedict in the
American colonies, he married his stepsister, Mary
Bridgham, who came on the same ship with him. They
became the parents of five sons and four daughters. All
were born on Long Island which was at that time
claimed by the Dutch. Later the Benedict family migrated to Connecticut where some of their descendants
still reside.

During the first century in the colonies, the members
of the Benedict family engaged in agriculture but in
the succeeding years their names are found in the early
records as ministers and lawyers. The first lawyer to
bear the name Benedict was Thaddeus of Redding,
Connecticut. Another, Noah Benedict, graduated from
Yale College in 1788 and practiced in Litchfield which
was a short distance from Kent.[3]

Although Litchfield was then an isolated town with
access only on horseback, or over rough roads by stage,
it was the site of the first law school in the American
colonies. Judge Tappan Reeve from Princetown estab-

---

[2] *Genealogy and Family History of State of Connecticut,* ed. Wm. R. Cutter
and staff, pp. 489-492.

[3] Henry M. Benedict, *Genealogy of the Benedict Family in America,* pp.
256, 272.

lished this famous school and the names of many noted lawyers may be found in the register of students, 1789-1833.[4]

One of the first lawyers of Kent was Barzillai Slosson[5] who was born there December 27, 1769. He graduated from Yale College in 1791 but instead of attending the Litchfield Law School, he chose to read law under Cotton Smith. After completing his study he opened an office in Kent.

The United States Census of 1790 reveals that, although the population of Connecticut was only some two hundred thirty-eight thousand, there were 120 lawyers. What influence the proximity of the law school and the lawyer of Kent had on Kirby Benedict may be judged by his experience in the years that followed.

When he was twenty-one, he began his westward journey to Ohio. Perhaps his widowed mother accompanied him as she spent the last years of her life with her daughter Maria (Mrs. James Crawford) near Delaware, Ohio.[6] That state received emigrants from Connecticut as early as 1803, but settlement was retarded by the War of 1812 and the hostility of the Indians. Furthermore, the sale of public lands fluctuated as the national economy rose or declined. Speculation and panic did not affect the thrifty settlers[7] from

---

[4] Samuel H. Fisher, *The Litchfield Law School, 1775-1833.*

[5] Mabel Seymour, "Barzillai Slosson, Lawyer of Kent," *Connecticut Tercentenary,* no. 47.

[6] John Benedict, father of Kirby, died Dec. 14, 1830; Chloe Benedict, his wife, is buried in the oldest section of Berkshire Cemetery, near Berkshire, Delaware County, Ohio, on the south side of U.S. route 36, three miles west of Sunbury. She is buried in the same plot with her daughter Maria Benedict Crawford.

[7] Lois K. M. Rosenbury, "Migration from Connecticut after 1800," *Connecticut Tercentenary,* nos. 28, 54.

Connecticut materially, as numbered among them were prosperous farmers, millers, merchants, and lawyers.

Kirby Benedict had not gone west to acquire land but to fulfill a latent desire to become a lawyer. He did not remain long in Ohio and soon was steamboating down the Mississippi to Natchez to study under the eminent lawyer, John Anthony Quitman. There were two hundred thirty-one steamboats on the river at that time. One of them, the side-wheeler "Arab," [8] was owned by Albert D. Benedict who belonged to another branch of the Benedict family.

John Anthony Quitman [9] had studied law under Henry Brush of Chillicothe and later moved to Delaware, Ohio. It is quite probable that Quitman met Benjamin Benedict who may have influenced his younger brother, Kirby, to study under this lawyer. Quitman was licensed to practice law in Ohio on December 4, 1821, but soon left the state to enter the office of William B. Griffith in Natchez. There he began his career as lawyer, state legislator, congressman, Mexican War hero, and eventually filibuster.

Under the tutelage of lawyer Quitman, a man of talent and volatile temperament, Kirby Benedict began the study of law as well as the French and Spanish languages.[10] Twenty years later, when appointed federal judge in New Mexico, his knowledge of Spanish was an important asset.

---

[8] *Deed Records of Adams County, Natchez, Miss.* Book U, (July 3, 1833), p. 206. William M. Lytle, "Merchant Steam Vessels of the United States, 1807-1868," *Steamboat Hist. Soc. of Amer. Pub.*, no. 6. The "Arab" was built in Cincinnati 1831.

[9] J. F. H. Clairborne, *Life and Correspondence of John Anthony Quitman,* vol. 1; Harnett T. Kane, *Natchez on the Mississippi,* 220-235. Quitman was owner of Monmouth Plantation.

[10] John W. Smith, *History of Macon County.*

Saint Andrews Episcopal Church, Kent, Connecticut

The Housatonic River flows between the church and 1200-foot Mount Algo in the background. See text page 15. From John Warner Barber's

Between Natchez and his own home on the Housatonic in Connecticut, there was a marked difference. The contrast was not only between the climate of north and south but in the entire social structure. The Mason and Dixon Line already had been designated, and South Carolina had passed her Nullification Act.

On the bluff overlooking the Mississippi were the mansions of the wealthy planters. Here luxuriant gardens were cultivated by their slaves; in his Connecticut garden young Kirby had pulled the weeds. Even the reverberating sounds were strange. Negro mammies sang soft lullabies to little children while intermingled with the whistle of the steamboats was the lusty "Roustabout" song of the river men.

> Ducks play cards and chicken drink wine;
> And de monkey grow on de grape vine;
> Corn starch pudding and tapioca pie,
> Oh! de gray cat pick out de black cat's eye.[11]

Underlying the plaintive harmony of the negroes, Kirby sensed the plight of the captives. Seared so deep in his memory were the scenes that he never forgot and became the champion of freedom for the slaves when the great struggle began.

He was admitted to the bar in Mississippi but since the early records have not been preserved, the exact date cannot be determined. It did precede October 23, 1834, when he married Charlotte Curtis of Delaware County, Ohio. Her parents, Carlos and Mary Curtis, had migrated from Connecticut when Charlotte was but one year old. After living near Delaware City for

---

[11] Herbert and Edward Quick, *Mississippi Steamboatin'*, 247.

almost a quarter of a century, the Curtis family moved to Round Prairie near Springfield, Illinois.[12]

Kirby and Charlotte, the bride and groom, also sought a new location; not a farm, but a frontier town where a young and ambitious lawyer could prosper. They first settled in Sangamon County then moved to Decatur, Macon County, in March 1836.

The future prospects of Decatur were encouraging. Illinois had inaugurated an extravagant program of "internal improvement" that year and Decatur was selected as the site for the junction of the Northern Cross and Illinois Central railroads. Speculation was rampant for a few years.

Macon County was established by an act of the Illinois legislature, approved on January 19, 1829. A twenty-acre tract of prairie with no inhabitants, houses, or even a footpath, was named Decatur and made the county seat. By the end of the first year, a few log houses, a store, tavern, and courthouse were built. This first one and a half story log courthouse was twenty feet square and contained a large fireplace. The roughly-hewn logs were notched, chinked with concrete, and laid on a stone foundation. John Hanks, the cousin of Abraham Lincoln's mother, received the sum of $9.87 for "chinking and daubing" the building.

The first term of the court was held May 6, 1830. During this springtime, twenty-one year old Abraham Lincoln with his family drove through the village and settled on the Sangamon River a few miles west.[13]

12 William E. Nelson, "Dr. Ira Curtis," *Ill. Hist. Soc., Jour.* vol. v, (Oct., 1912). *U.S. Census. Ill., 1850* (Microfilm Los Angeles Public Library).

13 Mabel E. Richmond, *Centennial History of Decatur and Macon County, Ill.,* pp. 76, 141, 147.

The rude courthouse was seven years old when Kirby Benedict was admitted to the Illinois Bar, September 5, 1837. One year previous, September 9, 1836, another young lawyer, Abraham Lincoln, received his license.[14] The two young barristers soon met when they rode the Eighth Judicial Circuit and a lifelong friendship developed. Sometimes they defended the same client but on other occasions, argued against each other.

Benedict was the second resident lawyer to open an office in Decatur. Jerome Rinaldo Gorin was his partner. The same year that Benedict was admitted to the bar, he accepted the office of probate judge of Macon County and held that office for six years. He was also president of the Decatur Board of Trustees and it was his duty to help solve some of the problems of that ten-year-old prairie town.

Gleanings from the early district court records yield scant information. The reasons are varied. One is that at the fourteenth session of the legislature, on February 21, 1845, an act was passed which provided that the clerks of the district courts no longer would be required to make complete records unless specifically ordered by the court and then only if paid for by the litigants. The passing of more than a century obscures the many other causes for the loss of these valuable papers. The records of the supreme court are extant.

The publicity accorded Lincoln's activities on the judicial circuit has overshadowed those of his contemporaries. Yet by careful scrutiny, fragments of information may be pieced together to provide an inkling of the attorneys who rode the circuit with him.

---

[14] Records of the Illinois Supreme Court, Springfield, Ill.

On one occasion, Abraham Lincoln, Stephen A. Douglas, and Kirby Benedict together, defended Spencer Turner who had been indicted for murder May 22, 1840, in the district court at Clinton, DeWitt County.[15] David B. Campbell and Wells Colton represented the state. Turner was charged, "for not having the fear of God before his eyes but being moved and seduced by the instigation of the Devil." He had attacked Matthew K. Martin with a stick of wood and inflicted a mortal wound on his right temple. Lincoln entered a plea of not guilty to the indictment and with the assistance of Douglas and Benedict convinced the jury of Turner's innocence.

How these early lawyers eked out a living is almost incomprehensible. The chief justice received an annual salary of $1,000, a circuit attorney $250. The fees of the probate justices were exceedingly meager. For administering an oath, twelve and a half cents was charged; for swearing a jury, twenty-five cents; examining inventories and bills of sales, fifty cents; and for issuing letters of guardianship and recording same, one dollar. For Benedict, there was promise of extra income soon.

---

[15] De Witt County was organized 1849 with the county seat at Clinton and was included in the Eighth Judicial District. This was Lincoln's first case in Clinton.

A Fledgling Politician

The spring of 1844 brought more than the resurgence of verdure to the prairie of Macon County. The election of members of the state legislature was scheduled for midsummer. Candidates of the Whigs and the Locofoco [1] political parties challenged their opponents in public meetings where taxes, the tariff, and internal improvements were debated.

Kirby Benedict was a Locofoco candidate to represent Macon and Piatt Counties in the house. At Decatur, on March 16, 1844, he engaged in a debate on the tariff with E. O. Smith, a Whig. Benedict assailed the tariff while Smith defended it.

A letter to the editor of the *Sangamon Journal*,[2] reveals the opinion of one correspondent who was present at the meeting. He asserted that, although the friends of Benedict considered him one of the ablest and most talented attorneys in Illinois, such a failure to convince an audience never before had been witnessed; and that instead of logical argument, the judge resorted to facial contortions and epithets. The other

---

[1] *Dict. of Amer. Hist.*, III, (1940), 292. Locofoco was a term applied to the National Democratic Party from the year 1837 until 1860. The name originated during a meeting of the Democrats in Tammany Hall, on Oct. 29, 1835, when the radical Democrats gained control of the city caucus by lighting candles with locofoco matches after the conservatives had endeavored to break up the meeting by turning off the gas lights. The National Republican Party was then designated the Whigs.

[2] *Sangamon Journal*, March 8, 1844. *Ibid.*, Aug. 15, 1844, election returns.

candidate, farmer Smith, marshalled a strong array of facts to support his statements. The debate commenced at eleven in the morning and continued until ten in the evening. In spite of the opinions expressed in the *Journal,* Benedict won the election and served for one term.

When the House was organized, Kirby Benedict was assigned to the judicial committee which consisted of eight members.[3] He was also a member of the committee to escort Governor Thomas Ford to the joint session of the legislature which had been convened to hear his message.[4]

In order to guide the legislators in their deliberations, the governor described the conditions that had existed during the past two years. The crops had not been as abundant on account of disastrous floods. Forty pounds of butter at from five to eight cents a pound would only pay for eight yards of calico to dress the wife of the farmer; ten bushels of corn would scarcely outweigh the value of eight pounds of sugar; and a hog had to be a large one to liquidate the price of a pair of boots.

His message contained recommendations for more schools, a special report on the Mormon crisis in Hancock County, and a plea for immediate revision of the laws. No adequate change had been made for twelve years although the previous legislature had repealed forty-seven laws and revived seven.

When the laws were first enacted, the state was a

---

[3] Judicial Committee: Kirby Benedict, Richard Yates, Julius Manning, Stephen T. Logan, E. S. Janny, H. P. Boyakin, Peter Lott, N. D. Strong.
[4] *Jour. of the House of Representatives, Ill., 1844-1845,* Jan. 2, 1845.

wilderness and the hardy pioneers found rifle and strong arm more efficient protection than the law. They had little time for legislation as they contended with the untried soil and climate. Yet under circumstances so disadvantageous, the laws passed reflect the sagacity and legal ability of those who framed them.

The legislature adopted a resolution containing the provision that revision of the laws be under the supervision of a committee composed of members of both houses. Governor Ford appointed Mason Brayer,[5] personally to make the necessary revisions and submit them to the legislative committee for approval.

Those who were appointed to serve on the committee were Senator David Davis from McLean County, Richard Yates, and Kirby Benedict from the House, together with thirteen others. This experience was of benefit to Kirby Benedict twenty years later when he was appointed as a member of a committee to revise and codify the laws of New Mexico.

Kirby Benedict supported the governor in his economy drive. At a public meeting in Decatur, his constituents adopted resolutions objecting to an increase of taxation for any purpose whatsoever; that there should not be the appropriation of another dollar for the completion of the Illinois-Michigan Canal unless retrenchments were made; and that a fifty per cent reduction be made in the salaries of all state officers. The members of the House then received $3.00 a day and an extra

---

[5] Mason Brayer, 1813-1895; admitted to New York bar; editor *Buffalo Bulletin, Louisville Advertiser,* and *Illinois Journal;* practiced law in Ill. 1842; held a special commission from Governor Ford to settle the differences between the Mormons at Nauvoo and their hostile neighbors; served in the Civil War.

allowance for travel exceeding twenty miles. These resolutions were duly presented to the House by Benedict and referred to the committee on finance.

The previous legislature had reduced the state expenditures by repealing the act which provided for the payment of bounties for wolf scalps. During the years 1840-1842, the sum paid by the treasury amounted to $12,037. The next two years the wolf hunters received only $4,057.50. This was not enough to relieve the shortage in the treasury.

The cattle men and farmers objected to the repeal of this measure. As a result of successful lobbying, the legislature enacted a new Wolf Scalp Bounty Law by which a certificate would be issued for a scalp provided that the ears were attached and that it was presented within ninety days after the wolf was killed. Furthermore, an oath was required. The law provided that the certificates would be accepted in payment of taxes.

As representative from Macon and Piatt Counties, Benedict introduced a petition from the citizens to declare the Sangamon River navigable and to provide for its improvement. For the benefit of the entire state, he introduced a resolution that the members of Congress, "be instructed and urged at all suitable times and in all judicious modes, the propriety of granting the state of Illinois each alternate section of land for six miles on each side of the Northern Cross Railroad."

Elementary schools and colleges received much attention during this session of the legislature. At that period the schools of higher education were classified as seminaries or academies which were privately owned and incorporated by legislative acts. While Benedict served in the House, thirteen schools were incorporated and the charter of Rush Medical College[6] amended. To encourage the education of the youth of Illinois, schools, churches and their camp grounds were exempt from taxation.

Road building was an important item on the legislative agenda. The labor problem was solved by the enactment of the Road Labor Law which provided that every able-bodied man between the ages of twenty-one and fifty years should contribute not more than two days work or less than one to building state roads.

Many of the privately-owned roads were constructed of planks and financed by tolls. Before the roads could be built or operated, it was necessary to obtain a charter from the legislature. The acts of incorporation carefully specified the amount of toll for various distances for man or beast. Toll gates were stationed at five mile intervals. A man on horseback could travel five miles for two cents; if he drove a one-horse wagon or buggy, the price was eight cents; if two horses, ten cents; four horses, twelve and a half cents; droves of horses were charged one cent a head; and hogs, goats and sheep, one-fourth cent. The price was doubled for ten miles. When the snow fell, sleighs were permitted to glide along at half price.

These "Plank Road Companies" were incorporated for a period of twenty years or more. The capital stock ranged from $200,000 to $500,000 and shares were priced at $25 each.

The most controversial issue before the legislature was the repeal of the charter of the Mormon city of

---

[6] Rush Medical College incorporated 1837; first graduating class 1848.

Nauvoo, Hancock County. In the spring of 1844, Joseph Smith, the Mormon prophet, and his brother Hyrum were murdered as a result of a riot. Although the citizens abhorred such violence, they did not condone some of the practices of the Mormons. When the measure was introduced into the House, Kirby Benedict was most vociferous in his denunciation of that religious sect.

He frequently made the headlines in the local newspapers. The *Republican,* under date of January 18, 1845, published a lengthy article about the controversy. A. W. Babbitt, who represented Hancock County,[7] argued in defense of the Mormon charter in accordance with written instructions from Mormon leaders.[8] When he had finished speaking, Benedict obtained the floor and occupied it until after candle lighting and the adjournment of the House. The news correspondent said that Benedict made one of the most forcible, withering, and convincing speeches that had been given during the entire session. He boldly claimed that he was in favor of the unconditional repeal of the charter on account of the flagrant abuses that had been perpetrated by the Mormons and which had been satisfactorily disclosed in the report of the commission on banks and corporations. He denied that he was governed by religious intolerance in his opposition to the charter but wished to prove that the leaders had selected the "cloak of religion" as a shield by which

---

[7] Hancock County had a population of 9,946 in 1840 and was allowed two representatives, A. W. Babbitt and J. B. Backentos.

[8] Private letter of Sarah W. Davis to her father, William P. Walker, January 28, 1845. David Davis MMS, Chicago Hist. Soc. Benedict copied the Mormon instructions for the amusement of his friends.

they more successfully could serve the devil and plunder the deluded masses over which they exercised unlimited control.

The speech was so well received that it brought applause from those in the gallery, which would have been repeated if the speaker had not warned that he would direct the sergeant-at-arms to clear the gallery.

Benedict declared that no man was more strongly wedded to his party and its principles than he. Yet he would prefer defeat rather than see his party cringe to the Mormons who held unheard-of powers in a free government.

An entire week was spent in arguing the Mormon question. The charter was repealed by a vote of 76 to 36.[9]

This speech was Benedict's political "swan song." It was proposed that he be a candidate from the Locofoco party for lieutenant governor in 1846. He failed to receive the nomination as it was quite evident that the Mormons would not vote for him.[10]

---

[9] *Jour. of the House of Representatives, Ill. 1844-1845.*
[10] *Sangamon Journal,* Feb. 26, 1846.

Circuit Riders in Illinois

Through the dust and heat of summer and the rain and mud of winter, the attorneys jogged along in horse and buggy or on horseback over the many miles of the Eighth Judicial District. Three months were required to visit the county seats of the fourteen counties. Twice a year they made the journey. Some of the cities were seventy miles apart but the average was approximately thirty miles.[1]

In their letters to their families, these pioneer attorneys have bequeathed an illuminating picture of their faithful services. A few excerpts from the letters of Judge David Davis reflect the light and shadow of that picture:[2]

> During the rainy days at Shelbyville, I read one novel called the *Polish Orphan,* a very old book which interested me greatly. The balance of the time, Judge Treat, Benedict, Thornton, and myself played whist to pass away the time. We thought that the rain would cease by Sunday morning and waited until then

---

[1] County seats, of the Eighth Judicial District of Ill.: Metamora, Pekin, Bloomington, Springfield, Mount Pulaski, Clinton, Taylorville, Decatur, Monticello, Urbana, Shelbyville, Sullivan, Danville, and Paris.

[2] David Davis MMS, Chicago Hist. Soc. Davis from Decatur to his wife in Bloomington, Oct. 27, 1847.

David Davis 1815-1886. Studied law at Yale Univ.; arrived in Bloomington 1836; practiced law until 1844; member State Legislature, 1844; State Constitutional Committee, 1847; judge of Eighth Judicial District Ill. 1848-1861; Lincoln appointed him to U.S. Supreme Court in 1862. In 1877 resigned as justice and elected U.S. Senator from Ill.; Pres. pro tem of Senate, 1881-1883.

before going to Moultrie twenty miles distant; but it rained Sunday morning and we rode through the rain all day. Sullivan, the county seat of Moultrie County, is a new place, not any better than Clinton.

The discomforts of travel during the spring term of court were equally annoying. The weather was hot and the horses suffered exceedingly. Benedict rode with Davis from Monticello to Urbana then to Danville. They made the journey from town to town in one day.[3] A month later Davis writes to his wife in Bloomington:

I left Decatur last Sunday morning with Benedict in my buggy in the rain and over a blind road and poor country to Taylorville, which is a new place but prettily laid out and tastefully arranged with trees and shrubs. We came to Springfield Tuesday evening over a good road and tomorrow I wend my way to Bloomington.[4]

The year 1849 was a restless year in the United States. Two major events had occurred; the acquisition of the vast territory to the West by the treaty with Mexico and the spreading of the news of the discovery of gold in California. Kirby Benedict took stock of the years he and Charlotte had lived in the prairie town of Decatur. The high expectations for the vast internal improvements had not materialized. There were then only a few more than 3,000 people in the entire Macon County. In a letter to Judge Davis, Benedict writes:

. . . Now, Davis, suppose I tell you that I should like, if circumstances are favorable, to go to California, not to dig out much gold, but to practice law permanently. Had I enough money at my command for such an enterprise, I surely would go. . .

[3] *Ibid.* Danville, May 7, 1848.
[4] *Ibid.* Springfield, June 9, 1848.

A second letter is a reply to one from Judge Davis:

Yours of last week came to hand and allow me to thank you for the expression of good wishes . . . and for your offer of pecuniary aid should a contingency occur requiring it.

As to California, I have no idea of going this coming season, if ever. My spirit of adventure is not sufficiently active to run me headlong upon any enterprise with the view of wealth. I do believe, however, that I would gather gold in California practicing law after the establishment of civil government, the laws, courts, etc. Every other good connected with the profession can be more permanently secured this side of the Sierra.

My view is on touring much. I intend, after the spring courts are over, to go and see how matters look. I am surely determined to leave this location. There is hardly anything to do here that cannot be done elsewhere. . . I am confident in my apparent destiny. I hope to arrange all my affairs so that I will be able, pecuniarily, to move from here without drawing upon the kindness of others for funds.

If, however, I shall find myself cramped so as to need temporary aid, I shall confidently let you know. I may want a few dollars for a short time and if so, I shall feel no hesitation in addressing your kindness and generosity. I shall, I trust, have my business so arranged so as not to tax my friends for any special assistance beyond a temporary loan of a few dollars which I should see the way to promptly return.[5]

Benedict concludes his letter by naming those who had sold their property and were fitting out for the gold country.

Kirby Benedict's friends by this time, had won distinction and been elected to public offices. Stephen A. Douglas was serving in the United States Senate; Abraham Lincoln and Edward D. Baker were members of the House of Representatives from Illinois.

---

[5] *Ibid.* Benedict to Davis, Decatur, Feb. 19, 26, 1849.

Although Benedict had served one term in the Illinois state legislature, his political career appeared to have ended. The success of his friends may have influenced his decision to move to Paris, Edgar County, where the population was almost four times greater than Macon County, and besides, his old friend Charles Emerson [6] had left Decatur for Paris.

He may have been influenced by his family also. The parents of his wife, Charlotte, had moved to Coles County near Oakland, a short distance from Paris. Kirby and Charlotte were then the parents of one daughter, Worthena Ceorda, who was born in 1848.

Benedict reached Paris, on November 22, 1849, to investigate the possibilities of moving his family there and opening a law office. In his letter to Judge Davis [7] he said that all the circumstances seemed favorable except locating a suitable house for the winter. He made arrangements to board at Mr. Earnest's who would provide a very good room for his family. He would share an office with Mr. Miller, the clerk of the court. Benedict then returned to Decatur to make arrangements to move to Paris as soon as possible. When he reached home, Charlotte told him that a letter from Kent, Connecticut, announced the death of his brother, John.

Less than six months after he moved to Paris, he was initiated into Prairie Lodge no. 77, A.F.A.M. on Feb-

---

[6] *History of Macon County,* p. 59. Charles Emerson was the first resident lawyer of Macon County; he came to Ill. in 1833; for one term attended Illinois College, then moved to Springfield to study law under Judge Keys; admitted to the bar and settled in Decatur in 1834. He resided in Paris from 1847 to 1850.

[7] David Davis MMS, Benedict to Davis, Paris, Nov. 23, 1849.

COURTHOUSE AT PARIS, ILLINOIS

Here Lincoln and Benedict argued their cases. In the upper story was the room of Prairie Lodge no. 77, A.F.A.M. See text page 36. Reproduced from a sketch by James E. Taylor, 1867, in his manuscript book.

Courtesy of the Illinois State Historical Society

ruary 25, 1850. He was the second Master of the new Lodge. The first meeting place was the second floor of the old brick courthouse which was erected in 1833.[8]

During the session of the Urbana circuit court in May, 1850, a correspondent of the *Illinois Citizen* was present and has furnished an appraisal of the abilities and personalities of the attorneys then present. His comparison between Abraham Lincoln and Kirby Benedict is quoted in part:

It is with reluctance that we introduce into this article the name of Kirby Benedict. This does not arise from any particular prejudice but from a consciousness of inability to do justice to our subject. We have never yet met Benedict's equal. He cannot be called a profound jurist, for having satisfied himself with the knowledge of the general principles of his profession, he is too impatient and fond of excitement to apply his energies to the acquisition of necessary legal details.

Abraham Lincoln and Kirby Benedict are the direct antitheses of each other and are as widely separated as heaven and earth. Benedict is easy, graceful and fascinating. Lincoln is rough, uncouth and unattractive. The former is kind, affable, and courteous; while the latter is stern, solemn, and unfamiliar.

Benedict has never been a deep thinker and, in his arguments, he depends almost entirely upon the resources of a rich and powerful imagination. As far as oratory is concerned, he transcends, by far, any member of the Bar on the Circuit; and it is perhaps true that he possesses more than all the others combined.

At one moment he dissects the testimony of a witness and over some trivial flaw, vents all the gall and bitterness of his invectives; then suddenly the mockery ceases and he solemnly and earnestly pleads for his client as his tones range from dulcet to fortissimo or the thunder of Niagara.

Yet with all his brilliancy and wit, the fascination of his

[8] *Centennial, 1848-1949,* Prairies Lodge No. 77, A.F.A.M., Paris, Ill. Prairie Lodge chartered Oct. 1, 1849, with only eight charter members.

eloquence and the sparkling joyousness of his disposition, he is never happy when alone. He lives only when his mind can be on the wing and like a caged eagle, pines when his pinions are fettered.

How different is Lincoln! He is gifted with a mind deeply imbued by study. His style of reasoning is profound; his deductions logical and his investigations are acute. In his examination of witnesses, he displays a masterly ingenuity and a legal tact that baffles concealment and defies deceit. When he addresses the jury, there is no false glitter or sickly sentimentalism. In vain we look for a rhetorical display of sublime nothings. His argument is bold, forcible, and convincing.

Such are some of the qualities which place Lincoln at the head of the profession in this state and although he may have his equal, it would be no easy task to find his superior.[9]

Benedict was not able to attend the spring term of court at Urbana in 1851 and thereby missed earning $50. Both he and his wife Charlotte were ill. He contracted a high fever and Charlotte probably suffered from an attack of arthritis as her left knee was misshapen and her hands and wrists distorted. But there was a happy note in his letter to Davis:

Our babe has done remarkably well although he has been nursed entirely from the bottle. He is a fine boy, good natured, grows finely, and plays, and laughs outright. My wife's mother (Mrs. Carlos Curtis) has gone entirely blind and will remain so, I presume, during the rest of her life. . . The situation of my family has been such that I have been unable to go to Decatur to attend to some business there . . . I expect to meet you at the Piatt Court. Mrs. Benedict feels grateful to Mrs. Davis for her solicitations about our domestic afflictions and . . . sends her best wishes for Mrs. Davis' health and happiness.[10]

[9] *Illinois Citizen,* Danville, May 29, 1850.
[10] David Davis MMS, Davis to wife, Urbana, May 1, 1851; Benedict to Davis, Paris, Feb. 20, 1851.

Six months later, Judge Davis was again riding the circuit. When he reached Danville he confided to his wife, "They say our friend Benedict is drinking. His wife is improving slowly but her limbs are distorted." A week later when Davis reached Paris, he was again reminded of the intemperance of Benedict. To the prevailing gossip, Benedict replied, "That Mrs. Harris is a busybody." [11]

The exchange of friendly letters between Kirby Benedict and David Davis tells of politics, court cases, and the activities of their friends. A loneliness pervaded their letters as each inquired how the other enjoyed himself during the long winter. Only twice a year could they conveniently meet to exchange their views and bits of gossip. One friend, "had been crushed to atoms in business;" another one, less respectable, "could not be admitted to young ladies' society." Would there be enough business to pay expenses? In Paris, there were no criminal prosecutions of importance, no prisoners in jail. "Yet," said Benedict, "I am beginning to long for the spring circuit so that we can be together again." An added note tells of political frustration. "I presume someone other than myself will get the appointment to carry the electoral vote to Washington but be that as it may." [12]

Hotels on the circuit were often unable to accommodate all the travelers, so four or more men were obliged to occupy the same room. On one occasion, Abraham Lincoln, David Davis, David Campbell,[13]

---

[11] *Ibid.* Davis to wife, Danville, Oct. 20, 1851; Paris, Oct. 27, 1851.

[12] *Ibid.* Benedict to Davis, Paris, Nov. 22, 1852.

[13] David Campbell, a native of New Jersey, arrived in Springfield in 1838, where he served as prosecuting attorney during the years 1848-1856. He rode the judicial circuit with Lincoln, Davis, and Benedict. He died in office in 1856.

and Kirby Benedict were assigned to the only vacancy, a room with two double beds. Lincoln and Davis occupied one and Benedict and Campbell the other.

One day Campbell said, "Benedict, you must ask the landlord to furnish you a bed to yourself."

"Well, suppose he hasn't one?" said Benedict.

"Then you must sleep on the floor or get the landlord to furnish you a berth in the haymow."

"What is your objection to sleeping with me, General David Campbell?" asked Benedict.

"Darn you," said Campbell, "I never did *sleep* with you but I have *lain* with you. To sleep with you would be impossible. You snore like a Cyclops and your breath smells of mean whisky.   . ."

"Well, General Campbell," said Benedict, "I shall show you that you shall sleep with me and if either of us has to sleep on the floor or the haymow it will be you, darn you, and not me."

"We'll see about that," said Campbell.

That night Campbell went to bed earlier than usual and about midnight along came Benedict pretty much "how-came-you-so." Campbell feigned sleep. "Hullo there!" said Benedict. "Dave, move over to the back of the bed and give me room on the front."

When Benedict crawled into bed, Dave quietly drew up one heel on which he had fastened a spur, and planted it on Benedict's leg just above his knee. He then gave a quick turn downward, crying, "Get up there! Get up there!" as though he were speaking to his horse.

Benedict gave a sudden leap and landed in the middle of the floor, yelling with pain, "Jesus! the darn fellow has the nightmare or delirium tremens and has taken me for his horse." [14]

From the bed on the other side of the room, Lincoln and Davis burst into uproarious laughter.

Benedict was not above the law, as he was sued for a debt of $33.53 plus cost $8.08 due Benjamin Dillehunt, a carpenter of Decatur. The case was appealed to the supreme court after judgment had been rendered in the justice of peace and circuit courts. Abraham Lincoln and Charles Emerson defended Dillehunt. Benedict was represented by Lyman Trumbull and Josiah Lamborn. The supreme court affirmed the judgment of the two lower courts and the appeal was dismissed January 17, 1842. Benedict was obliged to pay Dillehunt $41.61.

In spite of Benedict's temperament and indulgence in liquor, his legal tactics were respected by his fellow attorneys. Always he held the attention of his audience by his dramatic arguments. When naming an opponent, whom he especially disliked, he would turn his face to the left, limp as though injured, then shake his hand to the right to free himself from the contamination which he feigned he had incurred by even mentioning such a name.[15]

He was a master of satire. One moment he would convulse his audience with laughter and in the next bring tears. His voice was like a bugle note yet could be modulated to dulcet timbre. He was above medium height and of fine personal appearance but somewhat

---

[14] Usher F. Linder. *Reminiscences of the Early Bench and Bar of Illinois*, pp. 201-202.

[15] Jane M. Jones, *Personnal Recollections of Early Decatur*, Decatur Chapter D.A.R., 1912, pp. 267-8.

pompous in his manner and quite vain, fond of popular applause but very sensitive if he thought he was the subject of censure or ridicule.

Over a period of sixteen years Benedict was associated with Lincoln in the courts of the Eighth Judicial District of Illinois. The friendship of the two men never wavered. In later years, when Lincoln was President, his political friends attempted to persuade him to replace Benedict as chief justice of New Mexico; but Lincoln said that he had spent too many happy hours with Benedict in Illinois and that he would not disturb him.

The following tabulation reveals the type of cases tried during those early years, May 1840-May 1853, and the attorneys who rode the circuit. In the twenty cases, Lincoln opposed Benedict nine times but cooperated with him on eleven occasions.

> Clinton, De Witt County, May 22, 1840.
> *People* v. *Spencer Turner.*
> Lincoln, Douglas, and Benedict for defendant.
> Campbell and Colton for people.
> Turner indicted for murder. Acquitted by jury.

> Urbana, Champaign County, May 2, 1850. (3 cases)
> Lincoln, Howitt, and McRoberts for plaintiffs.
> Benedict, Gridley, and Somers for defendants.
>   1. *Nancy Jane Dunn* v. *Albert G. Carle* – a bastardy case.
>   2. *Zephaniah* v. *Carle* – trespass on the case of seduction, the defendant posts recognizances and files affidavits for continuance.
>   3. *Dunn v. Carle,* assumpsit, the defendant is permitted to plead over.
> May 3, 1850. Signing the names of all three counsels, Lincoln writes and files a demurrer in the bastardy case; in the assumpsit suit a jury hears arguments after which the plaintiff submits to a nonsuit.

Danville, Vermilion County, October 23, 1850.
Hickman v. *McCormack.*
Lincoln and Davis for plaintiff.
Benedict, McRoberts, Murphy for defendant.
Granted leave to withdraw their plea and plead again.

Paris, Edgar County, October 28, 1850.
Nancy Burr, et al v. *Seth Austin.*
Lincoln and Benedict file the final order of the supreme court in
accordance with which the case is reinstated on the docket.

Decatur, Macon County, November 16, 1850.
Froman v. *Pearson and Walton.*
Lincoln and Benedict for defendants.
Attorneys for plaintiff file proofs and Lincoln and Benedict are
ruled to answer for the defendant on April 1, 1851.

Paris, Edgar County, May 16, 1851.
Starr, et al v. *Cassidy.*
Lincoln and Benedict for plaintiffs.
Dill and Linder for defendant.
A bill to set aside a deed is submitted by Lincoln and Benedict.
The court dismisses the plaintiff's bill.

Decatur, Macon County, May 30, 1851.
Froman v. *Pearson and Walton.*
Lincoln and Benedict file defendant's answer.
Continued to November term, 1851.

Paris, Edgar County, October 27, 1851.
Nancy Burr, et al v. *Seth Austin, Adm. Elijah Austin,* an action
for a debt. Court dismisses the case, by agreement of attorneys.
Lincoln and Benedict for plaintiff.
Emerson and Steele for defendant.

Decatur, Macon County, November 13, 1851.
Froman v. *Pearson and Walton.*
Last before court on May 31, 1851. Suit is dismissed by agree-
ment.
Lincoln and Benedict appear for defendants.

Paris, Edgar County, May 17, 1852.
Munsell v. *McReynolds.*
Benedict for plaintiff.
Lincoln, Dill, and Linder for defendant.
A bill for settlement of a partnership is decided per agreement filed.

Paris, Edgar County, May 20, 1852.
Sizimore v. *Make.*
Lincoln and Dill for plaintiff.
The assumpsit suit in which a jury failed to agree on October 29, 1851; a jury finds for plaintiff and damage assessed at $260.

Paris, Edgar County, April 18, 1853.
Noblett v. *Duck* – an action on a covenant last before the court on May 17, 1852. Dismissed.
Lincoln and Benedict for defendant.
Emerson and Steele for plaintiff.

Paris, Edgar County, April 18, 1853.
Paddock v. *Snyder* – an assumpsit suit; leave granted to open depositions.
Lincoln and Benedict for defendant.

Paris, Edgar County, April 18, 1853.
Jaquith v. *Larkin and Burr* – assumpsit case.
Benedict for plaintiff.
Lincoln, Dill, Steele, Emerson, for defendant.
Case dismissed.

Paris, Edgar County, April 22, 1853.
Henderson v. *Reed* – assumpsit case.
Lincoln and Benedict for plaintiff.
A jury waived and case submitted to the court which takes it under advisement.
April 26, 1853, the court awards the plaintiff $100 and costs.

Paris, Edgar County, April 29, 1853.
  Davidson v. *Baily* – ejectment suit.
  Lincoln for defendant.
  Benedict for plaintiff.
  Court takes case under advisement.

Danville, Vermilion County, May 28, 1853.
  Phelps v. *Benedict.*
  Lincoln and Lamon for defendant, an appeal. (Lost three suits.)
  Plaintiff awarded $38.75.

Danville, Vermilion County, May 31, 1853.
  Campbell v. *Smith* – trespass.
  Lincoln, signing "Benedict, Lincoln, and Lamon," writes and
  files for plaintiff for $45.[16]

---

[16] Benjamin P. Thomas, *Lincoln, 1847-1853. Being the Day by Day Activities.* (Springfield 1936), pp. 175, 200, 201, 203, 229, 231, 253, 255, 282, 330, 331, 335, 336.

A Federal Judge in New Mexico

During the decade 1843-1853, Kirby Benedict witnessed the political success of his friends and close associates. Stephen A. Douglas was elected to the United States Senate; Abraham Lincoln, John J. Harden, and Richard Yates served in the House of Representatives. Now Benedict sought new opportunities. He prompted his friends to recommend him for a judgeship in Minnesota. Eleven prominent residents of Springfield addressed a memorial to President Franklin Pierce, on December 2, 1852, in which they testified to the merits, qualifications, and suitability of Benedict for the office. They expressed the hope that the president would bestow the appointment upon their friend.

From Palestine another associate, J. C. Allen, wrote the president:

> In filling any vacancy that may occur in the office of Judge in Minnesota, permit me to recommend for your consideration the Honorable Kirby Benedict. . . He possesses the character, ability, and legal attainments which eminently fit him for a position of that kind. His appointment would be highly gratifying to his numerous friends throughout the West.

The following year the Illinois delegation in Congress

unanimously voted that the name of Kirby Benedict be presented to the president for a judgeship in Washington Territory.[1]

Evidently the need for a competent judge was far greater in New Mexico than in the other two territories as President Pierce appointed Benedict, associate judge of the Third Judicial District of New Mexico, in 1853.

In the Springfield *Sangamon Journal* of July 19, 1853, there appeared the following news item: "Kirby Benedict Esq. has left Paris for New Mexico having been appointed judge for that Territory. It will be some time before he will return as United States senator."

The judge left his wife Charlotte and two small children in Illinois and crossed the plains to Santa Fe where he arrived on August 17, 1853. The contrast between the prairie land of Illinois and the mountains and desert of New Mexico was no greater than the difference between the pioneers of the two communities. Illinois settlements were scarcely more than half a century old while New Mexico proudly counted her age by three centuries.

Benedict was the offspring of New England Pilgrims who had fled their homeland to seek religious freedom. The New Mexicans did not migrate to escape the Church of their motherland but to spread the teaching of their faith among the native Indians.

Their laws are an integral part of their history. Those of the United States were patterned after the common law of England. In New Mexico, the genesis

---

[1] Appointment Papers, Office U.S. Attorney General Washington, D.C.; (National Archives) Springfield, Ill., Dec. 2, 1852; Palestine, Dec. 20, 1852; Washington, D.C. March 7, 1853.

of the courts was unique and differed from that of the other states. During the Spanish regime, the civil law of Spain and Mexico [2] became that of her American colonies. However, many legal enactments in force in Spain were never extended to the colonies. New laws and regulations were devised in the form of orders or decrees and were made to conform to the wants and exigencies of the emigrants.

After the independence of Mexico, her federal constitution provided for two general tribunals: national, and those of the state. The powers of these judiciaries were vested in supreme, circuit and district courts. Jurisdiction of these courts was very extensive yet not universal over all classes of Mexican society as large numbers of the population were exempted by *fueros* or specially privileged jurisdiction. These were chiefly the military and ecclesiastics.

Justice usually was administered by the alcaldes [3] or justices of peace. From the decisions of this class of officials, appeals were permissible to the governor and thence to the supreme court at Chihuahua or Mexico City. The proceedings before the alcaldes were unusual. The plaintiff made a verbal complaint to the officer who ordered the defendant to appear forthwith. If the latter did not obey this simple mandate, the alcalde sent him the *baston de justicia* or judicial staff, an ordinary cane on which a cross was carved and a black silk tassel attached. After receiving this notice, a refusal to appear was construed as a contempt of court and punished with severity.

[2] Gustavus Schmidt, *The Civil Law of Spain and Mexico,* pp. 91, 98.

[3] Brantz Mayer, *Mexico, Aztec, Spanish and Republican,* vol. II, 146-147.

An oath was seldom required of a witness but if so, he swore upon the cross on the *baston de justicia* or more frequently on a cross formed by placing the forefinger over the thumb on the upraised right hand. When no witnesses were subpoened, the alcalde would sometimes render judgment solely upon the statements of the parties in litigation. There was no written record of these proceedings.

Although there was no trial by jury there was a system of arbitration by which complaints were referred to what was called *hombres buenos*. This simulated a trial by jury.

One admirable and basically sound provision under the Mexican law was the "judgment of conciliation." In accordance with this ruling, the parties litigant were prohibited from beginning an action until they had procured from the alcalde a statement that judgment or arbitration had been attempted but failed.

The Provisional Code promulgated by General Kearny on September 22, 1846, and the Organic Act of 1850, resulted in the enactment of statutes which radically modified the old Spanish and Mexican laws and substituted those similar to the other states.

The judicial power was vested in the supreme, district, and probate courts and the justice of peace. The Territory was divided into three districts and a judge assigned to each. Under the 16th section of the Organic Act, the designation of the judges to their respective districts was left to the discretion of the territorial officers by a provision that, temporarily and until otherwise provided by law, the governor was empowered to define the judicial districts and assign the judges to

their respective circuits. Furthermore, the governor
possessed the right to designate the time and place for
holding court.

At the first and second sessions of the legislature, laws
were passed to define specifically the powers and duties
of the judges. The chief justice was required to reside
in the district in which the seat of government was
located. The law further provided that all judges
should hold court twice a year in each county of their
district. To prevent the passing of the court terms in
case of unavoidable absence of a judge, one of his fellows was obliged to hold court for the absent member.

The terms of court were so scheduled that the attorneys were enabled to represent their clients in the
courts of different districts and when necessary, one
judge could act for an absent judicial officer.

The supreme court met at Santa Fe annually for the
first three weeks in January except for a brief time
when it met in July. The supreme court members
exercised original jurisdiction in the district courts as
well as being members of the supreme court. The
review of cases appealed to the supreme court deviated
from the current procedures as the trial judge was a
member of the supreme court. His presence was likely
to obstruct the impartial administration of justice.

An early enactment of the New Mexico legislature
was a bill of rights modeled after the federal bill.
Although Judge Benedict found them inadequate to
meet all situations, many social laws had been passed
to assure good conduct on the part of her citizens.
Moral standards were protected by statutes that provided for Sunday closing, the restraint of gambling, the

arrest of drunks or any person who used scandalous language in the streets, and fines and imprisonment for those who had "no visible honest means of living." The sentences of the latter were reduced one-half upon the marriage of the accused.

Libel in the churches was curbed by an enactment which provided for the punishment of any minister or any other person who, by word or manner, slandered any person within the church. An attempt to preserve family unity resulted in the passage of an ordinance "to punish anyone who discovered faults of married couples or who interfered in private life, thus creating disagreement and thereby causing a terrible evil and injury to the family."

To prevent an outlaw from lurking behind a mask at any of the popular masquerade parties, the legislature enacted a law that required each masquerader to obtain a license and register with the probate judge his name, number of ticket, and description of his costume; and to take an oath to preserve the peace. Each person was obliged to wear his number in public view.

The life of these early pioneers is mirrored in numerous other laws. The buffalo was still the source of food even though the herds were diminishing and hunting was restricted to the Indians. Many New Mexican families depended upon wild game to supplement their meager rations. The legislature was induced to memorialize Congress to permit the people to hunt buffalo and to grant them the same rights as the Indians.

Racial discrimination was apparent in the law regarding the right of suffrage: "Voters must be white and not connected with the United States Army." A patriotic note was injected by the passage of a joint resolution which requested that the flag be displayed during each session of the legislature.

Judge Benedict soon made the acquaintance of the practicing attorneys[4] in New Mexico and began a thorough examination of all these laws by which he would be governed in rendering his decisions.

It is problematical that Judge Benedict could envision the vast extent of the Third District to which he had been assigned. It extended from the Colorado River on the west to Texas on the east; from approximately the thirty-fifth parallel on the north to the borders of Texas and Mexico on the south. From north to south the distance was three hundred miles. The total area of the district comprised nearly two-thirds of the area of the present states of New Mexico and Arizona.[5] It was thirty times larger than Benedict's native state of Connecticut and three times larger than Illinois.

Of the nine original counties of New Mexico, four, Bernalillo, Valencia, Socorro, and Doña Ana, were in the Third District. During the first year of Benedict's judgeship, the district was increased by the addition of the Gadsden Purchase to Doña Ana County.

This was a large circuit to cover by horse and buggy or on horseback. The perils of the journey were not forgotten for many years. As the judge crossed the *Jornada del Muerto,* he fancied that every bush con-

---

[4] J. J. Davenport, chief justice; Joab Houghton, associate justice, Second District; Hugh N. Smith, Charles Beaubien, John S. Watts, Merrill Ashurst, Theodore D. Wheaton, Spruce M. Baird, William Claude Jones, James A. Lucas, and others.

[5] Arizona made a separate county of New Mexico at ninth session of New Mexico Legislature, 1859-1860; county seat at Tubac.

cealed an Apache, every branch of the Spanish bayonet was an Indian headdress, and that hostile Indians skulked in every gulley.[6]

On the circuit ride in the spring of 1854, Benedict was accompanied by W. W. H. Davis[7] who kept a journal in which he noted some of the most significant incidents of the journey. Davis left Santa Fe early in April to join the judge at Albuquerque. He selected a sturdy mount for the long ride and into his saddlebags he crammed two shirts, two pairs of socks, and shaving equipment. In addition to his scant wardrobe, he tucked in one small Bible, two law books, some stationery, and the customary brace of pistols.

Attorney Joab Houghton and a New Mexican rode with Davis. They crossed a dry level plain to the six-mile canyon of the Rio Santa Fe. When they left the canyon, it was necessary for them to dismount and lead their horses up the two-hundred-foot zigzag trail to the summit of the mesa where they galloped their horses until they descended to the valley of the Rio Grande near the San Domingo Pueblo. Here they crossed the river, rode on to San Felipe, and before sundown reached Algodones where they remained for the night.

The following day they passed Bernalillo, Sandia, and Los Ranchos. The latter was formerly the county seat of Bernalillo County. When they arrived at Albuquerque, they found Judge Benedict already on the

---

[6] *New Mexico Union,* March 6, 1873. Kirby Benedict, editor and proprietor.

[7] W. W. H. Davis, *El Gringo,* p. 345. W. W. H. Davis, 1820-1910; born in Mass.; died, Doylestown, Pa.; secretary New Mex. Territory, 1853-1857 and was acting governor for 11 months during absence of Gov. David Merriwether; author of *El Gringo, Spanish Conquest of New Mexico,* and *History of 104th Pennsylvania Regiment.*

bench in a modest "mud" building on the eastern edge of the town. The United States Army depot was then located in Albuquerque's "Old Town" and here the circuit riders were entertained at the army mess hall.[8]

The district court records for those early years are missing. What criminal and civil cases were tried by Benedict remain unknown except those that were appealed to the supreme court.

Tome, then the county seat of Valencia County, was next on their itinerary. Their first day's ride ended at twilight at Baird's Ranch. Early the next morning, the judge in his buggy, and the other men, saddled and mounted, rode along the eastern side of the Rio Grande past flocks of sheep guarded by faithful shepherd dogs. They passed Isleta and Peralta and soon reached Tome.

Spring came early on the Rio Grande that year. The bordering cottonwoods on the plaza were just beginning to flaunt their shimmering leaves in the sharp clean air as Judge Benedict hurried to the courthouse. The one-story adobe building was long and low with a platform slightly elevated at one end of the courtroom where the judge presided. A small table was provided for members of the bar and a few benches for the audience.

There were few cases of importance on the docket and when the one-week term was completed, the judge in his jolting buggy started south toward Socorro with his companions on horseback. They encountered a sand storm at Casa Colorado and were obliged to spend the night at La Joya. The next morning the horsemen

---

[8] The army depot occupied the building that was owned by Mrs. James Henry Carleton at that time.

decided to cross to the west side of the river. Due to the spring thaws in the Rockies, the water was too deep for the judge's buggy so he continued along the east bank.

An old canoe, hollowed from a cottonwood log, was located and in this the horsemen prepared to cross. Saddles and bridles were removed and a rope tied around the neck of each horse. At first they balked but when they were finally coaxed into the river, they splashed away for the opposite shore and floated the canoe and its occupants safely across.

The dripping horses were saddled and the attorneys rode onward. When they reached Lemitar they crossed the stream again and here they rejoined the judge. They stopped for lunch at the home of the late General Manuel Armijo. The canopied beds, brass bedsteads, and heavy wooden benches appeared to be incongruous companions for the velvet-covered chairs and the beautiful "Turkey" carpet. The time-stained beams that supported the roof were reflected in twenty gilded mirrors around the room.

The journey was resumed at three in the afternoon and all the travelers reached Socorro before dark. The courthouse fronted on the plaza and backed against a fine vineyard. There was no jail nor had there ever been one. The usual mode of punishment was by means of fines, whippings, or selling the labor of the law violator for a stated period of time.

Their next desination was Las Cruces, county seat of Doña Ana County, one hundred fifty miles to the south. Before them lay the *Jornada del Muerto,* the journey of death. Careful preparations were made for the passage of this scorched land. Water kegs were filled, and the wheels of the buggy were soaked to prevent the shrinkage of the wooden tires which would result in loose steel rims. Horses and men rested from eleven in the morning until five in the afternoon. They traveled at night and by three in the morning they were sixty miles nearer the end of the circuit. After a two-hour stop, they plodded on and by noon reached Robledo, the southern terminus of the *Jornada*. In another night ride they arrived at Doña Ana and the following morning were on their way to Las Cruces, the last court on the Rio Grande.

Old court records occasionally disappeared from their original depository and were found years later in the archives of a neighboring county. Such was the case of the records of Doña Ana County for the years 1854-1856 when Judge Benedict served in that district. After an absence of eighty-four years they were discovered in Albuquerque and were returned to Las Cruces through the efforts of public-spirited citizens.[9] According to the following notation, the old records may have been in Mesilla during the Confederate invasion: "Confederate States of America, Territory of Arizona, County of Arizona, October 7, 1861, First Judicial District at Courthouse, town of Mesilla. Judge Hare."

There was great negligence in preserving early court records and some of those remaining are disappointing in their brevity. Nevertheless, an account of one early case was published in the *New York Daily Times* February 2, 1854.[10]

[9] L. A. Cardwell, deputy district clerk, and Judge Bryan G. Johnson, Albuquerque. *El Paso Times,* Feb. 1, 1940.

[10] The article is quoted from the *Missouri Republican,* Dec. 22, 1853, and was written by a correspondent from Albuquerque.

It involved the trading of a horse for a mule and the connivance of the traders. A man named Bourale (Pedro José Borule) sold a horse to a discharged soldier with the understanding that the latter trade it for one of Apache Chief Cusenas Azalas' mules. After the transaction, Bourale approached the chief and claimed the horse as his property. The chief refused to surrender it and appealed to the prefect at Las Cruces who decided that he had a legal right to the horse.

Chief Azalas with his band and the horse, left Las Cruces late the same day and proceeded toward Doña Ana where they camped near the town. Azalas drew a mark across the road and warned his men not to cross it; but evidently it was quite proper for the chief to visit the town.

Meanwhile Bourale sneaked cautiously behind and after the chief became intoxicated, lured his victim to a secluded spot where he was beaten to death. The murderer escaped across the Rio Grande to Mesilla, then a part of Mexico. A warrant was issued for his arrest but when Sheriff John Jones [11] arrived and demanded the accused, the authorities at Mesilla refused to comply. A requisition was made on the commanding officer at Fort Thorn for aid of the troops stationed there but this was rejected.

Nevertheless, the case came before Judge Benedict's court for trial at the May term, 1854 in Las Cruces. Three bands of Apaches camped within a short distance and watched the proceedings of the white man's court with great interest.

---

[11] John Jones was the first sheriff of Doña Ana County. Later he won the distinction of being the "Paul Revere of the Southwest." Aurora Hunt, *Army of the Pacific, 1860-1866*, pp. 115-116.

In an interview with Judge Benedict they stated that
their chief had come to the settlement at the invitation
of the whites; that they were peaceable; that they had
received from the President of the United States, a
medal upon which his image was impressed; that he
had called them his red children; that they would not
act hastily but wait and see how we administered our
laws; and that they wanted justice and if we did not
give them justice, they had laws of their own and knew
how to get satisfaction.

They had lost their chief, a man they had loved and
respected. He was wise and they obeyed him. He had
instructed them to remain at peace; they had done so
and were now without a head to direct them. If the
Americans did not give them justice, they could not say
what their young men might do.

The court record of this case is extremely brief. First
there was a request for a continuance until next term.
Then James A. Lucas, attorney for Bourale, asked the
court for permission to enter a *nolle prosequi*. This was
granted and entered to the indictment with the familiar
phrase, "The defendant go hence without day." The
crime was committed in Mexico and was not within
the jurisdiction of the district courts of New Mexico.

The acquisition of the Gadsden Purchase resulted in
numerous "Declarations of Intentions" to become
citizens of the United States. There were men from
Ireland and England who renounced allegiance to
Queen Victoria; one from Russia who no longer wished
to be a subject of Alexander II; and another, a citizen
of Mexico, relinquished his allegiance to His Serene
Highness Antonio Lopez Santa Ana.

The cases of trespass and ejectment by Judge Benedict provide evidence that some of the Americans were squatting on the property of Mexican citizens. This may have resulted from the ineffectual surveys and boundary markings. The verdicts were invariably in favor of the Mexican land owners. The judge ordered the properties surrendered and the trespassers fined ONE CENT.

Since Las Cruces was near the border of Chihuahua, smuggling was a common practice. Nineteen of these cases were tried before Judge Benedict during one court term. In another instance no attempt was made to secrete the passage of twenty *carretas* across the border but misinformation was given concerning the contents and value of the caravan. Consequently, the owners were sued for libel of information.

When a United States citizen was brought to trial, he frequently waived a jury trial and submitted to the court without the intervention of a jury. It was apparent that he placed greater confidence in Judge Benedict than in a native jury.

There were charges for unlawful assembly, for using false weights and measures and a few cases of assault and battery. For disturbing the peace of a religious meeting, the accused was fined five dollars and one hour in jail.

One evening during a respite from official duties, Judge Benedict invited the Catholic priest, Reverend Cardenas, to deliver a sermon. The attorneys organized a choir and sang three hymns, one of which was:

How tedious and tasteless the hours
When Jesus I no longer see!
Sweet prospects, sweet birds and sweet flowers,
Have lost all their sweetness to me.
The fields strive in vain to look gay
But when I am happy in Him
December's as pleasant as May.[12]

The judge's satisfaction in having completed the court term at Las Cruces was diminished by the realization that the dreaded *Jornada del Muerto* must be recrossed before he reached Albuquerque. A disappointment awaited him there. He had completed his first year of judgeship only to learn that he was the only judge in the entire territory. Chief Justice Davenport was absent by permission and the newly-appointed associate justice, Perry E. Brocchus, had not arrived.

There was then a notable murder case on the docket in Santa Fe and it devolved upon Benedict to substitute for Judge Davenport in whose district the case was tried. Richard H. Weightman,[13] delegate to Congress from New Mexico, had stabbed and killed Francois X. Aubry. A witness reported that Aubry met Weightman in the La Fonda bar room and accused him of publishing an article in his newspaper, *Amigo del Pais*,

[12] John Newton and William Cowper, "The Olney Hymns," *Plymouth Collection of Hymns and Tunes*, no. 1211, p. 389.

[13] William A. Keleher, *Turmoil in New Mexico, 1846-1868*, p. 125, fn 44. Richard Hanson Weightman was born in Maryland 1818, and died while commanding a brigade at Wilson's Creek, Mo., on Aug. 12, 1861. Weightman's newspaper, *Amigo del Pais*, published in Albuquerque in 1853. Aubry was a Santa Fe trader, explorer, and the most famous long-distance rider of his day. His diaries of 1853 and 1854 portray his successful attempt to make a wagon road from California to New Mexico along the thirty-fifth parallel.

that reflected on the honor and integrity of Aubry.
Whereupon the latter threw a glass of whisky in the
face of Weightman and drew his pistol. Weightman
then stabbed Aubry through the heart. By the able
arguments and pleadings of Benedict, Weightman was
acquitted.

At the close of the fall term, 1854, Benedict asked
President Pierce for a four months leave of absence so
that he might return to Illinois to bring his family to
New Mexico. He hoped to make the journey in less
time if he could join one of the large merchant mule
trains that was scheduled to leave Kansas in May or
June. If he joined the train, he would be more secure
from Indian attacks.

Due to the absence of his fellow judges, Benedict
stated that he was obliged to hold all the fall terms in
every county in New Mexico. In order to accomplish
this, he had taken his seat upon the bench and continued in session, without adjournment for refresh-
ments, from eight in the morning until eleven at night.

He indicated the confidence that when Judge Davenport returned, he would faithfully attend to the judicial
interests of the Third District. Benedict concluded his
communication by saying that it would not be possible
to receive an answer to his request in less than three
months but he hoped for a reply at the very earliest
date so that he could leave for Illinois as soon as the
first of April, 1855.[14]

In his second term in office, a number of his decisions
were appealed to the supreme court. Of special sig-

---

[14] Letter to William S. Marcy, Secretary of State, Washington, D.C.,
written Nov. 21, 1854, Las Cruces, New Mexico (National Archives).

nificance are those between the Acoma and Laguna pueblos. These and others will be reported in another chapter.

After completing the spring court term 1855, Judge Benedict returned to Paris, Illinois, to move his family to New Mexico.[15] Nearly two years had passed since he had seen his son and daughter and wife, Charlotte. Kirby Jr. had outgrown his babyhood and was four years old. Worthena greeted her father's return as a young lady of seven years plus.

They followed the same route traveled by thousands who had passed before them, when they returned together to New Mexico. No doubt, the two children frequently questioned the judge about the long wagon trains, the bullwhackers, and the seemingly endless prairies that separated them from their destination.

When Judge Benedict had found a house for his family in Albuquerque, it was time for the fall term of his court. For three more years he administered justice in the Third District. Not once during five years in that district did he miss holding court in each county twice a year. The records for the years 1857-1858 have not been located.

The information regarding the following case has been obtained by devious procedure. The crime committed was first brought to the attention of Judge Benedict when he received a letter from General John Garland who was then in command of the military department of New Mexico.

The general was greatly perturbed. He had been

---

[15] *Springfield Illinois Journal,* May 26, 1855. "Hon. Kirby Benedict arrived in this city today. He came from New Mexico for his family who have been residing in Edgar County during his absence."

ordered to New Mexico to protect the whites from the Indians. Now he was confronted with the problem of dealing with the New Mexicans who attacked the Indians. He asked the advice of Judge Benedict in a letter from Santa Fe, dated April 22, 1858.

Another outrage has been perpetrated by some men purported to be from Mesilla. The particulars of which will be found in the enclosed papers. The case is a grave and important one, new to me, being somewhat at a loss as to the proper course to be pursued.

I desire your advice upon the subject. We have neither a United States Judge (Chief Justice), a District Attorney, nor a Governor in Santa Fe at this time with whom to consult. It is quite possible that an effort will be made to get this band of murderers out of military custody under a writ of "Habeas Corpus" by some of the local magistrates. In such case, should the writ be obeyed? What is the proper course to be followed in order that they be committed for murder?

In case of committal, can the murderers be taken by the military to Fort Craig and held in custody until the Civil Court holds its session at Socorro or can they be bailed? Will you do me the favor to send instructions to the United States District Attorney who is said to reside somewhere in the vicinity of Mesilla? It would not surprise me to hear that he is Chief Counselor in these acts of terror.

(Signed) GENERAL JOHN GARLAND

General Garland's aide-de-camp made the ride from Santa Fe to Albuquerque in one day to deliver the reports to Judge Benedict so that he might advise the general regarding the proper legal course of action.

The reports[16] revealed that at about daylight April

---

[16] 35 Cong. 2 sess. Sen. Ex. Doc. no. 1, p. 284-290 (Ser. 975). Report of Gen. Garland to army headquarters, Washington, D.C. March 1, 1858. Reports of Lt. Col. D. S. Miles and Lts. W. H. Wood and J. W. Allen; U.S. Dept. Int. 1857-1858, 549; Michael Steck, Aug. 10, 1858.

17, 1858, a party of armed New Mexicans from Mesilla charged into the Indian camp near Fort Thorn and indiscriminately butchered men, women, and children. The garrison was immediately ordered under arms. While the Rifles were saddling their horses, Lieutenant W. H. Wood and his infantry succeeded in capturing all of the thirty-six men who participated in the crime. When the Mounted Rifles arrived at the scene, the prisoners were marched to the Fort where they were confined under heavy guard.

The soldiers then were ordered to collect the dead, wounded, and survivors. Three men, three women, and one boy were killed. They were all interred near Fort Thorn Cemetery.

Judge Benedict at once started the necessary legal procedure. He received the complaint of Lieutenant Craig, under oath duly sworn, and issued a warrant for the arrest of the accused returnable before him at Socorro and sent it by swift messenger to the sheriff of Socorro County. General Garland gave orders to his officers at Forts Craig and Thorn to aid the sheriff with all the guards that might be required to bring the prisoners before the judge.

Benedict proceeded to Socorro to examine the accused and committed all of them to await trial at the next session of the court at Mesilla the first Monday in June, 1858. Evidently their case was continued until the fall term as the record discloses that when court met in November of that same year, the entire party was released on $500 bail.

Public opinion was in sympathy with the accused as this band of armed men were reported to be held in high esteem by their townsmen. They were known as the "Mesilla Guard" and were always in readiness to pursue the Indians and recover the citizens' property when stolen.

Here again, the records are missing. However, in a letter to President Lincoln dated June 2, 1861, Judge Benedict wrote, "I tried thirty-six men for murder upon the same indictment but I met no uncommon trouble and no resistance." [17]

Whatever the outcome of the trial of the Mesilla Guard was, the citizens of the community received a sharp rebuke from General Garland. When he evacuated Fort Fillmore, a petition bearing 634 signatures was presented by the residents to protest the removal of the soldiers and to avow that their alleged "barbarous atrocities" were greatly exaggerated.

To this General Garland replied,

> Your request cannot be complied with. Mesilla is the strongest settlement in New Mexico. There are two posts within forty miles of the town. With every disposition to protect the lives and property of the citizens, I regret to say that instead of receiving their aid, they have, by their acts of outrage, provoked the attacks by the Indians. It is proper for me to say that those who perpetrate acts of violence and outrage have no claim to the protection of the military and will receive none.[18]

[17] Kirby Benedict MS, Attorney General's Office, Washington, D.C.
[18] 35 Cong. 2 Sess. Sen. Ex. Doc. no. 1 (Ser. 975), pp. 291, 293.

Chief Justice

Throughout his first term as associate justice, Benedict made frequent and detailed reports to the attorney general in Washington but as his term drew to a close, his letters increased in length and numbers. He emphasized the difficulties and dangers in traveling over his district which was three hundred miles from north to south and of great width from east to west. The long desert ride across the *Jornada del Muerto* remained clearly etched in his mind for years afterwards. The heat, dust, and thirst; and the suffering of the horses were less to be dreaded than the hostile Indians. In one of his reports he tactfully commented:

. . . I hope I shall be excused in alluding to my continuance in the office I now hold, although in this costly and primitive country, the salary is barely sufficient to support a Judge and his family in a becoming manner. Yet under all existing circumstances, I say frankly that I am anxious to remain in a Judgeship in this Territory if it shall be the will of the President and the judgment of the Senate.

This is my fifth year of service and I have brought my family here and find their health improved in this dry, bracing atmosphere. I am acquainted with the people, their customs, and peculiarities. I have learned enough of their language to charge juries and to conduct the business of the Court without an interpreter.

I have a deep solicitude in striving to aid in the establishment of a sound and well-directed system of jurisprudence in New Mexico. . . I am not informed that any complaints have

Mexico, I have nominated, by the advice and consent of the Senate, and do appoint him to be Chief Justice of the Supreme Court of the Territory of New Mexico and do authorize and empower him to execute and fulfill the duties of that office according to the Constitution and Laws of the United States and to have and to hold the said office with all the powers, privileges, and emoluments, to the same of right appertaining to him, the said Kirby Benedict, for the term of four years from the date thereof.

In testimony thereof, I have caused these letters to be made patent and the seal of the United States to be hereunto affixed. Given under my hand at the City of Washington the fourteenth day of June in the year of our Lord, one thousand eight hundred fifty-eight and of the Independence the eighty-second.

(Signed) JAMES BUCHANAN, President [5]

As chief justice he was assigned to the First District [6] with headquarters at Santa Fe. Now the problem of moving his family and household goods confronted him. He was just recovering from a "villainous" attack of diarrhea however, he must make provision for his family. He wrote Alexander M. Jackson, secretary of the Territory, to find out whether or not a house in Santa Fe could be rented or bought.[7]

He depended upon his friend, Charles P. Clever, to contract for two hundred burro loads of wood at twenty-five cents each; and to ascertain how the building of his furniture was progressing and how Charles Blummer, treasurer of the Territory, was succeeding with his well. Benedict, himself, was hard at work with his men making kraut.[8] No doubt Charlotte was diligently

---

5 Attorney General MSS. July 7, 1858.
6 Counties Rio Arriba, Taos, Santa Fe, San Miguel.
7 William G. Ritch, MS, no. 913, Huntington Library.
8 *Ibid.* no. 923.

supervising the packing of household belongings while Kirby Jr. and his sister Worthena scampered around in eager anticipation of the trip.

A week later another letter was dispatched to Clever. This time the judge requested him to see Joseph Hirsch, who had been freighting flour for the government to the army depot at Albuquerque, and learn when his wagons would make the trip from Santa Fe again. The wagons usually returned partially empty and this would be an opportunity for the Benedict family's household goods to be shipped to Santa Fe.[9]

At last the family was ready to start. Three mule teams with loaded wagons left for Santa Fe on November 22. The judge and his family left the same day, presumably in his carriage. They arrived in Santa Fe the following day.

In less than two weeks, on December 6, 1858, the judge and his wife purchased a ten room house and a large lot from Charles Blummer.[10] Of course, there was a barn on the property. The purchase price was $1,300 for this parcel of land situated in the northeastern section of the city, bounded and described as follows: On the north by hills and public land; on the east by a public road leading north from the plaza; on the south by the property of Manuel Alvarez, deceased; and on the west by lands and houses belonging to Tomasa Romero, Ysadora Romero, and Dolores Martinez. The property is readily located as part of a tract bounded by Grant Street on the east, Catron on the south, Bower

9 *Ibid.* no. 924.

10 *Deed Records,* Book C, (Santa Fe Courthouse, December 6, 1858) pp. 1, 2.

on the west and Arroyo Mascaras on the north. Judge and Mrs. Benedict later bought two adjoining lots.[11] Their holdings then comprised approximately four acres with other buildings in addition to their ten-room home. They subsequently rented one house to William F. M. Arny for $25 a month.[12]

The property purchased by the judge and Charlotte could have been considered a good investment. It lay within a few short blocks of the plaza and across the street from the capitol building which was in the process of being built.

Soon after the organization of the territory, Congress had appropriated $20,000 for public buildings. This amount was expended in laying the capitol foundation. Four years later on May 31, 1854, the sum of $50,000 was provided by Congress but this served only for erecting one and a half stories above the basement. In 1860 another appropriation was made but never paid.

The Capitol building remained a roofless shell for a quarter of a century, long after the death of the judge and precluding any opportunity to benefit by the increase in value of his investment. New Mexico finally built her own Capitol building and the government converted the unfinished derelict of sandstone into a federal courthouse which was not completed until 1890, forty years after money was first appropriated.

Although the First District to which the chief justice was assigned was not as large as the Third, it contained the greater proportion of the population. The

---

[11] *Ibid.* Book D, Oct. 24, 1863, pp. 300, 301. *Ibid.* Book C, May 24, 1864, pp. 557, 558.

[12] William G. Ritch MS, no. 1539.

rugged terrain and the freezing temperature of the winter storms in the Rockies equalled the discomforts and perils of the southern section of the territory.

When Kirby Benedict began his first term as chief justice, court was held in an old building that had been used as a storehouse for the quartermaster department in Santa Fe. The one-story adobe, 25 by 100 feet, was situated on the northeast corner of Palace at Washington Street. The roof was supported by a row of square pillars; large double doors opened into the street. The floor was of pine and comfortable seats were provided for witnesses, jurors, and litigants.[13]

From the pulpit-like rostrum, Judge Benedict rendered his opinions until the old building was torn down in 1862 to prevent its collapse. Rooms were rented until the new Capitol was under construction; then court was held in the first story of the unfinished building. Unfortunately, the L of the Capitol, occupied by the court, was burned on May 14, 1864, and many of the transcripts of records were destroyed.[14]

During the March term, 1858, many certificates of naturalization were granted. Among the European sovereigns who lost subjects were Queen Victoria of England, Louis Napoleon III of France, Frederick William IV of Prussia, and Oscar I of Sweden.

The chief justice and the prosecution attorneys, who accompanied him as he rode the circuit, were not above the law. The old court records of San Miguel County 1858-1859, reveal that Benedict fined himself $10 for

---

13 *Daily New Mexican,* March 11, 1940.

14 Ritch Collection MS no. 2216, Arny to Secretary of Treasury, Washington, D.C. Huntington Library.

gambling and levied the same amount against his companions.[15] The owner of the gaming table was fined $100. The fines were equally divided between the county and the territory.

The old plaza at Las Vegas, New Mexico, now so serene, once echoed to the cries of the auctioneer as he invited bids for the sale of the labor and services of a prisoner convicted of horse stealing. The case came before Judge Benedict at the March term, 1859. He pronounced:

> Take the prisoner to the middle of the public Plaza of San Miguel. Give him fifty lashes on his bare back, well laid on; furthermore, unless he shall pay the costs by the 20th of this month the sheriff shall then give him public notice in writing at not less than six public places in this county. Then at some day to be fixed not less than five nor more than ten days from the first day of publication, the sheriff will sell at public auction in the Plaza of San Miguel, between 10 A.M. and 4 P.M. the labors and services of said defendant. . . The sheriff shall make such sale in such manner and deliver the defendant to the purchaser to serve during the time bid and paid for.[16]

Angel is scarcely an appropriate name for a murderer, especially when a woman. Yet a jury in Las Vegas during the spring term in 1861 found Paula Angel guilty of murder in the first degree for the fatal stabbing of Miguel Martin.

The record may be found in Las Vegas where it is carefully preserved.

> March 28, 1861. This day came the Territory by her Attorney General and the defendant was led to this bar of the court in

---

15 Samuel Ellison, Hugh N. Smith, Richard H. Tompkins, and Merrill Ashurst.

16 Record filed in the archives of the Santa Fe County Courthouse.

custody of the sheriff. When asked if she had anything to say — said nothing.

She was then ordered to the jail to be kept securely by whatever chains and shackles necessary to secure the person of said Paula Angel until Friday the 26th day of April next; and that on said day, between the hours of 10 A.M. and 4 P.M. the sheriff was ordered to take the body of Paula Angel to some suitable place, to be selected by the sheriff, one mile from the church in the town of Las Vegas and there to be hung by the neck until dead.

An appeal to the supreme court was granted but it was ordered by the court that said appeal should in no manner operate a stay of execution but that said sentence should be fully executed as before ordered.

The fact that Benedict pronounced the death sentence for a woman did not necessarily mark him as a judge without just consideration for other offenders. His sympathy was frequently aroused when some of the Mexicans came before his court for minor offenses. He had sworn to uphold the laws even though he considered some of them unjust and cruel.

On one occasion he asked Governor Arny to pardon one Ysidro who had been guilty of stealing a hat. For this offense the judge had sentenced him to pay a fine of $10; but when he stole a coat also, Judge Benedict ordered him publicly whipped unless pardoned. Ysidro was a poor man and had a large family and through the petition of his neighbors and the judge he won a pardon.[17]

After a residence of ten years in New Mexico, Judge Benedict knew many of the New Mexicans personally.

---

17 Ritch Collection MS no. 1237, March 6, 1863.

Such was the case during the trial of Julian Chavez who had accepted a bribe of $60 and permitted Juan Jacobs Miera to escape the night before he was to have been hung. Chavez was a peon of Santa Ana County where he and his master had appeared before the judge in a suit several years previous.

The San Miguel County jail where Miera had been confined was neither well guarded nor securely built. Chavez was sentenced to five years imprisonment and had then served more than two years. Benedict recommended his pardon as he believed the cause of justice had already been served.[18]

The clemency of Chief Justice Benedict was further disclosed when he set aside the verdict of a jury at Taos and granted a new trial for Manuel Cardenas who had been found guilty of murder in the first degree. The judge ruled that the verdict was more severe than the evidence justified. Cardenas was permitted to withdraw his plea of not guilty and to plead guilty of murder in the fifth degree which degree was lawful at that time. The judge sentenced him to three years hard labor.[19]

A much publicized case was that of Jesús Maria Martinez who was tried at Taos during the spring term, 1864 and found guilty of murder in the first degree. All the original records of the case have been destroyed but the *Weekly New Mexican* provides the account of the trial and the execution of Martinez.

At the late Term (spring, 1864) of Court at Taos this man (Martinez) was tried for the murder of Julian Trujillo and found guilty of murder in the first degree and sentenced by Chief

---

[18] *Ibid.* no. 1152, Nov. 14, 1862.
[19] *Weekly New Mexican,* Oct. 7, 1864.

Justice Benedict to be hung upon the 13th of the present month (May).

The man killed bore the character of an industrious and useful man who worked at blacksmithing. The killing seemed to have been revengeful, vindictive, and wanton. Martinez fled the country immediately and went to Colorado. He ventured back and was arrested. He appeared to be about twenty-four years of age, small of stature, and supposed himself quite a handsome young man. He was quite dandyish in his dress and appearance. The expression of his face was sinister and wicked. His countrymen gave him a cruel and brutal reputation. He was married.

He bore his trial and sentence with great fortitude yet it was plain that his bitter and proud spirit was tortured. He labored to conceal all. He manifested great concern when informed by the Judge the means recommended to the sheriff to prevent his escape.

Martinez was defended by Merrill Ashurst, one of the most able attorneys in the Territory. The proof, however, was too full and overwhelming to be resisted. . .

The best of order prevailed at the execution. A great concourse of people were present at the gallows. Ever since the sentence of Martinez, the conduct of the county officers and the people have been entitled to much credit. The Judge of the Probate Court, Santes Estevan, gave the sheriff every assistance in his power. A guard was kept at the jail and the people, who were summoned to serve, did so cheerfully.

Sheriff Don Pedro Valdez asked the Brigadier General of the Militia for a company of soldiers to be present. All were promptly on the ground and all well armed. The prisoner was attended to the gallows by a priest. When he came within sight of the frame (gallows) all the bravado he had shown at his trial seemed to give way and desert the victim. At the gallows he had to be lifted, so completely unnerved was he. After he fell, he hung one-half hour.

So has perished another murderer. So has ended the life of one who practiced his brutal bravado upon the living. We give our sincerest thanks to the people and officers of Taos who have stood so faithfully to aid the execution of the laws.[20]

---

[20] *Ibid.* May 7, 21, 1864.

The legend of Judge Benedict's speech at this trial
still persists although the original was destroyed in a
fire that damaged the courthouse in Taos. In recent
publications, a discrepancy exists between the dates of
the execution and the name of the accused. If Jesús
Maria Martinez was the identical person reportedly
addressed by Benedict as José Maria Martin, a degree
of authenticity may be given the speech. Doubt exists
when the judge was alleged to have made the speech in
1861, three years before the news account above was
published.

No other remarks of the judge disclose such utter
lack of sympathy for the accused when he imposed the
death penalty.

> José Maria Martin, stand up! José Maria Martin, you have
> been indicted, tried, and convicted by a jury of your country-
> men of the crime of murder, and the court is now about to pass
> upon you the dread sentence of the law. As a usual thing, José
> Maria Martin, it is a painful duty for the Judge of a court of
> justice to pronounce upon a human being the sentence of
> death. . .
>
> You are a young man, José Maria Martin – apparently of
> good physical condition and robust health. Ordinarily you might
> have looked forward to many years of life, and the Court has no
> doubt you have, and have expected to die at a ripe old age; but
> you are about to be cut off in consequence of your own act.
>
> José Maria Martin, it is now springtime. In a little while the
> grass will be springing up green in these beautiful valleys, and
> on these broad mesas and mountainsides flowers will be bloom-
> ing; birds will be singing their sweet carols, and nature will be
> putting on her most gorgeous and her most attractive robes, and
> life will be pleasant and men will want to stay, but none of this
> for you, José Maria Martin. The flowers will not bloom for
> you, José Maria Martin; the birds will not carol for you, José
> Maria Martin; when these things come to gladden the senses of

men, you will be occupying a space about six by two beneath the sod, and the green grass and those beautiful flowers will be growing above your lowly head.

   . . . the Court was about to add, José Maria Martin, "May God have mercy on your soul," but the Court will not assume the responsibility of asking an allwise Providence to do that which a jury of your peers has refused to do. The Lord will not have mercy on your soul! . . .[21]

Some of the tales of Judge Benedict's circuit rides are still extant. In the early spring of 1864 he and five attorneys [22] left Santa Fe to hold the court terms in Las Vegas, Mora, Taos, and Rio Arriba. Four of them rode in Concord carriages and the others were on horseback. By the time they reached Apache Canyon, a strong east wind lashed snow and sleet in their faces. So thick was the snow that they could scarcely see the horses and mules yet by the trusty animals' instinct, the lawyers were able to follow the road as far as Martin Kosloski's public house where all spent the night except R. H. Tompkins who rode onward alone to stay with a friend at San Jose.[23]

For ten years Judge Benedict had never missed holding court in his district except once when the Confederate forces occupied Santa Fe. He determined to maintain his record for punctuality. According to law, if he did not reach Las Vegas by midnight, the legally designated time for court would have expired and no session could be held unless special provision was made.

---

[21] Ralph Emerson Twitchell, *Leading Facts of New Mexico History*, II, (1912), 394. *New Mexico Bar Association Minutes, 1890*, 56-7.

[22] *Weekly New Mexican*, April 9, 16, 23, 30; May 21, 1864. U.S. Attorney General Theodore D. Wheaton, Richard H. Tompkins, Charles P. Clever, and Merrill Ashurst.

[23] Don Pablo Antonio Sena.

The judge started for Las Vegas despite the inclement weather. Samuel Ellison and Charles P. Clever went with him. Clever had ridden with the judge all the way from Santa Fe so now he exchanged his seat in the carriage for Ellison's saddle horse. The judge and his two companions arrived at Las Vegas at ten in the evening. The sheriff was summoned out of bed, court was opened and adjourned. Thus the term was saved.

When court session was ended at Las Vegas, they left for Mora. The first town en route was Sapello where two saw mills were operated by the Sapello River. The demand for lumber to build military posts stimulated the business of the mills.

The next day they continued their journey to Mora. Court was immediately organized and business promptly completed. Praise was given the people of Mora County for having built such a good courthouse and the safest jail in the Territory. The court occupied the entire upper floor while the lower was divided to accommodate the jury and county offices. The jail adjoined the adobe courthouse and was built of rock laid in solid masonry. The fines assessed and paid upon conviction amounted to $90. Two men were tried for alleged participation in a lynching. Both were acquitted.

When the one-week court term at Mora was concluded, the circuit riders left for Taos in the afternoon. After riding twelve miles, they reached Guadalupita where a chronicler of the journey wrote during those war years, "Guadalupita is a place where one might exclaim with the Irish poet, Thomas Moore:"

If there is peace to be found in the world,
The heart, that is humble, might hope to find it here.

This small village at the foot of the mountains was the last the travelers would see on the road to Taos. The pines stood tall and straight at the mouth of the canyon from which Coyote Creek emerged to spread its waters among the farms in the valley. As Judge Benedict and his companions proceeded, the canyon narrowed, zigzagged upward, then swirled its snow water over and around the boulders blocking its course.

Nineteen times the judge urged his struggling team into the stream before he crossed to the opposite bank where there was scarcely enough room for the carriage wheels to turn without scraping the canyon walls. At another narrow passage, the road followed the stream bed for a distance of eight rods.

Good advice was given by one of these travelers. "When one is on wheels, he should be sure he has mules or horses that will never balk going up hill and will go down without alarm. The driver should be patient, steady and alert. The harness ought to be too strong to be broken and the carriage the best of Concords."

After emerging from the gorge, the road meandered over hill and down a steep pass to turn northward to Black Lake. Although there were still many miles to travel over more hills and through ravines, they were now near the Santa Fe Trail over which they could continue their journey with comparative ease to Taos.

On a previous occasion Benedict had gone to Albuquerque with Attorney General Clever to substitute again for a vacationing judge when an accident occurred. He stopped to speak to an old acquaintance when the horses became restive. Clever jumped from the carriage to try to quiet them but the reins broke and they ran away. One wheel struck a knoll which caused the carriage to lurch and pitch the judge out, injuring his back. As soon as possible he was taken to the home of Antonio Lerma where he received attention.

The people of that district had been afflicted with both uncertainty of the law and of the courts ever since Judge Benedict left after his promotion to the chief justiceship. Then when he was about to hold a special term, his accident prevented his doing so.[24]

Court cases did not occupy all of the attention of the chief justice. The battles fought on the eastern front, the invasion of New Mexico by the Confederate forces, and political dissensions all around him caused him considerable anxiety. Yet the future of New Mexico and her mineral wealth did not go unnoticed.

When Albert C. Benedict arrived in Santa Fe en route to the gold mines of Arizona, the judge's interest in prospecting was heightened. He referred to Albert Benedict as a "distant relative." [25] Portions of the latter's letters are quoted:

PIMA VILLAGES, ARIZONA   May 21st, 1863
HON. KIRBY BENEDICT, Chief Justice
Santa Fe, N.M.

DEAR SIR: Doubtless you wonder why I have delayed so long in writing to you. The reason is that until now we had not accomplished the exploration we intended nor the successes we

---

[24] *Rio Abajo Weekly Press,* Albuquerque, June 30, 1863.

[25] Albert Case Benedict was born at Barton, Mich., on Oct. 13, 1830. His father, Allen Benedict, was a miller at Port Huron. The letters were presented to the Arizona Pioneers' Society by the estate of his daughter, Mrs. Charles Wiswall, formerly Mrs. William C. Green.

Dan Ellis Conner, *The Walker Party in Arizona,* p. 103.

hoped for. I have not now sufficient space or time to give you a detailed narrative of all our travels since I left Santa Fe. I will, however, tell of our last prospecting trip.

Our party left these villages to search for gold on a stream northwest of this place. We consisted of twenty-five men with the well-known Captain (Joseph Reddeford) Walker as our chief and guide. We left on the 20th of April and returned on the 18th of the present month.

We went only one half of the distance we intended on account of some dissension in our party. We found the expected stream and travelled up it about eighty miles. For about sixty miles we found gold prospects not very encouraging; after that they became much better and the gold coarser. We arrived at the head of the stream where we prospected for three days. The results were favorable indeed. Each pan of dirt yielded from ten cents to a dollar. We found plenty of water and the mines are extensive. I think that considering the prospects we found, I can make from fifty to one hundred dollars a day, perhaps more.

These mines are situated in one of the most beautiful localities of New Mexico. . . The stream upon which the gold was found is not laid down upon any of the maps and was entirely unknown to the whites until a short time ago. . . The country east of the mines, as far as the eye can reach, is covered with a dense growth of pine. Captain Walker says that there is a fine agricultural country on the San Francisco river and that a good wagon road can be made from the mines to the Beale road. . . A road opened from the mines to Santa Fe would be the making of New Mexico.

While at the mines, a party of four of us went out about six miles from camp where we found what we consider of far greater value than gold. We found what we all pronounced to be silver lodes. These lodes are in great abundance and of a superior quality and I think they will lay Washoe in the shade. The facilities for working these silver lodes are splendid. Timber is abundant, water in every gulch, and the finest grazing country you ever saw. The Indians are friendly but how long they will remain so, I cannot tell. . .

Now, Judge, I have given you a plain unvarnished statement

of the discovery. I will now tell you what I am going to do and I want your advice how to proceed. I am the discoverer of the silver lodes and I believe I am entitled to the claim of the same. I am going to locate claims for some of my friends in Santa Fe. I send you a list of them. I wish to know if I can organize companies and locate claims for them and if the proceedings must be recorded in Santa Fe in order to secure legal rights.

Please write to me and direct your letter to Pima Villages, Arizona, to be forwarded to the Walker Mines, care of W. A. White, Esq. and I will be sure to receive same. Send by Military Express. I am, Sir, with great respect, Your friend and obt. servant   ALBERT C. BENEDICT

Two days later Albert Benedict again wrote to the chief justice having omitted some information from his previous letter. He gave a more detailed description of the terrain, the rivers, and mountains. Five Mojave Indians acted as guides for the first six days of the journey. These Indians had recently made a treaty with the Pimas and Maricopas. From Maricopa Wells he wrote:

HON. KIRBY BENEDICT, Chief Justice
Santa Fe, New Mexico

DEAR SIR: . . . Now, Judge, I will tell you what my opinion is in regard to the mineral wealth of that portion of New Mexico lying between the Beale road and the Gila river. It abounds in gold, silver and copper. There is not the same number of square miles on the American continent that contains the same amount of mineral wealth as does the section described. We found the gold in paying quantities on the river Prieto over two hundred miles from this place but the Indians were so hostile that we could not work there. It is only a matter of time when this country will be developed as another California and a Washoe. We need first to drive out the Indians.

When I left Santa Fe, Surveyor General Clark gave me a map of this territory and I promised to note down on the map any mistakes I might find; also any discovery I might make. Please tell him that I will do so when I get another opportunity to write and will send him the map corrected with these streams we found, their locality and sources.

I understand that a bill passed Congress for the organization of the new Territory of Arizona. Can you inform me where its present boundaries are? I wish to know whether or not our newly discovered mines are in the new Territory.

I have asked Captain Walker to write to General Carleton regarding our discoveries but he does not want to do so. I suppose his modesty keeps him from it. He says he cannot write well enough. Please communicate to the General what we have accomplished in searching for mines.

We get no war news here. We do not even know what is going on in Tucson. I send herewith a specimen of gold.

I am fraternally   Your friend and Obt. Servant
                    (Signed) ALBERT C. BENEDICT
Headquarters Dept. of New Mexico
Santa Fe, N.M.   June 25, 1864
Official   BEN C. CUTLER   Asst. Adjt. General

On August 8, 1863, Albert C. Benedict posted the following notice on a tree in the Yavapai District:

We, the undersigned, claim four thousand feet of this lode commencing at this tree upon which this notice is posted and running a southernly course along said lode for the distance aforesaid.

The signatures were Albert C. Benedict, Kirby Benedict, Kirby T. Benedict, Jr., Henry Carleton, Charles P. Clever, James Ellison, Merrill Ashurst, King S. Woolsey, John A. Clark, Peter Allison, Augustin W. Hunt, Joseph Cummings, Charles G. Parker, John C. McFerran, John H. Miner, James L. Johnson, George Lount, Gustave Ellsbury, and Jacob Omsbury (sic).

General James H. Carleton appointed Albert C. Benedict his attorney "to take up, locate and register, in accordance with the laws of the Territory of Arizona, mining claims upon any ledge, lode or vein of gold bearing quartz or of silver, copper, cinnabar or any other metal or ore; and as his attorney to hold the same for his use. . ." This was signed July 20, 1865.

Due Process of Law in the Indian Pueblos

THE STOLEN PORTRAIT OF SAN JOSE

Acoma v. Laguna

The Acoma and Laguna Indians were neighbors but not friendly ones. Two important cases were tried by Judge Benedict during his first term as associate justice. Both were appealed to the supreme court and his decrees affirmed.

Acoma Pueblo El Penol, the Pueblo on the Rock, is the only one of the southwestern pueblos that has not changed its site since the arrival of the Spaniards in 1539, although two villages, Acomita and McCartys, have been established twelve miles north where they have irrigated farms. The majority of the population live in these villages but all important ceremonies are held at old Acoma.

Captain Alvarado, a member of Coronado's expedition in 1540, reported that the village on the rock was so high that even a good musket ball could not reach the top. The one entrance was by a stairway which began on a gentle slope at the foot of the rock. The ascent continued by two hundred broad hand-hewn steps, then by one hundred narrower ones. The remaining distance was accomplished by mere toe holds.[1]

---

[1] Leslie A. White, "The Acoma Indians," Bu. Am. Ethnology, 47th Ann. Rep., 1929-1930, pp. 17-192.

On the summit of this almost inaccessible 400-foot mesa, these Indians had built about two hundred houses from two to four stories high. This village was enclosed by a stone wall of both large and small rocks which could be used to roll down upon the heads of their attackers without exposing themselves to their enemies. There was sufficient space on this "Sky Pueblo" to raise and store a large amount of corn. Water was supplied by cisterns constructed at the expense of their own backs. Their garments were made of buffalo and deerskin. Wild turkeys were domesticated and their feathers used for their robes which were woven from the fibers of the maguey plant.[2]

Their mission was built on the "rock" and here was hung the portrait of San José. The Saint is usually represented as a bearded man dressed in classical gown and mantle, holding the Holy Child in one arm and in the other, a staff crowned with flowers.[3] It was for the possession of this portrait that the Acoma Pueblo brought suit against the Laguna Pueblo before Judge Benedict in Tome, Valencia County, April, 1855.

It was alleged that under the pretense of a loan, the Pueblo of Laguna borrowed this painting of San José from the Acoma Pueblo for the purpose of celebrating Holy Week.[4] The Lagunas, having obtained possession, refused to return the portrait. The Acomas claimed that this was a fraud to deprive them of their Saint.

---

[2] Herbert E. Bolton, *Spanish Exploration in the Southwest.*

[3] Fray Francisco Anastasio Dominguez. *Missions of New Mexico, 1776.* Translation by Adams and Chavez, p. 361. St. Joseph, Señor, San José, Spouse of the Virgin, is seldom referred to in Spanish without the prefix Señor (Lord) and often with Patriarca before or after the prefix.

[4] Feast Day, March 19.

They appealed to their priest who was conceded to have authority and jurisdiction over the controversy. Thereupon, he directed the painting returned and caused the two pueblos to appear before him in Acoma. For the final settlement, he asked them to earnestly and fervently call on God and the saint for right and justice to prevail.

Then he proposed that they draw lots. Twelve lots were placed in a vessel in the church. All were blank except one on which a picture of the Saint was drawn. Two little girls were selected and placed on opposite sides of the vessel. One represented Acoma, the other Laguna. The first, second, third, and fourth lots were blanks. The fifth, drawn by the Acoma girl, was the sketch of San José. The priest then declared that God and the Saint had decided that the painting should belong to the Pueblo of Acoma.

But the Pueblo of Laguna, wholly disregarding the decision thus solemnly made and sanctioned by the priest, returned the same day, strongly armed, and threatened to break down the door of the church unless the painting was given to them.

The Pueblo of Acoma was weak and powerless against the strength of the Lagunas. They were advised by the curate to avoid bloodshed and to deliver the painting of San José to the Lagunas who retained it against the wishes and consent of Acoma.

The Pueblo of Laguna, through their attorney, testified before Judge Benedict that they knew nothing of the origin of the painting except from the traditions of their old men which clearly and conclusively established their right to it. It was universally believed that after the conquest of New Mexico by Spain, a bishop gave the painting of San José to the Pueblo of Laguna. They charged that the portrait was clandestinely taken from them and when they went peacefully to reclaim it, the Pueblo of Acoma refused to surrender it. Thereupon a Catholic priest proposed that they draw lots for it. To this the Acomas agreed but the Lagunas objected as they believed they held rightful title. They took it from the Acoma Pueblo as they claimed they had a right to do and have ever since that time continued to keep, use, and claim it as their own up to the time of the institution of the suit against them.

After all testimony was given and duly considered, Judge Benedict decreed that the painting of San José be restored to the Acoma Indians. Not content with the decree, the Lagunas appealed to the supreme court. The case was heard before Judge J. J. Davenport at the January term, 1857. Laguna was ably represented by Attorneys Spruce M. Baird and Hugh N. Smith. Merrill Ashurst argued the cause of the Acomas. The decree of Judge Benedict in the lower court was affirmed.[5]

After the conclusion of the trial, Judge Benedict made another one of his frequently quoted comments.

> The history of this painting, its obscure origin, its age, and the fierce contest which these two Indian pueblos have carried on, bespeak the inappreciable value which was placed upon it. . . This painting has well nigh cost these two pueblos a bloody and cruel struggle and had it not been for the weakness on the part of one of the pueblos, its history might have been written in blood instead of the Courts of the United States.

[5] Original records of this case may be found in the old district court records which are deposited in the county courthouse, Las Lunas, Valencia County. *Report of Cases in Supreme Court, New Mexico*, I, 220-226.

Such is the appreciative value that one witness swore that unless San José is in Acoma, the people thereof cannot prevail with God. All these supposed virtues and attributes appertaining to this Saint and their belief that the Throne of God can only be successfully approached through San José, have contributed to make this a case of deep interest, involving a portraiture of the feelings, passions, and character of the people.

However much the philosopher or Christian may smile at the simple faith of the people in their immediate and entire Guardian of their Pueblo, to them it was "a pillar of fire by night and a pillar of cloud by day," the withdrawal of whose light and shade crushed the hopes of these sons of Montezuma and left them victims of doubt, gloom, and fear.

This cherished object of the veneration of their long line of ancestry, this court permanently restores to the Acomas and by this decree confirms to them and throws around them the shield of the law's protection in their enjoyment of their religious love, piety, and confidence.

THE STOLEN DOCUMENTS DATED 1689

Acoma v. Victor de la O

This case was heard before Judge Benedict during the November, 1854 term of the district court at Socorro, Third District. By some means unknown to the people of Acoma, the title to their land had come into the possession of Victor de la O, Vicente Ariluead, and Ramon Sanchez who refused to return the documents unless the Acomas would pay the sum of $600. This was alleged to be fraudulent possession and extortion.

The court exonerated Vicente Ariluead and Ramon Sanchez but decreed that Victor de la O surrender the documents and be enjoined from destroying or disposing of them in any manner detrimental to the pueblo.

It was ordered that a copy of the decree be entered upon the records of the court and that it also be recorded in Valencia County where the lands of Acoma are situated.

From this decree, which taxed the costs against Victor de la O, he appealed to the supreme court. The case was heard by Judge Benedict at the January term, 1857. Theodore Wheaton was attorney for Victor de la O and Hugh N. Smith for the Acomas.

The Pueblo of Acoma, by their Governor Juan José Lovato, alleged that the pueblo was the owner of a certain tract of land in Valencia County which had been granted them by the king of Spain; that the titles had been made out in due form and deposited in the archives of Santa Fe; and that Victor de la O had no right to them.

Both documents, labeled A and B respectively, were dated September 20, 1689, in the Pueblo de Nuestra Señora de Guadalupe del Paso del Norte. They furnished proof of the rightful ownership of the land of the Acoma Pueblo.

These ancient documents, now deposited in the United States Land Office, Santa Fe, are still quite legible although written in old Spanish which differs somewhat from the modern. For that reason a literal translation is not presented.

His Excellency Don Domingo Jironza Petroz de Curate, Governor and Captain General, stated that by his authority in the Pueblo of Acoma, over the Queres Indians and over the apostates in New Mexico, he ordered the Indian Bartoleme de Ojeda to speak the truth and declare in his confession the condition of the Pueblo of Acoma and of the other apostates in that kingdom.

THE STOLEN PORTRAIT OF SAN JOSÉ
In the nave of the Mission San Esteban del Rey, at Acoma.
See text page 90. Courtesy of James M. Slack, Historical
American Buildings Collection, Library of Congress.

LAND GRANT TO ACOMA PUEBLO, 1689
Portions of the first and last pages of the three-page document.
Courtesy of the New Mexico Archives, Santa Fe.

AN AIR-VIEW OF ACOMA PUEBLO EL PEÑOL
Courtesy of the New Mexico Tourist Bureau, Santa Fe.

A VIEW IN PUEBLO ACOMA
From the Ben Wittick Photograph Collection, Laboratory of Anthropology, Santa Fe.
Courtesy of Miss Laura Gilpin.

LAGUNA PUEBLO

From a photograph by Kaadt. See text page 89. Courtesy of the New Mexico Historical Society.

Ojeda, who could speak the Spanish language and read and write, had been most conspicuous in the battles of the rebellion of 1680 and had been seriously wounded by a ball and arrow. He was examined before General Don Pedro Venero de Passada who had recently returned from New Mexico. The Maestro de Campo, Baninguas Mendoza, was also present during the examination.

Ojeda was asked his name, where he was born, his age and occupation, and whether or not he knew the conditions of the Acomas and Lagunas who were neighbors.

The Indian replied that his name was Bartolome de Ojeda, that he was a native of the Pueblo of Zia in the province of New Mexico; that he was twenty-one or twenty-two years old, more or less; that he had no other occupation than that of a warrior, and knew the condition of Acoma and Laguna because he was an apostate in the province of New Mexico.

He was then asked why the Lagunas and Acomas, being neighbors, disagreed so much and why the Acomas left their pueblo. He said that the Acomas had moved to El Peñol on account of the many wars between the two pueblos.

When questioned about the cause, Ojeda stated that the Lagunas had moved near Acoma on account of the abundance of water there but were permitted to use only the surplus. The infringement of the water rights of the Acomas led to many conflicts. Although the Acoma Pueblo had later moved to El Peñol, they had not lost their right to the water.

In defining the boundaries of Acoma, Ojeda said that the Prieto Mountains were on the north, Gallo

Spring west, Cubero Mountain lay opposite the old Pueblo of Acoma and the Peñol Rock was on the south. These boundaries were ratified by the Indian Poc-pec, a native of San Juan Pueblo and one of the Los Teguas tribe. He was obeyed by all at the time of the insurrection. Alonzo Cochiti, Don Luis Tipabu, and several other captains of these pueblos had also agreed that the water belonged to the Pueblo of Acoma and that Laguna was to collect only the surplus remaining.

Ojeda was asked to identify the pueblos by their legitimate names and to tell which ones were the most rebellious. He stated that those belonging to the Queres nation were the pueblos of Zia, Cochiti, Santa Domingo, Zemez (Jemez), Pecos, Tbanos, Teguas, Picuries, Peñol Acoma, Laguna, Moqui, and Zuni. (He omitted Santa Ana.)

The people of the Tbanos nation, whose pueblos are seven leagues from the city of Santa Fe, had deserted all but San Lazaro and San Cristobal. Of the eight pueblos of the Teguas, only Galisteo, San Juan, and San Dia (Sandia) were inhabited. The most rebellious pueblos during the insurrection were San Dia, Felipe, and Cochiti.[6]

The two documents, labelled A and B, were signed by Don Domingo Jironza Petroz de Cruzate and Bartolome de Ojeda and witnessed by Don Pedro Ladron de Guitarras (Guitterez).

---

[6] The present Keresan or Queres pueblos are Cochiti, Santa Domingo, San Felipe, Santa Ana, Zia, Laguna and Acoma. The Tanoan pueblos consisting of three groups are: Tiwa or Tigua group – Taos, Picuris, Sandia and Isleta; the Tewa or Tehua group – San Juan, Santa Clara, San Ildefonso, Nambe, Pojoaque, Tesuque and Hano on the First Mesa in the Arizona Hopi country; the Towa group – Jemez and Pecos but the latter is now extinct. The Piro and Tano groups are also extinct. San Lazaro was a Tano pueblo.

Victor de la O, through his attorney Theodore D. Wheaton, stated his conviction that he had the just right to the possession of these old documents. Judge Benedict ripped his testimony to shreds.[7]

De la O claims not only the right to retain the original documents but also refuses the people of Acoma a copy of the contract, allegedly made in 1850 between himself and the Pueblo, wherein the latter agreed to pay him $600 in money or lands for the return of the documents.

With much complacency he asserts that if the Acomas, by negligence or lack of care, have lost their copy, it gives them no valid right to take from him the original documents without compensation, which by the care and diligence of himself and his ancestors, has been preserved from loss and destruction until 166 years after execution.

A term not infrequently used to denote chancery powers is that "the arm of the chancellor is long." The expression is imposingly true if his arm can stretch itself through the long line of ancestral rank of this defendant and lay his hand on the tomb of him who somewhere at the close of the seventeenth century became the custodian of these ancient documents and by his care and diligence incurred a pecuniary debt against Acoma and handed the debt, the documents and their custody down from sire to son; the claim allegedly increased from new service rendered by each succeeding generation until at last this defendant became the lucky recipient of so many ancient merits.

As the chancellor's arm gathers the various and steady accumulations through the years, amounting to $600, from the property of the Indians of the Penol Rock of Acoma into the hands of Victor de la O, we will follow the defendant in his account of the circumstances under which he became keeper and possessor of the documents. The defendant calls his narrative which follows, "shedding further light upon the ancient document."

He states his age to be fifty-four years, birthplace Chihuahua,

---

[7] *Report of Cases in Supreme Court, New Mexico,* I, 226-237.

and that he is the only child of Gregorio de la O who died in 1810 near Corralitos at the age of sixty-four. His father was a lieutenant of the dragoons of Spain and a man of education and at his death owned many books and papers. But the defendant, by reason of his inability to read or write, did not know the value or nature of these books and papers so sold and squandered most of them.

In 1833 this only son of the learned father came to New Mexico. Three years later his wife joined him and brought the documents and other papers which have since been in his possession. The circumstance by which his father came into the possession of them was wholly unknown to this son but he presumed that it was by honest means – "these waifs floating upon the boisterous ocean of some of the revolutions of his day."

It seems unaccountable why such a literary Spanish father should have so cruelly neglected the education of his only son, sole heir to his house and heart. The child, left an orphan at the age of ten, was not taught to read and write by his literary father.

It is saddening when we infer that, when so noted a personage left no one who would look after the interest of the estate, the large amount of papers and books fell into the hands of the boy Victor to squander. It is a relief to know that it rarely occurred in those days that such an estate and such an orphan could find no one to look after them. An administrator would have been appointed to examine the books and papers, make an inventory and bring the "unclaimed waifs" to the attention of the probate court.

The magistrate would have quickly known where those titled and public documents belonged and taken steps for their restoration. . . In his childishness and utter ignorance of the value of the papers, young Victor was permitted to sell and squander them at his will and fancy. At what time he learned he had the title to the pueblo of Acoma the defendant has not given exact information. . .

Yet he was in "trade of pueblo titles" and made his appearance with documents in hand when the Indians were liable to fall victims of extortion and when their property could be wrung from them upon grounds wholly indefensible upon any principles of common honesty and equity. . .

The complainants (Acoma Indians) allege the titles in question were made out in due form and deposited in the archives in Santa Fe . . . The defendant (Victor de la O) does not admit that they were ever so deposited. His argument is that they were never deposited there or their existence would have been known to someone and the manner in which they were taken away or lost would have been accounted for. He further averred that he had a right to hold the papers from the Pueblo Acoma and the Secretary's office because said papers were purported to have been executed in El Paso which was then not a possession of the United States. . .

How does the defendant account for the manner the papers were taken from the archives? How did they escape and become waifs unclaimed? How and when did they desert their secure abode among the archives of El Paso and separate themselves from their companions on the shelf, wander like birds from their ark of safety, to be found lost and floating upon the revolutionary ocean which the imagination of the defendant has pictured. . . ?

His mind boldly moved around to imagine how the documents were found, snatched from destruction and preserved; but his spirit, tired and dropped from the effort in flight, his fancy retained no power to disclose how the documents left the custody to venture out to sea to endure so many perils, to be picked up by the literary lieutenant and finally rescued by his illiterate son as a profitable article of traffic in his trade in pueblo documents in New Mexico. . .

How does he assume the effrontery to come before the Chancellor and defend his action in detaining the documents from the Indians because a public duty is, in effect, upon him while in the same breath he prays the court to compel the Indians to pay him $600. . . ?

In view of all this, as if to make a parody of the recklessness of his conduct, he sold the title of the Lagunas to one unconnected with the Pueblo for $200. . . He saw nothing wrong in turning a document from a public archive into the field of trade and profit for himself. . .

We do not deem it irrelevant to remark that the recent abstraction of Pueblo titles from the archives of this Territory has become a matter of general notoriety on account of their nature and importance and the frequent attempts of extorting money from these Pueblos by means of these documents.

Perhaps these personal acts, at a period when the political power of Mexico passed to the United States and before the archives were possessed by the United States, could explain how the Pueblo titles were "floating upon the revolution of the day. . ."

We cannot admit that whoever comes into possession of a public document has the authorization to estimate its value and withhold it from its rightful owner until the sum estimated or demanded shall be paid. The wrongs, which might be perpetrated where such a doctrine would be recognized and enforced, can neither be counted or measured.

Every man's titles and all documents would become the prey to insecurity. The fraudulent men would riot in this species of plunder and the extortionist revel in his iniquity. We cannot regard the means used to obtain the promise of $600 other than an unconscionable attempt at extortion from the Indians. . . We are satisfied that the documents are the property of the Indians and that Victor de la O has no right to withhold them from their possession; that he has no lien upon the thing in controversy. . .

It plainly manifests that his hands, in time past, were stained in doing wrong to Indian Pueblos, relative to their titles; and by his defense he but deepens their discoloration to a repulsive blackness. . .

In this case, the title that Spain had given this Pueblo confirming to them the possession and ownership of their lands and the Rock upon which they have so long lived, was found in the hands of one professing to be of a better instructed and more civilized race; yet turned by him into means of extortion and money gathering from the unoffending inhabitants.

It is gratifying to us to be the judicial agents through which the ancient manuscripts, written evidence that established rights in their soil, their water rights, and their Rock, are safely restored and confirmed in their possession and keeping.

The decree of the district court was affirmed with costs. To Judge Benedict is ceded the distinction of having rendered the first decree regarding riparian rights in the Southwest.

Peonage and Slavery

For the first time it was the duty of Judge Benedict to examine and interpret the laws of New Mexico defining the relations and rights of masters and peons. The purpose of the court was to explain what the system really was, as well as to judge the evidence presented.

The case of *Mariana Jaramillo* v. *José de la Cruz Romero* was first heard before the justice of peace in the First District, then appealed to the district and finally to the supreme court in January, 1857.

Mariana was described as a servant who had abandoned the service of her master while owing him the sum of $51.75 advanced to her. The transcript showed that judgment was rendered against her for twenty-six months' work as a servant and for interest and costs; and that the plaintiff recover from Domingo Fernandez, Luz Jaramillo, and Juan Miguel Otero, the securities on her appeal bond, the sum of $56.21. In default of payment, Mariana was ordered to serve her master, José de la Cruz Romero, as a peon until the debt was paid. The price of the labor of a peon was variously estimated from $1 to $6 a month.

Upon examination of all available authorities,[1] Judge

---

[1] Joaquin Escriche y Martin, *Diccionario Legislativo,* I, 184. Gustavus Schmidt, *The Civil Law of Spain and Mexico,* pp. 113-114. White, *Recopilacion,* I, 201-202; 525.

Benedict was unable to find any law creating and defining the duties, rights, and civil and domestic relations, under the specific denomination of peon.

In 1846 the political relations of New Mexico were changed from Mexico to the United States. The president assumed political jurisdiction over the Territory and by his authorization, General Stephen W. Kearny proclaimed the "Kearny Code." Under this code the alcaldes were substantially justices of peace and had no powers beyond those expressly conferred upon them.

In these well-defined powers of the alcaldes, there was no special ruling regarding masters and servants. An alcalde could not proceed summarily against a fugitive servant. The same course of proceeding was given a master to recover his debt from his servant or peon as in the ordinary way from any other debtor; nor was any summary process provided to compel a peon to return when he had left his master's service.

These peons were not of any particular color, race, or caste. They were classified as servants, menials, or domestics and bound to some kind of service to their masters. One fact existed universally; nearly all were indebted to their masters. Yet it was an invariable rule that the peon could discharge himself from this service by the payment of his indebtedness to his master and the latter never supposed that he had any right to refuse to receive it and still hold him in service.

In order to clarify the relations between masters and servants and to define their respective rights, the legislature passed a lengthy act of sixteen sections.

Although the contracts were voluntary, the law provided for strict enforcement. Persons who contracted their services were required to labor from sunrise to sunset, to perform their duties punctually, and to use all vigilance night and day for the property under their care.

A father was permitted to bind out his children only when poverty demanded it and then he was obliged to use the meager salary for the support of his family. Any person was granted the right to advance his servant as much as two-thirds of his salary and the alcaldes or justices of peace were required to authenticate these accounts between masters and servants.

All servants were admonished to respect their masters as their superior guardians and all disobedience and insubordination was punished according to law. Masters who chastised or forced their servants to serve beyond the bounds of their contract, if found guilty, were fined not more than $25 nor less than $1. If a servant ran away, the law provided that the master could reclaim him.

Minors, who were subject to parental or guardian jurisdiction, were not permitted to make contracts as servants to masters; minors from fourteen to twenty years, who were *not* under parental or guardian control, were allowed the right.[2]

The only evidence presented before Judge Benedict was in the form of two documents signed in 1849, more than two years before the Peon Act became a law:

Territory of New Mexcio, County of Taos
THE CITIZENS: Francisco Ortiz y Delgado, Prefect of the County of Santa Fe, do certify as fully as I am permitted by law, that the citizen, José de la Cruz Romero, of the County

---

[2] *Laws of Territory of New Mexico,* 1851, p. 183. Masters and Servants.

of Bernalillo, has personally appeared before me, claiming a
servant of his who was taken from his service by her father,
José Jaramillo, without his consent. The servant's name is
Mariana Jaramillo and the sum claimed by her master is $51.75
and in order that the party interested may demand his servant or
his money from her father, who is the person who brought her
away, I give him the present document.

(Signed) FRANCISCO ORTIZ Y DELGADO
In SANTA FE,   May 21, 1849.

Territory of New Mexico, County of Bernalillo
To the Hon. Prefect and Hon. Alcaldes of the County of Santa
Fe: José de la Cruz Romero has represented in this office that
his servant, Mariana Jaramillo, has abandoned his service,
owing him the sum of $51.75 and that he is credibly informed
that his servant is in Santa Fe, and the party interested asks of
the undersigned Justice of Peace, letters requisitorial (ex horto)
for the apprehension of said servant, which the present judge
extends, requesting all authorities to be pleased to order that
said servant be delivered to her master or return to him the
amount she owes him. In so doing I will remain obliged to do
the same when I receive a similar request from you.

(Signed) AMBROSIO ARMIJO
RANCHOS,   June 5, 1849.

The judge argued that there was no proof of any
mutual agreement between the parties before any
magistrate, nor did any of them certify to the correct-
ness of any accounts owed by Mariana.

The paper issued by the prefect stated that Mariana's
father had taken her away and the document was given
in order that Romero might demand his servant or
money from her father. So far as this showed anything,
it strongly suggested that the debt, if any, was owed by
the father and not the girl. The inference was patent
that the girl was a minor and if held for a debt, it was

her father's. It was then (1857) nearly eight years since the prefect had issued the document.

If the debt were made on Mariana's account, it must have originated when she was not much more than a child. Since she then had "passed beyond her minority" she could not be held bound to service by her father's indebtedness.

In conclusion the judge decreed that the letters possessed no legal force as indebtedness from Mariana to Romero; the process or certificate of the Prefect of Santa Fe cannot prove her bound to service or her indebtedness; no notice or summons was given the girl, neither actual nor constructive; she seems in no form to have been brought within the prefect's jurisdiction. All was "ex parte."

The two documents were utterly insufficient to prove Mariana's contract of service or any indebtedness to Romero. The court reversed the judgment of the lower court with costs against Romero.[3]

The old system of peonage continued until March 2, 1867, when it was abolished by act of Congress. Peonage was not affected by the Emancipation Proclamation as it was not then considered slavery, but as a contract between servant and master.

The national slavery issue was a matter of direct concern to the residents of the Territory of New Mexico in the pre-Civil War years. The judicial opinions of Kirby Benedict were required, without doubt, in instances involving the Otero Slave Code during the years

[3] Charles S. Gildersleeve, *Report of Cases in Supreme Court, New Mexico,* I, 190-208. *Records Attorney General's Office,* Washington, D.C., MS Benedict to J. S. Black, January 29, 1858.

1859 to 1861, although specific reference to such cases is not available.

Slavery was abolished in New Mexico while she was still a province of the Republic of Mexico, and there were no slaves in New Mexico when she attained territorial status by the Compromise of 1850. Twenty-two negroes were enumerated in the United States Census of that year but these were recorded as being free. The two slaves, Hannah and Benjamin, that Lieutenant Carleton brought to the Territory and sold to Governor William Carr Lane in 1851, increased the number of negroes to an even two dozen. By the time the next federal census was taken there were about three times as many negroes. The exact number was sixty-four.

Although laws were enacted by the New Mexico territorial legislature in 1851 and 1853 to regulate contracts between masters and servants, it was not until January 29, 1857, that a law was passed to restrict the conduct and residence of negroes in the Territory. This latter act prohibited, under penalty of fine and hard labor in the penitentiary, the residence of free negroes or mulattoes in the Territory for more than thirty days. Any owner who might free a slave was required to transport him beyond the Territory within thirty days. This law did not apply to actual resident negroes but good behavior was mandatory. Furthermore, the marriage of a negro or mulatto, free or slave, to a white woman was prohibited.[4]

The next year, 1858, a proslavery faction advocated the enactment of laws for the protection of property in

---

[4] At the fifteenth assembly of the New Mexico legislature, 1865-66, the Act of 1857 regarding free negroes was repealed and the peonage law modified.

slaves. The following communication from Miguel Antonio Otero, delegate in Congress from New Mexico, reveals that this code had its origin by congressional, southern, and executive intervention.

HOUSE OF REPRESENTATIVES Washington D.C.
December 16, 1858

ALEXANDER M. JACKSON
Secretary of Territory New Mexico

I have been requested by General R. Davis of Mississippi to write you a letter requesting you to draw up an act for the protection of property in slaves in New Mexico and cause the same to be passed by our legislature.

I know that the laws of the United States, the Constitution, and the decision in the Dred Scott case establish property in slaves in the territories but I think something should be done on the part of our legislature to protect it.

You will perceive at once the advantage that will result from the passage of such a law for our Territory and I expect you will take good care to procure its passage. Immediately after its passage you will dispatch copies to all principal newspapers in the Southern states for publication and also a copy to the *New York Herald* very quick.

(Signed) MIGUEL ANTONIO OTERO [5]

Good care was taken to procure the passage of the slave code which later bore the title of the "Otero Slave

[5] Loomis Morton Ganaway, *New Mexico and the Sectional Controversy, 1846-61,* p. 68. Ralph Emerson Twitchell, *Leading Facts of New Mexican History,* II, 309-310.

Miguel Antonio Otero, Sr., 1829-1882; native of New Mexico; acquired English education in St. Louis and New York; passed the bar examination of Missouri and soon after returned to Valencia County, New Mexico; was appointed associate justice of the second district in 1846 by Gen. Kearny; member of the territorial legislature for the session 1852-1853; in 1855, was elected as delegate from New Mexico to Congress and reelected the following term; in 1861 returned to New Mexico and was president of the San Miguel National Bank of Las Vegas holding that position until his death.

Code." It was approved by Governor Abraham Rencher on February 3, 1859.

This slave code specifically affirmed that it in no way applied to peonage and that the word "slave" designated only a member of the African race.

Thirty-one provisions defined and defended the rights of slave owners but infringed upon liberties of the slaves. No slave was permitted to be away from his master's premises after sunset or before sunrise without a written pass. If this law were violated the sentence was not more than thirty-nine stripes on the bare back and confinement. If a slave was sentenced to pay a fine in addition to other punishment, all or part of the fine could be substituted for stripes or branding.

Runaway servants were ordered arrested and put to work at public or private hire so that they might be employed with security until their master could be informed and proceed to recover them. The sheriff was required to keep runaway slaves in custody until claimed by the owner. If unclaimed, the slaves were sold to the highest bidder at the door of the jail and the sheriff was authorized to give a bill of sale. If the sheriff failed to keep a slave in custody for his owner he might be fined $500 and also be liable in civil suit by the owner.

A fine of from $75 to $1,000 and imprisonment from three months to three years was imposed on any person who had given a slave a sword, dirk, bowie knife, gun, pistol, or other firearms and ammunition. A similar punishment was provided for insurrection, rebellion, or conspiracy.

As a further protection for the slave owners, section four of the Slave Code provided that

> No court in the Territory shall take cognizance of any cause for the correction that masters may give their servants for the neglect of their duties as servants.
>
> For as soldiers are punished by their chiefs without the intervention of civil authority, an equal right should be granted those persons, who pay their money to be served, in the protection of their property provided the punishment be not cruel or unjust.[6]

The following extract is from a letter written by a resident of the Territory of New Mexico to a member of the House of Representatives:

BARCLAY'S FORT, NEW MEXICO
April 10, 1860

At my solicitude, Judge (Levi) Keithly, Speaker of the House of Representatives of the Territory of New Mexico, introduced a bill for the repeal of the slavery law but as he is a plain, honest, straightforward old farmer he took no steps to get backers among the other members of the Legislature as he believed the bill would pass on its own merits.

The introduction of the bill came like a thunderclap on the corrupt office holders who had proclaimed the passage of the law. A Santa Fean rose and moved the bill of repeal be rejected at once. The motion found no favor in the House and debate began. Judge Keithly made a speech and was supported by two Mexicans who advocated the repeal.

The opposition to the repeal having nothing to say and dreading a free discussion of the question and public opinion, the House adjourned. What they despaired of accomplishing in open discussion, they determined to accomplish by outside pressure.

---

[6] Abraham Rencher, governor of New Mexico 1857-1861. *Eighth Territorial Legislature, New Mexico, sess. of 1858-1859*, p. 70-91. "An Act for the Protection of Property in Slaves."

Government officials kept open house that night. John Barley-corn did his work and "mint drops" were freely administered where other means failed. One of the Mexicans was offered the speakership in exchange for his vote. He was seated as Speaker the next morning as the former officer was absent.

Judge Keithly entered a protest and defended his right to express his opinion but gained no hearing. He demanded that the proceedings in his case should be entered in the Journal of the House but this was refused. He resigned his seat and returned home heartily disgusted with the leaders of the party with whom he had previously acted. He now understands exactly what "National Democracy" means.[7]

With this slave code on her statute books, New Mexico won the support of the southern states in Congress but aroused bitter opposition among the antislavery members. John Bingham, representative in the House from Ohio, introduced a bill in Congress to nullify the slave code of New Mexico contending that it was contrary to the Act of 1850 and that Congress had been given power under section seven which stated that all laws passed by legislative assembly and the governor of the Territory shall be submitted to the Congress of the United States and if disapproved, shall be null and void.

The opposition led by Miles Taylor argued that the passage of the bill to repeal the slave code would prohibit slavery in New Mexico by act of Congress and he questioned the right of Congress to interfere with legislation in the territories; that the Compromise of 1850 provided that the Territory of New Mexico would

---

[7] John A. Bingham, report and vote on the repeal of the New Mexico Slave Code. (Huntington Library).

be admitted with or without slavery as their constitution might prescribe at the time of her admission as a state; and that the legislative power conferred on the New Mexico legislative assembly had been exercised for nearly nine years. Furthermore, he said that the annulment of the slave code was a blow aimed at slavery itself. The bill passed the House but when it reached the Senate it was referred to the committee from which it never emerged.[8]

With a slave code for negroes, the New Mexico legislature attempted to extend the code to include male and female Indians that might be acquired from the Indian tribes. Governor Abraham Rencher vetoed this bill and in his message of December 6, 1860, explained his action:

> The act apparently is founded on the supposition that the Indians acquired from the savage tribes were slaves; which is not the case; neither is it in the power of the legislature to make them such. The legislature can neither create nor abolish slavery; it may only regulate it where it already exists, the same as any other species of property.
>
> If then, any Indian were found in a state of slavery under the laws of Mexico at the cession of this Territory to the United States, then the law above referred to could be applied to such property.

[8] 36 Cong. 1 sess. Ho. Rep. no. 508, Feb., 1860, pp. 1-7, 8-39 (Ser. 1069). Report of Miles Taylor on Ho. Rep. bill no. 64; Sen. Misc. Doc. no. 12.

Congressional Globe, 36 Cong. 1 sess. Dec. 5, 1859-June 25, 1860. Minority and majority reports regarding slavery in New Mexico, pp. 506, 2044-2045, 2059, 2744.

Congressional Globe, 36 Cong. 2 sess. December 3, 1860-March 2, 1861. Debates in Congress on slavery in New Mexico; the Otero Slave Code; admission of New Mexico as state; peonage; also New Mexico and Texas controversy, pp. 114, 378, 454-455, 514, 716, 1326.

The normal or native condition of our Indian tribes is that of freedom and by our laws they cannot be made slaves either by conquest or purchase.

We may hold them as captives or peons but not as slaves. When the Territory shall become a sovereign state, it may exercise jurisdiction over this subject which a territorial legislature could not claim.

(Signed)   ABRAHAM RENCHER, Governor [9]

There was strong opposition to the slave code among many of the citizens. William Need voiced his opinion in a letter written to Simon Cameron, secretary of war, September 27, 1861:

Why should this slave code, more odious and bloody than the Code of Draco, be longer suffered to pollute the statute laws of this territory where Daniel Webster declared that the Ordinance of God had forbidden its introduction and he was opposed to its reenactment; and where Henry Clay declared in 1850, that no earthly consideration, no power of man, should compel him to vote for the introduction of slavery to a territory that was free from its curse and crime. . .

Sir, it should be scorched out and will be at the next session of the legislature unless as heretofore the federal officers forbid the ban. . ." [10]

After being on the New Mexico statute books for almost three years, from February 3, 1859, to November 1861, the Otero Slave Code was repealed. By that time the soil of New Mexico had been invaded by an armed force of Texans commanded by Colonel John R. Baylor and reenforcements of Confederate soldiers

[9] *Fourth Annual Message of Governor Abraham Rencher, New Mexico.*

[10] *War of the Rebellion,* ser. 1, vol. 50, Part 1, 636-641. This letter was written at Fort Fauntleroy in the Navajo country. Need said that he had written the letter at intervals snatched from military duty as a sentinal in the watch tower.

were on the march from San Antonio. This time the Texans were confident that they could conquer New Mexico and at last regain complete possession of their "lost domain." [11]

[11] Aurora Hunt, *Army of the Pacific*, 1860-1866, p. 52-61.

Supreme Court Decisions
of Judge Benedict

These supreme court decisions provide an insight into the legal problems that confronted Judge Benedict in the new Territory of New Mexico where the Spanish and Mexican laws had been in effect for two centuries. When he arrived in 1853, the Territory was but three years old and the legislature as yet had not enacted adequate laws to provide a guide for the procedure necessary for the proper decisions of the law suits in his court. He was obliged to rely upon the laws and customs that prevailed during the old regime.

Even though he concurred in the judgments rendered by other judges, he occasionally voiced his personal convictions which were inscribed duly in the court records as "separate opinions."

The hardships and the meager salary did not always attract efficient lawyers, especially in the Third District. There were many "short term" judges. Some remained for only one year before resigning; others were appointed but failed to accept.[1]

Repeatedly Judge Benedict complained to Washington that he was the only judge in the Territory and that serious consequences resulted when court sessions

---

[1] Thomas B. Stevenson and Zachariah L. Nabers did not accept in 1858. William F. Boone, W. A. Davidson, James H. Holmes, W. G. Blackwood, Horace Mower, and C. N. Archibald served only part of their terms.

were not held. Criminal trials were postponed from term to term and frequently, indicted criminals, out on bond, left the Territory between terms and were never located again. The old records contain numerous cases of this nature and it is noted, "Case dismissed but with the right to re-instate." The presumption is that if the escapee was found, he would be brought to trial. Others, who waited in jail for their trials, remained incarcerated for months only to be proved innocent when their trials were finally held.

From 1854 to 1866, Benedict rendered twenty-two supreme court decisions. This was a far greater number than any of his contemporaries. From 1862 until the January term of 1867, his were the *only* decisions rendered. During the following years there were no supreme court decisions whatever: 1856, 1858, 1860, 1861, 1863, 1864, and 1865.

The diversity of the peoples involved in the cases tried by the judge was equal to the variance of the law suits. In the summer of 1856, private George McDonald, Company K, First Dragoons, brought suit against his commanding officer, Major James Henry Carleton.

McDonald was in the army and wanted to get out. He charged that his re-enlistment was obtained under duress when he was illegally confined in the guardhouse at Albuquerque by Major Carleton and that the re-enlistment was void because it was signed on Sunday.

From the testimony of Carleton and others, it was deduced that McDonald was drunk while on guard and asleep on post as a sentinel. He had been tried by court martial and confined to the guardhouse to await sentence.

Carleton testified that since McDonald had returned from the expedition against the Mescalero Apache country, after the death of Captain Henry W. Stanton, he had been in the guardhouse most of the time on sundry offenses arising out of the use of liquor.

A day or two previous to re-enlisting, McDonald asked Carleton to re-enlist him and have the charges against him withdrawn. To this Carleton agreed if McDonald would promise to refrain from getting drunk. He then could leave his papers in Carleton's care and obtain the $250 to $300 due him. If he did not re-enlist, he would probably be prosecuted and if convicted, lose his pay and receive a dishonorable discharge.

After re-enlistment, Carleton withdrew the charges. Carleton in good faith fulfilled his promise. McDonald received all his pay, bounties for re-enlistment, and clothing to which he was entitled at the expiration of his first term of service.

When Judge Benedict rendered his opinion he explained that such an exact and just fulfillment of the agreement by the government should have admonished McDonald to show good faith on his part instead of cultivating vain hopes that the civil tribunals would absolve him from his legal duties as a soldier which he had solemnly bound himself to perform. To be a soldier of the United States should inspire him with a high and inflexible spirit of honor and duty and he should not permit, even for a moment, the feeling that there is demerit or degradation in his profession.

The judge reminded him that it was not the purpose of the civil arm of justice to stretch itself within the guardhouse and snatch him from under sentence by which he was properly confined.[2]

A similar case was reviewed by Judge Benedict during the same term. One Daniel Green brought suit against Captain Richard S. Ewell for unlawfully restraining his liberty. Green attempted to prove that he was a minor when he enlisted and sought his discharge by habeas corpus proceedings.

It was established that the descriptive roll at the time of his enlistment showed that his age was recorded as over twenty-one years. He had received pay and subsistence as a properly enlisted soldier without objection. The presumption was in favor of the regularity of the proceedings of the enlisting officer and that the recruit was of lawful age. Opinions as to age are very uncertain and unsatisfactory when judged from personal appearance. The judge commented, "Green is rather too smart; has got to preaching law lately." The judgment of the lower court was then affirmed. Green remained in the army.[3]

During the first year of his term as chief justice, Benedict rendered eight important supreme court decisions. The question of naturalization was raised in a trial for the murder of Juan Duro.

In the case of *George Carter* v. *Territory of New Mexico,* in an appeal from Santa Fe County to the supreme court in July of 1859, the appellant pleaded that the Territory of New Mexico ought not to further

---

[2] *Records Supreme Court, New Mexico, January Term 1857,* pp. 172-182. Appealed from third district, John S. Watts for appellant; Hugh N. Smith for appellee.

[3] *Ibid.* pp. 166-172. Appealed from Third District, John S. Watts and Hugh N. Smith for appellant; Theodore D. Wheaton for appellee.

prosecute the indictment against him because Anastasio Sandoval, one of the jurors, was not then a citizen of the United States; that he had retained the character of a Mexican citizen in pursuance of the eighth article of the Treaty of Guadalupe Hidalgo.

A substantial part of the opinion of Judge Benedict is quoted:

If we were disposed to shrink from the heavy responsibility to be assumed in the discussion and decision in this case, there are points of practice and technical merits upon which the court might repose and avoid the examination and adjudication intended to be presented in this appeal. Such shrinking, however, would be unworthy of the independence and dignity of an intelligent tribunal of justice.

We may take judicial notice of the public and notorious acts which have constituted a portion of the history of New Mexico during the past thirteen years. The question of the retention of the character of Mexican citizenship has been exciting and disturbing. By the Treaty of 1848, the people of New Mexico could either retain the title and rights of Mexican citizens or acquire that of citizens of the United States. But they shall be under the obligation to make their decision within one year from the date of the ratification of that treaty. Those who remain in the Territory after the expiration of that year without having declared their intention to retain the character of Mexicans, shall be considered to have elected to become citizens of the United States. . .

Anastasio Sandoval did declare his intention within one year to retain his right to Mexican citizenship and his name was signed and certified according to requirements. However, he later declared his intention to become a citizen of the United States. . .

The war dismembered the Mexican Republic and one portion, New Mexico, was conquered by the United States troops in 1846. In this region there was a large number of native born Mexicans. Few of them were aware how deeply the Mexican government felt in insisting upon a treaty stipulation that would secure to those citizens, beyond cavil or dispute, the right to retain their Mexican citizenship, should they prefer to do so, in preference to becoming citizens of the United States. These instructions express the extreme unwillingness of Mexico to cede this Territory.

These well-deserving Mexicans were abandoned to their fate, very frequently without protection, not even shielded from the incursions of the Indians, yet, notwithstanding all this, they have been the truest Mexicans and most faithful patriots. Could our government sell Mexicans like these as they would a herd of sheep?

There was much diplomatic correspondence before the eighth article was finally adopted. . . Although Mexican citizens did retain right to Mexican citizenship, still the treaty failed to prescribe the form and manner, by the observance of which such citizens could avail themselves of the stipulations in their favor; but as Congress passed no act to aid these persons and defined no special form by which they could declare their intentions, they remained wholly without remedy. Consequently, that portion of the eighth article was ineffective, a dead letter among the supreme law of the land and void as to any power to retain rights under its provisions.

Mexicans had to make their choice. Those wishing to retain Mexican citizenship simply registered their names in the office of the state secretary. Those wishing to secure United States citizenship did nothing but remain passive for one year and this passiveness was declared to be evidence that they had chosen to be citizens of the United States.

When such nonaction was to be proof of the solemn act of changing allegiance and citizenship on one part, was the other part left without remedy or compelled to seek it through some modified declaration under oath analogous to that provided by naturalization laws?

In our government and also in the Mexican, no declaration concerning citizenship could be made without the aid and presence of some public authority. Varied as were the forms in both governments, there was one element ever present and universal and without which no such declaration in any form was known to our laws. Some court, magistrate, or council received the declaration and preserved the imperishable evidence of the act. Neither government ever trusted to memory the preservation of so solemn an act as that of the assumption of allegiance – an unchanging and undying record was ever required.

The Romans were not the only people whose sons, by the simple utterance that they were "Roman citizens," averted danger and commanded protection in whatever country they might wander. Modern powers render protection to their citizens in similar manner.   .   .

From the moment that proof appeared that a Mexican had elected to retain his Mexican citizenship, he was excluded from all places and share in the administration of the laws of the Territory. He was turned from a seat as a juror and deprived of his functions as a local or county officer.   .   .   In the Organic Act it is expressly stated that the right of suffrage and of holding office shall be exercised only by citizens of the United States, including those recognized as citizens by treaty with Mexico, February 2, 1848. Congress clearly intended to draw a distinction regarding the ineligibility to hold office or to vote of those who had preserved their Mexican citizenship.

It is implied in the provision that Congress knew that *a class of men were here who were not recognized as citizens*. For nearly two and a half years, a large number of men were recognized, by the official authorities and the entire population, as not being citizens of the United States because they had recorded their names in the records of the prefect as retaining the rights and titles of Mexican citizens.

In the first session of the legislature in 1851, an election law was enacted which declared that no person prevented by the Organic Law of the Territory should be entitled to vote or hold office. For disobedience of this law, a fine not exceeding $500 or imprisonment for more than one year was imposed.

These provisions had not been repealed at the time Judge Benedict rendered his opinion in 1859.

He emphasized the privileges of citizenship and his opinions are applicable to modern conditions among the nations of the world:

> To be a subject under a depotism is to be naked of political rights. To be a citizen of the United States in New Mexico elevates a man to being virtually his own legislator. This is a position not to be lightly esteemed. This great right should not be trifled with by those who enjoy it.
>
> Those who knowingly and willingly pushed it aside or trampled it under their feet after the treaty offered it, must place to their own charge their great loss. They should have estimated more fairly the strength, progress, and justice of the government inviting their allegiance. As deeply as we may regret this, still it is one of their own seeking and from which they have a mode of extrications.
>
> The pathway of the bench is where law and duty lead them. They are not to suffer their ears to be corrupted by the whispers that some people have personal political interests involved in this question.
>
> If relief is to be found, other branches of the government must give it and not the judicial, however gladly an individual judge might interpret an act lessening the disabilities under which the Mexican citizen labors.

Judge Benedict ruled that Anastasio Sandoval was a citizen of the United States at the time he served as juror during the trial of George Carter and that the latter was fairly and justly convicted by the lower court.[4]

Other Supreme Court decisions of Judge Benedict are set forth in the appendix of this work.

---

[4] *Ibid.* pp. 317-347. Merrill Ashurst for appellant; R. H. Tompkins for appellee.

Revision and Codification
of New Mexico Laws

Judge Benedict found it increasingly difficult to interpret the laws and render just decisions. Since his arrival in New Mexico, the legislature had not enacted essential laws to protect the rights of the people.

In a letter to Attorney General J. S. Black, he explained that much careful research was required to discover the true rules of law and practices that were in force during the Mexican regime. The isolated condition and great distance from the city of Mexico exposed the people to great abuses and to arbitrary acts regardless of the laws under the Mexican government. Under the ruling authorities, many changes were made although the general principles of the body of civil law, as understood in the prosperous days of the viceroys, continued in force. Few books could be found that contained those principles. General Manuel Armijo, when governor, sometimes substituted his own will in place of all law. Many of the cases adjudicated in the supreme court of New Mexico had necessitated the finding and interpretation of these ancient laws and usages. These were illustrated in the opinions of the judges. Benedict stated in 1857:

> There is a strong desire on the part of both races that the opinions of the supreme court be published in the Spanish and English languages. . . At the last session of court my

brother judges made an order requesting me to prepare and report the decisions and opinions for publication. This labor I have undertaken. A great difficulty is in the way. Not one dime can be expected from the Territory to aid in the printing and binding. This deeply seated abhorrence of the people against direct taxation has not been removed. Can we hope for any assistance from the government for translation? . . . Cheerfully I gave my own services. . ." [1]

This was not the first attempt to revise and codify the laws. As early as December 18, 1852, the legislature resolved that a committee of five be appointed to correct the acts passed previously. Two years later the governor was authorized to appoint some person to revise the laws again as the volume printed in 1852 contained errors and many parts were not exact copies and translations of the originals on file in the secretary's office. Five hundred copies were ordered printed and distributed among the members of the legislature, the territorial officers, attorneys, and judges. Two more years passed. This time a committee composed of three members from each house of the legislature prepared a revision but it was not published. [2]

Once more, on January 3, 1859, the legislature prodded the governor to action. This time the law was more specific:

The governor of this Territory is hereby authorized and required to appoint a commission, of two or more competent persons, to collect, revise, and put in systematic order the laws now in force in this Territory; and it shall be the duty of said commission so appointed to revise carefully the code and statutes,

[1] Justice Department Records, Attorney General MSS, Benedict to Black, May 29, 1857.

[2] Legislative assembly, Dec. 18, 1852, Feb. 9, 1854, Dec. 29, 1856.

to extract from them all the laws in force, and to present and return to the next term or some other legislature, and to his excellency, the governor, a list of all the laws in force and also of all those repealed; and the said commission, before entering upon their duties, shall take an oath truly and faithfully to discharge the duties of their appointment. The governor is authorized to award to the commissioners a just and adequate compensation, to be paid out of the money appropriated for the contingent expenses of the legislative assembly.[3]

After another lapse of time, in 1862, Governor Connelly, by authorization of the Act of 1859, appointed Kirby Benedict, Charles P. Clever, and Facunda Pino as a committee to revise the laws. On account of the death of Pino and the results of the invasion of the Texans, the revision was delayed.

Finally work was begun in the spring of 1864,[4] after the governor had appointed Diego Archuleta to fill the place vacated by the death of Pino. In his message to the legislature at the December term, 1864, the governor said that the "high character of the committee in legal -attainments gives assurance that the work will be creditable to the revisers and useful to the people."[5]

When the revision was completed it was submitted to the legislature for approval. On January 24, 1865, that body enacted the following:

That the revision of the statutes, each and all of the articles and chapters, is hereby declared to be the Revised Statutes and Laws of the Territory of New Mexico, and as such shall have full force and effect in all courts thereof. . .[6]

---

[3] *Laws of Territory of New Mexico, 1858-1859,* Chap. 1, sec. 1, 2. Jan. 3, 1859.

[4] *The New Mexican,* June 3, 1864.

[5] Governor's Message, Dec. 6, 1864.

[6] *Laws of New Mexico, 1864-1865,* Jan. 24, 1865, p. 742-746.

The next problem was to obtain an appropriation from Congress to pay for the printing. The revised statutes would be double the size of that of other territories as both the Spanish and English versions were imperative. Fifteen hundred copies were ordered by the legislature.

Evidently it was decided that a junket to Washington was necessary, so Secretary Arny asked permission from Secretary W. H. Seward for a leave of absence to supervise the publication of the revised code. Arny's letter was signed by the governor, the members of the legislature and Chief Justice Benedict.[7]

The revision committee was concerned about the pay for their services. In answer to their inquiry, Arny suggested that $100 each would be ample compensation and that an appropriation of $1200 from Congress would be just and equitable both to the United States and to the committee.[8] The completed volume was printed in St. Louis and contained 856 pages.[9]

The war years necessitated new laws for minors.[10] Some of them appeared to have been patterned by the Commandment, "Honor thy father and thy mother. . ."

Even though there appeared to be no law defining the speed limit in Santa Fe, several persons were arrested and fined for riding horseback through the streets at a reckless pace and endangering the lives of "foot passengers."[11]

---

[7] *Arny's Letter Book MS,* Dec. 23, 1864.   Huntington Library.

[8] *Ibid.* p. 111, Feb. 2, 1865.

[9] *New Mexican,* Nov. 3, 1865.

[10] *Laws of New Mexico, 1863-1864,* Jan. 1, 1864, p. 28.

[11] *Weekly New Mexican,* Santa Fe, Nov. 10, 1865.

Washington Correspondence

Judge Benedict's letters [1] *are still preserved in the National Archives and included among them are newspapers which are rare indeed. His bold handwriting is undimmed even though the record of his legal services on the frontiers of America has been almost obliterated.*

SANTA FE   February 17, 1861

HIS EXCELLENCY   ABRAHAM LINCOLN
Washington, D.C.

SIR: Before this reaches you, you will have been inaugurated the Chief Magistrate of this Great Republic. Permit me to express my pride and gratification of one with whom, but a few years since, I was so much associated in our prairie land, now so distinguished by the fame of her sons.

May all the good spirits assist you in becoming what I assure you my friends and the people here know to be your daily and nightly prayer, that is a great and good President. You go to the helm of State at a trying time and in the midst of stirring events.

These have been maturing for thirty years. Your election is only the pretext for the revolutionary dismemberment now going on. In the midst of all, it is

---

[1] Just a few words in Benedict's letters are illegible. In some instances, only excerpts have been quoted as the deletions were irrelevant. The letters are in the Justice Department Records, National Archives, Washington, D.C.

pleasant to see the personal merits and character of the elected so well appreciated and esteemed throughout the land.

With unreserved labor and energy and stern and unsullied integrity, you will have won your "pride of place." I say not this because in you is vested so much of the nation's power and patronage . . . I say it because my spirit is full of the truth of my utterances.

Since last we met in the defense of poor David Campbell, whom I so well loved, I have been through many scenes and now find myself rapidly passing into the "vale of years." I have now been longer in office than any federal officer, civil or military, in New Mexico.

Much of the time, I have been the only judge here and have performed the duties incumbent upon others rather than see my branch of service blamed and justice not administrated. This has been expensive in this expensive country with my comparative small salary. My term as chief justice will expire in the summer of 1862.

As I now feel, I say to you frankly, that I have a desire to remain during my term. As a judicial officer, I have striven to keep myself apart from the parties or factions that sometimes rage mid this people.

I have learned the language so that I seldom need the assistance of an interpreter. I have studied the Spanish and Mexican laws and the character of the people. I have held court in all parts of this Territory and I see no evidence that I have not the full confidence of the people.

I have my family with me but I now expect to ask your leave to be absent long enough to go to the states

with my wife and children and place the latter in
school. My only absence in nearly eight years service
was in going for my family and returning.

I have written to Senator (Lyman) Trumbull[2] and
will shortly again touching upon the interests in New
Mexico, officers, appointments, etc.

I have the honor to be with sentiments of highest
considerations,   Your Obt. Sevt.

KIRBY BENEDICT
Chief Justice, New Mexico

SANTA FE, NEW MEXICO
June 2, 1861

HIS EXCELLENCY   ABRAHAM LINCOLN
Washington, D.C.

SIR: Early and kindly associations over the prairies,
about courthouses and at the bar in our beloved Illinois,
will allow me to address you an entirely private letter.
Your necessary and controlling connection with the
great events, now transpiring in our once peaceful and
happy Republic, does permit thoughts of solicitude for
your every public movement and act.

The energy and directness of your administration in
combining the means to repel and punish aggression,

---

[2] Lyman Trumbull, 1813-1896; born in Colchester, Conn. At age of twenty,
went to Greenville, Ga., where he taught school and studied law; was
admitted to the bar in 1836; moved to Belleville, Ill., in 1837 where he
practiced law; soon entered politics; was elected to Illinois legislature in
1840; resigned the next year to accept appointment as Secretary of State of
Illinois; was removed by the Governor in 1843; practiced law until 1848
when elected chief justice of Illinois; in 1852 reelected but served for only
two years when elected U.S. House of Representatives; before taking his
seat, a three-cornered contest resulted in his being sent to the U.S. Senate
where he remained for three terms, 1855-1873.

suppress rebellion, and crush out anarchy, is having its effects even here. Rampant secessionists are more reserved in their public abuse of yourself, the Union, the Government, and the North.

It was not agreeable to President Buchanan to give any of the free states much chance in the appointments for New Mexico. Judge Boone [3] from Philadelphia, a Catholic, was the only one I remember that was sent here from any free state and he died after having been in office over a year. I was already here and so was Dr. Michael Steck,[4] Indian Agent. Southern extremists were usually sent here. . . There are a good many European Jews and other traders that I do not include in speaking of Americans. These Southern men, whether in office or out, are violent secessionists and sympathize with the Davis Confederacy.

The entire Mexican and Spanish population has remained calm and quiet while the convulsions have been so rapid in the states. Since your recent powerful movements that have cheered the hearts and raised the hopes of all Union men, the secessionists have insiduously labored to produce discontent among the Mexicans, telling them the government was destroyed; that the Confederacy was carrying everything before it; that Missouri was sure to secede; and that New Mexico must do as that state does.

At all of my recent courts, in my charges to the grand

---

[3] William F. Boone, associate justice, New Mexico, 1859-1861.

[4] Michael Steck, 1818-1883; born Hughesville, Penn.; graduated from Jefferson Medical College and practiced in Miffenville for a few years; in 1852 President Millard Fillmore appointed him Indian Agent for the Mescalero Apache Indians; made superintendent May 23, 1863, replacing James Collins. Steck resigned May 1, 1865, and returned to Pennsylvania. He died near Winchester, Va.

juries, I talked to them and explained the condition of things; enjoined the people to remain quiet and without alarm, assured them that the government *would* and *must* be maintained and that they would receive the same protection as heretofore. This I did in their own language and all gave evidence of feeling entirely safe and satisfied.

But for this conservative feeling among the Mexicans and their unwillingness to be disconnected from the government of the Union, . . . the Southern secessionists would have driven this country into anarchy and towards the Davis Government. I have, myself, as a man and magistrate, stood directly in the way and opposed all secession schemes and disorders. On the bench and off the bench, I have calmly and decidedly been against all infidelity to the Union or the Government. Yet in this situation, I have had to stand almost alone among the federal officials at this place.

Governor Abraham Rencher [5] from North Carolina is a Confederacy sympathizer and says he must do as his state does, and if she "goes out" he must share her fate. So far, . . . his opinions, sentiments, and sympathies are all against the Union and the Government and tend in favor of the secessionists and those who are trying to carry out their long-plotted scheme to overthrow the United States. As an executive he is of no further value, whatever, aside from the plain details imposed upon him by law. If a crisis should arise where a man of energy and action . . . would be required, he will not be worth two cents. I never

---

[5] Abraham Rencher, Governor New Mexico Territory, 1857-1861. He was from North Carolina and before coming to New Mexico had served in the U.S. Congress and as United States Minister to Portugal.

feel his arm to lean upon in the midst of any official responsibilities any more than if he were but ten years old. . .

In what you all call Arizona, the governor has appointed a probate judge (a very important office here) whose name was appended to a call for a convention which passed the resolutions of March 16. There will be no trouble in Arizona if you will keep a competent judge in that district and back him with an executive who will make himself felt for good.

There will be no kind of difficulty with the Mexican population. When I was associate justice, Arizona was within my district and I had to take some great responsibilities. At one time, I tried thirty-six men (Mexicans) for murder upon the same indictment but I met no uncommon trouble and no resistance. Both races have petitioned me within the last few months to hold court for them but to do so I would have to spend between two and three hundred dollars and I have done so much gratuitous service of this kind at my own "proper costs and charges," that my salary will not enable me to continue such labor however much I may desire to gratify the people's wants and to see no judicial requirements omitted.

Time and again the other judges have not been here and the Government has permitted their absence while I performed their duties and they received their salaries. Sometimes I have been to every county in every district to hold all the terms in the Territory. One time I was the sole judge for a whole year and I let not a day of court go unheld in the Territory. I learn that you have appointed Sydney A. Hubbell [6] judge and he will

6 Sydney A. Hubbell, associate justice second district 1861-1865

serve in the Arizona District. He is from Connecticut and is a man of much energy and experience. I trust he may succeed well. He speaks Spanish fluently. I expect you will correct the abuse of men who hold office and take their salaries while not at their posts.

A good many military officers here have resigned and gone home or to the Davis Government. Colonel W. W. Loring [7] has sent his resignation to Washington. He is a brave and gallant officer and as commandant of this Department could be relied upon for his high integrity and good faith. Still his state is Florida and his feelings and sympathies are undisguisedly and strongly with the South and the Confederacy. Of course the moral might of his opinions and feelings give encouragement to the enemies of the Government. Allow me to suggest, Sir, that if Colonel W. W. Loring should be relieved from his command that Colonel Edward R. S. Canby can be fully relied upon. I have conversed with officers of high character and intelligence and they assure me that Colonel Canby [8] is in every way fitted as a man, a gentleman, and soldier for the command of this Department at this crisis and that all things will be safe in his hands and treason find no encouragement.

Permit me further to suggest the real friends of Union and government in New Mexico ought not to be neglected. No man either civil or military officer should be entrusted with high powers and duties when his feelings, wishes, opinions, and sympathies are ad-

---

[7] Colonel W. W. Loring was in command of the Department of New Mexico in 1860 but resigned to join the Confederate army. He was replaced by Colonel E. R. S. Canby.

[8] Aurora Hunt, *Army of the Pacific,* 1860-1866, pp. 54-68; Max L. Heyman, Jr., *Prudent Soldier: E. R. S. Canby.*

verse to the duties he has to perform. Such men better leave here at once than be shedding a disastrous influence. Better let your military officers of tender feet and Southern sympathies get away from here and begone. You should trust no one here in important position whose whole heart and soul is not loyal to the Union and Government and who does not support all measures necessary to preserve this Republic, vindicate her wrongs, and go where duty calls even to the "bitter end," if the crisis should demand, through "blood and flame."

I fear that in the midst of your great and trying anxieties and labors, you can hardly spare the time to read this long "scroll" I have written in candor and sincerity and I am sure you will so appreciate it from me. I want you to know how we are here.

As for myself, I stand by the good old Union and all the means to maintain her. Let not expense be thought of. The people are ripe for the fray. Better a thousand battlefields than anarchy. The appointments you have made here are, in the main, . . . excellent. Those from the Mexicans are the best you could select among that people.

And now, Sir, permit me to hope that you and the Government will more sternly, grandly, and triumphantly [pass] through all the perils that surround you. Your name will then be great among the Nations of the Earth and through all time.

With sentiments of the highest consideration,

> I am your Obt. Sevt.
> KIRBY BENEDICT
> Chief Justice, New Mexico

SANTA FE, NEW MEXICO
June 9, 1861

HON. EDWARD BATES [9]   Atty. Gen. U.S.
Washington, D.C.

SIR: I have thought it not improper to bring to your notice some of the facts in connection with the Judicial of this Territory. My trust is that upon your being truly informed, your solicitude may be so engaged that you will see that in the future out here a more just and equal distribution of services, responsibilities, and expenses shall be enforced among judicial officers than heretofore.

This should be done in justice to those who spare themselves in no way to meet and supply the public and official wants and necessities. It should be done in fairness to the people, for the honor of the administration and for the credit of the Government in New Mexico.

I entered upon the discharge of duties here first, as Associate Justice in the summer of 1853. Within one year I found myself alone. One judge had resigned and his successor, although appointed early, delayed his coming until I completed holding the terms in the district which pertained to him.

Chief Justice Davenport [10] had gone to the States without leave, as I understand, so it fell upon me either to see the judicial service unperformed to the great detriment of the Government and the people or perform the duties myself at whatever sacrifice.

---

[9] Edward Bates was born in Virginia on Sept. 4, 1793; was licensed to practice law in Missouri, Nov., 1816; elected to Congress 1826; was Attorney General under Lincoln but resigned Nov. 24, 1864.

[10] James J. Davenport was Chief Justice of New Mexico, from 1853 to 1858. He was from Mississippi.

I did not hesitate in doing the latter. So from East to West and from Taos to Doña Ana, a distance of 400 miles, I went into every district and held courts in all the counties in the Territory. I assure you that the expenses incident to such services in New Mexico are enormous.

In the following spring the bench was full and each district, as it should, had its resident judge. In the summer (1855), by the approval of the President, I went to the States and brought hither my wife and children. Yet I did not leave until I had completed the sessions in my district and I returned long before time for the fall terms.

As the fall terms approached in 1857 . . . Judge Brocchus wrote me a letter informing me that deafness was fast growing upon him and that he needed to immediately go to the States to consult an occulist (sic) and desired me to go to his district and hold court. Of course, I at once notified him that I would do so and thereupon he left for the States and I fully complied with my engagement.

In October of that year, Chief Justice Davenport also left with his family and neither he nor Judge Brocchus [11] returned to the Territory at any subsequent period. The result was that I was again alone upon the bench until September, 1858. In the meantime, I held all the sessions in all the districts except one in Taos.

[11] Perry E. Brocchus, native of Baltimore, Md.; before coming to New Mexico was associate justice of Utah, appointed by President Fillmore; first appointed associate justice of New Mexico in 1857 by President Buchanan; served until 1859. He was also appointed in 1861, but owing to his inability to cross the plains, did not qualify. He was associate justice from 1867 to 1869 when he was removed by President Grant.

I was prevented by serious sickness in my family from doing this.

Judge Boone from Philadelphia, appointed to the vacancy occasioned by my appointment to the Chief Justiceship, arrived here in September, 1858. I agreed, from courtesy and friendship, to take my carriage (the Concord) and go with him to his first court in his district as he was wholly unacquainted with the language of this country and new to the forms of the proceedings of the courts.

It fell out, however, that the night previous to our departure he became suddenly indisposed so that he could not continue upon the fatigues of the trip. Again it happened that the judicial service had to be left undone or I must attend to it. I decided upon the latter and went through at great personal sacrifice and expense.

Judge Boone's illness was of short duration and he was relieved from going upon his bench at all, even to hold one day session in his district courts until the spring of 1859. He left in December of that year and died within a few days after reaching his family.

After Judge Blackwood [12] was appointed, I went into his district and held the court in the spring session previous to his arrival the first of July, 1859. . .

After all this, Sir, so flagrantly abusive and fraudulent upon the Government – so well calculated to inspire disgust and indignation in a member of the

---

[12] William G. Blackwood, associate justice, took his oath June 18, 1859. Ritch Collection MS, no. 936. Blackwood was a native of South Carolina. He was preceded by L. L. Nabers and followed by William A. Davidson who apparently were appointed but did not serve.

bench, situated as I was, I went down October last and held another two weeks term in the County of Bernalillo and then proceeded down in the district hoping to be able to reach Mesilla court in Arizona, when near the close of the end of a week's term in the County of Valencia, I fell violently sick with a fever and had to yield up the trip and remain in the district until I had recovered.

From this narrative, you can see how much one member of the bench has had to shoulder the duties incumbent upon others. . . I had to do what I have done or see the civil interests entrusted to my department of administration fall into confusion and great embarrassment, the public injured, and the Government dishonored.

It is needless for me to say that I have not, in the remotest degree, received in any form as much as *one cent* of reimbursement from any source whatever for any of my costs, charges and expenses, enormous as they have invariably been in this country in the performance of *extra services.* . .

I have consoled myself in the confident belief that abuses, such as I have mentioned, will be corrected by President Lincoln and his department when brought to his attention.

From former years in Illinois of personal and professional intercourse in the same judicial district with Mr. Lincoln, now President, I feel the utmost assurance from his sound and upright character, his clear and enlightened mind, and his loathing and detestation of all remissnesses and corruption in official and public duties, that he will be prompt to enforce faithfulness and devotion to duties in all clothed with official authority. I expect he will require of those who hold offices and draw their salaries to be at their posts and shirk not.

I am alarmed at the size to which this communication has grown but after once commencing, I wished to give you a full narrative of the matters to which I have called your attention. I have alluded to my own official services, not for the purpose of "vaunting" what I have done but because I deemed it not improper in explanation of the past judicial history to which I have referred.

As extended as this is, there are matters of serious import which I shall beg leave to lay before your consideration – matters not far disconnected from the great convulsion through which the Government and the people are now passing in the States.

With sentiments of the highest consideration,

I am your Obt. Sevt.   KIRBY BENEDICT

SANTA FE, NEW MEXICO
June 16, 1861

HON. EDWARD BATES,   Attorney General
Washington, D.C.

SIR,   The Mesilla affair [13] is one of the most brazen affairs anywhere to be found. It flippantly talks about that portion of the Territory seceding and openly advocates an adhesion to the Southern cause.

The published proceedings of the meetings and conventions, if they have been anything more than "paper meetings," show you the demoralized state, as

---

[13] Mesilla Convention March 16, 1861, to seek union with the Confederate states. Aurora Hunt, *James Henry Carleton, Frontier Dragoon*, p. 208, 260-262. *War Reb.*, ser. I, vol. IV, part I, 39. Report Mesilla Convention.

far as government is concerned, to which a portion of the people in Arizona have arrived. With but few American inhabitants, the newspaper is published only in the English language.

When I was associate justice, Arizona was in my district and as long as the law required courts there, I held them and found the native people as obedient to civil authorities as in any other part of New Mexico.

I do assure you, Sir, that the disorders, now so prominent, will disappear if the judge, now installed in that district, exercises firmness and is sustained by his own department and the Government. I have abundant evidence in my possession that the New Mexican population (seven-eighths of the people) have little sympathy for the disorderly and revolutionary movement to which some have given so much prominence.

The secession movement should be crushed out at once and the faithful population made to feel the protection and assurance of the Government as guaranteed by the Treaty of Hidalgo and the Gadsden Purchase. A reliable and capable district attorney is needed out here.

Treason can be committed as easily in Arizona and New Mexico as in any other part of the country and the heavy consequences can overtake this region as well as other parts of the United States.

Mr. Theodore D. Wheaton,[14] the present district

14 Theodore D. Wheaton came to New Mexico with Gen. Kearny; belonged to the First Missouri Volunteers under Colonel A. W. Doniphan. After the war, practiced in the courts of New Mexico and assisted in the prosecution of the murderers of Gov. Charles Bent; was speaker of the house of the territorial legislature during the second and third sessions; from 1861 to 1866, district attorney. He died at Ocate, New Mexico, 1875.

Santa Fé New Mexico
June 2° 1861

His Excellency
Abraham Lincoln
Washington. D.C.

Sir,

Early and kindly
associations over the Prairies about Court house
and at the Bar in our beloved Illinois, will
allow me to address you, an entirely private
letter. Your necessary and controlling connection
with the great result now transpiring in and
_____

And now Sir permit
me to hope that you and the
government will more sternly
grandly and triumphantly through
all the perils that surround you—
Your name will then be great among
the nations of the earth and
through all time—
With sentiments of the
highest consideration
I am your Ob't Serv't

Kirby Benedict

BENEDICT'S LETTER TO LINCOLN, JUNE 2, 1861
Portions of the first and last pages of this twelve-page letter. See text page 135.
From Record Group no. 60, The National Archives, Washington, D.C.

BURRO LOADS OF WOOD

Judge Benedict ordered 250 loads, valued at twenty-five cents per load. See text page 72.
Courtesy of the Santa Fe Museum Library; photographer unknown.

attorney, is little fitted in spirit, action, or disposition for a tumultuous period. In a crisis like the present, let me suggest that you stir him up and with unmistakable directions instruct him at once in the general line of conduct the Government requires of him.

We have few lawyers here. The language is a handicap. Unfortunately, those who are here have become so deeply compromised with secession opinion, sympathies, and virtues, as to necessarily preclude them from any United States trusts in New Mexico during the present difficulties. . . Mr. Wheaton lives at Taos. I have not yet heard what his interests and sentiments are. I am *not* counseling his *removal* but do suggest you *wake him up, stir him about.*

The *Gazette,* published by Collins,[15] Indian Agent, is now and for the most part of the past year been edited by a Mr. Russell,[16] a former Indian Agent who was removed by Lincoln. He is from Virginia. You will see by the package sent (newspapers)[17] that he is against the President, the North, the Government, and

---

[15] James Collins, born, Crab Orchard, Ky., Feb. 1, 1800; emigrated to Booneville, Mo., in 1819; in 1826 made first trip across the plains to Santa Fe with a pack train; from Santa Fe went to Chihuahua in 1828; engaged in business there until the war with Mexico started, then returned to Santa Fe; in 1852, established *Weekly Gazette,* publishing it until 1858 when he was appointed Indian Agent by President Buchanan; reappointed by President Lincoln; took active part in the Civil War in the west in 1862; was in the battles of Valverde and Glorieta; on June 6, 1869, was killed by robbers who stole $100,000 from the U.S. Depository. Three days later $65,000 was found in an adjacent brewery.

[16] John T. Russell, editor *Gazette;* in an editorial July 13, 1861, advocated neutrality in New Mexico. Neither abolitionists or secessionists should mix in her affairs – she wanted only to be left alone.

[17] The package of newspapers included the *Mesilla Times,* Feb. 13, March 2, 16, 30, May 17, June 1, 8, 1861; *Gazette,* May 4, 11, June 15, 1861. National Archives, Justice Department Records, Attorney General's Office MSS, Kirby Benedict appointment papers.

the Union. The paper's influence is pernicious.   .   .
The *Gazette* has the contract to print the laws of the
last legislature.

The former secretary of the Territory of New Mexico is anxious for Collins to change the columns of his
paper. Russell does not directly denounce the Government   .   .   .   but some articles offend the people.

I have the honor to remain very respectfully

Your Obt. Sevt.   KIRBY BENEDICT
Chief Justice, New Mexico

SANTA FE   June 25, 1861

HON. EDWARD BATES   Attorney General
Washington, D.C.

SIR: Last week I sent you a long letter in reference
to matters out here. I also sent you some newspapers.
Every week develops something in this Territory that
should be known in Washington.

Herewith, please find the *Mesilla Times* sheet of the
15th inst. and the editorial column of the *Santa Fe
Gazette* of June 22, 1861. From the paragraph marked
in the latter, you will perceive that the editor has
omitted the expression of his own sentiments and writes
in behalf of the Davis organization and leaves his
readers to believe or disbelieve as suits pleasure or
inclination.

The *Times* is open and avowed in its treasonable
sentiments and designs. In this it is encouraged by the
expected presence of Texans troops at Fort Bliss (El
Paso) fifty miles below Mesilla. The Americans in
Mesilla, who appear "ripe" for rebellion, doubtless

have promise from the Texas forces in the Southern organization.

You are aware of the reference made to Arizona in the proceedings, acts, and proclamations at Montgomery. Sir, I am unhesitating in urging upon you and through you, the President and his cabinet that the turbulence, the menace, and the treasonable avowals and designs in Arizona should be crushed out at once and with as much quickness of strokes as legitimate practice and the laws can exert.

The Government should act with energy, unstinting energy, complete energy, in its military and civil departments in New Mexico. Then will government and political demoralization "go to its end" in all this Territory as it was brought to a sudden "stand" and a "stop" in the States by wonderful and powerful movements of the President, the Government, the friendly and faithful States and their people.

A letter has arrived from Las Cruces, written by Don Lorenzo Labadie, United States Indian Agent assigned to duty in Arizona, in which he reports to Superintendent Collins that he has been waited upon by a committee from Mesilla who showed him the "resolutions" (I sent you last week) that no appointment by the Republican and Lincoln administration would be recognized in that country and that it would be resisted by all their power. Furthermore, a barrel of "tar and feathers" was prepared for any Lincoln appointee who should attempt the exercise of his office. The agent is alarmed for his life although he is among the most intelligent, brave, and competent of the Mexicans.

Jones,[18] the previous collector of this Department and now sutler at Fort Fillmore, seven miles below Mesilla, is said to be commissioned by the Montgomery organization as collector and is really collecting revenue for that body. Now, Sir, how long is this state of affairs to be tolerated within United States territory? One of the deputies, as the *Mesilla Times* has published, has fled down into old Mexico and carried with him all the United States money on hand.

You cannot but reflect how important is the holding of a United States court in that district and the action of the judge and district attorney. I mentioned the latter in my last letter. The people in Arizona are not in favor of transferring Arizona to the Davis plan. Sidney A. Hubbell, the new judge for that district, has but slight judicial experience but his intentions are all right.

The death of Senator Douglas [19] falls with all the force of deep pungent grief upon his friends here. In times now past by many years, I used to travel the circuit in Illinois in the practice of law in company with Douglas, President Lincoln, and Senator Trumbull of Illinois; Baker [20] of Oregon, and McDougall [21]

[18] Samuel John Jones, native of Virginia; listed in the U.S. Census 1860, as U.S. Customs Collector for Las Cruces. In March 1862, was nominated marshall of Arizona by Jefferson Davis and continued to espouse the cause of the Confederacy.

[19] Stephen A. Douglas, born, Brandon, Vt., 1813; admitted to the bar and practiced at Jacksonville, Ill., in 1834; judge of Illinois Supreme Court 1841-1843; member Illinois House of Representatives; U.S. Senator 1847-1859; died 1861.

[20] Edward E. Baker, member California bar; shortly before the Civil War he went to Oregon where he was elected to the United States Senate but resigned to serve in the Northern army and was killed at Ball's Bluff.

[21] *The National Encyclopedia of American Biography,* vol. XI, 331. James Alexander McDougall, born, Bethlehem, N.Y., Nov. 17, 1817; studied law

of California. I have felt greatly sad since the news of the decease of Douglas arrived here.

I have the honor to be your Obt. Sevt.

KIRBY BENEDICT
Chief Justice, New Mexico

SANTA FE   October 5, 1861

HON. EDWARD BATES   Attorney General
Washington, D.C.

SIR: I have the honor, herewith, to enclose to you the Oath of Fidelity and Loyalty taken by me as prescribed by Congress for all the officers in the civil department of the Government. I took this oath at once and I will add with pleasure that I required the same to be taken by the clerk of my district and the supreme court. Likewise, I have administrated and caused to be administrated the same to every sheriff in the district and all their officers who have been sworn by me since the arrival of the notice of this act of Congress. I have not stopped to inquire whether the act included them nor waited for any instructions from Washington.

Governor Connelly [22] took the same oath at my hands.

---

and settled in Cook Co., Ill., 1837; elected attorney general 1842; reelected 1844; in 1849 left Illinois to seek gold in Arizona; started for California but lost his way and arrived there in rags. In 1850, elected attorney general; member House Representatives in Congress 1853-1855, declined renomination; U.S. Senator 1861-1867; died September 3, 1867.

[22] Henry Connelly, born 1800 in Spencer County, Ky.; graduated from medical school and opened an office in Liberty, Mo.; gave up practice to join a party of traders bound for Chihuahua; many years engaged in trade between Missouri and Mexico; served as emissary to General Manuel Armijo from General S. W. Kearny. After the war he established trading centers in Peralta, Santa Fe, Albuquerque, and Las Vegas; was appointed Governor of New Mexico by President Lincoln in 1861, reappointed in 1864; died at Santa Fe, August 12, 1866.

There are some officers, clerks, employees, and others somewhat connected with the civil administration who have not taken it. They say they have not yet been required to do so by the chiefs of their departments. Judge Knapp [23] took the oath before me yesterday.

We have suffered great mischief in New Mexico, since the rebellion broke out, from those whose opinions, sentiments, and sympathies utterly disqualify them for the confidence of the Government. . . I wrote to you a month since that it would not do to confide power to such men.

Yet it required some time to disclose prominently the weakness or treachery or both of such infamous beings as Major (Isaac) Lynde [24] of Fort Fillmore's surrender and shame.

I propose shortly to write to you some of the chief events that have transpired here of late. We are anxious for Colonel Canby to drive the rebel Texans from Arizona. May all the good and energetic powers speed him.

I have the honor to remain very respectfully,

Your Obt. Sevt.   KIRBY BENEDICT

---

[23] Joseph G. Knapp, born Moravia, Cayuga County, N.Y., 1805; died in Florida, July 2, 1888; ordained a Methodist minister but within a year, united with Episcopal church and attended college at Geneva, N.Y. and the Theological Seminary, New York City; was appointed missionary to the Six Nations at Green Bay, Wisconsin. In 1838 he moved to Madison where he lived for more than twenty years; was editor and publisher of the *Wisconsin Inquirer,* first paper published in Madison; next, was superintendent of public property for Wisconsin; during that time, studied law and was admitted to the bar in Dane County; in 1861, appointed associate justice of the third district in New Mexico with headquarters at Mesilla. Early in the summer of 1864, Judge Knapp went to Washington where Lincoln accepted his resignation.

[24] Aurora Hunt, *James Henry Carleton, Frontier Dragoon,* p. 207-208. *War Reb.,* ser. I, vol. IV, part I, 4, 9, 13-14, 16-30, 49, 62-63.

SANTA FE   October 20, 1861

HON. EDWARD BATES   Attorney General U.S.

SIR,   I have the honor to acknowledge the receipt of yours enclosing a commission appointing Mr. (C.M.) Archibald, U.S. Marshall for the District of New Mexico. Mr. Holmes, our new secretary, arrived here the 17 inst. and handed me your letter. As soon as Mr. Archibald shall appear I will see to his making his bond. I am informed that he had resided in this Territory and is now somewhere within its limits. Holmes [25] has taken his oath of August 6th and entered upon the duties of his office.

In my last letter to you I mentioned those lawyers in New Mexico who are not secessionists. I take this early occasion to state that two others declare themselves in favor of the United States principles and the Government measures. They did not occur to me while writing my last letter as they are very little connected with practice yet have licenses. The one is C. P. Clever,[26] late marshall, and the other H. K. Johnson Esq. The latter is usually not in good health as he is afflicted with epilepsy. Clever is merchandizing.

Colonel Canby is preparing to move his forces to La Mesilla to expel the invading Texans. We pray him speed and success.

The latest news from Missouri causes some uneasiness among us. Can it be that General (John C.) Fre-

---

[25] James Henry Holmes served for only one year.

[26] Charles P. Clever, born Cologne, Germany, Feb. 23, 1830; after arrival in Santa Fe, formed a partnership with Sigmund Seligman, oldest firm in Santa Fe. He served as adjutant general during Henry Connelly's term as Governor and was delegate to the 40th Congress, 1869-1871. He died in Santa Fe, July 8, 1874.

mont must, with the disadvantage of inferior numbers on his side, fight (Sterling G.) Price? Fremont's fame will be eagle-winged if he conquers captains or disperses the secession hosts. If he loses the battle, which Heaven forbid, our difficulties out here will multiply. If the rebels subjugate Missouri, they will be able to give aid and comfort to their friends in this direction.

We look anxiously for the news and cannot believe that Fremont will risk a decisive battle without having under his command the elements to work out, through blood and courage, complete success.

I have the honor to remain very respectfully,

Your Obt. Sevt.

KIRBY BENEDICT

Chief Justice, New Mexico

SANTA FE   February 2, 1862

HON. EDWARD BATES   Attorney General U.S.

SIR, . . . All causes were determined at the last term of court except *Bautiste Vigil* v *United States.* This case was postponed until next term because Theodore Wheaton had the smallpox. You are aware that it is a land suit with the Government involving a claim to an immense tract of land and was instituted in pursuance of an Act of Congress for that purpose. Wheaton still is ill but not regarded as dangerously ill. The smallpox still rages out here.

I enclose a number of the *Santa Fe Gazette* containing the preamble and resolutions in regard to myself passed unanimously by both houses of the legislature at the session just ended. I also enclose to you a letter from C. P. Clever Esq., United States Marshall, relative to a malignant, unfounded, and scurrilous attack upon me in a Leavenworth, Kansas, paper.

The Texans have reenforced Mesilla with nearly 3,000 men of General Sibley's command. His proclamations [27] have been scattered among the people. It is said that the Texans are marching upon Fort Craig. Our entire militia, volunteers and regulars, have gone and are marching to the seat of the expected conflict.

Governor Connelly is there with Colonel Canby. Three militia companies were mustered into the territorial service and took their oaths. I hope to be able by next mail to give you further and better news.

I have the honor to remain very respectfully,
Your Obt. Sevt.   KIRBY BENEDICT
Chief Justice, New Mexico

By the year 1862, the popularity of Judge Benedict reached a high level. For reappointment as chief justice he received recommendations from approximately one hundred fifty persons. These included all the members of both houses of the legislature, the army officers, citizens, and his friends in Congress and in Illinois.

The preamble and resolutions covered several printed pages. One paragraph begins: "Whereas, the said Chief Justice is eminently known throughout the Territory for his patience, impartiality, energy, integrity, justice, learning, and abilities in his judicial acts and duties; for his maintaining the rights of the poor equally with the rich; the feeble as well as the

---

[27] *War Reb.*, ser. I, vol. IV, part I, 89-90, 157-158. Aurora Hunt, *Army of the Pacific*, p. 56.

*powerful; for his kindness, consideration, and for-
bearance in the administration of the law upon the
ignorant and misguided; and his vigilance and firmness
upon the willful and undoubted criminals. . ."*

CLINTON, ILLINOIS May 8, 1862

HON. A. LINCOLN

MY DEAR SIR,   Knowing that you are troubled with
applications for office, I have refrained from writing
you many letters. Feeling, however, great solicitude
that our old friend, Benedict, should be retained in
office, I have ventured to address you this note.

Judge Benedict, I conscientiously believe, ought to
be retained. From all information received from New
Mexico, I feel that I know that his reappointment
would be acceptable to the people of New Mexico –
eminently acceptable to them.

Having always entertained feelings of warm friendship for Mr. Benedict, I have naturally watched his
course there and obtained all possible information in
reference to his standing as a judge. The uniform
testimony is in his favor.

During these troublesome times, he has been the most
loyal of the loyal. Sound policy requires that when a
public officer is satisfactory to the people and is loyal,
he should be retained.

A territory like New Mexico needs officers that
people are attached to them. They are a peculiar people
and in their present condition, new men put over them
would exasperate and not conciliate.

I know you have the kindest feelings to Judge Benedict so do not hesitate to re-appoint him unless state
policy, in your opinion, required it. I most respectfully

submit, that the state policy that must be satisfactory to the people of New Mexico, requires that he should be re-appointed.

With high respect,   your friend,

DAVID DAVIS [28]

WASHINGTON, D.C.   June 12, 1862

HON. EDWARD BATES   Attorney General U.S.

SIR,   I have the honor to acknowledge a letter from your office dated the 10th inst. enclosing a commission appointing me, by and with the consent of the Senate, Chief Justice of the Supreme Court of New Mexico. Be pleased, Sir, to receive my warmest sentiments of gratefulness toward yourself, personally, for the high consideration, which I am assured, I have received at your hands.

I beg of you to make known to His Excellency, the President, that I keenly appreciate the confidence he has manifested in continuing in my hands the high trust he has renewed. Coming from one who has so long known me, imparts additional and great value. The best return I am able to make, is to assure him that my efforts will be ceaseless to scrupulously and thoroughly perform all the duties my office shall enjoin.

I shall arrive at Santa Fe as early as practicable in July and take and forward my official oath. I was born at Kent, Litchfield County, Connecticut.

I have the honor to remain with sentiments of highest consideration,   Your Obt Sevt.

KIRBY BENEDICT

Chief Justice, New Mexico

---

[28] David Davis, see footnote at page 34.

WASHINGTON, D.C.

June 12, 1862

HON. EDWARD BATES   Attorney General U.S.

SIR, The disastrous results that fell upon New Mexico by reason of the untoward circumstances of the battle of Valverde, Fort Craig, are not unknown to you. The enemy marched up the country of the Rio Grande taking possession as they went.

On March 2, the district commander of Santa Fe issued orders for the removal of military stores and the military abandonment of the city. Upon the next day, March 3 and 4, the removal was completed.

The enemy was within seventy miles and advancing. We had no means of successful defense left us. I would not consent to fall into the hands of the Texan marauders. I therefore left with my family upon March 4, and traveled to Fort Union, a point one hundred miles from Santa Fe and to which place the stores and military were moved.

My judicial district was in a few days overrun by Texans to such an extent that the effective exercise of judicial functions became impossible. No reenforcements had arrived to assist the loyal.

I had intended to ask leave of absence to allow me time to bring my children to the States to place them in school after the spring term should have been held. I have two children, one of them being a daughter of fourteen years of age. It was of first importance, with a view to her proper education, that she should be placed at school in the States.

So under all these circumstances, I concluded to rely upon the just judgment of yourself and the President and cross the plains with my family while there was a suspension of the means to enable me to exert my judicial functions and authority.

I did so and brought my family to Illinois where my children are now in school, to them indispensable. My object in writing this is to explain my leaving New Mexico without first procuring leave, as required by statute and the administration and also to seek the "certificate" of his Excellency, the President, that no impediment shall be found in the way of my being paid my salary.

I shall return under my new appointment so as to commence the terms in my district. The term will begin the first Monday in August. I trust yourself and the President will pronounce my absence, in the manner and from the motives I have detailed, as being "proper and necessary."

As I am about to leave the city to visit some friends in Connecticut, my birthplace, please do me the favor to make known to the Hon. John S. Watts,[29] delegate in Congress, what you and His Excellency, the President, shall determine as to this application.

I have the honor to remain with sentiments of highest consideration,   Your Obt. Sevt.

KIRBY BENEDICT

Chief Justice, New Mexico

----

[29] John S. Watts, native of Indiana; studied law and was admitted to the bar in that state; appointed associate justice, second district, New Mexico, by President Fillmore when New Mexico was organized as a territory; succeeded by Perry E. Brocchus in 1854; Watts then moved to Santa Fe and practiced law; in 1861 elected delegate to Congress; appointed Chief Justice of New Mexico after the death of Slough; died in Indiana, 1876.

SANTA FE   August 17, 1862

EDWARD BATES,   Attorney General

SIR: Owing to a severe casualty which befell my
son in Illinois, eleven years old, and whom I left to
attend school,[30] I was delayed in making my journey to
this place some few days longer than I had intended.

However, I arrived in time to hold my term of court
which has just closed in this county and I proceed to
hold sessions in the other counties in my district.

I have found the inhabitants giving very desirable
manifestations of being gratified at my reappointment
and seem cheerful and hopeful at the resumption and
exercise of judicial authority in their midst and in the
recovery of their civil rights and remedies now that the
rebel Texans have been compelled to completely
abandon our Territory.

I am sorry to have to say that on some of our out-
skirts, marauding parties have been formed that excite,
alarm, and threaten the settlements with mischief. They
do not appear to be stragglers from the Texans who
invaded the Territory but are made up of restless and
unprincipled persons from various parts who avail
themselves of the disturbed state of affairs to work out
their evil natures.

The court, just closed, has been highly interesting
and important. I have seen the liveliest zeal on the part
of the juries and the ministerial officers to thoroughly

---

[30] N. M. Baker, "The Pioneers of Macon County," *Ill. State Hist. Soc.,
Jour.,* vol. IV, 98-99. Kirby Benedict, Jr. attended the Presbyterian Academy
at Mount Zion a few miles southeast of Decatur. The school was founded in
1856 and continued until 1872. A fellow student of Kirby, Jr. has reported
that the Judge's son was first named Lamar after the distinguished South-
erner, L. C. C. Lamar, but after Lamar joined the Confederacy's cause,
young Benedict's name was changed to Kirby T.

perform their duties and in this they were eminently successful.

Mr. Cutler,[31] the newly appointed marshall, has arrived and yesterday entered upon the duties of his office. So far, he appears very well indeed, and I hope he will make a good marshall which the conditions here will greatly need.

Enclosed you will find the oath of office (transcript) taken by me. I have not seen the additional one that has been recently prescribed by Congress. I have, however, included what I understood to be its substance. If there be anything deficient, I shall perform whatever is required as soon as I ascertain what further, if anything, is needed.

I have the honor to remain very respectfully,
Your Obt. Sevt.   KIRBY BENEDICT
Chief Justice, New Mexico

SANTA FE   October 25, 1862

HON. EDWARD BATES   Attorney General, U.S.

SIR, I have the honor to inform you of my arrival at this place on the 6th of August and on that day announcing a term of court in my district. I continued and concluded the sessions in all the counties. I also went and held court in the counties of Taos and Arriba in Judge Knapp's district.

For eighteen months no term had been held in the latter county and none in the former for twelve months. It was of first importance that they should be held and I had evident reasons to know that the holding of them

---

[31] Abraham Cutler, U.S. Marshall, August 16, 1862-April 23, 1866. Aurora Hunt, *Army of Pacific*, 268-272.

was productive of highly beneficial public effects. I was induced solely by public and governmental consideration. . .

I forward to you a copy of Judge Knapp's letter informing me of his inability to be in his district in time to attend to his fall terms. Mention was made in the letter by the judge that he would pay my expenses while on the bench in his district.

For fear of being misunderstood, I avail myself of this occasion to state that I at once informed Judge Knapp, upon his recent arrival at this place, that I would not and should not receive any pay from him in reimbursement of my expenses. I performed the duties which pertained to a brother judge wholly from my regard to public requirements, the people's rights, and the Government. I have so many times done the same thing during my occupancy of the bench in New Mexico without any other compensation . . . than that which my own mind and spirit supplied. . .

I deem it not reprehensible to state that the grand juries in each of the counties in this and Judge Knapp's district, where I held courts, formally and in writing, expressed to me their gratification at my reappointment and my again assuming official duties among them.

On trials in proceedings of "Habeas Corpus" I had to determine the case of a negro woman claimed as a slave and also an Indian captive woman. Both were declared "free and set free."

General Carleton now commands this Department. I have the honor to remain with sentiments of the highest consideration,   Your Obt. Sevt.
KIRBY BENEDICT
Chief Justice, New Mexico

SANTA FE, NEW MEXICO
December 19, 1863

HIS EXCELLENCY   ABRAHAM LINCOLN
Washington, D.C.

SIR, When you re-appointed Judge Kirby Benedict last year it was with the understanding that he quit his inebriety and you requested me to inform you if he did not keep his promise.

He has lapsed into his old habits and his promise violated in the most public manner. In these moods he visits the gambling Hells and drinking saloons and with a swagger and bluster defiles his judicial robes in such manner as to forfeit the dignity of his position and, of course, respect. This conduct affects your administration.

Kirby Benedict is at dagger points with the legitimate personnel of the courts and has meddled in local and political strifes. On his last circuit he was provided with an escort of armed men by the commanding general of this Department (Carleton) when no necessity existed for such a guard.

He overawed the people of Taos County and produced irregularities in the election there which have taken the legislature some valuable time to rectify. All this is very disgraceful.

. . .   It is very painful to perform a task like this. His bar companions demand the removal of Kirby Benedict. He has been drunk in the streets.

W. F. M. ARNY [32]
Secy. State, New Mexico Territory

---

[32] W. F. M. Arny, secretary of New Mexico Territory, 1862-1867; served as acting governor fifteen months during absence of Governor Henry Connelly.

SANTA FE   January 3, 1864
HON. EDWARD BATES   Attorney General, U.S.

SIR,   It has been communicated to me "upon the square" according to my informant, that Secretary Arny of this territory was secretly, either alone or with others, writing Washington something to my prejudice. Now this Arny is a moronic maniac, an egotist, and general mischief-maker among us here.

The clerk of my court, a short time since, went without my previous knowledge to the office of the secretary and talked very plainly under a sense of personal wrong. Among other things, he slapped the face of the young man Arny had in his office.

I write this to ask of you that if anything should arrive at your office, from or through Arny, please let me know the charge and complaint. I hope to vindicate myself without difficulty. Mr. Arny is obnoxious to many people here. He is malicious and spiteful toward those who cannot be annoyed by his follies.   . .

Enclosed is the *New Mexican,* an unqualified paper for the Union and for which I give some of my time, somewhat "incognito" to writing its editorials.

I have the honor to remain very respectfully,
Your Obt. Sevt.   KIRBY BENEDICT
Chief Justice, New Mexico

SANTA FE   July 10, 1864
HIS EXCELLENCY   ABRAHAM LINCOLN
Washington, D.C.

SIR,   . . .   Judge Knapp paralyzes judicial procedure by a quarrel he has had for about eighteen months with General Carleton, who commands the Department. Knapp's residence is about 300 miles from here at Mesilla upon the southern side of New Mexico.

He did not attend the last January term of the Supreme Court assigning the cause that *he would not take a pass from the military to travel to Santa Fe.*

. . . When court went into session last Monday (July term, 1864) Judge Knapp then presumptuously refused to join in the fixing of the terms and places and announced his settled determination to transact no business of any kind in that court until General Carleton should revoke absolutely his orders concerning passports [33] in the Territory.

He adhered to his determination for two days. It was impossible to do any business so concurred on an adjournment of the term. Each day he delivered speeches from his seat on the bench to all present against Carleton and the military in New Mexico. His mind seemed in a quixotic state whenever the military are present in his thoughts. His speeches were made with much warmth and he used very strong expressions. The military were in no way concerned with the business of the court.

He refused to hear any motion in any cause from any attorney present. I was powerless to transact any business because the other associate justice (Perry E. Brocchus) was not present. . .

. . . I do assure you that I have no conflict with the military; neither General Carleton nor his officers

[33] Aurora Hunt, *James H. Carleton, Frontier Dragoon.* Passport Controversy, 248-252.

obstruct or oppose the court. On the contrary, I receive from General Carleton cordial aid and assistance.

Three judges are needed in this Territory. According to the present devaluation of the currency and high prices, it is too expensive to repeatedly go into a *district of an absent judge.* I do not know the cause of Judge Brocchus's omission to come to his place of duty. Perhaps he has resigned. If so, I implore you to appoint his successor.

This is not like a new country. It has been settled for centuries and has long established laws and a population of 80,000. Business has been long established. The duty here is different from that in the States.

Send us good men. A narrow and mischievous mind and spirit should never be sent here. No one should be sent here who is not courageous, persevering, and of the highest integrity. He should have manners, deportment, and the bearing of a gentleman with good sense enough to make no wanton or unprovoked controversies. He should promote and not paralyze others in the performance of their duties and cultivate harmony with the officers.

. . . I learn that Judge Knapp is about to leave for the States. If he goes, I will be the only judge in the Territory. Your unanimous recommendation for the Presidency imparts much gratification to all of us in this region.

I have the honor to be with sentiments of the highest consideration,   Your Obt. Sevt.

KIRBY BENEDICT

SANTA FE   May 16, 1865

To His Excellency Andrew Johnson
President U.S.

SIR,   Permit me in this mode to express my deep gratification at the announcement you have made so clear and determined against the perpetuation of slavery.

Every man in this Territory whose sympathies have truly been with President Lincoln . . . rejoices in the confidence that you will be nobly just and that your powerful arm will be vigorous in the punishment of those who willfully supported the rebellion.

To me, President Lincoln was a personal friend for a quarter of a century. We practiced law in the same court until I came to this country in 1853, twelve years ago. The enclosed paper will show how his death affected this mixed population. The grief was deep and sincere. The articles in the paper headed "Abraham Lincoln" and signed "Friend," and "Andrew Johnson" signed "Patriot," were written by myself.

I trust you will hold me excusable in saying that I desire to stand fair before you as judicial officer in your administration. I have been upon the Bench many years in this Territory. I take the liberty of enclosing a *copy* of a communication addressed to President Lincoln and signed by every representative and councilman at the last session of the legislature and by other persons also. The *original* was sent to President Lincoln while this copy was retained.

I deemed it but respectful to him, from whom I received my latest appointment as chief justice, to furnish him the evidence that the performance of my duties was satisfactory to the people.   . .

It shall be my endeavor, Sir, while I occupy my present official position, to so discharge all the duties of my office that you will find in me no cause for condemnation.

With fervent prayers for your safety and the prosperity, peace and happiness of the country, I have the honor to be with sentiments of the highest regards,

Your Obt. Sevt.   KIRBY BENEDICT
Chief Justice, New Mexico

The judge was generous in the use of his encomiums as he penned the following article for the New Mexican, *but it was of no avail as President Johnson failed to reappoint him chief justice of New Mexico.*

In the midst of so great a calamity as that which has befallen the nation in the assassination of President Lincoln, it is a matter of the greatest thankfulness to all patriots that so experienced, able, decisive, and tried statesman as Andrew Johnson succeeds to the presidency. A weak, temporizing, vacillating chief magistrate would be a fearful stumbling block.   . .

President Johnson had been an eminent statesman in Tennessee and the nation long before the rebellion.   . .   He took a bold stand against the rebellion. In the United States Senate he asserted and maintained his ground with all his well known powers of argument and eloquence.

He left the Senate when appointed by President Lincoln to the military governorship of Tennessee.

He steps to the presidency at one of the most momentous periods of this or any other nation's history. The eyes of the world will be turned upon him. Patriots of this and every other land will hope that he will be equal to the requirements of his position and that peace will be preserved. . .   (Signed)   PATRIOT

The following are excerpts of an eulogy to President Abraham Lincoln which was written by Judge Benedict:

. . . The faithful of no nation ever wept in deeper bitterness of spirit at their loss of their most beloved and trusted leader, servant and chief. The mind cannot conceive nor the soul explore to full consciousness the extent of the unexampled loss. . .

Yet while the true, the just, the downtrodden, and oppressed among all civilized people ponder and mourn over his death, we, his countrymen are now sure of his reputation and his deathless celebrity. Neither is longer subject to changes, accidents, or chance. We may seek some consolation in this reflection when grief shall calm itself.

Enmity has robbed him of longer enjoyment and usefulness among the living, but his death at this period of his career, hands his deeds and character over for imperishable inscription upon the brightest scroll, where time and history engrave the loftiest names. . .

All patriots in this nation will hereafter glow with pride that Lincoln was their countryman. Parents and teachers will point to his private and public life as examples for their children to imitate. His career will be a "pillar of fire" to beckon and lead onward the future sons of freedom and just government.

The principles and motives for which the President lost his life, will now accelerate their spread, growth, and strength. The blood of the martyrs, it has often been said, "is the seed of the Church." The voice of the blood of Abraham Lincoln will never cry in vain to Heaven from the free ground upon which it has been shed.

(Signed)   FRIEND [34]

34 *New Mexican,* May 5, 1865.

Civic and Social Affairs

Judge Benedict took an active interest in civic affairs and helped organize the Historical Society of New Mexico. The first meeting to consider preliminary proceedings met in the council chambers in the Governor's Palace on December 15, 1859. The next meeting on December 26, was held in a hall rented from Bishop Lamy for $12 a month.

Colonel John B. Grayson was elected president. Kirby Benedict, together with C. P. Clever, Dr. W. J. Sloan, Major J. L. Donaldson, and Colonel Grayson served on the constitution and by-laws committee. The judge was appointed on the history committee along with Joab Houghton and Colonel Grayson. Other committees of note were those on the Indian races, geology, antiquities, and natural history.

The minutes of the society [1] for those early years reveal the endeavors of the judge to further the progress and usefulness of the organization. He introduced a resolution to name as honorary members: His Excellency, President James Buchanan, Henry Rowe Schoolcraft, Lieutenant Matthew F. Maury, George Bancroft, Louis Agassiz, General John Garland, Lieutenant Amiel W. Whipple, and John C. Breckenridge. Photographic art was in its infancy, yet Benedict sensed its

---

[1] *Laws of New Mexico, 1860,* p. 688. Historical Society of New Mexico charter granted.

importance to posterity. By further resolution he sought possession of "an admirable melainotype likeness from Col. Grayson, the first president of the society. . . ; ambrotypes of Colonel B. L. E. Bonneville, Colonel E. V. Sumner, and General John Garland. . ." All of these were to be hung in the hall of the Historical Society.

With the exception of those made in court, very few of the numerous speeches of Judge Benedict are extant. His Anniversary Address [2] delivered before the society at Santa Fe on December 31, 1860, is an exception. Excerpts are quoted:

> Our minds are so endowed and our sympathies so governed that all the universe within our range of contemplation, from the marching armies of the stars . . . down to the gentle flowers . . . fail in their deepest sensibilities until man, the thinking conscious being, is seen in brotherhood with them.
>
> 'Tis now one year since this association was wrought into form. It sprang from a profound mental want in our natures. It flowed from the deep restless desire of the cultivated mind to seize upon all objects which may aid in the solution of that most interesting of all problems – Man's Existence and Destiny.
>
> The Cross is an instrument the humblest artist could construct and the gentle hill is common to every eye; but raise that Cross on Calvary's summit and the soul writhes in all its power and sensibility as the malignant and the bigot nail the form of Him who "spake as no man spake," who was Pure Intelligence, doing nothing but good and bringing life and mortality to light, teaching men to escape from errors, falsehood, and all sins and to live in the pure and the true. . .
>
> From the great act of sacrifice then accomplished, the faith, devotion, sentiments, and manners of the world were to be

---

[2] Address published by resolution of the Society. A copy, autographed, "Charles P. Clever, Attorney General, Regards of his friend Kirby Benedict," is deposited in the Huntington Library, San Marino, Calif.

changed; and even the far-off and unknown New Mexico, throughout her mountains and vales, would receive the "Symbol" of the instrument upon which the spirit and form of Jesus suffered – suffered for no wrong to man's highest and holiest nature – suffered as the Divine Revealer of purity, inspired knowledge, and spiritual truth. . .

All people who have developed to any noticeable degree of mental progress, strive by some means to perpetuate the remembrance of whatever occurs in their societies of marked public or private character. . .

When this society was formed, it was believed that New Mexico had been fertile in events worthy to be embodied with the record we of the present period are forming for the generations which soon must fill our places in the march of life.

We have opened a new and fresh field of research and materials. New Mexico is the only important peopled Territory added to our matchless Union during its unparalleled march, whose story has not as yet been thoroughly told by historians. Though a glance at some special points has now and then been given, no compact, detailed, and full narrative has ever gone to the world. . .

The cause of this neglect of New Mexico is not to be charged to dearth of interest in matters that would have fallen under review of historic pen. On the contrary, during more than three hundred years since the print of white man's foot was made upon portions of the Rio Grande, periods have arisen and passed, and deeds have been done upon this soil which, when faithfully written, will seem more like the facsinating pages of romance than the stern realities of facts. . .

The judge briefly reviewed the accomplishments of Christopher Columbus, Alvar Nunez Cabeza de Vaca, Alonzo del Castillo Maldonado, Andreas Dorantes, Hernandos Cortes, and the black Moor, Estefancio.

What induced the chivalric men and women of Spain to come so far, contend with so many dangers, and bear so many hardships to make their homes in this region midway between two oceans? By what spirit were they moved and sustained?

It was not to escape from the authority and worship of their religion – for they brought the creed and worship of their fathers and the altar and its ministers with them and set up the Cross and kneeled to its sanctified memories, even here, where we are now, and endowed this city with the name Santa Fe or Holy Faith.

It was not to cast off the rule of sovereign power, for the ideas of democratic liberty had but slightly tinctured the Spanish mind of that day. Indeed, among the strongest traits which marked the Spaniard wherever he went, was an unenquiring devotion to his sovereign.

He brought with him a love of personal daring and superiority to pain and danger, that, had his mind been enlightened with the true ideas of freedom, would have made him the most formidable character upon the face of the earth.

Members of the Historical Society of New Mexico! Are we enough impressed with the task we have assumed in this organization? Do we feel as we should regarding the duties we have chosen? Do we realize the expectations we have raised abroad among men of worth, literature, science, and eminence, as manifested by our monthly correspondence? It is full time we arouse ourselves and let "that one waiteth not for another."

The New Mexican historian stands at the base of the height of more than three hundred years of the white man's life. The Muse of History looks up through this long vista of the past and brings to her pen the gathering treasures of a great period.

These centuries now seem to beseech that their story be told so that they may no longer march in the solemn tread of ages in darkness and neglect. The historian stands here, too, in the presence of four classes [3] of men with annals and modes of life as varied and distinct as the sun paints the hues of light upon the bow of Heaven. . .

---

[3] The four classes mentioned were the Spanish, Americans, pueblo Indians, and those then classified as wild Indians.

Judge Benedict continued his review of the history of New Mexico and discussed the services of Don Francisco Xavier Chaves, General Manuel Armijo, Don Antonio Sandoval, Juan Felipe Ortiz and the priest, José Antonio Martinez of Taos. In addition, he promised, "with colors just and faithful," he would portray the patriotism, deeds and lives of the mountain men of Taos – Bent, Carson, St. Vrain, Beaubien, Maxwell, Leroux, and Bishop Lamy. . .

He closed his speech by saying: "My task is ended and if I have quickened an impulse in the right direction for the promotion of the intellectual interest of this society, I shall not in vain have received your attention on this occasion." [4]

In December, 1861, Benedict was elected vice president and the following year was chosen president. The war years brought change. On September 28, 1863, it was resolved that the room of the society be surrendered and the furniture and other property, as may be designated, be sold and the proceeds applied to the debts of the society. An amendment provided that the curator, August M. Hunt, be instructed to preserve and care for such property or donations that shall be retained until further disposition shall be made by the society. The sale was scheduled for October 3, 1863. No inventory of the property of the society can be located. Recorded in the minutes are gifts of many foreign coins and valuable relics. The society was reestablished December 27, 1880.

The judge, as a historian of the society, delivered a

---

[4] The speech was delivered in English and read in Spanish.

lecture on the revolution of 1837 in New Mexico.[5] He spoke of the great and bloody tragedy that terrorized Santa Fe before its acquisition to the United States. He related how the irritated and the unhappy gathered together in the city to protest against the administration of Don Albino Perez who was their governor and chief.

President Santa Ana and his party had destroyed the federal system of 1824 and established the central system which invested the governor with great powers. Instead of bringing about corrections of the causes of discontent in New Mexico, the new governor only further aggravated the people. He did not see, or pretended not to see, the approaching riot which fell in its ghastly fury upon his head. He found himself without power to resist the force.

The people of del Norte, especially in Taos, armed themselves and marched upon Santa Fe and Señor Perez. Still considering their force and their intentions of no great importance or peril, Governor Perez, with a small force, marched north to Santa Cruz de la Cañada where they were completely vanquished. Those who could, escaped in consternation to Santa Fe.

Perez, with some friends, hurried south toward Isleta but all were captured one by one and cruelly put to death. After Perez was killed, his head was severed from his body. The insurgents had made their encampment outside Santa Fe near the Chapel de Nuestra del Señora del Rosario. Here the head of Perez was passed around among them in triumph and the whole night long they reveled in their inhuman orgy. They amused themselves in their bloody ven-

---

[5] *El Novo Mejicano,* Enero 2, de 1864. Santa Fe.

geance by offering indignities to the head of Perez and kicked it over the ground. Then fell Abreus, Alarid and Sena, and others of note. They left orphans who are now young men and are numbered among our most energetic, useful, and influential citizens.[6]

Before joining the Historical Society, Judge Benedict had affiliated with Montezuma Lodge No. 1, A.F.A.M. on December 3, 1859, by transfer from Prairie Lodge No. 77, Paris, Illinois. He held the office of Worshipful Master from 1861 to 1865. During his term of office, a new two-story building was erected on the northwest corner of the plaza on a lot 90 by 130 feet. The upper story was occupied by the Masons and Odd Fellows. This was quite a pretentious edifice of twenty-six rooms. The materials for its erection consisted of 300,000 feet of lumber, 150,000 adobes, and 90 kegs of nails. The five winding stairways that led to the upper floor were reported as "elegant specimens of workmanship."

After the Masons had dedicated their hall, they formed in procession and, preceded by the military band, marched around the plaza to the Hall of Representatives to hear the anniversary address of the Worshipful Master Kirby Benedict. "As usual the oration was interesting, able, and eloquent as was to be expected from the learned chief justice, evidencing as it did, a thorough understanding of his subject and a soul-felt enthusiasm in his theme. At two P.M. dinner was served at the El Dorado saloon. A large cake, decorated with Masonic emblems, was served."[7]

---

[6] (Translation by courtesy of Herschel Moxley.) Don Ramon Abreu, Alcalde; Don Santiago Abrue; Don Jesús Maria Alaria, generally known as Alarid.

[7] *Weekly New Mexican*, Jan. 6, 27, 1865.

Not only did civic and fraternal affairs engage the attention of Judge Benedict, but social ones did also for he occasionally performed marriage ceremonies. In the bridal month of June, 1865, he officiated at the wedding of Teresina T. Bent, daughter of Charles Bent, first governor of New Mexico. The groom, Elois Scheurich, was then engaged in trade at Taos. The wedding was a brilliant affair and well attended by a large number of the prominent citizens of Taos.[8] Teresina has been honored and her name still lingers on a street in Taos called Teresina. There is a Bent Street also to remind future generations of the sacrifice of her father.

It is regrettable that in a section of the United States as old as New Mexico, so many of the ancient documents have been lost, sold, destroyed, or stolen. April 16, 1870, the following announcement was published:

> Inasmuch as great indignation has been expressed by a number of prominent citizens relative to the destruction of the public archives of the Territory of New Mexico, all who feel interested in this matter are requested to attend a meeting to be held at the council chambers this (Saturday) evening at 7 o'clock to ascertain who is responsible for said destruction and to provide measures for their better security in the future.[9]

The announcement was signed by Benedict and many other prominent citizens. Following the meeting, Librarian Ira Bond placed a notice in the *New Mexican* requesting the return of any papers removed from the palace since their value was underestimated.[10]

---

[8] *Weekly New Mexican,* June 16, 1865.
[9] *Daily New Mexican,* April 16, 1870.
[10] *Ibid.* April 22-23, 1870.

Judge Benedict addressed the citizens' Indignation Meeting. He claimed that, for the antiquity of the documents alone, they were of value and that any man who could not regard them as such must be a miserable sort of brute.

To illustrate he said, "Why, gentlemen, what would not any of you give to be the possessor of *just two inches of the fig leaf apron which Mother Eve wore to hide her sin. Not the whole apron, gentlemen, but just two inches.*" [11]

---

[11] Ritch Collection MSS, no. 2104.

Loss of Office and Prestige

As the time approached for the reappointment of Benedict as chief justice, his enemies began an aggressive campaign to exploit his weaknesses and discourage President Johnson from continuing him in office.

Then, as now, the greatest publicity was obtained through the press. Some of the editorials were unusually critical:

> Chief Justice in the opinion of Chief Justice is one of the most remarkable men of his age, that is, if we are to believe what he says in his editorials about Chief Justice Benedict.
>
> He turns his court into an electioneering machine and threatens litigants with the displeasure of the chief justice if they do not conform to his political notions. Grand jurors and witnesses are summoned to attend the United States courts not to investigate offenses against the law or give evidence but to make party capital. Then he comes home from his circuit and says he has been holding courts and lauds himself to the skies for having done that which other men would have blushed to have been guilty of doing under similar circumstances.
>
> The demagogism of Judge Benedict is so ingrained and he imagines himself such a shrewd politician that he forgets where courts end and caucuses begin. He merges the two so completely that the courts are lost sight of and the caucuses are all that can be seen by the litigants.
>
> He must dabble, dabble, dabble in the dirty pool of politics which he, himself, stirs up and from which he constantly bespatters himself with the most filthy mire.

> Who does not remember how he, but a comparatively short time ago lampooned Major John Greiner in his article entitled *The Dog, the Owl, and the Snake,* which he wrote and carried about the streets to read with accompanying explanations to admiring crowds.[1]

Benedict compared the traits of men to those of the animals, reptiles, and birds and emphasized the characteristics of the jackal, fox, snake, owl, and eagle. About two rival candidates for public office, he said that the one is by nature and practice as much superior to the other in truth and manliness as is the eagle in his flight to the slithering, hissing serpent in the grass.

The *Gazette* unceasingly condemned the chief justice:

> Benedict attacks all men [2] in public office; he appears in court beastly drunk and desecrates the Sabbath by appearing on the streets reeling while citizens are going to church. He sits in judgment, upon presentments of the grand jury of his own court, against himself for gambling and unblushingly approves of his own fine for violating the law which is his duty to uphold and enforce.[3]

It was insinuated that there was trouble in his family as his wife and children were not with him. He had taken them to Illinois three years previous, however, his wife and son returned to Santa Fe and were with him during the last years of his life.

A letter to President Lincoln, signed by both Sidney A. Hubbell and Francisco Perea, contained the following information:

---

[1] *Santa Fe Weekly Gazette,* Oct. 21, 1865.

[2] Francisco Perea, General James Henry Carleton, John S. Watts, and José Manuel Gallegos.

[3] *Santa Fe Weekly Gazette,* Nov. 18, 1865.

It is a painful duty to ask the removal of Judge Benedict and the appointment of a good sober man. The judge has taken to his cups again worse than ever before. He was so drunk when he took his seat on the bench he could hardly sit in his chair and it was with difficulty that he could articulate at all. I (Hubbell) was obliged to adjourn court until the next day to allow Benedict to sober up.

It is exceedingly mortifying to see the chief justice of New Mexico so drunk that he is unconscious of the place he occupied. It was undignified and brings disgrace upon the court and your administration.[4]

His friends in the legislature promptly rallied to his support and passed the following resolutions:

Be it resolved by the Council and House of Representatives of the Territory of New Mexico: That we see with indignation, the calumnies and gross insults contained in the *Santa Fe Gazette* last week, relative to the official and private conduct of the Hon. Kirby Benedict, Chief Justice of the Supreme Court of this Territory, and that we most solemnly censure the editors of that paper; and denounce them as vile calumniators, direct enemies of our interests and of the present Administration.

Be it further resolved: That the Hon. Kirby Benedict, Chief Justice of the Supreme Court of this Territory, and Judge of the First Judicial District Court thereof, has always conducted himself in the discharge of his duties as an impartial, just, and independent judge and has at all times merited the confidence of our people for his ability, energy, and integrity.

Be it further resolved: That his many services rendered to the people of our Territory entitle him to our highest consideration and we, in the name of the people of our Territory and as representatives of the interests thereof, do not find in his official or private conduct, anything detrimental to the interest of our country, and therefore, we do most solemnly declare and recognize him as a most energetic judge and one who thoroughly

---

[4] Records of Attorney General's Office, Appointment Papers of Kirby Benedict. MSS, March 18, 1865.

understands the customs and wants of our people, a faithful friend of our interests, and the pillar and defender of our rights.

Whereas, the Hon. Kirby Benedict, Chief Justice of the Supreme Court of the Territory of New Mexico, has served as a District Judge and Judge of the said Supreme Court, for more than twelve years and during all which time has been distinguished for his punctuality, impartiality, capacity, and integrity as a judge; for his fidelity and honor as a man, and for his correct deportment, usefulness, and loyalty as a citizen.

Therefore, be it resolved by the Council and House of Representatives of the Legislative Assembly of the Territory of New Mexico: That His Excellency, the President of the United States of America, be, and hereby is, earnestly requested to reappoint said Kirby Benedict to the said office of Chief Justice of said Territory when his present term shall expire. In so doing he will satisfy the wishes of the people of this Territory.[5]

Judge Benedict also received the endorsement of his old friends of the Eighth Judicial Circuit of Illinois. David Davis was then a member of the United States Supreme Court; Richard Yates and Lyman Trumbull served in the senate.

SUPREME COURT HOUSE   Washington, D.C.

Jan'y. 10, 1866

HIS EXCELLENCY   ANDREW JOHNSON

President of the United States

MY DEAR SIR,   I am advised that an effort is being made to remove the Hon. Kirby Benedict, the present Chief Justice of New Mexico.

I should regret this exceedingly for I know Judge Benedict intimately and advised his re-appointment. He is an honorable man and upright judge and thoroughly loyal – His course in New Mexico has been overwhelmingly sustained by the people of New Mexico in the election of Col. Chaves, the present member.

---

[5] *Journal of the Legislative Council of the Territory of New Mexico,* Dec. 4, 1865, Resolutions 5, 9, p. 251.

I believe all opposition to him is factious — I practiced law with Judge Benedict for many years and know him to be pure and above reproach. Although a Whig in politics, I recommended his appointment to Gen. Pierce.

Mr. Benedict was a Democrat until the war broke out and immediately devoted himself to the Govt. I most earnestly request that he be not removed. I would with equal earnestness recommend his re-appointment when his present term expires.

With High Respect, Yrs. Most Truly   DAVID DAVIS [6]

WASHINGTON, D.C.
July 10, 1866

HIS EXCELLENCY ANDREW JOHNSON
President of the United States

SIR: We are informed by the honorable Mr. Chavez, the delegate from New Mexico, that an effort is being made to remove Hon. Kirby Benedict, Chief Justice of that Territory.

Judge Benedict was formerly from Illinois where he had the reputation of an honest man and a good lawyer; Mr. Lincoln knew him well and reappointed him to his present position, he having originally been appointed by Pres. Pierce.

He has been a long time on the bench in New Mexico, understands the Spanish language well, has been thoroughly loyal, and we are assured that he is an able, honest, and upright judge and very satisfactory to the people.

We feel that it would be a misfortune to remove such a man and respectfully recommend his continuance in office.

LYMAN TURNBULL
RICHARD YATES [7]

The majority of the attorneys who had been closely associated with Benedict for so many years and had crossed and recrossed the desert and mountains with him in his Concord carriage wholeheartedly defended him and passed the following resolutions:

---

[6] Records Attorney General's Office. Benedict Appointment Papers. MSS.
[7] *Ibid.*

Whereas, we the members of the bar of the supreme court of the territory of New Mexico, have seen with deep regret that an unjust, and as we deem, a malicious attack has been made upon Hon. Kirby Benedict, chief justice of this territory, by W. F. M. Arny.

Be it therefore resolved — that we have always had and still have an abiding confidence in the honesty, integrity, and uprightness of the Honorable Kirby Benedict.

Resolved further — that the people of the territory are greatly indebted to him; not only for unremitting attention to his own duties but also for his attention to the duties of his associate justices by holding their courts during their absences from the territory.

Resolved further — Chief Justice Benedict is entitled to full confidence of the administration not only for his ability and legal attainments but also for his experience as well as his strict attention to his duties, to the interest of the United States and to those of this territory and that we would look upon his removal as a serious misfortune to the interests of the people of this territory as well as the government of the United States.[8]

Letters and commendatory resolutions were unable to influence President Johnson so Kirby Benedict was replaced by Colonel John P. Slough. It was at Las Vegas, San Miguel County, that Benedict voiced his last judicial words: "It is ordered by the court that all causes, motions, and proceedings be continued until next term of this court and that court adjourn until court at cause."

Then the distinctive signature appeared once more in the old court record but the hand that held the pen trembled and the lines wavered.[9]

Four days later is the notation: "John P. Slough present and presents his commission as Chief Justice of

[8] Ritch Collection MS, no. 1598.
[9] District Court Records, Las Vegas, March 10, 1866.

the Supreme Court of the Territory of New Mexico to whom the oath of office is administered by Court when he takes his seat upon the Bench."

Regardless of the faults and inebriety of Judge Benedict, his failure to be reappointed caused considerable regret. The *New Mexican* staunchly supported him:

> Chief Justice Benedict, who for twelve years has been connected with the judiciary of our Territory, at this time needs no encomium at our hands. He is widely known throughout the entire Territory and during the whole time of his judgeship the courts of his district have never failed.
>
> He has stood like a *wall of adamant* and been the only refuge *for justice* at times when there was *not another judge* in the whole Territory. The hardships of mountain travel, the rigors of winter, and dangers from hostile Indians, have never deterred him from discharging his official duties.
>
> His knowledge of the language of the people, the customs of our people and our mired system of jurisprudence, rendered him an able and efficient officer and his removal will not only be deeply regretted by the people of his district, but by a large majority of the members of the bar now practicing in the Territory. We only hope that his successor may prove as able a judge and render the same satisfaction.[10]

At a meeting of the members of the bar after the final adjournment of the district court, the following preambles and resolutions were adopted and unanimously signed by the practicing lawyers of this city:

> *Whereas,* We the members of the Bar of the City of Santa Fe, have intelligence of the removal of the Honorable Kirby Benedict from the position of Chief Justice of New Mexico, and
>
> *Whereas,* We feel it due to so deserving and able an officer of the Government, who has for more than twelve years been

---

[10] *Santa Fe Weekly New Mexican,* Feb. 16, 1866

connected with the judiciary of this Territory, to give some
expression of our high appreciation of his judicial worth and
official integrity, therefore,

Be it resolved, That we regret very much that in the disposition of government officials, it has become necessary to make
such changes as causes the removal of Judge Benedict: That in
all our intercourse with Judge Benedict as an officer he has in
all things conducted himself well, and his decisions have generally been characterized with wisdom and in accordance with
the principles of law and justice and we think fairly and
impartially.

Resolved, That on the whole, his entire administration during
the long period of twelve years in this Territory has given
general satisfaction and contributed largely to educate the people
and explain to them the fundamental principles of our government, and instill into their minds respect for her laws and
authority.

Resolved, That in taking leave of him in his judicial capacity,
we tender to him our sincere thanks for the uniform kindness,
courtesy, and consideration which he has manifested towards
every member of the bar and hope that success and honor will
attend him in whatever he may undertake in his future walk in
life.

(s) M. ASHURST;   R. H. TOMPKINS;   THEO. S. GREINER;
    C. P. CLEVER, Attorney General;   S. B. ELKINS [11]

---

[11] *Ibid,* March 16, 1866.

Richard H. Tompkins, born Louisville, Ky., Sept. 14, 1816; came to New
Mexico as clerk of the U.S. District Court in 1851; U.S. District Attorney,
1858, reappointed 1860; territorial librarian, 1880; died at Santa Fe, Jan.
14, 1888.

Merrill Ashurst, born in Alabama; came to New Mexico 1851. U.S. District
Attorney, 1852-1854; 1867-1869; died 1869.

New Ventures Follow Disbarment

Kirby Benedict faced his advancing years and loss of office with courage and determination. One of his first undertakings was to join an expedition to the gold fields near the headwaters of the Gila river.

All who wished to join the party were admonished to go armed, mounted, and with subsistence for ninety days. The departure was scheduled for July 20. In addition to Kirby Benedict were Associate Justice Joab Houghton; Charles P. Clever, U.S. district attorney; John Greiner, receiver U.S. depository; Chief Justice John P. Slough, and other territorial officers. They returned from their treasure hunt November 2, 1866.[1] There is no available record of their success or failure to find gold or to invest in any claims.

Kirby Benedict was duly sworn and admitted as an attorney of the court on January 8, 1867. His first advertisement as counsellor at law appeared in the *New Mexican* December 29, 1866. For six years his notice was printed in the same column with his contemporaries. The last date of publication was September 10, 1872.

As a practicing attorney he and Stephen B. Elkins defended William Logan Rynerson at his trial in the district court for the death, on December 15, 1867, of Chief Justice John P. Slough who had been in office less than two years.

---

[1] *Weekly New Mexican*, April 27, Nov. 3, 1866.

The "true bill" presented by R. M. Stephens, foreman of the jury, offers an inkling of the procedure.

The grand jurors of the Territory of New Mexico . . . that William L. Rynerson . . . on the 15th day of December 1867, . . . having the fear of God before his eyes, but being moved and seduced by the instigation of the devil, in and upon one John P. Slough, who then and there being feloniously, maliciously, willfully, of his malice aforethought, and with the premeditated design to effect the death of him (Rynerson) did make an assault, and that then and there the said William L. Rynerson, a certain pistol of twenty five dollars, then and there loaded and charged with gunpowder and leaden bullets, which pistol he (Rynerson) then and there had and held to, against and upon John P. Slough . . . did shoot and discharge . . . on the left side of him (Slough) a little above the left hip . . . did strike, penetrate and wound . . . one mortal wound of the breadth of one inch and of the depth of six inches . . . of which (John P. Slough) died on the 18th of December.   M. ASHURST
Atty. Gen. of
Territory of New Mexico [2]

[2] John P. Slough, born, Ohio; studied law and was admitted to the bar; moved to Kansas; candidate for governor, 1857; moved to Colorado, 1860; practiced law and elected to Minors' Court; during Civil War, was colonel of the Colorado Volunteers and defeated the Texans at Glorieta; later commissioned brigadier general and appointed military governor of Virginia; returned to New Mexico and was appointed chief justice by President Andrew Johnson to succeed Kirby Benedict.

William Logan Rynerson, born, Hardin Co., Kentucky, 1836; walked to California in the early 1850's to seek gold; enlisted in Company C, First Infantry, California Volunteers, Jan. 1, 1862; to Company B in April, 1862; advanced to captain and appointed assistant quartermaster of volunteers; served in Arizona and New Mexico until 1866; settled in Mesilla but later moved to Las Cruces; was admitted to the bar and practiced in the third district; served as district attorney and was a member of the Constitutional Convention, 1889; member of the council of the legislature, 1869-70; died at Las Cruces July 4, 1893. War service of Rynerson, *War Reb.* ser. 1, vols. XV, XLVIII, L. *Records, U.S. Dist. Court, County of Santa Fe, 1853-1858,* p. 246; Indictment, cf. file no. 175 a.

Ill will was first generated by a scathing remark that Secretary H. H. Heath had made concerning the chief justice. It was alleged that Heath influenced Rynerson to introduce into the legislature a resolution denouncing Judge Slough. As a result, the judge vented his rage against Rynerson.

According to witness S. B. Wheelock, Rynerson, at the time of the fracas, was playing billiards in the La Fonda while Judge Slough was seated on a sofa talking to a friend. The witness testified:

> The first I heard from Slough was, "There is a strange combination but one which is frequently seen in the world – a gentleman associated with a damn thief. I allude to that seven-foot s . . . b playing billiards with Colonel Kenzie. He (Rynerson) is a lying thief and a coward; he stole when in the army, stole since he came out, and stole his seat in the legislature. I here denounce him a s . . . b, a thief, and a coward but the damn scoundrel has not the courage to take it up."

Witness Wheelock continued, "In the course of the evening while I was at my store, I repeated to Rynerson what Judge Slough had said."

Further testimony was provided by J. Howe Watts, "A few days before the shooting, Judge Slough asked me if I had a Derringer. I told him that I had. He said that he wanted to be well heeled as he was under the impression that Heath would fight. I gave him the Derringer. . ."

Judge Slough was also credited with saying that Rynerson should wear a collar inscribed, "I am Heath's dog."

One witness declared that the judge had been drinking more than usual the evening of the fight. Others testified that when Rynerson entered the La Fonda, the judge had both his hands in his pockets and kept them there as he walked to the fireplace, then to the billiard room door where he paused and faced the bar room.

Rynerson approached the judge and said, "You have used language which you must take back." The judge replied, "I do not propose to take anything back."

The judge then took both hands from his pockets and with his left extended said, "Hold! Hold!" Then Rynerson fired.

The judge stood for a second or two, then fell. The Derringer dropped from his right hand. It was loaded and capped but not cocked.[3]

Rynerson was indicted for murder, but Judge Benedict, assisted by Attorney Elkins, succeeded in winning his acquittal. As an aftermath of the tragic affair, Heath was burned in effigy at Las Vegas in January, 1868. A sign bore the inscription, "I am H. H. Heath don't hurt me. I was forced to sign that certificate." An eye witness reported, "The torch was applied and as the flames hissed and cracked around him; the general (Heath) looked down upon his persecutors with stoic indifference, nor uttered a word of reproach nor cry of pain."[4] However, a joint resolution passed by the Eighteenth Assembly, 1867-1868, expressed confidence in Secretary Heath by proclaiming that his official conduct was correct and proper.

Joseph G. Palen was appointed chief justice to succeed Judge John P. Slough.

When the Legislative Council, during its 1868-1869

---

[3] *Santa Fe Gazette,* Jan. 11, 1868, p. 2. District Court Records, 1868.
[4] *Santa Fe Gazette,* Jan. 18, 1868.

session, sent a memorial to Congress to remove Joab
Houghton,[5] associate justice of the Third District,
Kirby Benedict aspired to fill the impending vacancy.
There was considerable prejudice against Houghton on
account of various suits that were the result of the
confiscation of property during the Civil War.

When it became known in Congress that Benedict
had applied for the position held by Justice Houghton,
his old friends from Illinois rallied to his support.
Richard Yates sent a personal letter [6] to President
Grant recommending Benedict's appointment as associate justice of the Third District where he had first
served in New Mexico in 1853.

All the Illinois members of Congress added their
names to a letter that requested the appointment of
Benedict and testified to his excellent qualifications for
the office. Mark W. Delahay, United States Justice for
Kansas, also recommended Benedict and reported that
their friendship had continued for twenty-five years
and that he was an able lawyer and a true gentleman.
In the letter that J. H. Moore, Illinois congressman,
wrote to the United States attorney general, he reminded him that Benedict had been a close friend of
Lincoln and had served as judge in New Mexico for
thirteen years but was removed by President Johnson
for refusing to endorse his policy.[7] Yet soon after the

---

[5] Ralph Emerson Twitchell, *Old Santa Fe,* p. 348. Joab Houghton, born,
New York, 1811; came to New Mexico 1843, the following year was appointed U.S. Consul to New Mexico; was partner with Eugene Leitensdorfer;
appointed judge by General Kearny 1846; served as associate justice of
Third District 1865-1869; practiced law in Santa Fe after his retirement from
bench; died at Las Vegas, 1877.

[6] Appointment Papers, Kirby Benedict MS, April 2, 1869.

[7] *Ibid.* April 1, 1869.

death of Lincoln, Benedict wrote to President Johnson to congratulate him and to approve of his announcements.[8]

However, Benedict had not yet outlived the abuses heaped upon him while chief justice, as the following letter discloses.

WASHINGTON, D.C.
April 5, 1869

E. ROCKWOOD HOAR   Attorney General
Washington, D.C.

Hearing that Kirby Benedict is applying for a judgeship in New Mexico, I feel it my duty to appraise you that he was dismissed from the position of chief justice in New Mexico a few years ago for habitual inebriety and incidental misconduct.

He has not reformed but is a confirmed inebriate and may be seen every day about the drinking shops in the city, more or less intoxicated and sometimes, sitting publicly asleep in open daylight in that condition.

His habits designate him a very improper man for any official trust and especially one so delicate as that of judge. These statements may be verified by a number of people who are daily observers of his dissolute conduct.

J. FRANCISCO CHAVEZ
Delegate from New Mexico [9]

At a session of the supreme court in January, 1871, when Joseph G. Palen [10] was serving as chief justice, new rules of practice for the supreme court and for the

---

[8] *Ibid.* May 16, 1865.

[9] *Ibid.* April 5, 1869.

[10] Joseph G. Palen attended both Yale and Amherst but did not graduate from either. He studied law in Hudson, N.Y. and was admitted to practice in 1838. For ten years he practiced law there until his health failed. He then went to the Northwest where he bought and sold real estate. He was appointed chief justice by President Grant, April 15, 1869, and arrived in Santa Fe in July. In September 1870, he went east and as a result, no court was held. He died December 21, 1875.

BIRD'S-EYE VIEW OF SANTA FE

Judge Benedict's ten-room home was in the lower left corner, next to the hills,
between Grant and Arny Streets. See text pages 200, 225. From a lithograph by
Beck & Pault, Milwaukee; courtesy of the Santa Fe Museum Library.

district courts were adopted. One of them made it necessary for attorneys to file briefs upon points of law that they relied on for reversal or approval and to give citations. This rule further provided that unless this was done, counsel would not be heard.

One day Benedict rose to argue a case in which he was counsel for the appellant. The court asked for his brief and learned that none had been filed. Benedict protested that he had not understood the new requirements. The rule was read to him and the case postponed in order to give him time to prepare his brief and comply with the ruling of the court.

When he reappeared in court, his statement of facts was, "The facts of this case will be found upon the record."

He stated his first point and his citation, "Vide United States Statutes at Large." There were thirteen volumes at that time.

The citation for his second point was, "Vide Phillips, Starke, and Greenleaf on Evidence."

The court informed him that his so-called brief did not meet the requirements of the new rule and gave him further time to perfect it. He brought it into court once more still unimproved. Whereupon the court announced that he would not be heard and directed the opposing counsel, Charles P. Clever, to proceed with the case.

Clever proceeded with his argument of the case while Benedict remained in his seat, commenting, muttering, and swearing. The court called him to order several times and finally directed a rule to be entered against him to show cause why he should not be suspended or otherwise punished for his misconduct.

His answer to the ruling further aggravated his offense for instead of offering an apology he bitterly assailed and villified the court. Then, promptly he was suspended from practice in the supreme and district courts until further order of the court.

At the following session of the supreme court, Benedict walked in without an apology and demanded that he be restored to practice. The court took no action. At the next term he repeated his request for restoration. Once more the court took no action.[11]

These new court rules imposed by Judge Palen resulted in financial loss to Benedict who found it necessary to offer some of his real estate for sale. He had owned two vacant lots adjoining his residence for more than seven years. He sold one for a $50 profit and the other for a loss of $50. Both lots were described by meets and bounds. One of the lots, priced $70, is described as follows:

> Beginning at a stone placed in the ground forty-eight feet, more or less, from the northeast corner of the dwelling house (Benedict's) running eastward in line with Benedict's house to arroyo (Mascaras) ; from said stone thence running on a line westward 160½ feet to a stone placed in the ground upon the eastern side of the land of Auguste Nicholas, and which line before reaching said stone and fence, passes through a corral of poles now standing, and thence from said stone running northern and with the line of the land of said Nicholas to the middle of the arroyo (Mascaras) eastward on a line until it intersects with a line from said corner of said house (Benedict's) and the stone first mentioned.

---

[11] *Report Supreme Court Cases, New Mexico, 1852-1879,* compiled by Charles H. Gildersleeve, p. 53-57. *New Mexico Bar Association Minutes,* p. 54.

The total amount realized from the sale of the two lots was $225. However, at the market price at that time, his family probably fared quite well. He could have bought 900 burro loads of wood for that amount if the price had not raised since 1858 when he first moved to Santa Fe.[12]

Although he had not profited from his investment in Santa Fe real estate, he had the greatest confidence in the ultimate benefits that would be derived from the completion of the Central Pacific Railroad and the telegraph lines.

As early as 1863, the New Mexico legislature passed an act to incorporate the Kansas, New Mexico, Arizona, and California Railroad and Telegraph Company. The proposed route began at the eastern border and crossed the entire Territory "in the direction of San Francisco." The company was obligated to begin work within three years but nothing was accomplished.[13]

Four years later, in 1867, the legislature sent a memorial to Congress requesting aid for the construction of telegraph lines that would accommodate the Government and increase the commerce and mineral wealth of New Mexico.[14]

Before a rail was laid in New Mexico, the legislature passed an act for the regulation and management

---

[12] *Deed Records, Santa Fe County.* Cf Book D, (Oct. 25, 1863), pp. 300-301; cf Book C, (May 24, 1864), pp. 557-558; cf Book L, (Jan. 21, 1871), pp. 97-98; cf Book E, (April 12, 1871), pp. 513-515.

[13] *Railroad Act,* approved December 30, 1863. Among the members of the R.R. Company were Henry Connelly, Ceran St. Vrain, L. B. Maxwell, José Manuel Gallegos, Diego Archeluta, H. S. Joynson, Anastacio Sandoval, Joseph Beuther, and Ambrocio Armijo.

[14] 40 Cong. 1 sess., Ho. misc. doc. no. 14, March 1867. (ser. 1312.)

of railroads. Safety was one of the first considerations. One requirement was the installation of a twenty-pound bell which the engineer was obligated to ring when within eighty rods of a crossing. Failure to ring the bell to warn both the natives and the stray cattle from the tracks was punishable by a fine of $100. Sobriety of both the engineer and conductor was mandatory. If found guilty of drunkenness, they could be fined $1,000.[15]

When the New Mexico and Gulf Railroad was incorporated, Benedict bought five shares. The capital stock was valued at 20 million; 200,000 shares were offered at $100. The proposed route extended from the northwest boundary of New Mexico as near as practicable at the junction of the San Juan and Rio Mancos, through Santa Fe and down the Pecos River to the vicinity of Eagle Pass, then to San Antonio, Austin, Columbus, and Galveston. It was also provided that, at the option of the corporation, telegraph lines would be constructed along any or all of the railroad routes.[16]

There was jubilation in old Santa Fe when Congress passed the law entitled, "An Act to Authorize the Building of the New Mexico and Gulf Railroad and for Other Purposes."

According to this act, the new railroad company was

[15] *General Incorporations, Railroad Laws of New Mexico,* Chap. VII, pp. 45-52.

[16] Corporation Commissioner's Office, Santa Fe. File no. 0324 a & b. Members – Albert Rupe, New York; William Rencher, James Yeoman, Charles P. Clever, James Cowan, W. F. M. Arny, Christian H. Schaap, C. William Schaap, Santa Fe; William F. H. C . . . y (not legible). New Mex. & Gulf R.R. Inc., Feb. 12, 1872; expired February 21, 1922.

granted a strip of land one hundred feet wide on each side of the center line of the railroad. In addition, land was provided for depots, stations, side tracks, and other needful uses in operating the railroad and telegraph line, not exceeding twenty acres at any one place.

A restricting clause provided that the rights granted should not preclude the construction of other roads through any canyon, defile, or pass on the route.[17]

Although chartered for fifty years, this railroad was never built. Consequently, neither Benedict nor any of the other stock holders became "king of the rails."

Benedict never lost his absorbing interest in politics. As President Grant's first term drew to a close Benedict wrote his old friend David Davis who was then a member of the United States Supreme Court:

SANTA FE   March 25, 1872

HON DAVID DAVIS   U.S. Supreme Court
Washington, D.C.

DEAR SIR: You can hardly imagine how intensely I am now watching the . . . coming presidential canvas and election. The interest with me is especially intensified by the prominent positions you and Senator Trumbull occupy. It seems to me that either you or he is almost bound to be the candidate against Grant.

I trust that your friends will not become antagonistical in such manner as to mar harmony in the canvas. *There is too much at stake.* Should you be elected, Trumbull would be very useful in some important place in support of your administration. Surely the Democrats will not make so silly and suicidal a mistake as to hope success with an . . . (not legible).

[17] *The Republican Review,* Albuquerque, July 20, 1872, p. 2, col. 5, Congressional Act, June 8, 1872.

I think you have more favor than Trumbull though his conduct and efforts during the present Congress entitle him to my
great consideration among all the elements in opposition to
Grant. I pray for a large convention of talent, influence, and
patriotism at Cincinnati. It must be wise in its promulgations of
principles, platforms, and issues. I hope there will be no foolish
gabblings about matters of theory which serve to mystify the
people without obtaining voters.

Sweep in November is the first thing. That accomplished, the
events, interests, wants, and conditions of the country will
determine legislation. Had I the power, . . . I can think
of no needed sacrifice I would not make to promote your election
should you be settled upon by the elements whose desire is always
change and that is my great one in the executive administration.

In this Territory a change would be the heavenly manna. You
can hardly conceive what a scurvy set of federal officers, with but
few exceptions, we have here. "Skeesicks" is a very imputable
term to name them. They are small creatures without dignity
of mind or spirit or character. They are miserable truckling
sycophants who dare not be mistrusted of a thought which they
fancy would not recommend them to the Grant influence at
Washington.

I live in hope that the days may come when we shall be rid of
the disquieting nuisance, and new gentlemen, honest and capable
ones, be put in their places.

The poor creatures begin to tremble in their boots with fears
that Grant will be beaten. There is no fraud or falsehood they
would not attempt to serve any contemptible or base motive. If
you should be elected, I expect they would soon have to give
place to new men who would be a credit to the Government and
its people.

I should like much a few lines from you, if you time admits.
It would be confidentially kept. . .

I remain as ever your friend and Obt. Servt.

KIRBY BENEDICT [18]

---

[18] David Davis MS, Chicago Hist. Soc.

However, Grant was re-elected and there was but little change among the federal officers in New Mexico. The so-called "Skeesicks" continued to be the recipients of Benedict's attacks.

The Judge Becomes a Journalist

Judge Benedict displayed an early interest in journalism and confessed to Attorney General Edward Bates in 1864 that he wrote editorials incognito for the *New Mexican*.[1] An incomplete manuscript, undated and unsigned but in the indisputable handwriting of the judge, announced that the undersigned had purchased the press and materials of the *New Mexican* printing office and was then editor and sole proprietor.
The policy of the paper was briefly outlined:

> We will sustain the Government in its efforts to oppose and put down the Rebellion. We believe that ample powers exist in the constitution to accomplish the desired results. . .
>
> We shall be the friend to all officers, civil and military, federal and territorial, of whatever service or grade, who faithfully discharge their duties and hold their obligations . . . above personal gratifications, private interests, or vain and selfish ends. . .
>
> Meritorious men and measures may expect our constant and cheerful aid. We shall hope to live in harmony with other peoples in the Territory and that our honest differences of opinion upon principles . . . shall not beget personal discord or vituperations. We shall oppose the election of José Manuel Gallegos to Congress and believe him unworthy of[2] . . .

---

[1] Appointment Papers MS, National Archives, Jan. 3, 1864. Attorney General's Office. Benedict to Attorney General Edward Bates.
[2] Ritch Collection MS, no. 2174.

Of what, was not disclosed as the page which should have followed was lost.

The rivalry between the *New Mexican* and the *Gazette* resulted in many charges and countercharges. The volume of controversial articles left no doubt about the freedom of the press in Santa Fe. The editor of the *Gazette* emphasized his opinion of Benedict:

> From June, 1863 until the latter part of May, 1864, it was well known that the *New Mexican* was under the direct editorial control and management of Chief Justice Kirby Benedict. The names of others appeared at the head of its columns during the whole of that time but no one doubted that the judge was responsible for its contents. In May, 1864, it was rumored that he had no further interest in the paper and would devote his entire time to his official duties. He is viewed as the masked instrument from which came the disruptable articles. Therefore the *Gazette* will consider *him* the editor and when it speaks of the editor, it will mean Benedict.[3]

Such a statement only intensified the conflict and resulted in the following affidavits:

> W. F. M. ARNY affidavit: I do solemnly affirm that Chief Justice Kirby Benedict came to me ten days ago and proposed that I take an interest in the printing office of the *New Mexican* and give to that establishment the printing of the laws and journals of the present legislature. He said he was interested and we could make a good thing of it. . . My reply was that I did not want any interest in any newspaper in New Mexico and that I could not be bought. Previous to that time, I gave all the printing to Judge Benedict's paper, the *New Mexican,* but when an effort was made to bribe me, I ceased to give him any more. Given under hand and seal, January 2, 1864. Sworn before THEODORE S. GREINER, Notary Public.

---

[3] *Santa Fe Gazette,* Nov. 26, 1864.

KIRBY BENEDICT affidavit: I, Kirby Benedict of the Supreme Court of said Territory, in the presence of the Most High God and upon the Holy Evangelists, do solemnly swear – That I have seen a copy of the affidavit made January 2 by W. F. M. Arny in reference to myself, printing, and the *New Mexican*. Furthermore, that so far as that affidavit professes or pretends to set forth and state any proposition or words from me, it is absolutely false and untrue in letter, substance, and spirit. Subscribed and sworn to, January 8, 1864.

Judge Benedict explained:

I loaned $10 to one of the printers which amount Manderfield agreed to assume. He feared his printing paper had been snowed in upon the plains for the winter. I purchased for him and paid for two reams of paper. These items comprise my pecuniary relations and interest in the *New Mexican*.

Second, I have had no confidential relations or conversations with Arny for over twelve months. For nearly a year he had become very malignant and vindictive against me and many of my personal friends for reasons which I can easily explain when necessary.

In the meantime, we became thoroughly convinced, from his conduct among men in this country, that he was so depraved as to personal truth, honesty, and veracity that it would be imprudent and even dangerous to the reputation of any of us to be alone with him or without the presence of some truthful person or else with some person whom Arny had no sordid means of influencing or controlling. This was mutually understood among us and notoriously known in Santa Fe. This had been mentioned twice on public occasions – once in Arny's presence and in the presence of Governor Connelly, General Carleton, Kit Carson, Colonel Collins, and in a large crowd during a reception speech made last May to Governor Connelly upon his return from the States. . .

Arny's office I have studiously avoided unless business has required my presence. The last time I was there was the second week of the legislature when I was present a mere "glance" of time to obtain a list of the members. I have even avoided my customary visits to the library for its doors connect with Arny's office and I am not willing to expose myself to being misrepresented by him.

About the middle of last December as I was passing from the Palace portal to the corner of the Johnson building, Arny called to me in quite a patronizing manner and began explaining what he had done with some printing. I at once gave him to understand that it was no business of mine.

He then told me that he was authorized by the Secretary in Washington not to send his printing of the laws and journals to the States but to give them to some press in this Territory or buy a press himself, and have the printing done on it.

He said, "They have been trying to get me to help 'em in getting a press brought out for a newspaper."

I saw his drift and said to him cautiously, "Well, why don't you help them?"

He replied, "Oh, I don't want to."

I did not ask him who the "they" were nor did I care about knowing. I desired to relieve myself of his presence so left him. Arny now says I took his affidavit in self defense in consequence of a personal attack upon him in the newspaper of January 2, 1864.

In an article under the heading, "The Public Printing," it is true that he was told that if he should have any transactions with the *New Mexican* office, he would be required to observe the principles of manhood and be truthful and act in good faith. He told one of the printers that in a little while he would have plenty of printing for the *New Mexican* office. I now say that he never gave a dollar's worth of printing to me in my life and that I do not own nor have I ever owned any printing press in this place. Now I leave this affair but am ready to resume my vindications as events may require.[4]

---

[4] *New Mexican*, Jan. 9, 1864, p. 2, col. 3-4.

During the time of this battle of words between Arny and Benedict, the former lived in one of the judge's houses. Old rent receipts reveal that Arny paid $150 for six months during the years 1863-1866. The indication is that he was in arrears some of that time.[5]

It was not until a decade later that Benedict attained his ambition to become the recognized editor of the *New Mexico Weekly Union,* owned by N. H. Gregory.[6] To further his journalistic ambition he later purchased the paper. The first known copy, issued after the change of ownership, bears the date July 3, 1873, Kirby Benedict, editor and proprietor.[7]

From contemporary newsmen his paper received favorable comment.

> We are gratified to learn that Kirby Benedict, editor of the *New Mexico Weekly Union* has become proprietor of that sheet and that he will, as announced in the last number, continue to run it in the independent manner heretofore maintained. We must give the *Union* the palm for typographical appearance over all papers in the territory.   . .[8]

The *Las Vegas Advertiser* highly praised the *Union* and its new owner:

> We hear with pleasure that this leader of journalism has been delivered from the ownership of strange hands and has become

[5] Ritch Collection MS, no. 1539. *Arny Letter* Book 365. (Huntington Library, by permission.)

[6] N. H. Gregory, proprietor; Francisco Sandoval, Simon L. Snyder, publishers; Melquiades Lopez, printer.

[7] Deposited in Huntington Library. Terms of subscription – one copy per year $5.00, six months $3.00, three months $1.75.

[8] From "Mining Life," Silver City, New Mex. Pub. in *New Mexico Weekly Union,* July 3, 1873.

the property of its editor. We predict for the readers new treats of investigation and general information. The *Union* had been a sharp battle axe fighting against wrong and will probably hereafter be a *matrailleuse* against our socio-political evils.

Let us hope that its subscription will soon justify its present owner to issue a daily sheet in order to increase its valuable reading matter and make it more effective with the frequency of explanations and duly impress the public on the selected topics of sheep raising, mineralogy, agriculture, etc., which so distinguish this paper ever since its foundation though controlled by unseen power of off-ownership. Now free and uncontrolled as it is, it will show all its characteristics more definitely and all its views will be better defined and explained.[9]

A correspondent from Socorro repeats the encomiums heaped upon the editor, Kirby Benedict:

The *Union* is a friend to New Mexico. Through its columns the capitalists and working men of the country must be informed of the wealth awaiting investment here.

There is no buncombe about the editorials and what is published in the paper is believed because your information is reliable. Therefore, go on and tell people everywhere what we have here, dependent only on capital and industry. Your articles on sheep raising have influenced thoughtful men to invest heavily. Colonel J. Francisco Chavez has from 10,000 to 12,000 sheep. . .[10]

After acquiring ownership of the paper, Benedict announced his own policy:

We intend that the *Union* shall discharge its duty to the public in advancing the main interests upon which the future wealth and prosperity of New Mexico depends. The most permanent industry is cattle and sheep raising.

[9] Pub. in *New Mexico Weekly Union,* July 3, 1873.

[10] *Ibid,* Jan. 29, 1873. Correspondence signed, San Antonio.

Ibid, May 15, 1873. Article about the Gen. Harrison Gray Otis goat farm on Guadalupe Island.

We advocate planting trees for shade and fruit. When we first
came to Santa Fe in 1853, the only trees then growing were the
few standing in front of the governor's residence. Since the
enclosure of the plaza, thrifty cottonwood trees have been
planted. The military planted rows of trees along Lincoln Street
and elsewhere. What Bishop Lamy and the Sisters Convent
have done by cultivating choice fruit trees, can be done by
others. . .[11]

Editor Benedict exchanged papers with numerous
other publishers including the *Springfield Republican;*
the *Mining and Scientific Press,* San Francisco; and
the *Western Guide,* Indianapolis. He subscribed to the
Daily Congressional Globe, the *Weekly Patriot* and
the *Capital,* Washington, D.C.; the *Weekly Tribune
and Herald,* the *Daily Press,* and *Leslie's Weekly,* New
York; and the *Tri-Weekly Tribune,* Chicago.[12]

The judge, as a newsman, performed the civic duties
of a one-man chamber of commerce. He published an
inventory of Santa Fe which he hoped would serve as
a reference for posterity when "men, things and ap-
pearances had changed in fact and substance." He
enumerated the churches, schools, banks, wholesale and
retail stores, jewelers, tailor shops, shoemakers, brew-
eries, flouring mills, the large number of *lendejones* or
dram shops, and one musical saloon where weekly
fandangos were held. He commented that the native
families did not patronize the latter.[13]

Considerable space was devoted to brief biographies
of the early lawyers [14] with whom he had been asso-

11 *Ibid,* May 8, 1873.

12 Benedict to Davis, March 25, 1872. Chicago Hist. Soc., by permission.

13 *New Mexico Weekly Union,* Jan. 2, 1873.

14 *Ibid,* April 17, 1873. Lawyers: Hugh N. Smith, Spruce M. Baird, John S.
Watts, Theodore W. Wheaton, Merril Ashurst, A. M. Jackson, Joab Houghton, Thomas H. Hopkins, William Claude Jones, and Charles P. Clever.

ciated. He maintained that they held a prominent place in the annals of that period and that no others rendered more valuable services. He also extolled the business men, doctors, clergymen, and educators.

Transportation made headline news. The Denver and Rio Grande Railroad had been completed as far as Pueblo, Colorado. Colonel Bennett and Company's mail coach "whirled out of Santa Fe behind six splendid horses that trod the air and earth as though there were springs beneath their feet." The mule and ox teams that poured into the city seemed to have no rest. Goods were never so abundant or so cheap as then. Every wholesale house was crowded with supplies. The telegraph rates were reduced to the following: Santa Fe to Las Vegas, 40 cents; Cimarron, 50 cents; Kit Carson, $1.00; and to all points in Iowa, Missouri and Illinois, $2.00. Benedict advised the citizens to cheer up and look for good times.[15]

The Land Office was doing a lively business and the editor was pleased to know that so many people were obtaining the nation's soil for the purpose of cultivation. "Those," said he, "are good signs. If surveyed, portions of the public lands in New Mexico would sell rapidly." Taxes were promptly paid in the Third District.

> This promotes the security of the treasury of the government and cuts the chance of grabbing vampire clerks snatching into their pockets such fees as they choose to charge against some innocent citizen who might not know that his taxes were delinquent. . . This government was not made for officials to eat out of the people's substance.[16]

[15] *Ibid,* Feb. 27, March 13, July 3, 1873.
[16] *Ibid,* July 3, 1873.

VOLUME 1.

The New Mexico Union.

SANTA FE, NEW MEXICO.
PUBLISHED EVERY THURSDAY.

KIRBY BENEDICT, Editor and Proprietor.

TERMS OF SUBSCRIPTION,
(INVARIABLY IN ADVANCE.)

ONE COPY, per year, - - - - - $5 00
" " 6 months, - - - - - 3 00
" " 3 months, - - - - - 1 75
No subscriptions received for a less
period than three months.

RATES OF ADVERTISING.

ONE SQUARE, (ten lines Minion type),
first insertion, - - - - - - - $2 00
Each subsequent insertion - - - - 1 50
Special and local notices, twenty-five cents
per line for each insertion.
All transient advertising must be paid in
advance.
Regular advertising payable on the last
day of each month.
Yearly, half-yearly and quarterly advertise-
ments inserted at liberal rates.

BENEDICT AS A JOURNALIST
The *Union's* masthead, July 3, 1873. See text page 211.
Courtesy of The Huntington Library, San Marino, California.

The alert editor gave timely advice during the cholera epidemic which was most prevalent in the Southern states. He warned that the pestilence might some day reach New Mexico notwithstanding the clear skies, pure air, and the absence of the filth of large cities. Always there appeared to be in the conscience of the judge an inerasable memory of his intemperance and consequent loss of prestige. He wrote:

> Temperance and regularity in eating and drinking and the avoidance of all ruinous excesses will promote security, happiness, and well being of all, cholera or no cholera. It will save time, strength, money, morals, conscience, and many a heartache. It will not plant the seeds of wasting regrets and self-inflicted remorse. To cultivate a composed and serene state of mind it is well to take heed of these observances.

The judge did not neglect to report the activities of the ladies. A group of them accompanied Major Nash, chief commissary, to Fort Stanton for a short visit. Here again the editor assumes the part of a publicity agent, by explaining that such excursions refresh the spirits, arouse attention to the varied scenes, form valued acquaintances, promote health, and generally put persons in better spirits with themselves and the world. As a sports editor he informed his readers that a baseball club had been organized.[17]

He defended the bull whackers who had been stigmatized by some of the writers on the Atlantic seaboard. The clumsy appearing whip of the teamsters had a short handle and a very long and heavy lash. When not in use, the handle lay on the driver's shoulder while the cruel lash dragged its slow length on the ground

---

[17] *Ibid,* July 3, 1873.

behind him. Professional bull whackers used the lash with the greatest ease and even with admirable grace. They could switch a fly from one of the oxen so deftly that scarcely a hair was disturbed. . . To his honor, the bull whacker, despite his name, seldom used his fearful weapon as an instrument of torture. He made it bark rather than bite and delighted in swinging the lash around his head and cracking it with reports as loud as those from a rifle. The teamsters or bull whackers were of every race and class. Among them were many eminent and influential men who crossed the plains on foot, with whips in their hands, driving ox-teams. They sought new homes which could be acquired free by their own labor and enterprising spirit.

Benedict had more to say about the population trends. The government of Prussia was alarmed at the emigration of its subjects to America at that time so a law was passed prohibiting the emigration of any person over the age of nineteen. Said the former chief justice, "Come on, we say and snap your fingers at the Kaiser and let him snarl and growl if that gives him any consolation. Land is cheap in America!"

To the prospective emigrants from Ireland, Benedict had this to say:

> Let them come to America as soon as they can get away from the old country "rile" and if they will be sober, industrious, and save their earnings, they will, in a short time, not only have their "half acre" of the Almighty's precious earth, but 40, 80, 160, or more acres with cows, sheep, hogs, and other property. In other words, he may be his own man and independent, a blessing which is richer than either glory or power. . .[18]

---

[18] *Ibid,* Oct. 30, 1873.

In addition to foreign, local, and political news, Benedict occasionally published advice to the youth of New Mexico. He warned the girls to forego the use of slang and leave that to their brothers. "I bet" and "you bet" were taboo. The conscience of the former New Englander was disturbed and he discouraged the scheme of one girl when she disclosed that "she intended to go for him." The inference is apparent.

His text for his admonition to the young men was provided by six incongruous words above the door of a respectable business house that faced the plaza. To provide the certainty of attention, an index finger aimed at an inscription, THE ENTRANCE TO HELL IS HERE. The judge surmised that this inevitable warning was painted before that particular occupant had moved in. It has been rumored that over another doorway in Santa Fe an equally inappropriate sign, THE SALOON OF THE LITTLE CHURCH was once printed. Itinerant ministers of that era frequently preached to the men who congregated in the frontier saloons so perhaps the rumor does contain some truth.

The judge explained that he did not mean the old orthodox hell of material fire and brimstone but the abyss of moral ruin and misery, the mind's anguish and the character's wreck:

> The insidious serpent ALCOHOL does not wind all his slimy folds around the young victim at once but tightens the windings with every cup that is taken after the habit is formed. It is easy to crush the monster upon his first approach but the more you familiarize with his seductions, the more surely will you be held within his fatal unyielding coils. Hard will it be then for the irresolute spirit to grapple with his hated enemy, rend and unwind his folds.

When the young man is led away by the fascination of the gambling table until he has become fevered with his losses and seldom winnings, he may exclaim in agony, "MY ENTRANCE TO HELL IS HERE." . . . When he has learned to scoff at conscience and his accountability to his Creator, his soul is then fast sinking away from the light of reasoning and preparing its leap into dismal depravity. . .

Scarcely ever have we met a victim who did not, in his soul, desire to be loosened and set free. The power and means lie within himself whenever he has the will and the courage to exert them. By so doing, he will pour coals of fire upon the heads of his human enemies. These are the ones who will hate to see you rise in your spirit and mind and assert and maintain your manhood. . .[19]

This editorial reveals the agony, the remorse, and humiliation he, himself, suffered. A few years previous he was bitterly reproached personally, in the press, as well as to officials in Washington. Kirby Benedict, Jr. was then twenty-two and his father's warning may have been written to influence him.

Judge Benedict indirectly inferred that he had overcome the curse and risen again to espouse right and justice and prove to his enemies the injustice of their accusations. In a letter to his old friend, Judge David Davis, then serving in the United States Supreme Court at Washington, he wrote, "Allow me to state that in all respects I am in the sedate, *sober,* and well regulated issue of life, *so to remain.*"[20]

---

[19] *Ibid,* Oct. 30, 1873, p. 2, col. 5.

[20] Appointment Papers MS. National Archives, Attorney General's Office. Benedict to Davis, March 25, 1872.

Before the Tribunals of Man and God

Three anxious years passed after Benedict's disbarment and he had not yet been reinstated. Finally, he presented his petition, dated January 16, 1874, to the supreme court in session at Santa Fe and requested the court to remove him from the judgment of suspension from practice as an attorney and counsellor at law in the courts of New Mexico.

In the spirit of respect, obedience, and supplication he asked this. He confessed to have committed disorders, improprieties, and contempt and rightly judged that he should be punished. He sincerely craved the pardon and forgiveness of the court and promised to make atonement for his offenses. He pledged that upon being relieved from the suspension he would not indulge in any "excessive habits" or any disorders or improprieties within the courts. He concluded,

> Accumulating age, want and desolation press upon me and I desire to be at peace and maintain just and honorable relations with the courts, judges, and others in my remaining days, in as much usefulness as possible to my family and others in the practice of the profession of my life.
>
> I beg your honors may heed this petition at least in generous clemency and grant me the relief I pray for and which is in your power to limit.

A few days later Chief Justice Palen appointed attorneys Sidney Hubbell, Joab Houghton, and William Breeden to investigate the general character of Kirby Benedict during the three years following his disbarment and report his conduct and attitudes toward the judges and the court.

They were ordered specifically to procure files of the *Santa Fe Post* and ascertain whether or not Benedict was responsible for the publication of articles that reflected upon the personal and official conduct of the judges. The *New Mexico Union,* edited and published by Benedict, was also scrutinized for defamatory news items.

There was sufficient evidence that Benedict wrote editorials not too complimentary to the territorial officers. In the *Union* of March 13, 1873, he outlined one of his policies: "It was not to amuse but to inform the public of the injustices, follies, and crimes of public officers, whose only importance arose from the fact that they held public office but commanded no other distinction. . ."

On the seventeenth of the following month he published an article that alleged that some of the attorneys were disgusted with the conduct of the judge of the district and had little confidence in receiving justice from the bench. These men, who had years of honorable practice, would not submit to the wrongs to which they and their clients were subjected. Some of them, including Charles P. Clever, had "wholly disappeared from the courts of the district." Benedict emphasized his objections to the policies of the court by reprinting from the *Las Vegas Advertiser* an article which criticized Judge Palen.

The investigating committee was further instructed to learn what connection, if any, Benedict had concerning the effort of the legislature, 1871-1872, to destroy the independence of the judiciary of the Territory and to disgrace and degrade a justice of the court; to inquire what part he had in the attempt to pass a law which would compel the courts to permit him to practice as an attorney and counsellor. The measure was passed in the house but defeated in the council.

Benedict's personal habits, particularly the excessive use of intoxicating liquor, were studied as they affected his qualifications and standing as an attorney.

For the purpose of enabling the committee to successfully pursue its investigations, it was authorized to administer oaths to witnesses and to procure from the clerk of the court process of subpoena for the attendance of witnesses.

The investigation was never undertaken for in less than a week after Chief Justice Palen had so meticulously outlined the procedure to be followed by the committee, Benedict, through his attorneys, Sydney Hubbell and Joab Houghton, withdrew his petition and application.

Inscribed in the old *Records* January 23, 1874, is Judge Palen's ruling: ". . . It is ordered that the proceedings herein and the same are hereby dismissed and the referees (committee) appointed discharged from further consideration of the matters referred to them. . ."[1]

---

[1] *Records of the Proceedings of the Supreme Court, New Mexico,* nos. 375, 382.

Only a brief month later, death came to Kirby Benedict, on February 27, 1874. He had proved himself a man of many talents, which he had multiplied by his service to all who had appeared before him in the courts of the United States in New Mexico. He had sentenced transgressors to pay the full penalty as prescribed by the laws of his fellow men, but he had judged impartially and honestly and had shown mercy to those deserving of its consideration. He who had been the judge became the judged before the Highest Tribunal. He now could let his record stand before him, and expect fair and honest judgment — the kind he had striven to give.

His last day began as usual. The family breakfast in the Benedict home was followed by the departure of the husband and father for his business office. During the day as he was walking along the street, he received his final summons and slumped to the sidewalk. Solicitous friends immediately took him home where all possible aid was given to the dying judge.

Funeral services were conducted by Montezuma Lodge No. 1 A.F.A.M. on March 1. The United States Eighth Cavalry Band played the dirge as it led the long procession through the muddy streets to the Masons' cemetery where the Worshipful Master, W. W. Griffen, read the last rites. The Masons first owned a section of the Rosario Catholic Cemetery but later the bodies were moved to the present Fairview Cemetery. There lies the judge far from the graves of his Connecticut forebears.[2]

---

[2] Minutes of Montezuma Lodge No. 1 A.F.A.M. 1873-1874. The Cavalry Band received $85 for their services. *Daily New Mexican,* March 2, 1874, p. 1, col. 3.

Thirty days after the death of Judge Benedict the following notice was published:[3]

> Letters of administration upon the estate of Kirby Benedict, deceased, having been granted to the undersigned by the Honorable Probate Judge of Santa Fe County, all persons indebted to said estate are notified to come forward and pay their indebtedness within the time prescribed by law and all persons having claims against said estate will present them to the undersigned within the said time or they will forever be barred.
>
> (Signed) EDWARD MILLER, Administrator [4]

The inventory of the estate revealed that Benedict held notes ranging from $10 to $370 due him from forty-nine different people. The total debt was $2542.80. A list of his clients showed that twenty-four persons relied upon him to collect a total of $5,349. His fee was not noted. Delinquent subscriptions to Benedict's *New Mexico Weekly Union* amounted to $30.[5]

His other assets consisted of a ten-room adobe house, four other rooms, a stable and the land surrounding the buildings appraised at $1,500; five shares of stock nos. 118-122 in the New Mexico and Gulf Railroad, valued at $100 each; and two shares, C no. 22, in the U.S.M. Telegraph [6] at $50 each. It was undetermined what part he owned in the Merced Junta grant. The record in the inventory is, "Copy of Merced Junta Grant; mention of interest in Grant; Gomez to Lopez to K.B." There was nothing to indicate his interest in the Ari-

---

[3] *Weekly New Mexican,* March 30, April 7, 14, 28, May 5, 1874.

[4] Original Field Book, *U.S. Census, 1870,* Edward Miller, age 40; occupation, maker of willow furniture; native of Saxony.

[5] *Journal of Probate Court,* Cf. Book D, Wills, Letter B, pp. 216-217, 221-223. Inventory of Kirby Benedict estate, received by Edward Miller from John Risque, attorney for Charlotte Benedict, April 8, 1874.

[6] U.S. Military Telegraph.

zona mine, the Blue Lode of Yavapai District that was promoted by Albert Chase Benedict August 8, 1863.[7] According to the United States census of 1870, the valuation of the judge's personal property was $5,000 and his real estate $8,000.

Apparently nothing escaped the prying eyes of the unknown appraisers. Carefully recorded is the following unsigned statement:

> TERRITORY OF NEW MEXICO, COUNTY OF SANTA FE
> We, and each one of us, the undersigned, do solemnly swear that we shall correctly and faithfully evaluate, to the best of our knowledge, the goods of the estate of the deceased, Kirby Benedict, according as we see and understand the same; and, as the said evaluators, we shall fulfil such a charge truthfully, correctly, legally, and scrupulously. So help us God.[8]

That used Concord wagon, designated as a buggy, together with the harness was appraised at $100; the two saddle bags, $2; the horse $75; but the cow and calf were not evaluated. No mention was made of the praiseworthy newspaper, *The New Mexico Weekly Union.*

Everything was listed and hauled away: The homemade rug under Charlotte's feet, her cape, hoops and petticoats; the beds, five mattresses, the blankets and bedspreads; the stove, pots, pans and dishes – even food, a bucket of preserves, eight pictures in gilded frames from her walls, the tables and nineteen chairs, and $15 in cash that was found in a chest.

The personal belongings of the judge were not over-

---

[7] Albert Chase Benedict MS, Arizona Pioneers' Hist. Soc. Tucson, Ariz.
[8] *Journal Probate Court,* Cf. Book "B", p. 355.

looked. There was his gold watch, his Masonic outfit, white vests, underwear and socks, the garden tools, a buffalo skin, and rifle. Four cupboards and books were appraised at $250. His writing desk and contents, together with a leather chest and papers, were recorded. The information in these papers was not revealed.[9] Where were the letters from Lincoln?

The court granted Edward Miller, administrator, permission to sell the personal property as inventoried at public auction.[10] Before the sale, John Risque, attorney for Charlotte Benedict, presented to the court a sworn statement from Kirby Benedict, Jr., declaring the following was his private property: The horse, buggy, harness, one mattress of straw and another of wool, one pillow, one rifle and double-barreled shotgun; and gifts from his father, two books of two volumes each, leather bound, entitled the *History of Napoleon Bonaparte*. Also claimed for the son as private property and which he had bought with his own money were an overcoat, a riding saddle, five volumes of the *History of the Reformation,* one volume each of *Pilgrim's Progress, Beyond the Mississippi,* and *Bookkeeping*. In addition he claimed a powder flask or horn, *un frasco polvoroso*.

Charlotte presented an affidavit of her private property: paintings in color in gilded frames, one of a mountain scene, another a flower and a war scene; a mirror, a rocking chair and a book entitled the *History of the Bible*. She was permitted to keep the judge's

---

[9] *Ibid.* Cf. Book "D", Wills, Testaments, Report of Inventories, pp. 209-210.

[10] *Journal of Probate Court, Special Session,* March 31, 1874, p. 307.

Masonic regalia, a symbol of the Masons' pledge to protect the widow and the orphan.[11]

After the notice of the auction was published as prescribed by law, the old plaza, as in centuries past, once more became the stage where the drama of joy and sorrow, loss and gain, was enacted May 13, 1874. The total amount realized in the auction was $318.15. To this was added the $15 cash, making a total of $333.15; but the expense of the auction was $222.70. Only $110.45 remained to apply against the debts of the estate.

The procedure practiced at that time exaggerated the expense. The personal property was hauled from the Benedict home to the house of the administrator, Edward Miller, who charged storage during the time the goods were in his home. The cartage cost was doubled on account of moving the goods to Miller's house, then to the plaza. Even the horse was taken from his stable and forage charged for sixteen days at a rate of $1 a day. Then, too, it cost $2 to bring the cow to the auction. The town crier who gave notice of the auction with his bell received $2. The greater part of the expense was incurred by the administrator, the clerk of the court, and the sheriff.[12]

Those who held claims against the Benedict estate were not slow in making public their demands for payment in full. Carlos Ayala presented his claim of $26.70 due him for his services in the office of the *New Mexican Weekly Union.*

---

[11] *Ibid.* May 8, 1874, p. 315.

[12] *Journal of Probate Court.* Cf. Book D, pp. 218-220, receipts and disbursements. Sheriff, Charles M. Conklin; Clerk, Ambrosio Ortiz.

While Benedict was serving as chief justice and during the year following, he was appointed guardian of several minors and obligated himself to pay twelve per cent interest on the money entrusted to him. The total amount was $2,088.04. During the intervening years prior to his death, his income dwindled and he was unable to meet the interest payments when due. He paid no interest on one sum for five years and on others seven years passed without compensation to the minors. The total accruement was $3,995.26.[13]

José Manuel Gallegos was another one of Benedict's creditors and on February 10, 1874, signed an affidavit to the effect that Benedict owed $519.62 for money lent and interest accrued; and that he (Benedict) had fraudulently disposed of his property and effects so as to defraud, hinder, and delay his creditors.[14]

As the result of the suit against Benedict, his property which had been attached, was ordered sold at public auction May 11, 1874. Charles M. Conklin postponed the sale until May 13. The ten-room house was appraised at $979. Thomas B. Catron bid $653 and as there was no higher offer, received a deed to the property.[15]

Catron retained ownership of the Benedict property for only two years when he sold it to W. F. M. Arny, one of the former antagonists of the old judge. Arny

13 *Ibid.* Cf. Book B, pp. 119, 307-311. Minors: Miguel and Ricardo Gomez; Pantaleon, Agueda, Amada and Soledad Estes.

14 *District Court, County of Santa Fe Records,* no. 553, Feb. 1874. Benedict sold two lots for $225 in 1871.

15 Deeds, R no. 2, p. 9. Charles M. Conklin, Sheriff, to Thomas B. Catron.

improved the property by inclosing it with a new and modern fence.[16]

Law suits seemed to continue ad infinitum.[17] The sheriff sued the administrator and the administrator pressed his suits against the debtors of Benedict.

On July 14, 1874, Miller, administrator of the Benedict estate, was served with a summons to answer to Sheriff Conklin for goods, wares, and chattels alleged to have been *lost* by Conklin and *found* by Miller, who "did convert and dispose of said goods to his (Miller's) own use to the damage of Conklin for $1,000."

The case was continued twice in 1875 and then a change of venue to Albuquerque resulted in more postponements until it was appealed to the supreme court in 1879. The property of Miller was ordered sold to satisfy judgment. The case did not rest there. Both Miller and Conklin were insolvent, as was attorney Sidney Hubbell who represented Miller.[18]

An attempt was made by Edward Miller, administrator, to collect from the many persons who were indebted to the Benedict estate. At the February court term, 1875, a suit was entered against Joseph Hirsch and William White, his security. On March 2, 1867, Hirsch had given his promissory note to Benedict for $194, payable within twenty-five days without discount or defalcation. Eight years had then passed and neither interest nor principal had been paid. The sum due at that time was $325 with costs.[19]

---

[16] *The Daily New Mexican,* April 2, 1876.

[17] District Court Records, County of Santa Fe, Case nos. 542, 587, 619, 913.

[18] *Ibid.* no. 957, p. 12, 39.

[19] *Ibid.* Case no. 619, p. 27.

The grieving widow Charlotte, then homeless and penniless, returned to Illinois accompanied by her son and daughter. Here the narrative ends.[20]

[20] The daughter, Worthena, married James Smith and lived near Moweaqua, Ill.; Kirby, Jr., a bachelor, lived with his two cousins, Cordelia and Carlos Curtis in Tuscola, Ill. The two cousins were unmarried also. Kirby, Jr. was reported by his neighbor, Librarian Elsie M. Williams, Tuscola Public Library, as a sober and hard working carpenter. Cordelia and Carlos Curtis were affectionately known as Cordie and Carlie. Both are buried in Tuscola Cemetery, Douglas County.

Appendix

Appendix

NEW MEXICO SUPREME COURT
DECISIONS OF BENEDICT

1. JUSTO PINO *v.* ALEXANDER HATCH [1]
   January 1855. Appeal from Santa Fe County.
   Spruce M. Baird and Hugh N. Smith for appellant.
   Merrill Ashurst and John S. Watts for appellee.

When a plaintiff in ejectment is endeavoring to prove a prescriptive right to land of which he claims to have entered into possession in 1823, evidence is admissible to show what was the custom under the Spanish and Mexican governments with respect to obtaining possession of public land.

The political chief of the province of New Mexico, under the government of Mexico, after the separation from Spain, had no power to grant away any part of the public domain. Rights under the Mexican grants are protected by treaty. Property rights acquired under Mexican grants in New Mexico, prior to the cession of the United States, are fully protected by the Treaty of 1848 and cannot be disturbed.

---

[1] *Report of Cases Argued and Determined in the Supreme Court of the Territory of New Mexico, 1852-1879,* pp. 125-145.

2. DAVID WALDO, JACOB HALL, WILLIAM McCOY *v.* HUGH N. BECKWITH [2]

January 1857. Appeal from Santa Fe County.

Theodore D. Wheaton for appellant.

Merrill Ashurst and Hugh N. Smith for appellee.

This case had been six years in litigation and was before the court on appeal in 1854. Beckwith brought suit to recover pay for the wintering of a drove of working oxen.

The cattle in question were oxen that had been driven from the States and arrived in Santa Fe with a train late in the fall. Forty-four cattle were receipted for. Three or four died the night they arrived; by spring only one or two were living. Witnesses testified that the oxen were in extremely poor condition when they arrived.

The loss and misfortune was heavy upon the company but that does not exonerate them from paying Beckwith. The damages found by the jury seem large and doubtless they are but are they so much as to require this court to send the cause back to be again tried? We think not.

It was a matter peculiarly fitted for a jury to determine. Two juries have found in Beckwith's favor. The corn and fodder was a great price that winter. The anxiety and trouble to Beckwith must have been great and if the damages are somewhat excessive, they are not so great as to justify this court in reversing the judgment of the court below. Judgment is affirmed with costs.

3. FRANCISCO SANCHEZ *v.* RAMON LUNA [3]

January 1857. Appeal from Socorro County.

Hugh N. Smith and Spruce M. Baird for appellant.

Sydney A. Hubbell and John S. Watts for appellee.

The points upon which the court passes are, the possession of the land by Luna and the stealthy and fraudulent entry of Sanchez. The evidence is that Juan Gaveldon had the keys and put Sanchez in possession; that the latter took possession publicly and in the daytime and under color of right by purchase from the heirs of the land. Judgment reversed and new trial ordered.

---

[2] *Ibid.* pp. 182-190.

[3] *Ibid.* pp. 238-246.

4. ALLEN T. DONALDSON *v.* COUNTY OF SAN MIGUEL [4]
   January 1859. Appeal from district court, San Miguel County.
   Joab Houghton and John S. Watts for appellant.
   Theodore D. Wheaton for appellee.

A county may be sued. It is a quasi corporation, a body politic.

An almost reckless regard of the usual forms of pleading is apparent throughout the whole of the petition of this cause. The second count is too loosely drawn in form, but there is no averment that the plaintiff was acting in the capacity of sheriff or jailer at the time the account accrued nor that any promise had at any time been made to him by the county nor any warrant has even been drawn upon the treasury nor that the county had become liable in any way to pay him.

The act of the judge of the district court approving and allowing the claim was extra judicial and of no binding effect upon the county. The judgment of the district court reversed. Leave to amend reversed and remanded.

5. RAMON ARELLANO *v.* RAFAEL CHACON [5]
   January 1859. Appeal from district court at Taos.
   Theodore D. Wheaton for appellant.
   Merrill Ashurst and R. H. Tompkins for appellee.

An election contest for justice of peace in Taos County, 1855. This was an appeal from the probate court. Chacon was declared elected but Arellano contested the election and won. Chacon then appealed to the district court.

The judge explained that the officers known as prefects and alcaldes under the provisional government were, by the Organic Act and by common consent and construction, respectively succeeded by the probate judges and justices of peace.

Furthermore, new trials are peculiar to courts of common law where jury trials prevail and a rehearing belongs to chancery jurisdiction, but as the probate court is not provided with a jury and has no chancery jurisdiction, it cannot grant a new trial or rehearing after deciding a contested election for this office under the statute.

Judgment of lower court is reversed and cause remanded to district court with directions to dismiss the appeal.

[4] *Ibid.* pp. 263-268.
[5] *Ibid.* pp. 269-279.

6. JOHN C. MOORE *v*. WILLIAM J. DAVEY, RICHARD OWENS, AND
   GEORGE H. ESTES [6]
   July 1859. Appeal from Rio Arriba County.
   Merrill Ashurst for appellant.
   Hugh N. Smith and R. H. Tompkins for appellee.

John C. Moore filed a bill to foreclose a mortgage against Davey.
The mortgage was executed in Santa Fe County, June 23, 1853, and
recorded in Rio Arriba County where the land was situated on July
2, 1853. The executions were in proper form and levied. The levy
was kept alive until the lands were sold by Owens and Estes.

Said Benedict, "From the *silence of our statutes at the time the
mortgage in question was made,* as to its qualities and legal consequences which followed its execution, we are to *turn for information and authority* to the Spanish and Mexican laws in force at the
time of the Treaty of Guadalupe Hidalgo. In view of that law (still
in force where not repealed or modified) this was a conventional
mortgage. The person in whose favor the mortgage is given has the
right to seize the property for the satisfaction of his debt or claim, in
whatever hands said property may be found."

Judgment was rendered in favor of Owens and Estes. Benedict
quoted a maxim well known to lawyers: "The law favors the
diligent."

7. LEVI SPEILBERG *v*. JOHN H. MINK, ADMINISTRATOR, ESTATE
   OF ELIAS SPEILBERG [7]
   July 1859. Appeal from Santa Fe County.
   R. H. Tompkins for appellant.
   Merrill Ashurst for appellee.

Mink claimed compensation for appraising the estate of Elias
Speilberg. Benedict announced that it was not for Speilberg to
repudiate the fair demand of an appraiser. The allowance of claims
against a decedent's estate is so peculiarly within the province of a
probate court, that another court will not be disposed to disturb its
action if the proceedings appear to have been fair and regular.
Judgment of district court affirmed with costs.

[6] *Ibid.* pp. 303-307.
[7] *Ibid.* pp. 308-314.

8. MARIA ENCARNACION ROMERO *v.* LUGARDA MUNOS [8]
   July 1859. Appeal from Rio Arriba County.
   John S. Watts for appellant.
   Merrill Ashurst for appellee.

A case of trespass and ejectment. Munos repeatedly trespassed upon the lands of Maria Romero. He attempted to take possession; pulled up and destroyed her crops. In utter contempt of the force of law and the sanctions in favor of the plaintiff, the defendant again re-enters her lands and deprives her of her lawful possessions. "How many times must she be remitted to the deprivations of her possessions and the same lawsuit with all the harassments and expenses before she can find relief. . . ? The injured party is not compelled to lie still and submit to trespass until her wrongs or her ruin shall be complete." The cause reversed and remanded.

9. ANTONIO MATIAS ORTIZ *v.* JESUS MARIA BACA Y SALAZAR [9]
   January 1862. Appeal from District Court of Santa Fe.
   Merrill Ashurst for appellant.
   Theodore Wheaton for appellee.

A suit to collect an inheritance of $307.50 with interest. The case was tried by a jury March, 1858 and appealed by Ortiz. The suit was founded on a document in Spanish made in 1823. When the instrument was made, the plaintiff was about three years old. It had been agreed that the sum of the inheritance should remain in the possession of Rosa and Antonio Matias Ortiz without interest in the capacity of guardians until Jesús Maria should receive it May 1, 1841, when he was twenty-one.

The judgment of the court below was affirmed with an additional sum for interest on plaintiff's claim from May 1, 1841, at the rate of 6 per cent, amounting to $372, which sum added to judgment on record totaled $679.56.

---

[8] *Ibid.* pp. 314-317.
[9] *Ibid.* pp. 355-359.

10.   JAMES THOMAS *v.* DAVID W. MCCORMICK [10]
      January 1866. Appeal from Mora County.
      Theodore D. Wheaton for appellant.
      Merrill Ashurst and R. H. Tompkins for appellee.

Proceedings begun September, 1863. Lost note, averments in action on – A petition in an action on a lost or destroyed note, distinctly averring the facts of its loss or destruction without showing the manner of its loss or of the diligence used to find the note is sufficient, these facts being merely matters of evidence.

In an action in a lost note, the testimony showing that the note was filed with the clerk in a previous action and that making diligent search afterwards in the clerk's office, the note and other papers could not be found, is sufficient proof of the loss.

The judgment of the district court affirmed and assesses the interest which has since accrued and also 6 per cent damages against appellee. The judgment now rendered shall draw interest at 12 per cent, that being the rate agreed upon in the note.

11.   AARON L. CRENSHAW, JAMES PORTER, JAMES L. BARRON *v.* SIMON DELGADO, ADMINISTRATOR ESTATE OF OLIVER P. HOVEY [11]
      January 1866. Appeal from Santa Fe County.
      Charles P. Clever for appellant.
      R. H. Tompkins for appellee.

This was a bill in chancery. Hovey's estate was insolvent and could pay but 30 or 40 cents on the dollar. The principal inquiry in this was whether or not Crenshaw, Porter, and Barron, as judgment creditors, were entitled to their full pay out of the insolvent estate.

"The court cannot fail to regret that during the fifteen years of territorial legislation, the Assembly of New Mexico has omitted to pass acts fully defining and establishing liens upon property, upon renditions of judgments and the manner of distributing among creditors the assets of insolvent estates of deceased persons.

"In the absence of such legislation, the courts are often troubled . . . in the search to find rule or law among the civil laws of Spain and Mexico to aid or guide them in their decisions."

Demurrer was properly overruled in court below.

---

[10] *Ibid.* pp. 369-376.
[11] *Ibid.* pp. 376-382.

12. WILLIAM TIPTON *v.* JOSE MANUEL CORDOVA [12]
    January 1866. Appeal from district court of Mora County.
    Theodore D. Wheaton and Charles P. Clever for appellant.
    R. H. Tompkins for appellee.

This was an action of forcible entry and detainer by Cordova against Tipton before a justice of the peace, in which upon trial, judgment was rendered against Tipton and he sought to appeal and entered into bond for such purpose but omitted to place a revenue stamp of 50 cents upon the bond.

In the district court the appellee moved to dismiss the appeal for the lack of a revenue stamp upon the bond. Permission was granted to amend the appeal bond and affix the stamp.

The court, after the correction was made, dismissed the appeal upon the ground that the original bond upon which the cause was taken from the justice's court to the district court was not stamped in conformity with the requirements of an act of Congress, approved 1864.

Judge Benedict affirmed the judgment of the court below with costs.

13. TERRITORY OF NEW MEXICO *v.* GREGORIO MIERA AND JACK COLLINS [13]
    January 1866. Appeal from Santa Ana County.
    Charles P. Clever for appellant.
    R. H. Tompkins and Merrill Ashurst for appellee.

A case of punishment. Omitting "unlawfully" contained in a statutory description of the offense is fatally defective. In the charge "did beat, bruise, and wound Guadalupe Lopez," the word "unlawfully" was omitted.

There are many "strikings" which are not "unlawful," such as parents correcting their children or officers executing sentence of court, etc. So, too, one may lawfully beat, bruise and wound another in the necessary defense of himself, his wife, or child.

Judgment of the lower court is affirmed.

---

[12] *Ibid.* pp. 383-387.
[13] *Ibid.* pp. 387-388.

14. Jose Secou et al. *v.* Louis Leroux and Esteban Ortiz [14]
     January 1866. Appeal from Mora district court.
     Charles P. Clever, Atty. Gen., for appellant.
     R. H. Tompkins and Merrill Ashurst for appellee.

The case involves the omission of the war revenue stamp. The stamp was omitted from the appeal bond but permission was requested to affix the stamp "nunc pro tunc" and the refusal of the court is assigned for error.

In the other case, no such motion was made but the party stamped the papers as he willed. The affixing of the stamp is done at the discretion of the court and the refusal is not an error to be examined and corrected in this court.

The courts in this Territory have been liberal in allowing parties in appeal cases from the justice courts to amend defensive papers or proceedings in the furtherance of justice.

They have not hastened to turn litigants from the tribunals on account of the unskillfulness or omissions of their counsel or the ignorance, want of education, or mistakes of inferior courts on appeal. Courts interpret and administer – do not make laws. The stamp requirement is an act of Congress.

15. Leandro Gutierres *v.* Maria Refugio Pino and Miguel
     Romero y Baca [15]
     January 1866. Appeal from San Miguel County.
     Charles P. Clever for appellant.
     R. H. Tompkins for appellee.

This was an action in chancery for an injunction. The suit was tried before a justice of peace who rendered judgment in favor of the plaintiff, then the defendant appealed to the probate court of which Don Migul Romero y Baca was judge. The bill charged fraudulent conduct by the judge who falsely represented to the complainant that the appeal was not pending in his court; then he clandestinely tried the cause "ex parte" and rendered judgment against him that he "should deliver a cow to Maria Refugio Pino."

Judge Baca denied the charge that he had not informed the complainant that the case was pending and swore that she was represented by an agent. After hearing the case the probate court dismissed the case.

The opinion and judgment of the supreme court was that the decree of the court below was correctly rendered and affirmed.

Bibliography

Bibliography

MANUSCRIPTS

David Davis Collection MSS. Chicago Historical Society

Historical Society of New Mexico Minutes, 1859-1860. Original. Museum Library, Santa Fe, New Mexico

Justice Department Records, Attorney General MSS. Papers of Judge Kirby Benedict, 1852-1869. National Archives

New Mexico and Gulf Railroad Certificate, February 2, 1865. Original. Corporation Commissioner's Office, Capitol, Santa Fe

Records of the Proceedings of the Supreme Court, New Mexico, 1852-1866. Original

Ritch, William G. MSS, nos. 909, 912-13, 917-18, 923-25, 1237, 1539, 1598, 2075, 2104, 2174, 2216. Kirby Benedict Correspondence. Huntington Library

——. New Mexico Slave Code, nos. 329, 475, 839

United States Census: New Mexico, 1860, 1870. Original Field Books. University of New Mexico, Albuquerque

——. Illinois, 1850. Microfilm of Original. Courtesy of Los Angeles Public Library

U.S. GOVERNMENT DOCUMENTS

30 Cong., 1 sess., Ex. doc. no. 52, (ser. 509). Mexican citizenship

35 Cong., 2 sess., Sen. doc. no. 1, March 1, 1858 (ser. 975). Reports from Gen. John Garland, Lt. Col. D. S. Miles, Lt. J. W. Alley, Michael Steck

36 Cong., 1 sess., Ho. rept. no. 508, Feb. 1860 (ser. 1069). Report of Miles Taylor on House Bill no. 64. Sen. misc. doc. no. 12

36 Cong., 1 sess., 1859-1860. Congressional Globe. Minority and majority reports regarding slavery in New Mexico

36 Cong., 2 sess., 1860-1861. Congressional Globe. Otero Slave Code; debates on admission of New Mexico as state; and Texas-Mexico controversy

40 Cong., 1 sess., Ho. misc. doc. no. 14 (1867) (ser. 1312). Memorial from New Mexico for aid in the construction of telegraph lines

United States Statutes, vol. XIII, 38 Cong., 1 sess., 1863-1864. War Stamp Act

———, vol. XVII, 42 Cong., 2 sess. June 8, 1872. An Act to authorize building of New Mexico and Gulf Railroad and land grants

———, vol. XVI, June 17, 1870. Salary of U.S. Circuit Court Judges. (41 Cong. 2 sess.)

Deed Records Adams County. Book U. Natchez, Miss.

Deed Records Santa Fe County, Books C, D, E, L, R-2. Records of the Benedict property transfers

General Incorporations Act – Railroad Laws of New Mexico, chap. VII, 1867

General Laws of New Mexico. Including the unrepealed laws from the promulgation of the Kearny Code in 1846 to the end of the Legislative session of 1880. Compiled and edited under the direction of L. Bradford Prince. New York, 1880

Journal of the Probate Court, Santa Fe County, 1865-1883. Book B, Letters of Administration and Bonds. Book D, Wills and Testaments; report of Inventories

Journal, House of Representatives, Fourteenth Assembly, Illinois, 1844-1845

Laws of Illinois, Fourteenth Assembly, 1844-1845

Report of Cases in Supreme Court, New Mexico, vol. I, 1852-1879. Compiled by Charles H. Gildersleeve. San Francisco, 1881

Revised Statutes and Laws of New Mexico in force at the close of the session of the legislative assembly, February 2, 1865. St. Louis, 1865

Records of the United States District Courts, Territory of New

Mexico: Doña Ana County, 1854-1856, 1861. County Archives, Las Cruces

———— Rio Arriba County, 1853-1865. Santa Fe County Archives

———— San Miguel County, 1851-1853; 1859-1860. Santa Fe County Archives. 1861-1866. County Archives, Las Vegas

———— Santa Fe County, 1853-1866. Santa Fe County Archives

———— Socorro County, 1854-1856. County Archives, Socorro

———— Taos County, 1862. Santa Fe County Archives

———— Valencia County, 1854-1856, 1860. County Archives, Las Lunas

NEWSPAPERS

El Novo-Mejicano, Santa Fe, N.M. Enero 2 de 1864. Santa Fe Museum Library

Illinois Citizen, Danville, Illinois, May 29, 1850. Chicago Historical Society

Illinois State Journal, Springfield, 1847-1855. State Library, Springfield, Illinois

Illinois State Register, Springfield, June 1849. Chicago Historical Society

Mesilla Times, February 23, March 2, 16, 30, 1861. Library of Congress

New York Daily Times, Feb. 2, 1854. Clipping only. Santa Fe Museum Library

Republican Review, Albuquerque, N.M., 1870-1873

Rio Abajo Weekly Press, Albuquerque, N.M., 1863-1867. Santa Fe Museum Library. Incomplete file

St. Louis Republican, Independence, Mo., April 5, 1849

Sangamon Journal, Springfield, Illinois, 1832-1847. Illinois State Library

Santa Fe Gazette, 1851-1869. Santa Fe Museum Library

Santa Fe New Mexican, 1848-19——. Santa Fe Museum Library

Santa Fe Weekly Post, 1874. Library of Congress

Santa Fe Weekly Union, 1873. Kirby Benedict, Ed. and Prop. Library of Congress

GENERAL WORKS

Abbott and Downing. Catalog no. 44

Allis, Marguerite. "Historic Connecticut," Connecticut Triology. New York, 1934

American Guide Series. Mississippi. New York, 1941

Americana, vols. XXIX, XXX

Anderson, G.B. History of New Mexico, Its Resources and People. Los Angeles, 1907. 2 vols.

Atwater, Francis. History of Kent, Connecticut, biographical sketches. Meriden, Conn., 1897

Baker, N.M. "The Pioneers of Macon County," Illinois State Historical Journal. vol. IV, 1911-12

Bancroft, H.H. History of Arizona and New Mexico, 1530-1888. San Francisco, 1889

Bandelier, Adolph Francis A. and Hewett, Edgar Lee. Indians of the Rio Grande Valley. Albuquerque, 1937

Barber, John Warner. Historical Collections of Connecticut. New Haven, 1831-1832

Bateman, Newton and Selby, Paul. Historical Encyclopedia of Illinois, vol. I, Chicago, 1912

Benedict, Henry Marvin. Genealogy of the Benedicts in America. Albany, N.Y., 1870

Bingham, John A. Report and vote on the repeal of the New Mexico Slave Law. (Huntington Library)

Boardman, David S. Sketches of the Early Lights of the Litchfield Bar. 1860

Bolton, Herbert E. Pageant in the Wilderness, Diaries of Silvestre Velez de Escalante and Fray Francisco Anastasio Dominguez. Utah State Historical Society, Salt Lake City, 1950

————, Spanish Exploration in the Southwest, 1542-1706. New York, 1916

Carriage Monthly, vol. XI, 1904

Century of Freemasonry in New Mexico, One Hundredth Anniversary, 1851-1951: Pioneer Freemasonry in the Winning of West. Montezuma Lodge No. 1, A.F.A.M., Santa Fe, New Mexico

Claiborne, J.F.H. Life and Correspondence of J. A. Quitman. New York, 1860. 2 vols.

Coan, Charles F. A History of New Mexico, vols. I, III. Chicago, 1925

Connecticut, Genealogy and Family History of the State of. Cutter, Clement, Hart, Talcott, eds. New York, 1911

Connecticut Historical Society Papers, 1590-1796. vols. VIII, XII, XXI. Hartford, 1924

Conner, Dan Ellis. The Walker Party in Arizona. Bethrong and Davenport, eds. Norman, 1956

Davis, William Watts Hart. El Gringo. New York, 1857

————. The Spanish Conquest of New Mexico. Doylestown, Pa., 1869

Deming, Dorothy. "Settlement of Litchfield." Connecticut Tercentenary, nos. 6, 7. Yale Press, 1933

Dictionary of American Biography

Dominguez, Fray Francisco Anastasio. The Missions of New Mexico, 1776. Translated and annotated by Eleanor B. Adams and Fray Angelico Chavez. Albuquerque, 1956

Duncan, Mrs. Rosalie. Life of Gen. John A. Quitman. Mississippi Historical Publications, IV, 1901, 2 vols.

Encyclopedia of American Biography (New Series), Winfield Scott, ed. New York, 1936. Contains Benedict family coat of arms and motto: Benedictus qui petitur (He who suffers is blessed, or He who endures is blessed)

Escriche y Martin, Joaquin. Legislativo Diccionario, 1784-1847. Madrid, n.d.

Espinosa, José Manuel. Crusaders of the Rio Grande. Institute of Jesuit History, Chicago, 1942

Firelands Pioneer, n.s., vols. XII, XIII (1899-1900). Firelands Historical Society, Norwalk, Ohio

Fisher, Samuel H. "The Litchfield Law School." Connecticut Tercentenary. Yale Press, 1933

Ford, Thomas. History of Illinois. Chicago, 1854

Fox, Col. Dorus M. History of Political Parties. Des Moines, Iowa, 1895

Ganaway, Loomis Morton. New Mexico and the Sectional Controversy, 1846-1861. Historical Society of New Mexico, Publications in History, vol. XII, Albuquerque, 1944

Greenleaf, Simon. A Treatise on the Law of Evidence. Boston, 1842-1846

Gregg, Josiah. Commerce of the Prairies, vol. I, 1849

Harrington, John P. Ethnogeography of the Tewa Indians. Bureau of American Ethnology, 29th Annual Report, 1907-08. Washington, 1916

Heyman, Max L., Jr. Prudent Soldier, a biography of Major General E. R. S. Canby. Glendale, 1959

Hill, Frederick Trevor. Lincoln, the Lawyer. New York, 1906

Hinton, Richard J. Hand Book to Arizona, its resources, history, towns, mines, ruins and scenery. San Francisco, 1878

Howe, Henry. Historical Collections of Ohio. An encyclopedia of the State. Cincinnati, 1902

Hunt, Aurora. The Army of the Pacific, 1860-1866. Glendale, 1951

—— James Henry Carleton, Western Frontier Dragoon. Glendale, 1958

Jones, Jane Martin. Personal Recollections of Early Decatur. Decatur Chapter D.A.R., 1912. Recollections of Rev. N. M. Baker, August 16, 1912

Kane, Harnett T. Natchez on the Mississippi. New York, 1947

Keleher, William A. Turmoil in New Mexico, 1846-1868. Santa Fe, 1952

—— The Fabulous Frontier, Twelve New Mexico Items. Santa Fe, 1945

Kilbourne, Dwight C. Bench and Bar of Litchfield County, Conn., 1709-1909

King, Clarence. U.S. Mining Laws under the State and Territory (Arizona) to which are appended local mining rules and regulations.

King, Willard L. "Riding the Circuit with Lincoln," American Heritage, vol. VI, February, 1955. A Biography of Judge David Davis

Linder, Usher Ferguson. Reminiscences of the Early Bench and Bar of Illinois, and an appendix by Joseph Gillespie. Chicago, 1879

Litchfield County, Connecticut: illustrations and biographical sketches. Philadelphia, 1881

Lummis, Charles F. Some Strange Corners of our Country, the Wonderland of the Southwest. New York, 1901

Lytle, William M. Merchant Steam Vessels of the United States, 1807-1868. Steamship Historical Society of America, pub. no. 6, n.d. Compiled from official merchant marine documents and other sources

Macon County, Illinois, History of, with illustrations descriptive of the scenery and biographical sketches of some prominent men and pioneers. Philadelphia, 1880

Mayer, Brantz. Mexico, Aztec, Spanish and Republican, vol. II. Hartford, 1853

Moore, William F. Representative Men of Connecticut. Everett, Mass., 1894

Moses, John. Illinois – Historical and statistical, comprising the essential facts of its planting, growth as a province, county, territory and state, with statistical tables. 1895, 2 vols.

National Encyclopedia of American Biography. 1893-19—

National Geographic Magazine, vol. VIII, 1897. Acoma Mission.

New Mexico Bar Association. Report of Committee on Legal Biography and Proceedings. Santa Fe, 1890

Newton, John and Cowper, William. The Olney Hymns. New York, 1857

Parsons, Elsie Worthington Clews. American Anthropologist, n.s. vol. XX, no. 2, April-June, 1918. Notes on Acoma and Laguna.

———. American Anthropologist, n.s., vol. XXII, no. 1, January-March, 1920. Notes on Isleta, Santa Ana, and Acoma

———. American Anthropologist, n.s., vol. XXX, no. 4, October-December, 1928. Laguna Migration to Isleta

Perrin, W.H. and Battle, J.H. History of Delaware County, Ohio. Chicago, 1880

Plymouth Collection of Hymns and Tunes. New York, 1870

Poldervaart, Arie W. Black-robed Justice, A History of Administration of Justice in New Mexico from the American Occupation in 1846 until Statehood in 1912. Historical Society of New Mexico, Publications in History, vol. XIII. Santa Fe, 1948

Prairie Lodge No. 77, A.F.A.M., Paris, Illinois: Centennial, 1849-1949

Pratt, Harry Edward. Lincoln 1840-1846; Being the Day by Day Activities of Abraham Lincoln from January 1, 1840, to December 31, 1846. Abraham Lincoln Assn., Springfield, 1939

———. Lincoln, 1809-1839, Day by Day, February 12, 1809, to December 31, 1839. Abraham Lincoln Assn., Springfield, 1941

Public Records of the State of Connecticut, from October, 1776 to February, 1778, with the Journal of the Council of Safety from October 11, 1776, to May 6, 1778, with appendix. Charles J. Hoadly ed. Hartford, 1894

Putnam, James W. Illinois and Michigan Canal; Illinois Centennial Publication; a study in economic history. University of Chicago, 1918

Quick, Herbert and Edward. Mississippi Steamboatin'. New York, 1926

Read, Benjamin M. Illustrated History of New Mexico. Santa Fe, 1912

Richmond, Mabel E. Centennial History of Decatur and Macon Counties, Ill. Decatur, 1930

Rosenberry, Lois Kimball Mathews. "Migration from Connecticut after 1800." Connecticut Tercentenary, nos. 54 and 28, 1934-35

Sangamon County, Illinois, History of, with sketches of its cities, portraits of prominent persons, and biographies of representative citizens. Chicago, 1881

Schmidt, Gustavus. The Civil Law of Spain and Mexico. New Orleans, 1851

Scholes, F.V. Church and State in New Mexico, 1610-1650. Albuquerque, 1937

Seymour, Mabel and Fergens, Elizabeth. "Barzillai Slosson, Lawyer of Kent, his account book, 1794-1812," Connecticut Tercentenary, no. 47, New Haven, 1933-36

Silver, David Mayer. Lincoln's Supreme Court. Urbana, 1956

Smith, John W. History of Macon County, Illinois. Springfield, 1876

Starke, Thomas. A Practical Treatise on the Law of Evidence and a Digest of Proofs. Boston 1828

Stevenson, Matilda Cox. "The Sia." Bureau American Ethnology, Eleventh Annual Report 1889-1890. Washington, 1894

Thomas, Benjamin P. Lincoln, 1847-1853; Being the Day by Day Activities of Abraham Lincoln from January 1, 1847, to December 31, 1853. Abraham Lincoln Association, Springfield, 1936

Tittman, Edward D. "The First Irrigation Lawsuit." New Mexico Historical Review, vol. II, 1927

Trumbull, J. Hammond. Public Records of the Colony of Connecticut, 1636-1776. Transcribed and published in accordance with the resolutions of the general assembly. Hartford, 1850-1890

Twitchell, Ralph E. The Leading Facts of New Mexican History, vol. II. Cedar Rapids, Iowa, 1912

—— "Chief Justice Kirby Benedict." Old Santa Fe, a magazine of history. Vol. I, 1913-1914. Santa Fe, 1914

—— Spanish Archives of New Mexico. Cedar Rapids, Iowa, 1914, 2 vols.

Ware, Francis M. Driving. New York, 1903

War of Rebellion. Compilation of official records of union and confederate armies. Ser. 1, vol. 50, pts. 1 and 2. Washington, 1897-1900

White, Alain Campbell. "A Brief History of Litchfield," Connecticut Tercentenary, 1635-1935. 1935

White, Leslie Alvin. "The Acoma Indians." Bureau of American Ethnology, 47th Annual Report, 1929-1930. Washington, 1932

—— "Report of Field Work at Acoma," American Anthropologist, vol. XXX, no. 4, 1928

Whitney, Henry Clay. Life on the Circuit with Lincoln, with Introductory Notes by Paul Angle. Caldwell, Idaho, 1940

Winthrop, Gov. John. Journals, History of New England, 1630-1649. Jameson and Hosmer ed. New York, 1908

Index

ABREU, RAMON (Alcalde): 179

Abreu, Santiago: death, 179

Absences, New Mexico Judges: 121, 134, 141-45, 163, 164, 167-68

Acoma Pueblo El Penol (Pueblo on the Rock): 65, 89; suit for recovery of portrait, 90-93; suit won but appealed, 92; documents stolen, 93; lawsuit, 94, 99-105

Acomita Indian village: 89

Agassiz, Louis: 173

Alaric (Alarid) Jesús Maria: 179

Albuquerque: court session, 56-57; court records discovered, 59; 65-66; residence of Benedict, 71; left, 73

Alcaldes: 51

Alcoholism: 219-20

Allen, J.C: lawyer, 49; recommends Benedict, 70

Alvarado, Capt: 89

Alvarez, Manuel: 73

Amigo del Pais: 63

Angel, Paula: trial for murder, 76-77; executed, 77

Apache Canyon: snowstorm, 81

Appraisal of estate: fee for, 238-39

Archibald, C.M: U.S. Marshal, 121 note; 155

Archuleta, Diego: on revision of laws, 131; railroad promoter, 201

Ariluead, Vicente: 93

Arizona Territory: organization of, 87, 138-39, 145-46, 151, 154

Armijo, Ambrosio: 110; railroad promoter, 201

Armijo, Gen. Manuel: home, 58; 129, 177

Arny, William F.M: rents Benedict house, 74; pardons Ysidro, 77; edits law revision, 132; letter to Lincoln condemning Benedict, 165; criticized by Benedict, 166; controversy with Benedict, 208-10; buys Benedict estate, 229

Arriba: 81, 163

Ashurst, Merrill: 55; fined for gambling, 76; counsel for Martinez, 79; circuit-rider, 81-84; invests in gold mine, 87; counsel for Acoma Pueblo, 92; 190, 235-42, 213 note

Assault and battery: 62

Aubrey, Francois X: murdered, 63

Auction: of Benedict property, 228

Ayala, Carlos: 228

Azalas, Cusenas: murdered, 60-61

BABBITT, A.W: in Ill. Legis., 30

Baird, Spruce M: 55; ranch, 57; counsel for Laguna Pueblo, 92; 235-36, 231 note

Baker, Edward D: congressman, 35; 152

Bancroft, George: 173

Barclay's Fort: 115

Baston de Justicia: 51-52

Bates, Edward, U.S. Atty. Gen: letters from Benedict, 141-57, 159-64, 166; 207

Baylor, Col. John R: invades N.Mex., 118-19

Beale Road, N.Mex: 86

Beaubien, Charles: 55, 177

Benedict, Albert Case: gold mine claims, 84-87, 226

Benedict, Albert D: 18

Benedict, Benjamin: 15-16; moved to Ohio, 16; 18

Benedict, Chloe: mother of Kirby, 15, 17 note

Benedict, Delilah: 15

Benedict, Germon: 15

Benedict, Grandison: 15

Benedict, John: father of Kirby, 15, 17 note

Benedict, John, Jr: 15; death, 36

Benedict, Kirby: 11, 12, 15, 17; law student, 18; admitted to Mississippi bar, 21; marriage, 21; moved to Decatur, Ill., 22; admitted to Illinois bar, 23; probate judge, Decatur trustee, 23; 24; Locofoco candidate, 25; elected Illinois legislator, member Judicial Committee, 26; member of committee to revise laws, 27; 28-29; address against Mormons, 30-31; defeated as candidate for lieut. gov., 31; 33-35; moved to Paris, Ill., 36; becomes Mason, 39; description of, 39-40; drinking habits, 41; as circuit rider, 42, 43; lawsuit, 43; association with Lincoln, 44-47; appointed New Mexico judge, 50; arrives in Santa Fe, 50; horse and buggy circuit, 55-59; murder trial of Bourale, 60-61; cases decided — trespass, ejectment, smuggling, unlawful assembly, false weights and measures, assault, disturbing peace, 62; murder trial of Weightman, 63; asks leave of absence, 64; moves family to New Mex., 65; trial of Mesilla Guard, 67-68; letter to Lincoln, 68; reappointed, 70; appointed Chief Justice, 71-72, 159; moves from Albuquerque to Santa Fe, 73; buys house from Blummer, 73; buys two lots, 74; fines self for gambling, 75-76; sentences pronounced by — horse thief, 76; Paula Angel, murder, 76, 77, on Ysidro, 77; Julian Chavez, bribery, 78; Manuel Cardenas, murder, 78; trial of Martinez, 81; circuit rider in New Mex., 81-84; injured en route to Albuquerque, 84; invests gold mine, 87; letters from Albert, 84-87; tries lawsuit, Acoma vs. Laguna, 89-93; tries lawsuit, Acoma vs. de la O, 93-94, 99-105; settles Acoma water rights, 105; hears peonage case, 107-11; cases tried by — McDonald v. Carleton, 122-23, Green v. Ewell, 124, Carter v. New Mex. Terr., 124-28; New Mex. law revision, 131; letters to Lincoln, 133-40, 165-68; letters to Bates, 141-57, 159-64, 166; takes loyalty oath, 153; recommendations for reappointment, 157-58; leave of absence for travel, 160-161; oath of office, 163; determines case of negro slave and Indian captive, 164; criticized by Arny, 165; criticizes Arny, 166; letter to Pres. Johnson, 169-71; eulogizes Lincoln, 171-72; address to Hist. Soc., 174-76; address on Revolution of 1837, 178-79; Master of Montezuma Lodge, 179; performs marriage ceremony, 180; addresses indignation meeting, 181; supported by legislature, judges, bar, newspapers, 185-90; on mining expedition, 191; private practice, 191; defends Rynerson for murder of Slough, 191-94; controversy with Palen, disbarment, 196, 199-200; sells lots, 200-01; buys railroad shares, 202; letter re Grant's election campaign, 203-04; editorial policy of *New Mexican*, 207; controversy with Arny, 208-10; editor and owner of *New Mexican Union*, 211; editorial policy of, 212-13; exchanges newspapers, 213; scope of newspaper contents, 213-20; letter to Davis, 220; petitions bar for reinstatement, 221; conduct investigated, 221-223; proceedings dismissed, 223; death and funeral, 224; burials, 224; inventory and appraisal of effects, 225-27; auction of property, 228; estate litigation, 230; Supreme Court decisions of, 235-43

Benedict, Mrs. Kirby (Charlotte Curtis): 21, 34, 36; illness, 40; 50; moved to N.Mex., 65; illness, 71; 72; visit to Ill., 160-61; effects inventoried, 226; returns to Ill., 231

Benedict, Kirby, Jr: born, 40; moved to N.Mex., 65; 73; invests in gold mine, 87; at school in Ill., 160-61; injured, 162; 220; effects inventoried, 227; return to Ill., 231 note

Benedict, Maria: 15; married, 17

Benedict, Noah: lawyer, 16

Benedict, Stephen: 15

Benedict, Thaddeus: lawyer, 16

Benedict, Thomas: 16; wife, 16

Benedict, Worthena Ceorda: daughter of Kirby and Charlotte, 36; moved to N.Mex., 65; 73; at school in Ill., 160-61; returns to Ill., 231

Bent, Charles (Gov. of Colorado): 177; street named for, 180

Bent, Teresina: married by Benedict, 180

Bernalillo: 56

Beuther, Joseph: 201

Bingham, John: congressman, 116

Black, Jeremiah S., U.S. Atty. Gen: letter from Benedict, 70, 129

Black Lake: 83

Blackwood, Wm. G: 121 note; 143

Bloomington, Ill: 33 note; 34

Blue Lode Mine: 226

Blummer, Charles, Treas. of New Mex: 72-73

Bond, Ida: librarian, 180

Bonneville, Col. B.L.E: 174

Boone, Wm. F: judge, 121 note, 136, 143

Bourale (Borule), Pedro José: murder trial, 60-61

Boyakin, H.P: 26

Brayer, Mason: lawyer, 27 note

Breckenridge, John C: 173

Breeden, William: 221-22

Brocchus, Perry E: judge, 63; absence, 142, 167

Brush, Henry: lawyer, 18

Buchanan, Pres. James: Benedict's appointments, 70-72; policy, 136; 173

Bullwhackers: 217-18

Burros: 72, 201

CABEZA DE VACA, ALVAR NUNEZ: 175

Cameron, Simon, Sec. of War: 118

Campbell, David B: lawyer, 24; Benedict's bedfellow, 41-42; 44, 134

Canby, Col. Edw. R.S: 139, 154-55, 157

Capitol, Santa Fe: building of, 74; part burned, 75

Cardenas, Rev: sermon of, 62-63

Cardwell, L.A: 59

Carleton, Henry Guy: 87

Carleton, James Henry: invests in gold mine, 87-88; as slave owner, 112; sued by McDonald, 122-23; commands N.Mex. Mil. Dept., 164; controversy over passports, 167-68; 184, 209

Carson, Christopher (Kit): 177, 209

Carter, George: suit of, 124-28

Casa Colorado: 57

Catron, Thomas B: purchases Benedict estate, 229

Central Pacific R.R: 201

Chapel de Nuestra del Señora del Rosario: 178

Chavez, Francisco X: 177, 187

Chavez, J. Francisco: letter Hoar disapproving of Benedict, 196; sheep raising by, 212

Child punishment: 241

Circuit riding: 42-43, 55-59, 81-84

Clark, John A., Surveyor Gen: gives map to Benedict, 86-87

Clay, Henry: 118

Clever, Charles P: 72; rides circuit, 81-84; invests in gold mine, 87; revision of laws, 131; 155-56; member of Hist. Soc., 173; 190; on mining expedition, 191; 199, 222, 240-42

Clinton, Ill: 24, 34, 44

Cochiti, Alonzo: 100

Collins, James: publishes *Gazette*, 149-50; 209

Colton, Wells: lawyer, 24, 44

Columbus, Christopher: 175

Concord carriage: 55, 57, 83, 226

Confederate troops: invade New Mex., 59; 81, 118-19, 136-37, 157; capture Santa Fe, 160; abandon New Mex., 162

Conklin, Charles M: 229

Connelly, Gov. Henry W: requests revision of laws, 131; takes loyalty oath, 153; 157; promotes railroad, 201; 209

Coronado Expedition: 89

Cortes, Hernando: 175

County: sued as quasi corporation, 237

Craig, Lt: 67

Cruzate, Domingo J.P. de: 94, 100

Cummings, Joseph: 87

Curtis, Carlos: 21

Curtis, Carlos, Jr: 231 note

Curtis, Charlotte: *see* Benedict, Mrs. K.

Curtis, Cordelia: 231 note

Curtis, Mary (Mrs. Carlos): mother of Charlotte, 21; lost eyesight, 40

Cutler, Abraham: U.S. Marshal, 163

Cutler, Benjamin C., Asst. Adj. Gen: 87

Danville, Ill: 33-34, 44-45, 47

Davidson, W.A: 121

Davis, David: 11; revision of Ill. laws, 27; 33-35, 41-42, 45; recommends Benedict, 158-59; letter to Pres. Johnson, 186-87; letters from Benedict, 203-04, 220

Davis, Jefferson: 152

Davis, Sarah W. (Mrs. David): 30 note, 40

Davis, W.W.H: 56; recommends Benedict, 70

Davenport, J.J: chief justice, 55, 63, 64, 71; tries lawsuit, Acoma vs. Laguna, 92; 141-42

De la O, Gregorio: 102

De la O, Victor: steals documents from Acoma, 93; lawsuit, 94, 99-105

Decatur, Ill: as county seat, 22; Benedict debate, 25; 33 note; 34, 36

Delahay, Mark W: recommends Benedict, 195

Delaware City, Ohio: 21

Denver and Rio Grande R.R: 214

Dill, M.M: 45-46

Dillehunt, Benjamin: sues Benedict, 43

Doña Ana: 59, 142

Doña Ana County: court records, 59

Donaldson, Maj. J.L: 173

Dorantes, Andreas: 175

Douglas, Stephen A: 11, 24; senator, 35; 44, 49; death, 152

Draco Code: 118

Dred Scott case: 113

Duro, Juan: murdered, 124

Education: 18, 160-61

El Paso, Tex: 94

Election contest: 237

Elkins, S.B: 190; defends Rynerson for murder of Slough, 191-94

Ellison, James: 87

Ellison, Samuel: fined for gambling, 76; rides circuit, 81-84

Ellsbury, Gustave: 87

Emancipation Proclamation: peons not affected by, 111

Emerson, Charles: 36, 43, 45-46

England: Benedicts from, 16

Entrance to Hell: 219-20

Estate, of Benedict: 225-27

Estefancio (the black Moor): 175

Estevan, Santes: as judge, 79

Ewell, Capt. Richard S: sued, 124

Fairview Cemetery: 224

Fernandez, Domingo: peonage case, 107

Ford, Gov. Thomas: message, 26

Fort Bliss (El Paso): 150

Fort Craig, New Mex: 66-67, 160

Fort Fillmore: 68, surrender, 154

Fort Stanton: 217

Fort Thorn, New Mex: 60; Indian attack, 67; Indians buried at, 67

Fort Union, New Mex: 160

Fraudulent conduct: of judge, 242-43

Fraudulent possession: 236

Fremont, John C: 155-56

Fueros: special jurisdiction, 51

GADSDEN PURCHASE: 55, 61, 146

Gallegos, José Manuel: 184 note; railroad promoter, 201; Benedict opposes, 207; creditor of Benedict, 229

Gambling: laws regulating, 53; lawyers fined for, 75-76

Garland, Gen. John: commands Mil. Dept., New Mex., 65; consults Benedict re attack on Indians, 66-68; hon. member of Hist. Soc., 173

Gazette (Santa Fe): 149-50, 156, 184; rivalry with New Mexican Weekly, 208

Gila River gold fields: 191

Gorin, Jerome Rinaldo: lawyer, 23

Grant, Pres. Ulysses S: 195, 203-05

Grayson, Col. John B: 173

Green, Daniel, Pvt: sues Ewell, 124

Gregory, N.H: publisher, 211

Greiner, Theodore S: 208

Greiner, Major John: 184, 190; on mining expedition, 191

Gridley, A: 44

Griffen, W.W: Masonic Master, 224

Griffith, William B: lawyer, 18

Guadalupe Hidalgo, Treaty: 146

Guadalupita: 82

HANKS, JOHN: 22

Harden, John J: lawyer, 49

Hare, Judge: of C.S.A., Ariz., 59

Heath, H.H: territorial sec'y., 193

Hirsch, Joseph: freighter, 73; debt to Benedict, 230

Historical Society of New Mexico: 173; Benedict addresses, 174-76, 178-79

Hoar, E. Rockwood (U.S. Atty. Gen.): letter from Chavez, 196

Holmes, James Henry: Sec'y. of New Mex., 121 note; 155

Hombres buenos: 52

Hopkins, Thomas H: 213 note

Horse stealing: punished, 76

Houghton, Joab: 55-56; member Hist. Soc., 173; on mining expedition, 191; resolution for removal as justice, 195; 213; 221-23, 237

Housatonic River: 15, 21

Howitt, E.L: 44

Hubbell, Sydney A: judge, 138; letter to Lincoln, 184-85; 221-23, 236

Hunt, Augustin W: invests in gold mine, 87; 177

ILLINOIS: legislature, 23; 8th Judicial Circuit, 23; lawyers' compensation, 24; legislators' salaries, 27-28; laws revised, 27; county seats, 33; Supreme Court cases, 44-47

Illinois Central R.R: 22

Illinois Citizen: Compares Lincoln and Benedict, 39-40

Illinois-Michigan Canal: 27

Immigrants: 61, 75, 218
Indians: *see* Acoma, Acomita, Laguna, Maricopa, Mescalero, Mojave, Pima, Queres, Pueblo, Tanoan, Tbanos, Teguas
Indignation Meeting, Santa Fe: 181
Inheritance: suit for, 239
Isleta: 57

JACKSON, ALEXANDER M: Sec. of New Mex., 72; 213 note
Janny, E.S: of Illinois, 26
Jaramillo, Luz: peonage case, 107
Jaramillo, Mariana: sues Romero, 107-11
Johnson, Pres. Andrew W: letter from Benedict, 169-71; 183; refuses to reappoint Benedict, 188; appoints Slough, 188; 195-96
Johnson, Bryan G: 59
Johnson, H.K: 155
Johnson, James L: invests in mine, 87
Jones, John: sheriff, 60
Jones, Samuel John: of C.S.A., 152
Jones, William Claude: 55, 213 note
Jornada del Muerto: 55-56, 58-59, 63, 69

KANSAS, New Mex., Ariz. and Calif. R.R. and Teleg. Co: 201
Kearny, Gen. Stephen W: 108
Kearny Code: 52, 108
Keithly, Judge Levi: opposes Slave Code, 115-16
Kent, Conn: birthplace of Benedict, 15
Knapp, Joseph G: takes loyalty oath, 154; absence, 163-64; controversy with Carleton, 167-68
Koslaski's Road House: 81

LA JOYA: 57
Labadie, Lorenzo: threatened, 151
Labor: sale of, 76

Ladron de Guitarras (Guitterez), Don Pedro: 100
Laguna Pueblo: 65; steal portrait from Acoma Pueblo, 89; sued for return of portrait, 90-93; suit lost, appealed, 92
Lamborn, Josiah: lawyer, 43
Lamon, Ward Hill: 47
Lamy, Archbishop John B: 173, 177
Land Office: in New Mex., 214
Lands: *see* Merced, Junta, Mexico, Northern Cross, Vigil
Lane, William Carr: buys slaves, 112
Las Cruces: 58, court records, 59; Court cases, 62-63
Las Lunas: 81
Las Vegas: sale of labor at, 76; execution at, 81-82; 188
Las Vegas Advertiser: 222
Laws: revision of in states, 27, 129-32; of New Mex., 53-55; *see also* slave code, Draco code, Spain, Wolf Scalp
Lawsuits: stolen portrait, 90-93; stolen documents, 93-94, 99-105; illegal confinement, 122-23; enforced army service, 124; Benedict's estate, 230
Lemitar: 58
Leroux, Antoine: 177
Lien on property of insolvent debtor: 240
Lincoln, Abraham: 11, 15, 22; admitted to Ill. bar, 23; 24; congressman, 35; character sketch, 40; 41-43; association with Benedict, 44-47; 49; letters from Benedict, 68, 133-40, 167-68; 144, 152, 159; letter from Arny, 165; death, 170; eulogy by Benedict, 171-72
Linder, Usher F: 45-46
Litchfield Law School, Conn: 17
Locofoco political party: 25 note, 31
Logan, Stephen T: of Illinois, 26
Lopez, Melquiades: printer, 211

Loring, Col. W.W: 139
Los Ranchos: as county seat, 56
Lott, Peter: of Illinois, 26
Lount, George: invests in mine, 87
Lovato, Juan José: of Acoma, 94
Lucas, James A: 55; attorney for Bourale, 60-61
Lynde, Major Isaac: surrenders Fort Fillmore, 154

MAIL COACH: 214
Maldonado, Alonzo del Castillo: 175
Manning, Julius: of Illinois, 26
Marcy, William S: 64 note
Maricopa Indians: 86
Martin, Matthew K: murdered, 24
Martin, Miguel: murdered, 76-77
Martinez, Dolores: 73
Martinez, Jesús Maria (José Maria Martin): trial and execution, 78-81
Martinez, José Antonio: 177
Mason and Dixon Line: 21
Masonic order: 36, 39, 179, 224
Maury, Matthew F: 173
Maxwell, L.B: 177; railroad promoter, 201
McCartys Indian village: 89
McDonald, George: sues Carleton, 122-23
McDougall, James Alexander: 152-53
McFerran, John C: invests in mine, 87
McRoberts, Samuel: 44, 45
Mendoza, Baninguas: 99
Merced Junta Land Grant: 225
Merriwether, David, Gov: recommends Benedict, 70
Mescalero Apache Indians: 123
Mesilla: occupied by C.S.A. troops, 59; 66-68, 155, 167
Mesilla Convention: 145
Mesilla Guard: attack Indians, 66-68
Mesilla Times: 149 note, 150, 152

Metamora, Ill: 33 note
Mexico: civil law of, 51, 52; federal constitution, 51; citizenship, 125-27; land grant titles, 235-36
Miller, Edward: administers Benedict estate, 225, 227-28, 230
Miner, John H: invests in mine, 87
Minors: laws regarding, 132
Mojave Indians: as guides, 86
Montezuma: 93
Montezuma Lodge No. 1, A.F.A.M: Benedict joins, 179; conducts funeral, 224
Monticello: 33 note, 34
Moore, J.H: recommends Benedict, 195
Moore, Thomas: quoted, 82-83
Mora: description of, 82
Mormon crisis: 26
Mortgage foreclosure: 238
Mother Eve: 181
Moultrie: 34
Mount Algo: 15
Mount Pulaski: 33 note
Mounted rifles: 67
Mower, Horace: 121
Murphy, John H: 45

NABERS, ZACHARIAH: 121
Nauvoo, Ill: repeal of charter, 29-31
Need, William: 118
Negroes: New Mex. laws on, 112; woman slave, 164
New Mexican Weekly: Account of Martinez, 78-81; 166; supports Benedict, 189; Benedict's advertisement, 191; Benedict writes editorials, 207; mentioned, 208-10
New Mexico: judicial district, 50, 55; laws, 53-55; supreme court jurisdiction and judges, 53; counties, 55; circuit ride, 55-59; judges, 121 note; territory sued, 124-28; revision of laws, 129-32; legislature resolutions, 185-86, 195; judges

support Benedict, 187-88; railroad legislation, 201-02; court decisions of Benedict, 235-43

New Mexico and Gulf R.R: incorporated and building authorized, 202-03; members of, 202 note; 225

New Mexico Weekly Union: Benedict edits, 211; praised by local newspapers, 211-12; scope of contents, 213-20; 222, 226; delinquent subscriptions to, 225; 228

New York Herald: 113

New York Times: 59, 60

Newspapers: list of exchanges, 213; policy and contents, 212-20; *see also* Gazette, Illinois, Las Vegas, Mesilla, New Mexican, New Mexico Weekly Union, New York, Springfield, Sangamon

Northern Cross R.R: 22; land grants, 28

Nullification Act: 21

O, VICTOR DE LA: *see* De la O

Oath of Fidelity and Loyalty: 152

Ojeda, Bartoleme de: 94, 99-100

Old Northwest: 16

Olney Hymns: 63 note

Organic Act of 1850: 52, 127

Ortiz, Juan Felipe: 177

Ortiz y Delgado, Francisco: 109-10

Otero, Miguel: recommends Benedict, 70; peonage case, 107; Slave Code, 111-18

Oxen: 236

PAGE, MRS. CORA BENEDICT: 12

Palen, Joseph G: made Chief Justice, 194; Benedict controversy, 196, 199-200; appoints committee to investigate Benedict's conduct, 221-23

Paris, Ill: 33 note, 36, 45-47

Parker, Charles G: invests in mine, 87

Passports: 167-68

Pekin: 33 note

Peonage: contracts for, 108-09; abolished, 111

Peralta: 57

Perea, Francisco: 184 note

Perez, Gov. Albino: death, 178-79

Pierce, Pres. Franklin: 49; appoints Benedict, 50; 64, 70

Pima Indians: 86

Pino, Facunea: 131

Plank Road Companies: 29

Poc-pec (Indian): 100

Prairie Lodge no. 77 A.F.A.M: 36, 39

Price, Sterling G: 156

Princetown: 16

Prospecting: 84-88

Pueblo titles: trade in, 102, 104

Pueblos: *see* Acoma, Laguna, Queres, San Domingo, Tanoan, Tbanes, Teguas

QUERES (KERESAN) NATION: pueblos of, 100

Quitman, John Anthony: 18

RACIAL DISCRIMINATION: 54

Railroads: 22, 28, 201-02

Reeve, Judge Tappan: 16

Rencher, Abraham, Gov: vetoes Indian slave bill, 111; 118, 137

Revenue stamps: 241-42

Revolution of 1837: 178-79

Risque, John: attorney, 227

Road Labor Law: 29

Robledo: 59

Romero, Jose de la Cruz: sued, 107-11

Romero, Tomasa and Ysadora: 73

Rosario Catholic Cemetery: 224

Roustabout Song: 21

Rush Medical College: 29

Russell, John T: ed. *Gazette,* 149; 150

Rynerson, Wm. Logan: trial for murder, 191-94

St. Vrain, Ceran: 177; railroad promoter, 201

Saloon of the Little Church: 219

San Domingo Pueblo: 56

San Felipe: 56

San José: portrait of, 89

Sanchez, Ramon: 93

Sandia: 56

Sandoval, Anastasio: citizenship questioned, 124-128; railroad promoter, 201

Sandoval, Antonio: 177

Sandoval, Francisco: publishes *Union,* 211

Sangamon Journal: 25, 26, 50

Santa Ana, Antonio Lopez: 61

Santa Fe: 66; judicial district, 72; captured by C.S.A. troops, 160; Capitol, 74-75; newspapers of, *see* New Mexico Union; New Mexican; Gazette

Santa Fe Post: 222

Santa Fe Trail: 83

Sapello: sawmills, 82

Schoolcraft, Henry Rowe: 173

Sena, Miguel: 179

Seward, William H: 132

Shelbyville: 33 note

Sibley, Henry H: proclamation, 157

Slave Code of New Mex: provisions of, 113-15; repealed, 118

Slavery: 17, 111-18

Sloan, Dr. W. J: 173

Slosson, Barzillai: lawyer, 17

Slough, Col. John P: appointed Chief Justice, 188; on mining expedition, 191; killed, 191

Smith, Cotton: lawyer, 17

Smith, E.O: Whig candidate, 25

Smith, Hugh N: 55; fined for gambling, 76; counsel for Laguna Pueblo, 92; counsel for Acoma Pueblo, 94; 213 note, 235-36, 238

Smith, Joseph and Hyrum: murder of, 30

Snyder, Simon: publishes *Union,* 211

Socorro: description of, 57-58; case of stolen documents, 93

Somers, William D: 44

Spain: civil war of, 51-52

Springfield: 21-33

Springfield Journal: 65 note

Stanton, Capt. Henry W: 123

Starke, Thomas: 199

Steck, Michael: Indian agent, 136

Steele, James: 45, 46

Stephens, R.M: jury foreman, 192

Stevenson, Thomas B: 121

Strong, N.D: of Illinois, 26

Sullivan, 33 note, 34

Sumner, Col. E.V: 174

Sunday closing: 53

Tanoan nation: pueblos under, 100

Taos: trial of Martinez, 78-81; 83, 142, 165, 178, 180

Taylor, Miles: 116

Taylorville: 33 note

Tbanos nation: pueblos, 100

Teguas nation: pueblos of, 100

Telegraph rates: 214

Teresina Street, Taos: 180

Texans: 119; reenforce Mesilla, 157; capture Santa Fe, 160; abandon New Mexico, 162

Tipabu, Don Luis: 100

Thornton, Judge Anthony: 33

Tome, Valencia Co., N.Mex: 56, 57; lawsuit at, 90-93

Tompkins, Richard H: fined for gambling, 76; rides circuit, 81-84; 190, 237-38, 240-42

Treason: 146

Treat, Judge Samuel H: 33

Trespass and ejectment: 62, 239

Trumbull, Lyman: lawyer, 43; 135, 152; letter to Pres. Johnson, 186-87; 204

Tucson: 87

Turner, Spencer: trial of, 24

U.S. Army Depot: Albuquerque, 57
U.S. Census: of 1790, 17; of 1850, 111
U.S. Citizenship: declarations of naturalization intention, 61; granted, 75
U.S. Congress: authorizes railroad building, 202-03
U.S. 8th Cavalry Band: 224
U.S. Statutes at Large: 199
Unlawful Assembly: 62
Urbana: 33 note, 34, 44

Valdez, Don Pedro: sheriff, 79
Valverde, New Mex: battle, 160
Venero de Passada, Gen. Don Pedro: 99
Vigil, Bautiste: land grant suit, 156

Walker, Joseph Reddeford: guide for gold prospectors, 84-87
Washington Terr: Benedict recommended for judgeship, 50
Water rights: 105
Watts, John Howe: lends derringer to Slough, 193

Watts, John S: 55; delegate to Congress, 161; 184; 213 note; 235-37, 239
Webster, Daniel: 118
Weightman, Richard H: delegate to Congress from New Mexico kills Aubrey, 63-64
Wheaton, Theodore D: 55; rides circuit, 81-84; counsel for de la O, 94; district atty., 146, 149; has smallpox, 156; 213 note; 236-37, 239-40
Wheelock, S.B: as witness, 193
Whig political party: 25
Whipple, Amiel W: 173
White, William: 230
Wolf Scalp Bounty Law: 28
Wood, W.H., Lt: 67
Wood: for fires, price, 72, 201
Woolsey, King S: invests in mine, 87

Yale College: 16, 17
Yates, Richard: of Illinois, 26; revision of laws, 27; 49; letter to Pres. Johnson, 186-87; 195
Yavapai District: mining claim, 87

WALLS OR BRIDGES

WALLS OR BRIDGES

HOW TO BUILD RELATIONSHIPS THAT GLORIFY GOD

JON JOHNSTON
Foreword by Ted Engstrom

BAKER BOOK HOUSE
Grand Rapids, Michigan 49516

Scripture references marked NASB are from the New American Standard Bible,
© 1960, 1962, 1968, 1971, 1973, 1975, 1977 by the Lockman Foundation; those
marked NIV are from the New International Version © 1978 by New York
International Bible Society; those marked KJV are from the King James Version;
those marked PHILLIPS are used with permission of the Macmillan Publishing
Company; those marked JB are from the Jerusalem Bible © 1966 by Darton,
Longman & Todd, Ltd. and Doubleday and Company, Inc.; those marked NEB
are from The New English Bible, © 1961, 1970 by The Delegates of Oxford
University Press and The Syndics of the Cambridge University Press.
Those marked RSV are from the Revised Standard Version © 1972 by Thomas
Nelson, Inc.

Library of Congress Cataloging-in-Publication Data

Johnston, Jon.
    Walls or bridges

    Includes indexes.
    1. Interpersonal relations—Religious aspects—Christianity.   I. Title.

BV4509.5.J646   1988   248.4   88-10509

ISBN: 0-8010-5224-6
    0-8010-5223-8 (pbk.)

To

Frank

J. Kenneth

James "Gene"

M.A. "Bud"

Norma

They built bridges
to my life
and
we crossed them
together.

Prayer of Unity

Our Father, we thank you for the privilege of being
together at this time and in this place.
As your people, we pray that your love will unite
us into a fellowship of discovery.
Cleanse us of everything that would sap our
strength for togetherness.
Unravel the knots in our spirits.
Cleanse the error of our minds.
Free us from the bondage of our negative
imaginations.
Break down the barriers that sometimes keep us
apart and cause us to drift along without a
dream.
As we go from here,
Explode in us new possibilities for service.
Kindle within us the fires of your compassion so
that we may not wait too long to learn to love.
May we be a people with loving purposes
Reaching out . . .
Breaking walls . . .
Building bridges . . .
Let us be your alleluia in a joyless, fragmented
world.
In the name of our Lord we pray
Amen.

Earl Lee

Contents

Foreword   **11**

Introduction   **13**

Part **1** **Bridges / Design:** *Healthy Relationships*

1   Our Chief Demolition Expert and Architect   **19**

2   Our Precise Blueprint   **39**

3   Our Essential Construction Materials   **54**

4   Our Dedication to Labor   **69**

Part **2** **Bridges / Destination:** *Wholistic Relationships*

5   Footbridges to the Devoted   **87**

6   Drawbridges to the Defiant   **106**

7   Causeways to the Different   **123**

8   Covered Bridges to the Distant   **140**

9

Part **3** **Bridges / Delivery:** *Holy*
            Relationships

9 Fruit Cluster #1: Love, Joy, Peace   **161**

10 Fruit Cluster #2: Patience, Kindness,
   Goodness   **179**

11 Fruit Cluster #3: Faithfulness, Gentleness,
   Self-Control   **197**

12 He Makes the Pieces Fit!   **214**

   A Parting Word   **223**

   Appendix 1 Stanford Shyness Survey   **226**

   Appendix 2 Stress Rating the Effects of Forty-
   Three Personal Crises   **237**

   Appendix 3 Highest and Lowest Pressure Jobs
   in the U.S.A.   **240**

   Subject Index   **242**

   Scripture Index   **248**

Foreword

Am I—are you—building walls or bridges? Jon Johnston poses this crucial question, the answer to which can result in life-changing, redemptive improvements in our lives.

Footbridges, drawbridges, the Golden Gate bridge, covered bridges, and causeways all bring great lessons concerning our relationships.

The Bible, God's manual for our daily living, has much to say about relationships. God himself established these: heavenly Father—obedient Son; husband-wife; parent-child; friend—neighbor.

We are reminded that Jesus built bridges so durable that they have lasted for two millennia, and so diverse that they connect all human beings with his Father.

Our Lord, the architect of rewarding, Christian relationships, guides us in the important process of tearing down walls and building bridges.

In our day of microwave cooking, fast-food restaurants, condensed seminars and fifteen-second commercials, we need to realize that meaningful relationships require time and energy. Author Johnston wisely brings this to our attention.

11

This book comes alive with the graphic imagery of walls and bridges. There's nothing stodgy in the author's scriptural references and applications.

The biblical principles—helpfully and interestingly applied in the book—will make better people of us. Our lives will become more fulfilled, enjoyable, and productive.

Jon Johnston, as in the previous books he has written, exhibits a marvelous sense of humor. I was amazed to come across terms like "flakes," "nerds," "bozos," and "klutzes." You will chuckle as did I. They are specimens of life's "irregular" people whom we all encounter. And bridges can be built to them as well. The author helps us to see this, and guides us in the process.

When you finish this book, I predict you will be determined to be a bridge builder. Expect to become a better, stronger person as a result.

Interestingly, this is the first book I have ever read in which helpful footnotes attracted my attention and demanded my reading them!

One word describes this book for me: captivating. See if you don't agree.

Ted W. Engstrom
President Emeritus
World Vision, International

Introduction

It began as a typical, crisp fall day in Malibu. Nothing special occurred—that is, until I attended our morning chapel.

The speaker, a former missionary to India and current minister to a church of several thousands, mesmerized students and faculty alike with his words.

He disclosed that his son was among the Americans being held captive in Iran. To most of us, he had every right to be angry and bitter. Many of us were, and we didn't even have a member of our family imprisoned. But not Earl Lee.

His message was one of forgiveness and understanding. Get this: He even spoke of his love for the Ayatollah Khomeini. We thought, tolerance maybe. But love? Isn't that carrying our Lord's Sermon on the Mount a little too far? Earl Lee showed us that it wasn't.

The world news services had caught wind of his startling declarations in recent weeks. News reporters now jammed into his worship services in order to film his sincere prayers for this nation's hated enemies.

On this particular morning, our speaker began to unroll his large American flag. The same one he raised daily

above his house and would until the hostages were released. It symbolized his lofty faith.

It was then that he cast his deep sentiments in a simple,
but powerful, theme: Walls or Bridges. And what he said
made a lot of sense.

In short, he declared that in all we do and say, we are
either building walls or building bridges between ourselves and others. We're putting up roadblocks or we're
establishing linkage.

This process is often unconscious, misunderstood, or
minimized in our thinking. Nevertheless, it occurs with
regularity and great significance.

Well, I left chapel that day with a kindled spirit. The
theme remained in my mind as I thought about its implications for my life.

Providentially, it wasn't long before I ran across Gloria
Evans' book entitled, *The Wall: A Parable*. And her
thoughts were along the same line. Walls protect, but
they also imprison. Freedom can only occur when walls
are destroyed.

At this point several questions entered my mind. Am I
building more walls than bridges? When I construct
bridges, are they of the right kind? And do I use them for
the right purposes?

This fact is certain: The quality of our relationships is
an important barometer of our spiritual well-being. When
we turn off others, by intent or neglect, three reputations
suffer: our own, that of the body of believers, and most
important, the reputation of Jesus Christ.

Those of us who claim to be twice-born must understand the dynamics of godly relationships. Then, with
God's guidance and power, we must demolish unsightly
walls in order to construct bridges to other people, regardless of our temperament or talent.

Walls or Bridges attempts to encourage us in this necessary task. It is primarily addressed to those of us who love
Jesus and who earnestly desire to live for him.

The book's three sections focus on the key components of bridge building.

Section one, "Healthy Relationships," invites us to construct reliable structures. Ones that will stand the tests of change and adversity.

Section two, "Holistic Relationships," focuses on the issue of destination. To where should our bridges reach?

Finally, section three, "Holy Relationships," pertains to the use of our bridges. After building strong, well-constructed bridges and making certain they link us to the right banks, we must begin transporting cargo. Otherwise, our bridges are merely lavish monuments.

What, specifically, must our bridges transport? The biblical answer is emphatic: the Fruit of the Spirit.

May our hearts prayerfully examine these dimensions, and may the Holy Spirit probe us until we respond in obedience.

Part **1**

Bridges/Design
Healthy Relationships

*The rich man thinks of his wealth as an impregnable
defense, a high wall of safety. What a dreamer!*
–Proverbs 18:11 LB

*People are lonely because they build walls instead of
bridges.*——Joseph Fort Newton

*A flea and an elephant walked side-by-side over a bridge.
Said the flea to the elephant after they had crossed, "we
sure did shake that thing, didn't we!"*

1

Our Chief Demolition
Expert and Architect

After our Southern California wedding,
Cherry and I jumped into our heaterless Rambler and
headed for Kansas City, where I planned to enter seminary.

Enroute, we ran into a blinding rainstorm, necessitating an extra night on the road. As a result, our meager
cash supply was evaporated. But we were much too naive
to worry.

Finally, we reached our destination, exhausted and
broke. Not knowing a soul in town, we resorted to telephoning the seminary president to explain our plight. He
rushed over to convey his condolences and to loan us ten
dollars.

Jobs were eventually located. I say "jobs," because each
was so low paying that we had to work at several. In
addition to being a nighttime bill collector in an ethnic
section of the city, I played the organ for a local funeral

home. Praying for funerals to occur, somehow never did seem right!

We moved into a one-room studio apartment, located above an old garage next to Tower Park. It was actually two rooms, if you counted the wardrobe closet which became my study when the clothes were pushed back.

Unfortunately, our landlord refused to fumigate. This delighted the enormous cockroaches. I recall hearing them walk across the linoleum floor at night. A high percentage of our grocery bill went for insecticide.

The landlady was an early riser. Her morning ritual began about 5 A.M., when she began cranking the starter on her antique Oldsmobile. Finally, the gas-guzzling engine would start, and she would race it for another ten minutes. Great quantities of carbon monoxide fumes would seep through the porous floor of our apartment. One good thing: The fumes did help us with the roach problem!

After a few weeks, our material needs began to be satisfied. We became quite content with our substandard living.

But then it hit us. We became painfully aware of our unmet social needs. We discovered that we were very lonely in this strange city, and it was then that we began groping for friendship. Since others refrained from inviting us to their homes, we decided to do the inviting. The results were as surprising as they were enlightening. Allow me to share three instances.

The first seminarian couple was invited to dinner. Prior to their coming, they expressed a definite preference for coffee. Not being coffee drinkers ourselves, we were forced to experiment. Cherry brewed and tasted coffee the entire day before our guests arrived. They came. One sip of my wife's coffee was enough. It was definitely *not* to their liking. Not only that. My well-intentioned wife was so saturated with caffeine that she lay awake staring at the ceiling the entire night!

Soon thereafter, we focused our attention on another couple, who were overheard complaining about their sad financial plight. We were far from affluent, but felt a strong compulsion to extend a helping hand. After all, these people were described as destitute.

They arrived, and we all enjoyed a scrumptious meal. Then, a couple of weeks later, we were overjoyed to receive an invitation to their home for dessert. Upon arrival, we discovered that they owned a horse-sized dog. All varieties of dog food known to man were piled high on their kitchen table. It wasn't long before a dim light turned on in our naive brains. We realized that destitution is a very relative term.

But it was our third attempt to reach out that took the cake! This couple had been having serious marital problems. It was the Christmas season, and Cherry once again prepared a delicious meal. She even displayed some homemade, festive decorations for the occasion.

The couple entered our humble abode accompanied by their pug-nosed little girl. The catastrophe began. For starters, the youngster began making deep furrows in the maple coffee table with a brass candleholder. After receiving a mild rebuke from her father, the mother and child began repeating these words in unison: "Daddy is a dumb-dumb."

Bored with that, the small aggressor began unwrapping the Christmas presents under the tree. The suspense of wondering what we were getting that year quickly subsided! Both parents laughed convulsively as the gift contents were revealed.

After completing this demolition project, the miniature delinquent disappeared into our bathroom. While we visited, it became apparent to me that she had been in there much too long, even though it was actually no more than five minutes. Her mother decided to check on her well-being. What she saw made her go into hysterical laughter.

Unable to find any small boats or ducks to play with, the sweet young thing had taken my toothbrush and was floating it in the toilet! This time I couldn't help myself. I began to laugh—while grinding my teeth.

More Lesson Than Loss

Cherry and I had attempted to reach out for meaningful relationships. To build a few bridges.

The results were disastrous. In the first instance, we were embarrassed. In the second, we met deception. As for the last instance, we beheld a complete lack of respect for our property. Tell me. Would you have used that toothbrush again?

Our first reaction was to bow out of the bridge-building enterprise. Furthermore, we considered building some walls of our own, or at least some fences. It was Robert Frost who declared, "Good fences make good neighbors."

Good *neighbors*, maybe, but how about good *Christians*? After coming to our senses, we realized that even fence building can yield great spiritual damage. For in reality, fences are thin walls. And all walls have these functions. To break contact. To block communication. To keep what is inside inside. And what is outside outside.

Our physical world is already overdosed on walls! Probably more time, energy, and resources have gone into wall building than any other activity. There are

Long walls like the ancient one in China, which appeared as "earth's giant necklace" to lunar astronauts.[1]

1. This defensive barrier, erected by China's first Emperor, Qin Shi Huang, extends 3,700 miles from the Gulf of Bohai to the Gansu Province. Actual construction began during the Warring States period in the fifth century B.C. to ward off plundering nomads from the north. After Qin conquered and became the first emperor of a unified China (221 B.C.), he told general Meng Tian to link up these walls and to extend them. Three hundred

Short walls—the kind that border my backyard where flowering vines climb at will, along with tomcats.

Thick walls like those that surrounded Nebuchadnezzar's Babylon[2] and Alexander's Athens.[3]

Thin walls—the kind we've referred to as fences, which broadcast an emphatic "Keep Out!" to neighbors.

Admittedly, some walls are greatly venerated. The Western Wall where Jerusalem's devout pray.[4] And the

---

thousand people did the work. Reinforcement and renovation was carried out during successive dynasties.

Building a wall of this length and magnitude over mountain peaks, precipices and ravines was a stupendous undertaking. Moving stories connected with it reflect the misery it inflicted on the people. Since persons who died while working on it were buried beneath it, the Great Wall has been termed "the largest graveyard in the world." *Sixty Scenic Wonders in China* (Beijing, People's Republic of China: New World Press, 1980), pp. 1–4.

2. King Nebuchadnezzar II erected the three hundred-meter Procession Road (also called Feast Road) in 580 B.C. that led to the spectacular city of Babylon. It was lined on both sides by walls made of colored enamel bricks. Lions (holy animals of the Ishtar religion worshipers, goddesses of love, fertility and war) were etched in the glazed, blue walls. Also, there were dragons and bulls. The main gate to the city was called the Ishtar Gate. The front of the two gate towers has been located, refurbished, and moved to the Pergamum Museum in East Berlin, where it can be seen today (along with thirty meters of the Procession Road). It is a spectacular sight indeed!

3. Like most cities of the ancient world (except for arrogant Sparta), Athens built formidable walls of protection. They extended around their glorious city, and during their Golden Age ruled by Pericles, they extended side-by-side down to the seaport city of Pireas, which was also enclosed by walls. Such walls made Athens seem to would-be enemies almost impregnable.

4. The Western (or Wailing) Wall has been described as a "grim, gray, hyssop-tufted, architectural fragment." It towers about sixty feet above what was once a narrow, ninety-foot-long, stone-paved courtyard.

Jewish tradition maintains that this portion of the wall is the one remnant left of the containing wall of the outermost enclosures of Herod's Temple that has survived war and the elements. Many believe that when God's Shekinah Presence left the Holy of Holies of the Temple (at its destruction), the divine presence went to this section of the Western Wall and hovers over it to this day. As a result, Jews of all types gather there to pray, or send money to have others pray for them. Often prayers are written on notes and stuck in a crevice of the wall.

The Jews were shut out from this, their most sacred place of prayer, for nineteen years from 1948–1967. On June 6, 1967, when the Israeli army was recapturing ancient Jerusalem, their first act was to take the Temple Mount, then to march straight for the Western Wall to kiss its hallowed stones and weep. Today, the Western Wall, especially on Friday afternoons (the evening of the Jewish Sabbath) and on special holy days, is inundated with crowds of worshipers. G. Frederick Owen, *Jerusalem* (Kansas City, MO: Beacon Hill Press, 1972), pp. 106–110.

granite one that names 58,023 Americans who died in Viet Nam.[5] And then there are walls that only reflect hate and anger. Like the barbed, grotesque, graffitied Berlin Wall, which has become a symbol of heartbreak. It seems only yesterday that Cherry and I stood beside it at Checkpoint Charlie and soberly reflected on the unbelievable trauma it has caused. Divided families. Tragic escape attempts. Broken dreams.[6]

When it comes to physical walls, a lot of negative thoughts come to mind. perhaps that's why we have the expressions "I feel walled-in;" "up against a wall;" "about to climb a wall."

If this is true concerning physical walls, how much more is it so regarding the walls that block personal relationships.

Walls Do a Prison Make

In a classic poem titled "Walls Do Not a Prison Make," the author seems to be implying that walls aren't always incarcerating. Perhaps so. But more often they do imprison.

First, walls can separate us from God. 2 Corinthians 10:3–5 (NASB) tells us how:

For though we walk in the flesh, we do not war according to the flesh, for the weapons of our warfare are not of the flesh, but divinely powerful for the destruction of for-

---

5. The Vietnam Veterans Memorial Wall has been established on the mall in Washington, DC This is a 494-foot monument visited by thousands daily.

6. On August 13, 1971, a wall was built by the East Germans to separate East and West Berlin. It began with barbed wire, then stone, finally concrete. Today, it is heavily guarded by fifty thousand soldiers, wolfhounds, and land mines. The form of the wall varies, sometimes even being the side of a building. Numerous escapes have been attempted, such as hiding in car trunks, tunneling underneath, riding a balloon over. Prior to the wall's construction, hundreds of thousands of East Germans crossed over to freedom. The East German government felt that it could no longer tolerate such a mass exodus; thus, the wall was constructed to form an imprisoning ring around West Berlin. Rainer Hilderbrandt, *It Happened At The Wall* (Berlin, 1984), N.P.

tresses. *We are* destroying speculations and every lofty thing raised up against the knowledge of God, and *we are* taking every thought captive to the obedience of Christ.

Paul uses military terms to convey the kind of warfare that takes place in our minds.

In ancient times cities were constructed inside thick, massive walls.[7] Aspiring invaders were deterred by such protective shields. Towers were strategically built into or inside the walls, and from them defenders could pinpoint the locations of advancing troops.[8]

For enemies to take these well-fortified cities, they had to accomplish these three objectives:

1. Walls must be demolished or scaled.[9]

2. Towers must be invaded.

3. Men who planned military strategy must be killed or captured.

If these tasks were completed, victory to the enemy was assured. The battle was over!

The Scripture passage above illustrates this first-century warfare strategy. Author Charles Swindoll explains how it is a symbol of our own struggles.

---

7. Every ancient city had enormous walls surrounding it. Some walls contained chambers inside. There still exist some of the stones in the wall of the Temple enclosure at Jerusalem. They measure thirty feet long, eight feet wide, and three and a half feet high, weighing over eighty tons. *The Zondervan Pictorial Bible Dictionary*, Merrill C. Tenney, ed. (Grand Rapids, MI: Zondervan Corporation, 1963), p. 885.

8. Along the three thousand seven hundred miles of the Great Wall of China, there are massive watchtowers situated every few hundred yards.

Also in Jericho, reputed to be the oldest city in the world, archeologists have unearthed a nine thousand-year-old watchtower. It set back from the ancient wall, because people attached their homes to the latter, making it one side of their abodes. Most probably, it was in such a structure Rahab lived, and because of its proximity to the wall, she was able to help the two Israeli spies escape (Josh. 2).

9. According to our Israeli guide, unless they planned to demolish a city, the Roman soldiers did not pound the walls of a defending army with hammers. Instead, they simply dug away the earth under the wall, causing the entire structure to collapse.

Similarly, our God has no trouble destroying our walls, no matter how formidable they seem to us. He strikes them at the base by changing our hearts and minds.

He says that originally our minds were "enemy-held territories." And, we declare, "Surely I have been a sinner from birth, sinful from the time my mother conceived me" (Ps. 51:5; cf. Rom. 3:23). But then we suddenly became aware of God's love invasion taking place (cf. John 3:16). The enemy within us met his match and was forced to relinquish his control and power.[10]

But we've all found Satan to be an unbelievably determined enemy. He isn't quickly or easily conquered. He retreats fighting. Only with the greatest reluctance does he release his strong hold.

This is evidenced in the stubborn persistence of impure habits, which were deeply embedded in our natures when he controlled us. Paul vividly expresses this reality: "What I want to do I do not do . . . For I have the desire to do what is good, but I cannot carry it out" (Rom. 7:15b, 18b).

---

10. I feel that the Scriptures support the idea of dealing with our sin in two steps. First, we invite God into our lives through sincere confession. Past sins are acknowledged, then repented of (2 Cor. 7:10, Acts 17:30). We promise to do an about-face—to begin the new life of love (2 Cor. 5:17, Eph. 4:22–24). Then we accept by faith that we are forgiven (Rom. 10:9–10), based on the promise of God's infallible Word (1 John 1:9). The Holy Spirit confirms the reality of this in our hearts (Rom. 8:16–17). Result: We know that we've been born again. We are pardoned rebels.

Second, at a subsequent time we consecrate our forgiven lives to God. We surrender our will to his will. Such consecration is thorough and complete.

It was what Paul wished for the Thessalonians when he declared. "May God himself, the God of peace, sanctify you through and through. May your whole spirit, soul and body be kept blameless at the coming of our Lord Jesus Christ" (1 Thess. 5:23).

Paul's audience had already been born again. He previously spoke of their "work produced by faith," their "labor prompted by love," their "endurance inspired by hope" (1:3). He referred to them as "brothers loved by God" who had been "chosen" (1:4), "imitators of us and of the Lord; in spite of severe suffering" (1:6), and "a model to all the believers in Macedonia and Achaia" (1:7). He declared that he thanks God because they "received the word of God" and "accepted it" fully (2:13). The Thessalonians were forgiven sinners! Nevertheless, the Apostle beckons them to the second work of grace, namely entire sanctification.

In receiving this second gift, our sinful nature is instantaneously cleansed. Our original sin (in contrast to past sins that were forgiven in confession), which is inherited from Adam, is completely removed. We are purged of all uncleanness. More than pardoned rebels, we become intimate, obedient (though yet maturing) children of God—his transformed creation (cf. Rom. 12:1–2).

Our mighty conqueror rescued the apostle from his imprisonment, so that he could triumphantly declare, "Therefore, there is now no condemnation...because through Christ Jesus the law of the Spirit of life set me free from the law of sin and death" (Rom. 8:1–2; cf. Rom. 6:6).

Likewise, Christ desires to liberate all of us from Satan's power. His strategy is clearly outlined in 2 Corinthians, Chapter 10 (NASB).

1. He destroys "fortresses" and "speculations" (v. 4–5). These are walls encircling the mind—habits of thinking ingrained by Satan over the years, destructive, painful mindsets that especially inflict persons who have come to Jesus late in life. (Example: believing that we should punish our persecutors.)

2. He demolishes "every lofty thing raised up against the knowledge of God" (v. 5). These are mental blocks we've erected against spiritual viewpoints, carnal attitudes that typically intensify when we are under pressure and when we see our significant others reacting in sinful ways. (Example: blaming God for our misfortune.)[11]

3. His ultimate goal is to take "every thought captive to the obedience of Christ" (v. 5.). After striking down the old, he proposes to make all new. Romans 12:2 says, "Be transformed by the renewing of your mind." "His plan is to transform old thoughts that

---

11. Roger von Oech has written a book entitled *A Whack on the Side of the Head*. In it he lists ten common statements that hold us back from being what God would have us be. They cast gloom on our faith, and poison the atmosphere with a negative spirit. They are as follows: (1) The right answer. (2) That's not logical. (3) Follow the rules. (4) Be practical. (5) Avoid ambiguity. (6) To err is wrong. (7) Play is frivolous. (8) That's not my area. (9) Don't be foolish. (10) I'm not creative.

Roger von Oech, *A Whack on the Side of the Head* (New York: Warner Books, Incorporated, 1983), p. 9. Quoted in Charles Swindoll, *Living Above the Level of Mediocrity: A Commitment to Excellence* (Waco, TX: Word Books, 1987), p. 25.

defeat us into new thoughts that encourage us."[12]
And he realizes that this means repatterning our
whole way of thinking. (Example: knowing that God
desires the very best for our lives.)[13]

Second, in addition to separating us from God, walls
barricade us from one another.

In her book *The Wall: A Parable*, Gloria Evans testifies
to this fact.

> One day I realized that [my] wall was so high that I no
> longer saw anyone go by. I no longer heard anyone. Every-
> thing was quiet. "Is anyone there?" I yelled. There was no
> answer. It was dark inside the wall and the air was foul. I
> sat there for a long time. It was quiet and dark and lonely.
> Only the whispers of my memories could be heard.[14]

The walls that we build to isolate ourselves from others
refuse to remain stationary. They seem to inch their way
inward, aggressing our life space, invading our consciousness, inflicting discomfort on our daily existence.

It reminds me of the retractable walls used by the
Romans for capital punishment. Criminals were placed in
a room and the mobile walls came inward, one inch each
day. At one point they began touching the skin. Then, a
day or two later, bones were heard cracking along with
muffled screams.

In a similar way, the walls we erect turn on us. The
threat gets closer, inch-by-inch, until we become spiritual
casualties.

Cherry and I decided to resist the temptation to build

12. The word Paul uses for being transformed from the world is the Greek term,
metamorphousthai. Our word *metamorphisis* is derived from the same root meaning. It
implies the taking on of a completely new nature. We cease being "worms" and become
beautiful "butterflies."

13. Many of the ideas related to this point, that walls separate us from God, are taken
from the book previously referred to by Charles Swindoll, *Living Above the Level of
Mediocrity: A Commitment to Excellence.*

14. Gloria Jay Evans, *The Wall: A Parable* (Waco, TX: Word Books, 1977), n.p.

walls where our fellow seminarians were concerned. We saw that our only hope was to continue building bridges, even though our first three had collapsed.

How does bridge constructing differ from wall building?

Spanning Gaps and Gulches

Bridges—the kind made of wood and steel—appeared much later in history than walls.[15] And they are not nearly as plentiful.

There are reasons for that. Bridges usually cost more and are more difficult to construct. They require a greater variety of less accessible, more expensive materials.

Also, their upkeep is more necessary and tedious. When a wall collapses (usually only during an earthquake or a military attack), few of us take notice. But when a bridge crumbles, that is a different story.

Approximately 150 bridges in our country give way each year. The results are tragic. Also, it is estimated that one-fifth of our half-million bridges are unsafe. Hearing this fact alarms us much more than learning that 100,000 walls are unsturdy.

In contrast to walls that barricade and block, bridges help to join, connect, reach, link, and bring together.

They also add beauty to our natural environment. We need only to catch a glimpse of San Francisco's Golden Gate as it glistens jewellike in the sun and morning fog.[16]

15. The word *bridge* is not found in the English Bible. Nevertheless, the earliest idea of a bridge must have been suggested by a plank or fallen tree across a small stream. But the Israelites generally crossed a stream by a ford (Gen. 32:22, Josh. 2:7, Judg. 3:28) or in some cases by a ferryboat (2 Sam. 19:18, LB).

Although the arch principle was known early, as seen in two stones leaning against each other to bridge a small gap in Myceanaean ruins, it wasn't until the time of the Roman Empire that the magnificent arches, bridges and aqueducts appeared, at which time the bridge may be said to have come into its own. Merril C. Tenney, ed., op.cit. p. 132.

16. The Golden Gate Bridge was opened May 22, 1937. It spans 4,200 feet, connecting San Francisco and Marin Counties. The bridge was designed by Joseph Strauss, with two cables three feet in diameter. Each of these contains 27,572 wires. *Encyclopedia Americana*, Vol. 7, (Grolier, Inc., 1985), p. 532.

But all bridges, in spite of their beauty, size or composition—once again—share the same function, establishing linkage. So that what's over there can come here, and what's over here can go there. So that interchange can occur, whether it be transportation or communication. So that a connection can exist between separate parts.

The same can be said for those bridges that link us as human beings. Social bonding is essential. Even for our physical health. Epidemiologist Lisa Berkan's study of seven thousand persons between the ages of thirty and sixty-nine over a nine-year period reveals that extroverts (bridge builders) are more likely to live longer than introverts (wall builders). Gregarious persons are more resistant to heart and circulatory diseases, cancer and strokes, and less inclined to suicide.

John Donne is right; "No man is an island." So is well-known author Reuben Welch, who declares: "We really do need each other."[17] For fulfillment. For survival. Yet, many of us who realize this fact continue building walls. Walls that separate, seal off, and stifle.

Back to our seminary days. After we committed ourselves to building bridges, some very encouraging things occurred.

Those we reached out to came to learn that our bridges were meant to be permanent. Not like the pontoon kind used to help army troops cross a river. That kind is quickly put down, and then, just as quickly picked up. Our bridges were meant to stay. And when others became assured of this fact, they began to build permanent bridges toward us. And, we met somewhere in the middle.

Once linked up, we joined in mutual efforts to strengthen and reinforce the relationships. They became projects of constant upgrading. By the end of our three years at seminary, some very strong friendships had

---

17. Refer to Reuben Welch, *We Really Do Need Each Other* (Nashville, Impact, N.D.).

formed. And they are still very much intact today, having stood the test of time.

Perhaps it will be helpful to contrast the specifics of wall and bridge building. Here are the essential differences:

Wall Building	Bridge Building
primarily motivates us to *protect ourselves*	primarily motivates us to *help others*
focuses on *hoarding* what we have accumulated	focuses on *sharing* what God has entrusted to us
leads to a self that is *sealed off, ingrown, shriveled*	leads to a self that is *unleashed, outgoing, expanding*
causes us to see others as a *threat* to our security, but worthy of our impressing them.	causes us to see others as *essential* to our well-being and worthy of our accepting them
greatly *diminishes* our usefulness to God	greatly *enhances* our usefulness to God

I heartily believe the above principles in theory. But I also know that they hold true in practice.

At this point something more important must be fully understood. As Christians, our primary interest in bridge building is not based on a desire to maintain our physical or psychological health. Nor to make our lives more pleasant for ourselves or admirable to others. It's not even based on wanting to add a needed dimension to the lives of the needy.

As commendable as those motivations are, they pale in significance when compared to our primary rationale.

We are drawn to this activity, most essentially, because of the example and teaching of our Lord. It is he who destroys unsightly walls and designs beautiful bridges.

It is with him that we begin. He supplies all guidance, as well as the necessary blueprints.

Our Master Link

Satan prides himself on being the master wall builder of our planet. He constructs tall and thick ones that seem insurmountable. Between us and God. Between us and one another. Why? Because he knows that such isolation destroys our inner spirits and deprives those we might help.

By contrast, our heavenly Father constantly builds bridges. The beautiful rainbow that we behold after a rainstorm, with its fusion of colors, is his "bridge of promise" to all mankind. It testifies to his vow that our earth shall never again be destroyed by the kind of flood experienced by Noah. Genesis 9:8–14 (LB) declares:

> Then God told Noah and his sons, "I solemnly promise you and your children and the animals you brought with you—all these birds and cattle and wild animals—that I will never again send another flood to destroy the earth. And I seal this promise with this sign: I have placed this my rainbow in the clouds as a sign of my promise until the end of time, to you and to all the earth. When I send clouds over the earth, the rainbow will be seen in the clouds."

Then, nearly two thousand years ago, God's own son bridged the great gap between the creator and his creation. Jesus,

> Who, being in very nature God, did not consider equality with God something to be grasped, but made himself nothing, taking the very nature [form] of a servant, being made in human likeness. And being found in appearance as a man, he humbled himself and became obedient to death—even death on a cross! (Phil. 2:6–8).

As a result of this, we can now cross his bridge of mercy and grace and enter the very presence of God with boldness (Heb. 4:16). The middle wall that separated us from

God has been destroyed forever.[18] For this reason we sing these joyful words on Easter:

> Once our blessed Christ of beauty
> Was veiled off from human view,
> But thro suffering, death and sorrow
> He has rent the veil in two.[19]

The veil referred to was the thick curtain that separated the Holy of Holies from all people except the high priest, who made an atonement sacrifice there once each year. So in essence, the veil was a cloth wall that isolated God's presence from his people.

When Jesus died on the cross, that curtain was severed from top to bottom. This symbolizes the fact that now all persons everywhere and for all times have direct access to our Father. All because of our Lord.

But, in addition to the bridge he built to connect mankind with God, Jesus constantly built bridges to the persons he encountered. In doing so, he provided us a clear and wise architectural design for our bridge construction projects.

---

18. Ephesians 2:14 speaks of the "middle wall." This is a picture from the Temple complex which consisted of a series of courts, each one a little higher than the one before—with the Temple itself in the innermost court. First there was the Court of the Gentiles, then the Court of Women, then the Court of the Israelites, then the Court of the Priests, and then the Holy Place. Only into the first of them could a Gentile come. Between it and the Court of the Women there was a wall, or rather a kind of screen of marble. Inscribed into it were tablets that announced that if a Gentile came any farther, he was subject to instant death. In 1871 one of these prohibiting tablets was discovered, and the inscription reads, "Let no one of any other nation come within the fence and barrier around the Holy Place. Whosoever will be taken doing so will himself be responsible for the fact that his death will ensue."

Paul was very familiar with this barrier, for his arrest at Jerusalem—which led to his final imprisonment and death—was due to the fact that he was wrongly accused of bringing Trophimus, an Ephesian Gentile, into the Temple beyond the barrier (Acts 21:28–29).

The intervening wall, with its unpassable barrier, shut the Gentile out from the presence of God. It was that wall that was destroyed when Jesus died for all persons everywhere. William Barclay, *The Daily Study Bible: The Letters to the Galatians and Ephesians* (Philadelphia: The Westminster Press, 1958), pp. 130–131.

19. Taken from the hymn entitled "The Unveiled Christ." Words and score by N. B. Herrell. (Kansas City, MO: Lillenas Publishing Company, 1972), p. 97.

Let's eavesdrop on an encounter he had with a certain woman from Samaria. It is recorded in the fourth chapter of John's Gospel.

More Than a Wishing Well

Accompanied by his disciples, Jesus journeyed toward his home in Galilee. He stopped at Jacob's well to recoup and get a drink. His disciples left him in order to find some food.

Along came a Samaritan woman to draw water from the one hundred-foot deep well. She was so much of a moral outcast that probably she was prohibited from using the town of Sychar's supply.

In the dialogue that transpired, Jesus attempted to bridge, and she countered by erecting walls.

Jesus began by asking for assistance. "Will you give me a drink?" To ask a direct favor is an excellent means to begin a relationship. She turned in astonishment and informed him that it was inappropriate for a Jew to ask such a favor from a Samaritan. Wall number one firmly in place!

She spoke the truth. No love was lost between the Jews and their neighbors. They remembered how in 720 B.C. the Assyrians had invaded, captured, and subjugated Samaria. Afterwards, they transported most of the population to Media (2 Kings 17:6). In turn, foreigners from Babylon, Cuthah, Ava, Hamath, and Sepharvaim (2 Kings 17:24) were transported into the conquered province. The few Jews who still lived there began to intermarry with the foreign people, which the Jews in Judea saw as unforgivable.[20]

The superiority complex of the Jews over the Samaritans had remained firmly intact until that day. Jesus had overstepped his bounds.

---

20. In a strict Jewish household even to this day, a marriage between a Jewish son or daughter and a Gentile necessitates the conducting of a funeral service for the "lost" child. Such a person is dead in their minds.

Undaunted, our Lord began constructing another bridge. He spoke of his ability to offer her "living water." She took his statement literally, and threw up another barrier. From a well that collects rainwater? Such a claim was foolish! Who was this man, anyhow? He was purporting himself to be wiser and more powerful than Jacob, whom Samaritans claimed to be their "father."

Jesus kindly overlooked the insinuation.

Up went another wall. She said, in effect, "How can you even talk about drawing any (much less running) water, when you don't even have a bucket?" No doubt, like all travelers, Jesus possessed a leather container to retrieve well water. But his disciples had possibly taken it with them into town.

As before, our Lord calmly went around that barrier in order to proclaim spiritual truth. He spoke of offering her water that would quench her thirst forever! The thirst of her eternal soul!

By this time, she may have had a good idea of what he meant. Nevertheless, she put up another barrier of literalism. Her response was flippant, implying that such a gift would certainly save her a lot of future trips to the well.

How many walls would this woman construct? Could they be penetrated? Could Jesus ever build a bridge that would reach her heart?

By this time he had her curiosity. But now it was time to reveal his lordship. Suddenly he brought her to her senses. The time for verbal byplay was over.

"Go, call your husband and come back," he said. She stiffened, grew serious, and looked shocked. Why? Because now she was forced to see herself. And what she saw was not beautiful.

The maze of walls she had constructed began to crumble. She was forced to cease being trite and defensive. It started with an honest admission. "I have no husband," she told him.

Seeing a crack in her resistance, our Lord was quick to disclose his knowledge of her depravity. He said, "You are right when you say you have no husband. The fact is, you have had five husbands and the man you now have is not your husband."

He affirmed that she had spoken the truth, but not the whole truth. And she now fully realized that this man was a prophet.

But, wouldn't you know it, she just had to put up one more wall. The wall of diversion. In essence, she said, "Let's forget me for a moment. There's this question I've been wondering about. Where is the appropriate place to worship? here in Samaria on Mount Gerizim, or in Jerusalem's Temple on Mount Zion?"

Since she cared enough to ask, Jesus offered a quick but thorough reply. In building bridges, we must table our own agendas at times to respond to the concerns of the other individuals. This is a price that must be paid, and Jesus paid it.

Feeling some guilt, the woman was probably pondering where she should go to give an offering for her sin. In her mind, the only cure for sin was sacrifice. And where it took place was crucial.

The Savior offered another answer she was unprepared for. It mattered not where she went. A special location was not required. Anywhere would do. Then he added that this is not to say that the Jewish nation has no unique place in God's plan for salvation of mankind. Worship need not take place only in Jewish territory, but its special significance as his chosen nation is undeniable.

Jesus knew that the Samaritans were off track. They ignored all but the first five books of the Old Testament. Also, they adjusted Scripture and history to glorify their sacred mountain, Gerizim, claiming that it was the site of Abraham's intended sacrifice of Isaac. Being as inoffensive as he possibly could, our Lord exposed these errors.

Well, by this time, the Samaritan woman was bewildered and overwhelmed by her new vista of truth. It all seemed so amazing. So deep. So far beyond her mental grasp.

Her reaction was to construct a final wall—that of delay. In so many words she declared, "Thanks for the interesting discussion, but it's all too much for my shallow mind. I guess I'll have to postpone my conclusions until the Messiah gets here. Then I can ask him what it all means!"

At last she had focused her attention on the need for the Messiah to disclose truth. Here was our Lord's opportunity to reveal his full identity, to reveal that he was more than a nice and clever man who condescended to converse with passersby and greater than one of the many prophets. He was the authentic Messiah, who cared enough about her to patiently reveal the plan of eternal life.

He bridged. She crossed over. For this to occur, he had to transcend all the barriers. She was a Samaritan. She was living in sin. Reasons enough for him to completely ignore her that day!

But our Lord climbed over, went around, or penetrated each of these barricades. And he replaced each one with a bridge. Final score: Jesus 1, Satan 0.

The Samaritan woman had witnessed a masterful job of bridge building. It was only natural for her to begin constructing some of her own. She ran back to town and beckoned people to meet him, suggesting that he could be the Christ. They came, they believed, and they invited him to remain with them to tell others. He stayed for two eventful days.

Upon Jesus' departure, the people of Sychar delivered their final verdict to the Samaritan woman: "We no longer believe just because of what you said; now we have heard for ourselves, and we know that this man really is the Savior of the world."

Not content to go on hearsay, or to base their belief on her testimony, they ventured to cross the bridge themselves.

And to think, it all began with a simple request for a drink of water!

The Samaritan drew water that day. Today, we can draw lessons from the events that transpired. Lessons from the master bridge builder.

Focusing on his example is the first crucial step in learning the essentials of skillful bridge building. He wisely admonishes, "Take my yoke upon you and learn from me" (Matt. 11:29).

But in addition to his unparalleled example as our chief architect he provides us with a set of reliable and ingenious blueprints for our bridge construction. It's time for us to "check out the specs."

With your help I can advance against a troop; with my God I can scale a wall.—2 Samuel 22:30

Lay on me an anvil, O God. Beat me and hammer me into a crowbar. Let me pry loose old walls.—Carl Sandburg "Prayer of Steel"

[We all have] those moments when the lights are out, . . . the valleys deep, and the walls are high, thick, and cold.
—Charles Swindoll in *Growing Deep in the Christian Life*

2

Our Precise Blueprint

As a youth I excelled in all kinds of destruction, but displayed a pitifully small aptitude for worthwhile construction. Though leaving a trail of broken everything in my wake, I couldn't seem to make anything that looked good or worked.

The tree houses, club houses, and dog houses ignominiously collapsed. And the bicycle-built-for-two, engineered with great deliberation and care, ended up a bicycle-built-for-nobody!

Then, one Christmas my parents presented me with an Erector Set. They assumed that even a klutz like their son could follow the simple directions. Besides that, all the construction materials were right there in the box. And they were made of steel.

What occurred? You guessed it. Even an Erector Set couldn't make me look good. My engineering feats underwhelmed everybody. The miniature Eiffel Tower I made was a carbon copy of the Leaning Tower of Pisa. And the Golden Gate Bridge looked like a catastrophe!

With such traumatic memories anchored in my psyche, you can imagine why I pricked up my ears when a colleague began bragging about his son's ingenious construction project.

I learned that the lad and his fifth-grade classmates were challenged to build bridges. And they were restricted to using only toothpicks and glue.

The students were divided into groups, each containing no more than a half dozen. Then each child was assigned to a specific position such as being a designer, architect, construction superintendent, or budget manager.

According to the resourceful teacher, the pivotal position in each group was the architect. The plans had to be precise, clear, and complete.

The children realized this fact in the course of their construction. Some tried to change the blueprints after noticing mistakes. To stop these shenanigans, their teacher covered all architectural drawings with wax paper.

Well, finally all the bridges were finished. And the day of judging had arrived. All structures were required to undergo a weight test. Results? Amazingly, most of the toothpick bridges survived fifteen pounds. The sturdiest one supported twenty-three!

Unfortunately, other structures did not fare so well. One responded to the added weight by popping upward. When the weight was removed, it collapsed. Another buckled rapidly, as a chain reaction of weak links led to a small explosion. Wooden fragments flew everywhere.

While musing over this clever learning experience, I couldn't help thinking about the bridge building we are involved in as Christians. The parallel is remarkable.

His Plan Is Our Purpose

When we fail to build healthy, Christ-centered relationships, it is because of either or both of these reasons:

1. We are *following* the blueprints of the wrong architect, Satan; or

2. We are *failing* to abide by the specifications of the right one, Jesus.

In both cases, the collapse of our relationships is assured. Sooner or later the weight test will reveal the weakness of our structure.

Chapter 1 focused on our wall demolition expert and bridge architect. In this chapter we shall examine the reliable set of blueprints that he offers us. That is essential if our bridges are to be structurally sound.

Where are these blueprints located? In his holy Word. Therein are contained sound, timeless truths that—when obeyed—assure us of authentically Christian relationships. The kind that draw us into close communion with others and into intimate oneness with him.

How can we know for certain that the blueprints contained in God's Word are completely reliable? Because his Word is inspired. This means that its authority is not grounded in the response of the readers, nor in the subjective experience of the writers. Rather, the Bible is absolutely reliable because it comes directly from God.

Paul underscores this point when he announces, "All Scripture is God-breathed [given by inspiration of God, KJV] and is useful for teaching, rebuking, correcting and training in righteousness, so that the man of God may be thoroughly equipped for every good work" (2 Tim. 3:16).[1]

The Bible shapes us up so that we can effectively relate to those around us—for God's good purposes.

---

1. *Eerdman's Handbook to the Bible,* David and Pat Alexander, eds. (Grand Rapids, Mi: William B. Eerdmans Publishing Company), chapter entitled "The Bible Is Different," by David Cousins, pp. 32–36.

And because his Word is truly inspired, its impact on the reader is dynamic. Its words penetrate the deepest recesses of our minds and emotions as it bridges us with other persons in other ages.

Nehemiah, Chapter 8 records that Ezra the scribe read from the law of Moses to the returned exiles in Jerusalem. The people, we are told, "understood the reading." But, in addition, they were "weeping when they heard the words of the law" and made "great rejoicing." Furthermore, they returned the next day to build shelters for the Feast of Tabernacles in obedience to the law's commands. The act of hearing and understanding the Scriptures had aroused their emotions and propelled them to action.

Centuries later, biblical scholar and writer J. B. Phillips describes a similar experience he had while translating the New Testament. "Although I did my utmost to preserve an emotional detachment, I found again and again that the material under my hands was strangely alive; it spoke to my condition in the most uncanny way."

No wonder the Bible's author used vivid metaphors to describe the impact that God's Word had made on their lives. To them it was:

a hammer to break	a fire to warm
water to cleanse	milk to nourish
meat to invigorate	light to guide
a sword for the fight	a mirror to reveal
at work in believers	able to build you up
living	active
piercing	discerning[2]

The conclusion is obvious. When we approach these blueprints, we can expect to be transformed dynamically!

In addition to capturing our aesthetic interests and supplying us with historical and theological information,

2. *Ibid.*, chapter entitled "The Bible and Christian Living," by David Field, pp. 48–49.

The scriptural references are as follows: Nehemiah 8, Jeremiah 23:29, 1 Peter 2:2, Hebrews 5:13–14, Psalm 119:105, Ephesians 6:17, James 1:23–25, 1 Thessalonians 2:13, Acts 20:32, Hebrews 4:12.

the Bible has a dramatic impact on our lives. And it links us with people through the centuries who have followed its hallowed pages to align themselves with the Savior's will.

Prep Time

But before we can build bridges, God's plans call for our taking care of those walls. The ones that block us from Jesus and from one another.

Some we need to demolish completely, just as the Roman armies of Titus did to Jerusalem's walls in A.D. 70. I can picture the grotesque-looking battering ram relentlessly doing its destruction.

Walls of sin require such thorough annihilation. Walls bearing the identity of anger, greed, envy, jealousy, prejudice, strife, and the like must be destroyed. Romans 6:6 (KJV) speaks emphatically of this necessity; "Knowing this, that our old man [self] is crucified with *him* [Jesus], that the body of sin might be destroyed."

But there are other walls we encounter that are not inanimate, walls involving the entrenched wills of stubbornly disobedient persons. For certain, we are not advised to infract their personhoods or transgress their freedom. As someone put it, they were made before we became maker.

Rather, such walls must be transcended. Instead of a battering ram, the ancient siege engine comes to mind.

When armies found a wall too thick to penetrate, they would push a tall, wheeled structure against its surface. Then after climbing to the top, they would extend a bridgelike walkway over the top of the wall, enabling their warriors to cross into enemy territory.

There are times when we Christians must climb over walls that people have constructed. Walls that are intended to shut us out. We must rise above such barriers, just as our Lord did in the story of his conversation with the Samaritan woman at Jacob's well.

But the point remains. Whether it's through or over, we must conquer those walls!

Then, after effectively responding to the wall issue, we are ready to build bridges. And according to the "specs" in God's Word.

So turn up the lamp a bit. Move a little closer and lean down. It's time to take a penetrating look at what is penned in blue ink.

Approach this task with hope and vision, for here before us are God's plans for guiding us into the kinds of relationships that we need.

Descendants of Aaron; That's Us!

In Old Testament times, all priests were descendants of Aaron, the brother of Moses who performed priestly duties during the period of the Exodus. Also, in each generation the legal head of the house of Aaron came to be called the high priest.

Then Jesus came, and everything changed. Especially the idea of priesthood.

The Lord himself became the one high priest. Hebrews explains this so well: "We have a great high priest ...Jesus the Son of God..." (4:14). Continuing, the writer declares:

> Such a high priest meets our need—one who is holy, blameless, pure, set apart from sinners, exalted above the heavens. Unlike the other high priests, he does not need to offer sacrifices day after day, first for his own sins, and then for the sins of the people. He sacrificed for their sins once for all when he offered himself. For the law appoints as high priests men who are weak; but the oath, which came after the law, appointed the Son, who has been made perfect forever (7:26–28).

Because of this reality, all of us who are his servants can legitimately claim to be authentic priests. As Martin

Luther said in the statement that became the rallying cry for the Reformation, there is a "priesthood of *all* believers."

This is true because our blueprint says so. Revelation says, "To him who loves us and has freed us from our sins by his blood, and has made us to be. . .priests to serve his God and Father" (1:5b–6). Again: "You [Jesus] have made them [Christians] to be. . .priests to serve our God, and they will reign on the earth" (5:10; cf. 20:6).

But it is Peter who lays this truth before us in a very picturesque fashion:

> As you come to him [Jesus], the living Stone—rejected by men but chosen by God and precious to him—you also, like living stones, are being built into a spiritual house to be a holy priesthood, offering spiritual sacrifices acceptable to God through Jesus Christ (1 Peter 2:4–5).

Question: What does the fact of our priesthood have to do with our relationships? Plenty. The Latin word for priest is *pontifex* which means—you guessed it—"bridge builder."

The fact that we're all priests, obedient to our one high priest, means that our mission is to form linkages with others. But even more important, to link others with him. Just as our great high priest bridged us with his Father through his death.

So congratulations to all of us, the spiritual descendants of Aaron. We are charged with the awesome responsibility and offered the great privilege of being card-carrying members of his bridge-building union. Moreover, our Lord has fully paid—once and for all—our union dues!

To realize these truths is to give ourselves the green light. To admonish ourselves to discover just *how* our blueprint instructs us to relate as priests. Let's explore with open minds and hearts.

After prayerfully scrutinizing God's Word, it becomes apparent that two main planks must support the bridges that we build as Christians. Two undergirding principles are completely reliable, consistent, practical, achievable, all because of Jesus. What are they?

1. Compassion: An Eraser on a Pencil?

Former Vice President Hubert Humphrey had a unique way of expressing himself. Speaking to a group of Christian men while holding a long pencil, he said, "Gentlemen, just as the eraser (on this pencil) is only a very small part . . . and is used only when you make a mistake, so compassion is only called upon when things get out of hand." He concluded by saying, "The main part of life is competition; only the eraser is compassion. . . . In politics, compassion is just part of the competition."[3]

But that was Hubert Humphrey talking. Our blueprint considers compassion to be much more than an eraser. It's that too, all right, but much more.

Compassion is a quality of spirit highly valued by our Lord. The Gospel writer tells us, "When he saw the crowds, he had compassion on them, because they were harassed and helpless, like sheep without a shepherd" (Matt. 9:36). Then, in Luke 6:36 Jesus says to his disciples, "Be merciful [compassionate] just as your Father is merciful."

The word *compassion* is derived from the Latin words *pati* and *cum*, which together mean "to suffer with." To be compassionate means to enter the arena of pain, to share in brokenness and anguish, to cry out with those in misery.

We're quite willing to speak down to and advise those who suffer. After all, they are flat on their faces because of their own faults, we often think.

But the compassion Jesus speaks of and demonstrated so faithfully has nothing to do with this kind of insulting

---

3. Donald P. McNeill, Douglas A. Morrison, Henri J.M. Nouwen, *Compassion: A Reflection on the Christian Life* (Garden City, NY: Image Books, 1966), p. 6.

paternalism. He would, most likely, tell us to spare the needy our platitudes and advice that would only intensify their hurt.

Some of us are willing to reach down to the destitute in order to pull them up to our level. We're so noble.

Again, our Lord expects more than this expression of pity. For such an attitude masks inherent feelings of superiority. He'd likely tell us to forget such "favors," especially the once-a-year-at-Christmas-kind!

His clarion call is for us to get down with the hurting. To climb down into their trenches. To identify with their misery. And then to lovingly offer his help without expecting a return and without demanding improved performance. Compassion has no preconditions.

I have observed a pervasive hesitancy among Christians to assume such a lowly posture. Self-preservation and even self-ascendancy often seem to be their guiding stars.

This was clearly demonstrated among members of a church at one of their recent meetings. Their spacious, multi-facilitied church building was certainly not being taxed to the limit. Those who came seemed to rattle around in the large structure.

At this particular session, a self-supporting ethnic minister made a polite request to start a new congregation in their building. He assured them that he would worship at nonconflicting times, respect the property, and keep in close contact. Furthermore, he would be willing to pay for his keep.

In spite of these facts, one key board member responded, "If we grant this request, I fear that these people will take us over!" The wall of self- preservation went up, compassion went out the window.

Thankfully, this man's knee-jerk reaction wasn't allowed to prevail. Other members brought the discussion back to biblical basics. The request was granted.

We wince at this example, but how many of us have rejected opportunities for compassion? "Sorry, but I'm really too timid to contact absentees." "I just don't have the stomach for watching those guys at the mission eat." "Give to hungry children overseas? Never. God has given me my own hungry mission field."

Daniel McNeill, in his book entitled *Compassion*, states it well: "Jesus' compassion is characterized by a downward pull." That disturbs us, because we focus on the upward climb as we strive for better lives, higher salaries, more prestigious positions.[4]

Compassion means going directly to those people and places where suffering is most acute and building a home there. Just as Jesus did when he left the portals of paradise to "pitch his tent" among us.

> Who, being in very nature God, did not consider equality with God something to be grasped, but made himself nothing, taking the very nature of a servant, being made in human likeness. And being found in appearance as a man, he humbled himself and became obedient to death—even death on a cross! (Phil. 2:6–8).

Verse five of this convicting chapter says it all: "Your attitude should be the same as that of Christ Jesus." It's really not optional. Filled with his presence, we *must* be compassionate!

2. Community: Come on Board!

Quartets used to sing a toe-tapping ditty entitled "On The Jericho Road." The words begin, "On the Jericho Road, there's room for just two. No more or no less, just Jesus and you."

No way! Last month I traveled on that ancient highway

4. *Ibid.*, pp. 26–28. On page 26, the author makes this additional comment: "Instead of striving for a higher position, more power, and more influence, Jesus moves, as Karl Barth says, from 'the heights to the depth, from victory to defeat, from riches to poverty, from triumph to suffering, from life to death.'" [Taken from Karl Barth, *Church Dogmatics*, IV/I (Edinburgh: T and T Clark, Sons, 1956), p. 190.]

and saw for myself. The Jericho Road has room for a lot more than Jesus and you—or me. It will hold thousands.

Too many of our hymns emphasize wrongly, I feel, the isolated believer alone with God. Now, I'm sure that this kind of thinking squares with our go-it-alone culture. Admittedly, all of us do feel like we're in a sealed vacuum at times. And the feeling can get very uncomfortable, as intimated in this poem by Jim Long:

> Sometimes I feel isolated,
>   so completely alone,
>   as if I am entombed
> in a Plexiglass shell.
> I can look out.
> Others can look in.
> But we are separated . . .
> Some people tell me
> I should not have lonely feelings.
> I should climb out of my shell . . .
> as if I can instantaneously
> melt the plastic
> or will the shell to shatter.[5]

But with Jesus, and our brothers and sisters in Christ, it must be different. We're inseparably linked into a compassionate community of believers.

Forget any lonely journey on the Jericho Road. In a very real sense, the Christian's journey is more like what occurred on the Golden Gate Bridge some time ago. The occasion was the fiftieth anniversary of the celebrated structure. And did the people ever come to celebrate!

Over eight-hundred-thousand jammed onto the bridge with noisemakers and flags. Some feared that the tremendous weight might be too much for the old, steel monument. One person said that it did actually buckle a bit, but it held as thousands celebrated.

With Jesus as our reliable bridge, we the very large

5. Poem titled "The Lonely Quiet." Found in loose form, publication unknown.

community of disciples can rest our full weight on him and continually celebrate en masse. The very thought of this makes me want to write another song: "On the Bridge of Jesus Christ, There's Room for Millions." And here's the best part, as still another songwriter has penned, "Though millions have come, there's still room for one."

The message of the Bible is that the compassionate life is a life of living together, rather than being individuals with isolated personality traits or special talents. Paul exhorted the Philippian church to live compassionately in this manner:

> There must be no competition among you, no conceit; but everybody is to be self-effacing. Always consider the other person to be better than yourself, so that nobody thinks of his own interests first but everybody thinks of other people's interests instead (Phil. 2:3–4, jb).

How often we focus our attention on individual acclaim and personal advancement. Even (and maybe especially) in the church!

Case in point. I've heard persons in the clergy wax eloquently on the subject of servanthood, rightly saying that we must be willing to "decrease so that he might increase."

Yet, somehow, few whom I have known have willingly taken a step down on the political ladder. Moving to a small church is almost out of the question. And those who are elected to administrative posts are even less prone to relax their power grasp. The very thought of reentering the pastorate makes them cringe, for it seems like a backward step. They've become used to the perks, the power, the privileged position, and others' perceptions of them, too. Admit it or not, they are dug in, though they might articulate otherwise.

Again, the New Testament admonition is to think community welfare rather than individual advancement. Ours is a corporate identity. No wonder our blueprint uses the term *one another* in no less than thirty distinct manners![6]

And that's why the Good Book makes such a big deal of the term *fellowship*. New Christians after the Day of Pentecost devoted themselves to it (Acts 2:42; cf. 1 John 1:3). This word, in Greek *koinonia*, means two things: first, a "sharing together in partnership," and second, a "giving of what we have (and are) to others." *Union* and *communion*. Such activities are the expected outgrowths of true community.[7]

Compassion and Christian community do not exist in isolation. They have a deep and profound effect on one another.

The first is a God-given quality of heart that makes us want to completely identify with others' suffering. It is an individual matter.

New Testament community, on the other hand, refers to a kind of spiritual melting that makes many compassionate individuals into one, so that they might corpo-

---

6. The phrase "one another" is employed in the New Testament (NASB) in the following manners: exhort (encourage) one another every day (Heb. 3:13); edify (build up) one another (Rom. 14:19); admonish (instruct) one another (Rom. 15:14); through love be servants of one another (Gal. 5:13); bear one another's burdens and so fulfill the law of Christ (Gal. 6:2); teach and counsel (admonish) one another (Col. 3:16); comfort one another (1 Thess. 4:18); stir (stimulate) one another up to love and good works (Heb. 10:24); confess your sins one to another and pray for one another (James 5:16); offer hospitality to one another without complaint (1 Peter 4:9); be devoted to one another in brotherly love—honor one another above yourselves (Rom. 12:10); don't challenge one another or envy one another (Gal. 5:26); do not be conceited and live in harmony with one another (Rom. 12:16, RSV); be patient, bearing with one another in love (Eph. 4:2); speak truth to one another for we are all members of one body (Eph. 4:25, NIV); be kind and compassionate to one another, forgiving each other, just as Christ forgave you (Eph. 4:32); submit to one another out of reverence for Christ (Eph. 5:21, NIV); don't speak against one another (James 4:11); clothe yourselves with humility toward one another (1 Peter 5:5); if we love (*agape*) each other God lives in us and his love is perfected in us (1 John 4:12); we are members one of another (Rom. 12:5); seek to do good for one another (1 Thess. 5:15); do not lie to one another—there cannot be Greek or Jew, circumcised or uncircumcised . . . but Christ is all and in all (Col. 3:9–13); love one another earnestly from the heart (1 Peter 1:22); care for one another (1 Cor. 12:25); speak to one another in psalms and hymns and spiritual songs (Eph. 5:19); love one another, for love is of God (1 John 4:7); bear with each other and forgive whatever grievance you may have against another (Col. 3:13, NIV); a new commandment I give to you, that you love one another, even as I have loved you (John 13:34); by this all men will know that you are my disciples, if you have love for one another (John 13:35).

7. Jerry Bridges, *True Fellowship* (Colorado Springs: Navpress, 1985), p. 16.

rately respond to God's presence and others' needs. In a day when persons will stop at nothing to get ahead, an authentic Christian community is a refreshing oasis.

Speaking to his diversified audience, Paul announces:

> You are all sons of God through faith in Jesus Christ, for all of you who were baptized into Christ have clothed yourselves with Christ. There is neither Jew nor Greek, slave nor free, male nor female, for you are all one in Christ Jesus (Gal. 3:26–28; cf. John 17:11b).

As his priests, we must continually remind ourselves of our bridge-building function. Our highest goal is to become middlemen, helping his community to grow and become ever more tightly bonded.

In addition to constructing bridges, we must often become bridges ourselves. The imagery is captured in a recent incident that occurred in London.

That's Stretching It a Bit!

United Press International reports the unusual story about a bank official who literally stretched his six-foot-three-inch frame across a gap in order to allow twenty persons to reach safety.

Andrew Parker, seeing his family and other desperate, panic-stricken people stranded on the Zee-brugge ferry in the turbulent English Channel, came up with the emergency plan.

He sized up the situation. Between the sinking ship and a small island of metal was a six-foot-wide cascade of water, which "was too big for people to jump across." So, in Parker's words, "I just made a sort of a bridge."

His wife Eleanor was the first to try out the human structure. She said, "I stepped on his back and I was petrified!"

All of the people made it across. Once across, all of them clung to the small island until rescuers could throw a rope. Parker helped everyone climb the rope.

"People were screaming, and my daughter thought she was going to die," Eleanor Parker declared. "She said, 'Mommy, if I did something wrong, I didn't mean to do it.'"

But, in the midst of all the confusion and pandemonium, hero Andrew became himself a vital link to safety.

Our world is filled with gaps caused by sin. People, though attempting to appear calm, have an internal state of disequilibrium. They impulsively try to span their gaps with structures that are certain to collapse: drugs, alcohol, illicit sexual encounters, gambling. The list seems unending.

Only Jesus can truly satisfy their hearts and ensure their eternal safety. But he needs our help. He has anointed us as his priests, or bridges, to rescue the perishing.

Are we willing to become Andrew Parkers for him?

Well, after becoming thoroughly acquainted with our chief architect and gaining a full understanding of his blueprint, we are ready to collect needed materials. Otherwise, our structure will only remain in the planning stage.

So let's bring on the items that are necessary to build solid and trustworthy relationships.

I will tear down the wall you have covered with whitewash and will level it to the ground so that its foundation will be laid bare.—God to Israel, Ezekiel 13:14

Before I build a wall I'd ask to know
What I was walling in or out.
And to whom I was like to give offense.
Something there is that doesn't love a wall,
That wants it down.
                    —Robert Frost, "Mending Wall"

The youth gets together his materials to build a bridge to the moon . . . the middle-aged man . . . build(s) a woodshed with them.—Henry David Thoreau

3

Our Essential Construction Materials

Suppose we decided to build an expansion bridge over a wide, raging river, one that would support many heavy vehicles simultaneously.

We'd be certain to select just the right materials. Items such as bailing wire, paper, and scotch tape wouldn't even be considered.

There would be no cutting of corners. We would set out to gather only heavy-duty, reliable materials like cement, steel cable, and granite.

By contrast, if our task were to construct a wall, we wouldn't need to be so particular. We could use almost anything that we could get to stand up: plastic, dirt, block, wood, hedge.

Why the difference? The reasons are obvious.

Unlike the wall, our bridge must be made to counteract gravitational pull and to support greater weight.

Also, we realize that the bridge is less likely to survive any flaw or weakness. Remember the old adage, "A chain is no stronger than its weakest link?" The same is true for a bridge. Recall last chapter's toothpick bridge that buckled when one part gave way?

But there is one final reason, and it is the most important. When a bridge collapses, the tragedy is usually more pronounced than when a wall collapses.

For these reasons, it is apparent that great care must go into the selection of bridge-building materials.

The same principle holds for the bridge construction we do as Christians. Only the best materials will do. Why? Because our relationships must counter such gravitational forces as hardship and ill health. They must be able to support excess weight. And, without a doubt, their collapse is sure to yield great trauma to our lives.

How much easier it would be if we were building walls. The materials are cheaper and a lot easier to acquire. No farther away than a thoughtless deed! Some wall-building materials come to mind: an "I-wish-I-could-take-it-all-back" comment; a "make-my-day" hate stare; and "I'll-never-do-it-again-I-promise" affair. All are the stuff that barricades between people are made of.

But, to reiterate, our bridges, if they are to be sound and strong, must be built with only the best materials. We can't afford to scrimp with those that are inferior.

Case in point. Husbands often allow such intruders as "work mania" and "golfitis" to shortchange the quality of materials they invest in their marital relationships. The results are not good.

Often they use inferior materials like cards, candy, and flowers, to make up for noncommitment. Their wives are usually well aware of their antics. Some wives become suspicious and resentful of such counterfeit measures—cheap substitutes for the real thing.

I must add this qualification. The above items are very appropriate for husbands and wives to give to one another. But only if they are seen as supplements to, and not substitutes for the essentials. If they are "added-to," not "instead-of."

The point is clear. All relationships, regardless of their nature, require the costly investment of certain critical materials.

To place these essential items in proper perspective, let's focus on the foundation upon which they must lie.

The Bedrock of Commitment

There are many ways to reveal commitment. At Pepperdine University it is often expressed in "gallows humor."

Allow me to illustrate.

A few years ago, a faculty colleague of mine had his life threatened by a mentally disturbed student. When the news leaked out, our entire campus seemed upset. How would this touchy situation be resolved? The tension mounted.

Then, the faculty member's best friend—an administrator—did a very humorous thing. He made a sign and posted it on his bulletin board. In big, bold letters it read:

I DO NOT KNOW,
NOR HAVE I EVER KNOWN
BOBBY JOE GILLIAM
NOR DO I THINK THAT I WOULD EVEN LIKE HIM
IF I KNEW HIM!

In reality, this was only a joke. But it did serve to defuse the tension and assured that his best friend was committed to his well-being.

Humor aside, the *Random House Dictionary* defines commitment as "pledging oneself to" a thing, idea, or person.[1] It carries with it the idea of giving loyalty, re-sources, and attention in a total, hands-down manner.

Commitment goes much deeper, and is far more in-tense, than involvement—which implies mere participa-tion with or in. I like the distinction that someone made between these two concepts. "A chicken was involved in my breakfast. She laid the egg. But a pig was truly com-mitted. He furnished the bacon!"

What is commitment really? Think of the bridge again. Commitment is the bedrock far beneath the earth's sur-face on which is based the giant pilasters that support the superstructure of the bridges. Commitment is solid, strong, immovable.

The image that we receive here is one of *steadfastness*.

Our commitment to Jesus must consist of persever-ing—stalwart steadfastness—in order for our relationship with him to remain vibrant and intense. Paul says it well. "Stand firm. Let nothing move you. Always give your-selves fully" (1 Cor. 15:58).

When we commit ourselves to him in this way, we are then able to extend Christian commitment to those for whom he died. As a result, we will form the kinds of relationships that please him and make us fulfilled.

But it is important to realize that commitment is a topic that is also increasingly being recognized in our secular society.

Is It Your Heart's Habit?

According to the sociologist-author Robert N. Bellah in his best-selling book titled *Habits of the Heart*, this na-tion's baby boomers are seriously questioning the value of rugged individualism. A concept that is as American as Coca-Cola and hotdogs (called Dodgerdogs in Los An-geles) at baseball games.

---

1. *The Random House Dictionary*, Jess Stein, editor-in-chief (New York: Ballantine Books, 1980), p. 184.

The sizable and influential segment of our society seems to feel that both the "me generation" (narcissists of the 70s) and the "give-me generation" (materialists of the 80s) have taken individualism to a ridiculous extreme. They see that the results of these decades are rampant self-centeredness and myopia in epidemic proportions.

The only value of relationships is satisfaction of personal needs. If that goal is unmet, relationships are abruptly ended and thrown away with no thought given to their repair.

But refreshingly the author states that the boomers are calling for a return to authentic commitment in their relationships, so that they think "us" instead of "me."

Why do they feel this way? Because there is intrinsic worth in committed bonding. Through it we receive our significance as persons and it almost seems ironic, but we are the ones who receive the greatest payoff for developing committed relationships. Through them we become self-actualized, even though that is not our primary purpose in relating to others.

Implications? According to these young adults, it is time to say no to the pop psychologists who say, "Get in touch with your feelings; focus your attention on number one; go for it all, in order to die with the most toys." That kind of thinking no longer washes with many people.

Baby-boomer marketing consultant, David Wolfe, puts it thus:

> An uncommitted relationship is like living in an emotional amusement park—doing everything for yourself alone quickly burns itself out. I've found that there's no better way to find fulfillment in life than to focus on (i.e., be committed to)... (other) persons.[2]

Without commitment our bridge building doesn't stand a chance. With it, regardless of life's weights and

2. Robert N. Bellah et. al., *Habits of the Heart: Individualism and Commitment in American Life* (New York: Harper and Row, Publishers, 1985).

intrusions, survival is assured. And as the late author and educator Bertha Munro says, "We will not merely survive somehow, we'll survive triumphantly!"

Again, we must think of commitment as the supporting principle of our relationships. The other materials are built on this solid foundation.

Thinking of it in another way, each of the remaining materials is an expression of commitment.

Let's turn our attention to these manifestations of Christian commitment.

Start Glancing at Your Watch: Commitment of Time

The other day I wandered into a stationery and party supply store. As I walked down one aisle, I happened upon an entire section of things for a fortieth birthday. There were "It's all over" balloons, black napkins and plates, mourning paraphernalia, and the like. I recalled my recent trip to the local pastry shop, when I saw a fortieth birthday cake decorated with black and moldy-colored green frosting. On top was a tombstone.

It all seemed pretty amusing, that is until I realized that I had recently had *my* fortieth birthday. Then I recalled a statement credited to Winston Churchill: "The age forty may not be the beginning of the end, but it is definitely the end of the beginning."

Where had those years gone? But even more important, had I spent them wisely? All 14,600 days; 350,400 hours; 21,024,000 minutes of them?

Could I really consider myself to have been a faithful steward of my time? More important still, would I buy up my opportunities in a better way during the years that remain?

James 4:14 describes life as "a mist that appears for a little while and then vanishes." It's a simple case of hatch (birth), match (marriage—which is optional) and dispatch (death) in rapid succession.

How we all fritter away our precious hours! And when we waste time in sinful living, we give ourselves painful memories besides.

Then there is the great quantity of time spent in red-taped, monotonous duties. The kind that seem so inconsequential: pencil pushing, grocery shopping, and lawn mowing.

Many of us devote too big a chunk of this precious commodity to trifles and inconsequential hobbies, such as reading horoscopes, watching sports on television, excessive sleeping, and tinkering in the garage.

Of course, there is value in most (or some) of these activities—depending on our needs and interests. But *only* when they do not consume an inordinate amount of time. And when they prepare us, therapeutically or otherwise, for the important activities of life.

How much better it is, however, to create hobby-interests out of more substantive ventures, like Bible study and prayer, working on a project that assists others, such as volunteering at a senor citizens' home, and telephoning or writing people to offer encouragement.

Our use of time, like money, gravitates toward one of two polarities: ourselves or others. We increasingly become like either Howard Hughes or Mother Teresa: takers or givers. The former comes easily and seems like the natural course. The latter requires a conscious act of the will; it is like swimming upstream.

It is impossible to be simultaneously others-oriented and hoard our time. On the other hand, being willing to devote time to others means one thing: interruptions. We can bank on that.

But the truth of the matter is this. The interruptions by people who are in need are often the most productive times of our day.

For Christian bridge builders, establishing time priorities is essential. We must schedule hours to generate and nurture relationships. Frequently, this is done in person. People need us to be close by.

I heard about a small girl who was suffering in the hospital. In her anguishing moments, someone said to her, "Amy, don't you know that Jesus loves you?" Sobbing, she replied, "But I need someone with skin."

There is no touch like the closeup, personal touch, the intimate encounter where words, actions, and body language can communicate the message "I care." People need people "with skin" to be the virtual incarnation of Christ's love. And many times the most important thing is simply for them to be there and spend time.

Regardless of what we've heard, time does *not* fly. It moves at a steady, consistent pace. Also, there *are* enough hours in the day if we plan studiously and judiciously.

Nevertheless, our time is very limited. As my home-spun-philosopher father used to say, "The time that knows us now will soon know us no more." Also, "Our hearts beat like a muffled drum to the grave." But the most memorable statement he used to make was, "We must see all time in the light of eternity."

We must cease pretending that our lives on earth will last forever. This means focusing on people rather than things, on others rather than ourselves.

Bonnie Prudden put it right. "We can't turn back the clock. That is true. But we can wind it up again." Let's do just that, and as we do, I propose that we resolve to commit a lion's share of the future to others!

Begin Relinquishing Your Security: Commitment to Risk

Proverbs 28:1 speaks of the righteous as being "as bold as a lion." We all know that this king of the jungle rarely backs off from a challenge. His bravery is legendary.

As Christians, many of us roar within the protected confines of our churches. But when it comes to risk building *new* bridges for the Lord, we whimper.

Who needs new bridges? The old ones work fine! Old cliques are safe and comfortable. Old friends remain true.

And so we form cliques. Futhermore, the cliques we form give rise to other cliques—formed by those who resent our cliques. Before long, our churches have so many walled-in cliques that they resemble giant mazes.

Newcomers may vigorously attempt to break into our fellowship, but encountering such barriers is usually enough to generate discouragement and withdrawal.

An elderly couple began attending my own church. They had just moved to California from the hospitable Midwest. Being quite shy themselves, they were very hesitant to make bridge-building overtures. It was their feeling that others should build bridges to them, and they were right, but few if any did.

This continued for over a year. Then, in desperation, this lonely couple began groping for friendship. It was a Sunday evening. The church service had just concluded. The gentleman made a beeline for the targeted couple. After clearing this throat a few times he said, "My wife and I would like to have you join us at a nearby restaurant for a cup of coffee."

The response shot back, "Sorry, but on Sunday evenings we get together only with the same four people— our closest friends!" In other words, not this Sunday night, not next Sunday night, not *any* Sunday night. You're not good enough.

You can imagine the old fellow's reaction. His voice stammered, as he began backing up. After telling his wife, they went home devastated. In relating the story to me, he concluded by saying two words: "We cried."

In spite of our age gap, my wife and I attempted to establish a relationship with them, and we requested other couples to do the same. Fortunately they have, and the couple is becoming accepted as part of the church.

Sure, building new bridges does involve risk. To launch out in faith can, and often does, mean pain. But, as followers of the one who "learned obedience from what he suffered" (Heb. 5:8), we have no other option. To do otherwise is to invite spiritual atrophy and demise.

C. S. Lewis in his inimitable style articulates this fact in graphic terms: "Love anything, and your heart will certainly be wrung and possibly be broken. If you want to (keep) it intact, you must give your heart to no one. . . . Wrap it carefully around with hobbies and little luxuries; avoid all entanglements; lock it up safe in the casket. . . of your selfishness. But in that casket—safe, dark, motionless, airless—it will change. It will not be broken; it will become unbreakable, impenetrable, irredeemable. . . . The only place outside heaven where you can be perfectly safe from all the dangers. . . of love is hell."

Rather than waiting for others to approach us and make us feel comfortable, we must take the initiative. Jesus will help us to transcend propensities toward shyness. His Spirit will provide the words to say, and we will improve with practice.

But, once we approach others in love, what should our attitude be?

Make Encouragement Your Goal: Commitment to Affirmation

Robert Schuller said it, and I heartily concur: "Words can either be bombs or baths; bullets or blessings." And whichever they are is of crucial importance to our relationships.

USA TODAY reported the results of a survey of married couples. It was revealed that, while happy and unhappy couples self-disclose equally, the happy couples are characterized by upbeat positive communication patterns.

Those who admitted to being unfulfilled said they spend time alone reflecting on their anxieties, fears, and weaknesses. By contrast, the ones who felt that they had togetherness shared hopes and dreams. They focused on strengths and encouragement.[3]

3. Marilyn Elias, "Happy couples accentuate the positive," *USA TODAY*, p. 10.

Ditto in our churches. "Wet blankets" wreak havoc. It takes five upbeat persons to merely cancel one's gloomy spell. Get enough of these deadbeats, and any bridge-building energy is depleted.

As believers, we are called upon to be bridges over troubled waters. To provide hope and joy. To communicate that we really care. To link those who are discouraged with the master, who says, "Come to me, all you who are weary and burdened, and I will give you rest" (Matt. 11:28).

His real name was Joseph. But the disciples called him Barnabas, and with good reason. His new name means "Son of Encouragement" (Acts 4:36). He provides a refreshing example for all of us.

He was sent to Antioch to observe what God was doing there. "When he arrived and saw the evidence of the grace of God, he was glad and encouraged them all to remain true to the Lord with all their hearts" (Acts 11:23). Later, he strongly affirmed Paul at a time when the disciples were hesitant to accept him (Gal. 2:1, 9). That's our man.

Some years back I could have used his support. The small Christian college where I served as an administrator changed presidents. I was demoted. Barnabas, where were you?

My friends were at a loss for words. Trite words of encouragement might have intensified my grief.

They decided to have a party for me. Everyone came beautifully dressed. Food was plentiful and delicious. But words still came hard. There were a few tears. The atmosphere was tense.

All of a sudden, one of my colleagues decided to break the ice. In a voice that could be heard by all, he declared, "I don't know about you guys, but this is the first time in my life I've attended a demotion party!"

That did it. Everyone cracked up in convulsive laughter. The party instantly became enjoyable. And from that moment on, I felt encouraged.

Paul puts it straight in Ephesians 4:29:

Do not let any unwholesome talk come out of your mouths, but only what is helpful for building others up according to their needs, that it may benefit those who listen.

May we all remember the importance of committing ourselves to building up others.

But there is one more essential material for our bridges.

Consider Change Your Friend: Commitment to Flexibility

My father used to say, "Son, a rut is nothing but a grave with both ends kicked out." Saying it another way, Woody Allen once remarked, "A relationship is like a shark; it must constantly move forward or it dies."

Inflexibility is an enemy of healthy, Christian bridge building. Entrenchment, as the term implies, provides the mental image of wall construction.

Some of us are more prone than others to resist change—perhaps the powerful, the wealthy, those who live away from a large city. Also, those who are older.

Speaking of our senior citizens, I came upon this prayer the other day. It reveals a recognition of this pull toward inflexibility, and asks the Lord for grace:

Lord, Thou knowest I am growing older. Keep me from being talkative and possessed with the idea that I must express my self on every subject. Release me from the craving to straighten out everyone's affairs. Keep my mind free from recital of endless details. Give me wings to get to the point.

Seal my lips when I am inclined to tell of my aches and pains. They increase with the years and my love to speak of them grows sweeter with time. Teach me the glorious lesson that occasionally I may be wrong. Make me thoughtful but not nosey, helpful but not bossy. With my vast store of wisdom and experience, it does seem a pity not to use it all, but Thou knowest, Lord, I want a few friends at the end.[4]

But, again, older people aren't the only ones who become set in their ways. Not by a long shot. As a university professor and counselor, I meet inflexible people of all ages.

I had to laugh to myself as my friend told the story. Also a professor at a Bible college, he related an incident that sounded all too familiar.

It was term-paper deadline time. One of his students stumbled in with a long and somber face. The touching story began. It seemed as though his wife was in the last weeks of pregnancy. He felt that the Lord wanted him to drop everything, including the trivial term paper responsibility, and unite with her in enjoying the birthing process.

Now, my friend has a reputation for being very hard-nosed when it comes to making such concessions. But, somehow, this student had plucked a responsive chord in his heart. He agreed to setting back the due date, but only if the entire class could have the same favor.

He announced this concession at the next class session. Some students were upset. They had sacrificed to complete their project on time. Why encourage procrastination? Nevertheless, my teacher friend hung tough. It was high time that he showed himself to be more flexible, understanding, and compassionate.

Well, all the papers came in on the extended date—including that of the new father. The grading began. As the prof read through the masterpieces, one stood out for depth of thought and verbal sophistication. He glanced up at the name and it was, wouldn't you know it, the student he had made the concession for.

4. Entitled "cook's prayer," unpublished prayer contained in the news sheet "News From Oakie Acre," Fairfax, Virginia.

He thought, "This paper is so good that it could be published!" He couldn't help himself, he had to read it through again. It was then that he discovered the unvarnished truth: The paper had already been published! He recognized it, and went to the very source the student had copied.

The day of reckoning came. The poor fellow was summoned to his office. My friend began by complimenting him on the high quality of his work. The student beamed, saying that he was not surprised. He always knew that he had the potential. The professor could stand it no longer, and he confronted the young man with the evidence. He readily confessed and pleaded for mercy.

Knowing this professor as I do, I'm certain that the contrite plagiarist suffered the consequences.

The point is this. He had requested the professor to be flexible. Nevertheless, he had remained inflexible himself—as he held tenaciously to his undisciplined, irresponsible ways.

Once again, flexibility is essential in bridging to others. We must adapt to their thoughts, words, and actions until we arrive at a place of mutual respect.

And when we finally arrive at a communion of spirit, the assignment is not complete. Why? Because we grow at different rates. Therefore, we are forced to make many midcourse corrections with those we relate to. Never can (or should) we force them into our molds.

When we are flexible toward persons, we are showing them great respect. Also, we are revealing the depth of our own character.

Where from Here?

We have a clear and spectacular model for bridge building in Jesus Christ, our Lord. And his trustworthy blueprint reveals the precise specifications for following in his footsteps. Finally, we have the needed materials for construction within our grasp: commitment to time, risk, affirmation and flexibility. All we need is right here. Now it's time to go to work. To roll up our sleeves and, with his help, to begin our challenging and rewarding task. Let's get going.

No longer will violence be heard in your land, nor ruin or destruction within your borders, but you will call your walls Salvation and your gates Praise.—Isaiah 60:18

Stone walls do not a prison make,
Nor iron bars a cage.
          —Richard Lovelace "Lucasta. To Althea:
          From Prison"

The worst thing about crossing a bridge before you come to it is that it leaves you on this side of the river.—Old Proverb

4

Our Dedication to Labor

Recently, I spoke at a retreat in a beautiful, rustic monastery overlooking the Santa Barbara Channel. When arriving at the cell where I would be sleeping, I noticed this name over the entrance: St. Julian of Norwich.

Being inquisitive, I asked the monk to tell me about the life of this saint. He complied with enthusiasm.

It seems that Saint Julian lived in a small English town in the Middle Ages. While he was still very young, his church deemed him exemplary on all counts and decided to give him the ultimate recognition.

The day was announced, and everyone was there for the elaborate investiture ceremony. Singing was vibrant. Prayers were fervent. Praise to God for this saintly man was given.

Then it happened, just as everyone had expected. Saint

Julian was literally sealed into a small room that adjoined the cathedral. The walls were enclosed around him tightly, with only a small hole in the side. In that small, dark cubicle he would spend the rest of his life praying, administering blessings to passersby, and writing holy literature.

I thought to myself, "What a pity! Poor guy. That's worse than we treat our zoo animals today!" But wait. He wasn't the last good person to have sealed himself behind church walls. The church world is saturated with Saint Julians! And this reality strongly contributes to the fact that so few of us are building bridges to non-Christians.

Number Crunchers, We Hear You!

I've never been very impressed by statisticians, whom someone defined as "people who say that, if you put your feet in the oven and your head in the refrigerator, the middle of you will be the right temperature."

First, statisticians scare me. They tell me I don't have a chance. If I'm fortunate enough to escape drunk drivers and drug-crazed murderers, the disappearance of the ozone layer is sure to get me.

Second, the number crunchers insist on comparing me with something as uncomplimentary as a rat or monkey. They recently did this in their unsuccessful attempt to stop me from drinking diet soft drinks.

One more thing about the numbers guys. They twist statistics to support some pretty bizarre conclusions. I heard about one who used impressive figures relating human to stork populations in Europe, proof positive that storks really do bring babies. Now really!

But in spite of these misgivings, I must admit that one statistician recently got to me. His study found that only one in four hundred of us who claim to follow the master bridge builder is successful in linking someone to him each year. Think about that a moment. That's only one fourth of one percent.[1]

In our hearts, we realize that Jesus died so that such persons "shall not perish but have eternal life" (John 3:16). Furthermore, we know that he does not discriminate in his invitation, but desires that "all men [will] be saved and [will] come to a knowledge of the truth." (1 Tim. 2:4).

Unfortunately, our knowledge of this truth doesn't always spur us to action. Some of us remain apathetic, which the poet Thoreau describes as a state of "quiet desperation." Others of us labor, but hide behind thick walls. Encased. Entombed.

Is it not time that we who claim to be Christ's redeemed servants begin cutting yellow ribbons on scores of new bridges that will link us and our Savior with our desperately pagan world?

That means plenty of diligent and dedicated labor. Labor that is likely to tire us and maybe even make us look older. But is that really so bad?

Concerning our appearance, author Reuben Welch asks, "Shouldn't a Christian who has lived half a life look half used up? What are we saving ourselves for? To look good in our caskets?"

I say, Let's pull out all the stops. Let's jump into the thick of this God-ordained construction project. With rolled-up sleeves, let's use his model, blueprint, and essential materials to build bridges for him.

Our work assignment is divided into two important tasks. The first focuses on the initial construction, the second on maintenance. Both are challenging assignments.

---

1. Stated in Jon Johnston, *Christian Excellence: Alternative to Success* (Grand Rapids, MI: Baker Book House, 1985), p. 128.

Task Number One:
Building Reliable, Functional Structures

A man walked up to a workman who was digging trenches in New York City. After getting his attention, he asked, "Sir, what are you doing there?"

The laborer snapped back, "I'm making five bucks an hour!"

To satisfy his curiosity, the fellow went up to another ditch digger and asked the same question. The answer was much different. "I'm participating in the construction of a very impressive skyscraper."

Both were doing the same activity, but that is where their similarity stopped. The first was short sighted; the second visualized the great significance of his work.

We must see that the relationships our Lord helps us to build have eternal significance. Why? Because relationships have a crucial bearing on why most people affiliate with a church and become disciples of Jesus.

Win Arn says so, and he has plenty of support for his conclusion. In his scientific investigation, he found that 75–90 percent of all churchgoers identify a "relational factor" as being responsible for their attending.

Either a friend, relative, or neighbor networked them into the church body.

Another study found that 71 percent of all active church members today had responded to a "relational approach" to evangelism. This is contrasted with only thirteen percent who were drawn in by a content-oriented presentation of the Gospel.[2]

2. Quoted in "The Win Arn Growth Report: A Newsletter for the Leaders of Growing Churches," Number 15, Institute for American Church Growth, 709 East Colorado Boulevard, Suite 150, Pasadena, CA 91101, pp. 2–3.

For an enlarged discussion of this study and the application of the network principle of church growth, see the book *The Master's Plan for* Making Disciples, by Win Arn.

The author accentuates a concept made popular by Bible translators—dynamic equivalence. We must locate concepts that are dynamically equivalent in our culture today, that are relevant to both the secular world and God's Word. Then we can meaningfully translate biblical truth.

The bridge of content, whether constructed of lessons or sermons, is ineffective. Especially when unsupported by relationships.

So, fellow builders, as we establish links with others, we must be encouraged by the tremendous significance of our labor. We're doing more than depositing an hourly wage in the bank of heaven. Much more.

Seeing our work from this perspective should give us *inspiration*. Now we are ready for *perspiration* as we work at some very important tasks.

1. Personality Under Construction

In order to become skilled workmen we must allow Jesus to help us remove the rough edges from our personalities.

Whether by accident or intention, some of us are turn-offs. And the more we alienate others, the less we seem to be aware of the fact! As a result, people avoid us like porcupines, skunks, and growling dogs.

In what specific ways do we turn off others? Allow me to describe these three.

First, some of us are oblivious. We're so much into our own worlds that we don't have the foggiest notion about what is going on around us.

At Pepperdine University where I teach, 20 percent of our student body is from outside the United States. Of this number, many come from Third World nations where poverty is rampant.

By contrast, the students from these areas are typically very wealthy themselves. Their parents are, in fact, among the richest people in the world.

Recently, I was talking with a fellow who fit this cate-

In searching for these connecting bridges we must investigate the predispositions of Americans. How? By focusing on the content that is disseminated by the media.

Social scientists are saying that the predominant concerns today are friendship, love, and relationships. Perhaps that is why the great majority of Christians come to Christ and their church through social connections. They are, in effect, the dynamic equivalent of our culture on which we can build an effective evangelism strategy.

gory. He was from India. Without attempting to put him on the spot, I asked him about his concern for the destitute of his country.

Did the tens of thousands who anguished on the streets concern him? Did he lie awake at night worrying about their welfare? Did his heart ache when he saw the garbage trucks pick up the emaciated bodies of those who had starved?

Now, keep in mind that I was asking these questions of a well-mannered, responsible young man, whose smile lit up his entire face.

That's why I was surprised by his nonchalant answer. "No, prof, to be perfectly honest, I've never been concerned at all. I've never really seen those people."

In the same way, some of us have conditioned ourselves to avoid seeing. Or feeling. Or caring. Although we may not be isolated from those others, we've somehow insulated ourselves from them.

Jesus asks us to remove the scales from our eyes. To be truly sensitive to those around us, especially to those in need.

Second, more than a few of us are obnoxious. People can't stand to be around us. At best we're only tolerated.

We talk too much, or invariably say the wrong things. I'm reminded of a prayer that my mother shared. One that we're all well-advised to pray: "Lord, fill my mouth with worthwhile stuff, and nudge me when I've said enough."

Some of us have a well-rehearsed reservoir of annoying habits. We eat with our mouths open, chew on our fingernails, doze off during the pastor's message, have perpetual "doggie breath."

If only we could see ourselves as others see us. Perhaps then we would cease being so offensive and unappealing.

Third, a great number of us are ostentatious, always performing, forever on display in order to impress.

Matthew's Gospel declares, "Whoever humbles himself like [a] child is the greatest in the kingdom of heaven" (18:4). Similarly, James 4:6 says, "God opposes the proud but gives grace to the humble." Finally, the apostle whom Jesus called the rock admonishes, "Clothe yourselves with humility toward one another" (1 Peter 5:5).

Our Lord is unimpressed by our parading. So are other people.

These three o's—oblivious, obnoxious, ostentatious—must be eradicated from our personality no matter how deeply rooted they are.

2. An Inch at a Time

Bridge building requires more than placing six or eight massive beams across a river, along with a few side rails. Instead, there are millions of tiny parts—swivels, bolts, screws, metal slats. A good bridge is built by workers persistently connecting these small parts in a skillful manner.

Christian bridge construction must be just as deliberate and painstaking, done bit by bit with small acts of kindness and thoughtfulness.

I'm reminded of an incident that takes place regularly on a Philadelphia toll bridge. My friend, Anthony Campolo, crosses this bridge often.

If you have heard him speak or have read his books, you won't be surprised by a small act of kindness that he frequently renders.

When he pulls up to the collection booth to pay his toll, he invariably pays for the car behind him. It brings a little ray of sunshine to the other driver, raising by a fraction his confidence in mankind.

As he pulls away, Tony particularly enjoys seeing the toll receiver explain what has occurred to the recipient. It is a major production.

My point is this: We do our most effective bridge building in small increments, little acts of kindness, natural outgrowths of our love for Jesus and those for whom he died. With no glory or expected return.

Though seemingly insignificant, such acts combine to have a powerful effect, like the tiny snowflakes that melt together to form gushing mountain streams.

Bonaro Overstreet restates this important principle in verse:

> You say the little efforts that I make will do no good:
> They never will prevail; to tip the hovering scales,
>   where justice hangs in balance.
> I don't think I ever thought they would.
> But I am prejudiced beyond debate, in favor of my
>   right to choose which side will feel the stubborn
>   ounces of my weight.[3]

Jesus instructs us to not minimize our "ounces." Small gestures of kindness have great significance, even the giving of a cup of cold water.

> And if anyone gives even a cup of cold water to one of these little ones because he is my disciple, I tell you the truth, he will certainly not lose his reward (Matt. 10:42).

Relationships—the kind that are the most fulfilling and enduring—are constructed gradually. One smile here. A toll fee paid there. One sincere compliment here. A cup of cold water there. It all adds up. Not only that, it is multiplied by him just as the loaves and fishes were on two separate occasions.

Every morning we should ask, "What small gesture of kindness can I express to someone before this day is over?" In the Lord's eyes, it could be the most important event of the day.

Well, eventually the bridge is completed. The blueprints, tools, and excess materials are removed. In come the cleaners to make it shine. Bands, city officials, and crowds of onlookers gather to celebrate. Vehicles line up to be the first to cross.

---

3. Bonaro Overstreet, "Hands Laid Upon the Win" (source unknown).

We take a deep breath and say to ourselves, "At last, all of our labor is finished. We can enjoy what we have constructed forever. No more work!"

Right? Wrong. After building, we are only ready for the second essential task.

Task Number Two:
Maintaining the Bridges We Have Built

I must be naive. It seemed to me that after a bridge like the Golden Gate was completed and painted, that was that. Then someone clued me in.

An army of painters never stops painting. They start at one end, and continue until they reach the other end. Then they start over again. This has continued since the bridge's conception.

If they would stop their work, the salty ocean air would cause harmful corrosion. In a very short time the bridge would become unsafe as well as unattractive.

Like this paint crew, we must continually work at refurbishing and reinforcing the bridges we've built. Otherwise, they are likely to collapse. And this is true even for the bridges that we consider to be the most resilient. Allow me to illustrate.

I attended a Christian college on the West Coast. During those four years, some very sturdy bridges were built between me and my classmates. We were close. Even intimate. When we parted on graduation day, it seemed as though our bridges would remain firmly intact in spite of our separation.

Well, a few days ago Cherry and I attended my class reunion. It was an eerie feeling to walk into a roomful of strangers who were supposed to be close friends. We all had to wear name tags. Not only were names difficult to remember, but we looked much different.

What had occurred? To put it simply, we had neglected to maintain our bridges. Life's other priorities had intruded, causing us to relegate our relationships to the back burner.

Here's the good news. Our three-hour event was more than worthwhile. After becoming reacquainted, it was only a matter of minutes before we began to rekindle our relationships. As we laughed about old pranks (such as when "those other guys" somehow placed a sports car in the library) and requested prayers for special needs, we established a facsimile of old times. People relaxed. Communication became easy and fun. We had given the old bridges a fresh, new paint job.

Furthermore, we vowed to keep those brushes moving. Plans for a newsletter, notification of addresses, and another reunion are in the works. We realize now what it takes to keep even the closest relationships intact and growing.

What should we keep in mind while attempting to maintain and continually refurbish our relationships? I'd like to make a couple of suggestions.

Cultivate Contacts Consistently

We've all heard the adage, "Absence makes the heart grow fonder." That may be true for some people, or for most people during a short period of time. But in the long run, another common saying seems to be more accurate: "Out of sight, out of mind."

In sociology, we talk about a well-researched principle that concerns basic human nature. It is called the Homans thesis, after the person who formed and publicized it widely. In essence, it states: The more people interact under conditions of equality, the more they tend to like one another.[4] According to the researcher, the opposite is also true.

---

4. Refer to George C. Homans, *The Human Group* (New York: Harcourt, Brace, 1950), pp. 111–120; also discussed in Don Martindale, *The Nature and Types of Sociological Theory* (Boston: Houghton Mifflin Company, 1960), p. 480.

Establishing contacts with others can be enjoyable. Keeping them enjoyable is also very necessary if our relationships with them are to endure.

And when we approach this issue as Christians, there is still another important dimension. Our Lord expects us to take the time and go to the trouble of maintaining the relationships he has entrusted to us. That transcends the advice of George Homans, although it is consistent with it.

All of us have a particular sphere of influence. It includes immediate family members, work associates, neighbors, clerks, or anyone with whom we have or should have built a relationship. These are the people with whom we have an "in," more than with anyone else. When we speak, they listen.[5]

By making regular, caring contacts with them we are performing essential maintenance on important bridges. As a result, not only are our relationships with them strengthened, but so are those they have with one another and with our Lord.

Contacts can be made in many ways: In person. On the telephone. Through the mail.

My wife prefers the latter. She has committed herself to the task of writing approximately ten cards and letters each week. Usually they are targeted to persons who are sick, discouraged, lonely, or bereaved. In addition, she sends plenty to say "thank you" for kindnesses that have been extended to the Johnstons. It's her very own ministry—a way of keeping in touch. A way of bringing encouragement.

Her correspondence builds bridges, or lets others know

5. The Old Testament equates what we know as our sphere of influence with the Hebrew term that means "household," of which the several generations includes a family (Gen. 12:3 KJV). The New Testament uses the Greek term *oikos* to mean "household." Included in its meaning are friends, extended family, and associates. Win Arn says, "Bridges of *oikos* were used regularly as a means to a spread the Good News." After healing the demon-possessed man, Jesus instructed him to "go home to [his *oikos*] and tell them how much the Lord [had] done for [him]" (Mark 5:19). Following the ascension, *oikos*-evangelism caused the church to flourish. See Acts 16:15, 30–34.

that they are welcome to cross those we've already constructed. She lets others know that we care and are available for further contact.

Dean Martin used to close his television show with one
statement: "Keep those cards and letters comin'." My
admonition is similar: Keep those contacts comin'.
Whether they are cards and letters, conversations,
prayers, smiles, or telephone calls. They are absolutely
essential for enhancing and strengthening relationships.

Always Advocate Acceptance

Tower Bridge in London is an impressive, beautiful
structure. It would cost millions to build today. Nevertheless, in spite of its value, everyone is allowed to use it.
Kids wearing soccer caps. Killers carrying weapons. Doctors rushing to help the sick. Drug addicts on their way to
peddle destruction. The Tower Bridge is no respecter of
persons.

In this sense, the structure is like our bridge to Jesus
Christ. He accepts us, as Reuben Welch likes to say, *as* we
are, *where* we are, *how* we are, right now! We need not
shape up our act or take a crash course in righteousness in
order to approach him. Rather, we can "come boldly unto
the throne of grace, that we may obtain mercy, and find
grace to help in time of need" (Heb. 4:16, KJV).

Like our Lord, we are to manifest an accepting spirit
toward those with whom we have built relationships.
This implies such things as

listening intently to their concerns, while empathizing
with their feelings;

refusing to judge their behavior; and,

allowing for their weaknesses, even if the latter over-
shadow their strengths.

All of this means somehow communicating to them:
"It's okay to be you. I'll allow you as a divinely created son
or daughter of God that freedom."

And what if even this kind of acceptance doesn't produce results in others? What if they refuse to cross the bridges we have constructed so skillfully and caringly?

In such cases our acceptance of them must remain intact. We must leave the structures standing and continue to maintain them, in hopes that such persons will someday choose to cross.

I know of a warm, Christian parent who invested unselfishly in a bridge to his son. Like the prodigal son, this lad refused to cross—or even to acknowledge—that the bridge existed. This was very discouraging to the parent. After having invested so much, his natural reaction was to dynamite that bridge so that the boy could never cross. Have you ever had that feeling toward someone?

Well, after much prayer and thought, my parent friend resisted this impetuous idea. With Christ's help, he vowed to leave the bridge intact.

Again, like the prodigal son, the young man came to his senses and "returned to his father's house." And when he did, he received complete acceptance. I wish this were the end of the story. Unfortunately, the boy had more lessons to learn and recrossed the same bridge to the old life.

But his father isn't about to give up. The bridge still stands and will continue to stand for the duration. My prediction is that eventually this errant fellow will cross that bridge one final time. And he will be home to stay at last.

Acceptance also means letting go. Allowing others to make their own decisions, refusing to preach or lecture, to shame or scold. Simply letting go is described in this inspirational reading by Barbara Johnson.

To let go doesn't mean to stop caring; it means I can't do it for someone else.

To let go is not to cut myself off; it's the realization that I can't control another.

To let go is not to enable, but to allow learning from natural consequences.

To let go is to admit powerlessness, which means the outcome is not in my hands.

To let go is not to try to change or blame another; I can only change myself.

To let go is not to care for, but to care about.

To let go is not to fix, but to be supportive.

To let go is not to be protective; it is to permit another to face reality.[6]

Possessiveness and acceptance are like oil and water; they don't mix. Relinquishing control is essential to cultivating our relationships.

You might be saying to yourself, "This business of building relationships sounds like a lot of work." If so, you couldn't be more right. Work to build. Work to maintain. The important question for us all is: Are we ready to join in the labor? Furnished with Christ's example, presence, blueprints, and materials, will we show up at the work site?

Absolutely! For we realize that our labor of love is exceedingly worthwhile. Recalling Paul's words, our "labor in the Lord is not in vain" (1 Cor. 15:58). Similarly, the writer to the Hebrews declares, "God. . .will not forget your work and the love you have shown him as you have helped his people" (6:10).

What is the result of our labor? Sturdy, dependable, beautiful bridges that stand tall.

But, building such impressive structures is not enough. There is another important consideration—that of destination.

It would be foolish to build a bridge beside, rather than across, a river, or to construct it to extend back to its point of origin, thereby making a continuous U turn.

6. Barbara Johnson, "Letting Go," source unknown.

Rather, these structures must be aligned with the banks. To places where people want and need to go.

Likewise, our relationship bridges must extend to a variety of important destinations. They must reach over chasms and gaps in order to establish linkage with a wide range of people. In that sense, they must be holistic and inclusive, rather than parochial and restricted.

In the section that follows, we shall closely examine the four kinds of essential destinations to which our bridges must extend.

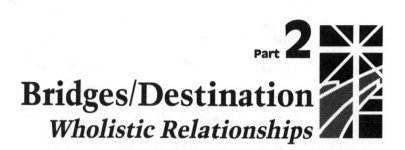

Part 2

Bridges/Destination
Wholistic Relationships

Friendship is the inexpressible comfort of feeling safe with a person, having neither to weigh thoughts nor measure words.—George Eliot

No man ever went to heaven alone; he must either find friends or make them.—John Wesley

Friendship is like money, easier made than kept.
—Samuel Butler

5

Footbridges to the Devoted

Historians inform us of an experiment that was performed by Emperor Frederick II of Prussia. It was his contention that every newborn child possesses an intuitive knowledge of Latin, "the language of the gods."

To offer proof of his bizarre notion, he isolated a large number of infants. The only human contact permitted them was during their feeding, which was done without a word spoken.

Frederick just knew that after a few months all of the babies would spontaneously speak a beautiful, untainted Latin.

Results? You guessed it. The infants began to die, until only a few remained alive, and these few had irreparable brain damage. Not one, at any time during the experiment, uttered a single syllable of Latin!

Why had the experiment failed? Because the emperor's theory was ludicrous. Why did the babies perish? Because they were deprived of necessary, nurturing relationships during these crucial, formative days.

We might have expected such a tragic ending. After all, these were newborn infants. But most of us are adults. Are we, too, dependent on nurturing contacts with others? Absolutely.

We all have a desperate need to hear comforting voices. To feel the warm touch of others. To sense their uplifting spirits of camaraderie. In short, we need to receive and give "strokes."

Of course, the main suppliers of such life-sustaining support are those who are devoted to us—our friends, family members, work associates, leisure-time cronies, or church companions.

These are the people who are up close, the first people with whom we need to build bridges.

I cannot help thinking of the small, arched, decorative footbridges I saw in Japan. In a garden there were as many as a dozen, punctuating the sculptured landscape with beauty and grace.

We all need to build footbridges that link us in true friendship with people near to us.

Let's take a closer look at the dynamics of friendship.

The True Blue Few

On the wall of the photocopier room at our university, there is a sign that reads:

> A friend is one who—
> knows you as you are,
> understands where you've been,
> accepts who you have become,
> and still gently invites you to grow.

Such persons are rare. It was Abraham Lincoln who said if we have but one true friend, we should consider ourselves wealthy.

Recently, a plethora of books on friendship has appeared. Some are best sellers. Their message is consistent: Meaningful human existence is impossible without friendship ties.

So what else is new? Of course, friends are valuable. But can we lump all we call by this term in the same bundle? Author Jerry White doesn't think so. His classification provides helpful clarification.[1]

Levels of Intimacy

Level 1 acquaintances

Level 2 casual friends

Level 3 close friends
  a) associate
  b) personal
  c) mentor

Level 4 intimate friends

Acquaintances are those ever-changing relationships that we form in the course of daily living. People we recognize, and smile or say hello to in the market. Those we interact with as they serve us, such dentists and gasoline station attendants. According to White, we are involved with 500 to 2,500 acquaintances each year.

Acquaintances constitute the pool from which we choose casual friends. These are persons we see somewhat regularly, know on a first-name basis, and meet socially on occasion. They number from twenty to one hundred, and their friendships may last from a few months to a lifetime.

Though important for social and economic reasons, casual friendships rarely satisfy our innermost social needs. They tend to be too oriented toward personal gain, and are thus too superficial.

1. See Jerry and Mary White, *Friends and Friendship: The Secrets of Drawing Closer* (Colorado Springs: Navpress, 1982), p. 30f.

But, some casual friends become close friends, who can be of three kinds:

1. associate friends: ones who emerge from mutual participation (example: those involved in a Bible study with us)
2. personal friends: ones who remain close, regardless of time lapse or distance (example: sorority sisters)
3. mentor friends: ones who have guided or taught us (example: former professor or counselor)

We have from ten to thirty active close friends, and about the same number of inactive (persons we're separated from). Concerning the inactives, it's amazing how quickly it becomes just like old times again when we see each other, no matter how long we've been apart.

A few of our close friends trickle into intimate friendships with us. Most of us have no more than four, due to the fact that they consume so much of our time, energy, and concern.[2]

To these persons we bare our souls and share our deepest needs and hopes. We enjoy their presence immensely, even when they criticize us.

In fact, some of us seek their sometimes painful analysis of our ideas and performance. We feel that they've earned the right to "fire away." Also, we know that they will be honest and have our best interests at heart. Furthermore, they're likely to be open to our critique of them.

We all need buddies. Best friends who are available when we need them and with whom we can have helpful and healthy interchange.

In summary, most of us relate to people on these four levels of intimacy, with the result that we receive and

2. Ibid.

give varying degrees of companionship, trust, and acceptance.[3]

But Christians' friendships provide another benefit. They draw us closer to the master. Our linkages with brothers and sisters in Christ help us to do such things as resist temptation, maintain spiritual perspective, be accountable, and receive encouragement and uplift.

Jesus generously supplies us with "spiritual kin" who possess compassionate hearts. Because he lives within us, we have a unity that surpasses anything this world can exhibit. An authentic, Christ-centered fellowship. The kind that makes our lives a fulfilling ministry.

But some of us are saying, "That certainly doesn't describe the people at my church. They are pretty vicious."

Granted. What we have portrayed is the biblical ideal. It is true that church environments can become war zones rather than havens of tranquility. Why is this so?

Doves or Bantam Roosters?

dove (duv), n.: bird resembling small pigeon; symbol of peace and gentleness; person who advocates peace.

---

3. According to the Bible, friends bring out the best in us. Specifically, they do this by providing us with: (1) emotional encouragement. "Perfume and incense bring joy to the heart, and the pleasantness of one's friend springs from his earnest counsel" (Prov. 27:9). (2) help in trouble. "A friend loves at all times, and a brother is born for adversity" (Prov. 17:17). (3) personal stability. Without friends we are rootless for they keep us from self-centered wanderings and rash decisions. (4) spiritual help and counsel. "As iron sharpens iron, so one man sharpens another" (Prov. 27:17). (5) freedom of expression. Friends encourage us to speak openly and freely without fear of being condemned, even if our ideas lack a logical basis. (6) protection from isolation. Without friends we turn inward as we grow older. With friends, we're forced to communicate, to be committed, and to be held accountable. (7) love and acceptance. We need to be loved for who we are, not just wanted for what we do or might do. "Faithful are the wounds of a friend; profuse are the kisses of an enemy" (Prov. 27:6, RSV). (8) opportunities to give. To be a friend to our friends, we must contribute. And that meets another basic need of our lives.

Ibid, pp. 33–42; 45–47. Also, on p. 30 the author portrays the constituent parts of the arch of friendship: (1) foundation: personal relationship with Jesus Christ (2) supporting columns: time and effort (3) connecting stones in arch: love, deep sharing, self-sacrifices, encouragement, stimulation, spiritual challenge, loyalty, and fun.

See also Alan Loy McGinnis, *The Friendship Factor: How to Get Closer to the People You Care For* (Minneapolis: Augsburg Publishing House, 1979).

bantam (ban'tom), n.: chicken of a very small size; small quarrelsome person.[4]

Most of us think of God's house as a retreat where we can come to find rest for our souls. People there are peaceful—a virtual nest of doves.

But, as admitted above, churches can become battle-grounds. People can engage in such warfare as refusing to speak, indulging in slander, giving backhanded compliments, and threatening legal action.

Often such childish behavior results in church splits (or prunings). One rapidly growing denomination attributes its expansion to this fight-split-begin-new-church pattern. Not exactly the New Testament ideal!

The question is "Why?" Why do such attitudes and behaviors surface in the hallowed precincts of our churches?

Our situation may not be as bad as it seems, especially when compared with secular institutions. It just *seems* worse for two reasons.

1. Nonchurch people expect more from us who make great claims. They squint their eyes to locate any flaw. When found, it is blown out of proportion so they can say, "See there, we're really not so bad in comparison."

2. In addition, we expect and demand more from one another than outsiders do. As a result, we're quick to condemn our brothers and sisters when they manifest the slightest weakness.

Now, the first of these is self-explanatory. But concerning the second, allow me to elaborate.

When we become Christians, we become truly new. 2 Corinthians 5:17 (KJV) says, "All things are become

4. *The Random House Dictionary*, ed. Jeff Stein (New York: Ballantine Books, 1980), "bantam," p. 69; "dove," p. 273.

new." In what ways do we become new? And how exactly, do these newnesses affect our relationships with one another?

First, we have a new aim. Prior to becoming Christians, we desired to fit into and conform with our world. Our invisible antennas constantly tested the winds of opinion. Once we determined what "they" were doing and thinking, sheeplike we marched in the same direction.

After receiving Jesus into our hearts, our primary intent is to please him rather than men. We manifest a new independence from the reactions of others.

Unfortunately, the pendulum can swing too far. We can begin to disregard what our Christian brothers and sisters think. We can become very insensitive. Our attitude can become "Let the chips fall where they may. I answer only to God."

We must learn to be nonabrasive. Hebrews 12:14 says, "Make every effort to live in peace with all men."

Second, as new Christians we have a new kinship. And with that comes certain new rights.

If we are not careful, our new rights can prompt us to become presumptive, to take others for granted.

I can't help thinking about how inconsiderate we often become toward members of our biological families, doing things like turning the bathroom into a virtual swamp after showers, failing to put gasoline in the car for the next driver, or neglecting to wipe off the catsup bottle. It's these little things than can make home life pretty trying at times!

We often become inconsiderate toward our spiritual families, too. We phone in the middle of the night, drop by unannounced, request their sacrificial assistance. Or, in the church setting we do such things as whisper and write notes during the sermon, sing too loudly, throw down our bulletin in the parking lot, dominate Sunday school class discussion.

To these obnoxious facts of commission we add equally offensive acts of omission. We neglect to say thank you, refuse to answer an RSVP for a class social, fail to make a necessary hospital call.

Never should we allow ourselves to use or presume upon the lives of others, regardless of how close we feel toward them.

Third, when the newness of Jesus enters our lives, we have a new love. *Agape* love. The kind that is unconditional, sacrificial, and available to everyone. This God-sent love fills our being, and we begin to feel a closeness with others that we have never felt before.

This kind of love can make us very courageous and honest. Like so many things, that can be both good and bad. Good when courage and honesty make us open and transparent. Bad when we can become extremely blunt with one another. In fact, we can become brutally frank— which is only permissible for brutes!

However, we must be candid with one another. The writer of Proverbs says, "Faithful *are* the wounds of a friend." Better are they, says this ancient sage, than the kiss of an enemy (27:6, KJV). Nevertheless, we must learn to express honesty at appropriate times and in a sensitive, caring manner.

It is most ideal to bare our hearts to Christian friends whom we have known for some time, have mutual confidence with, and who have requested our honest reaction.

Otherwise, our advice is likely to come across as preaching, lecturing, or shaming. And these often produce feelings of guilt and resentment.

Finally, when Jesus becomes our Lord, we become subject to a new law—the law of right.

While unconverted we conformed to the laws of self-interest and pleasure seeking. This made us in many ways a law unto ourselves.

But now things are different. We strive to be guided by the principle of rightness. To paraphrase a statement made by John Gray, no longer do we do what others consider to be great; we do what we consider to be right!

However, like the other forms of newness described above, this one can be pushed to the extreme. We can develop a detective complex: Here we go, Christian Sherlock Holmeses, setting out to preserve the faith by rooting out all heresy.

This approach can become very hurtful. It is obvious that our quest for rightness must be tempered with godly wisdom and love. We are ill-advised to become judge and jury for all Christendom.[5]

To summarize, as humble followers of Christ we must cautiously accept our newness in him with gratitude.

But in so doing we must always remember to not become too independent, to not presume on the rights of others, to not exhibit brutal frankness, and to not play detective. Our prayer must be the same as Earl Lee's: "Lord, please help me to be tolerant without being compromising. Obedient without being judgmental. And honest without being unkind."

The remedy for all of these potentially threatening maladies is to grow in grace, and a key way we mature through God's grace is by investigating his Word.

What, exactly does the Bible say about the friendship bridges that we should be building with God's people?

The World's Greatest Friendship Manual

The late comedian W. C. Fields was forced to enter the hospital because of health problems. A visitor entered his room and caught him reading a Bible. Surprised, he asked, "W. C., what are you up to? Why are you reading *that* book?"

The rotund comic shot back, "I'm just looking for loopholes!"

In exploring what the Word says about equipping ourselves for friendship, we must not search for loopholes.

---

5. Taken from lecture notes of Dr. Richard Taylor. Class entitled "Doctrine of Holiness," 1966–67. Nazarene Theological Seminary.

Rather, we must be completely open to guidance. The Bible offers just that: clear, direct, understandable guidance.

What are some of the important things that God's Word tells us concerning our friendships?

Jesus: He's Numero Uno

While I was traveling through London's Hyde Park, our guide pointed to the cemetery and said, "Over there is a tombstone that reads, 'Love to my best friend, my adorable dog, who treated me far better than any of my five husbands.'"

Many dogs have been tagged with best-friend status. So have cats, horses, books, flowers, and even chocolates.

Nevertheless, as Christians we can assure ourselves of this fact: The lowly one from Galilee is, without a doubt, the best friend we can have. He's at the top of the list. That is why, with intense feeling, we sing:

> A friend of Jesus! Oh, what bliss.
> That one so vile as I.
> Should ever have a Friend like this.
> To lead me to the sky!
>
> (chorus)
> Friendship with Jesus! Fellowship divine!
> Oh, what blessed, sweet communion!
> Jesus is a Friend of mine.[6]

We don't refer to Jesus as our friend in a half-convinced or glib manner. Why? Because our claim is staked in Scripture.

The writer of Proverbs is right when he says, "There is a friend who sticks closer than a brother" (18:24). He has loved us through eternity.

In the fifteenth chapter of John's Gospel, our Lord illuminates the nature of our friendship with him.

---

6. "Friendship With Jesus," *Worship in Song* (Kansas City, MO: Lillenas Publishing Company, 1972), p. 204.

First, he shed his own blood for us. That is very significant, for, he says, "Greater love has no man than this, that he lay down his life for his friends" (v. 13).

Furthermore, he hand delivered to us the most intimate secrets of his Father. He declares, "I have called you friends, for everything that I learned from my Father I have made known to you" (v. 15).

Finally, he is straightforward in telling us how we can make our friendship with him complete. We must respond to him in complete obedience. He says, "You are my friends if you do what I command" (v. 14).

Make no mistake about it. The gift-wrapped package of friendship that Jesus delivers to our front door comes C.O.D. We're expected to pay the price, which is loving and faithful obedience (see John 14:21 and 15:10, 14).

In summary, we can have a fulfilling, abundant relationship with Jesus. He can be our closest friend. He has bridged us to God and has delivered to us his Father's commands and compassion. All we need to do is respond in obedience. And he even helps us to do that.

When Jesus truly becomes our friend, and we sense his unfathomable love and power, good things begin to happen.

For one thing, we begin seeing ourselves as someone beautiful. Why? Because we see ourselves through his eyes of love. And what do his eyes see when they look at us? Our potential for living a totally abundant life (see John 10:10)!

Here is another bonus. When we transcend the wall of just being chummy with Christ and really become his friend, we discover that we become more like him every day.

The same thing occurs with other humans with whom we are intimate. Psychologists tell us that we even begin to look alike. Facial muscle contractions are learned through imitation. In short, we learn to smile and frown like the persons we are close to. We take on their countenance as well as their ideas and attitudes.

The same thing occurs when we are close to the Savior. We begin to imitate him. What he is becomes an ever-increasing part of us. D. L. Moody, evangelist of yesteryear, put it so well: We may start our friendship with Jesus by emulating him, but as we grow closer, we will begin exemplifying him. And what a friend to exemplify!

Furthermore, our friendship with him has a dynamic, spill-over effect on our other friendships. We will begin to relate to others as he does to us, which is nothing but good.

It is to our other friendships that we now direct our attention.

Caution: Pseudo Friends at Large

Some time after Abraham Lincoln had become President, a reporter said to him, "Mr. President, your intimate childhood friends never really made anything of themselves. Some even became involved in serious trouble. With such unsavory early influences, how did you ever become President?"

Lincoln answered, "Sir, you are mistaken. These weren't my intimate friends. My closest friendships were made with Jesus Christ, Paul, Peter, Moses, and the other writers of the Bible."

Abe Lincoln chose his intimate friends carefully and wisely. So should we. Paul is emphatic when he cautions, "Do not be yoked together with unbelievers. For what do righteousness and wickedness have in common? Or what fellowship can light have with darkness" (2 Cor. 6:14)?

Scripture is telling us to avoid getting too close to persons who are not Christians, to maintain a certain measure of detachment (See 2 Corinthians 6:17–18). Certainly, avoiding courtship and marriage with them is implied. But, also, we must not be tempted to become intimately involved with them in business and leisure activities.

This may even mean burning some bridges with people we were close to prior to becoming Christians. Persons who are enslaved by a sinful lifestyle or intent on causing us to fall.

Question: If we're not supposed to be best friends with unbelievers, how can we hope to influence them to become believers? Answer: We can still meaningfully relate to such persons on a nonintimate basis.[7]

Recall the previous statement that most of us retain no more than four best friends. We are admonished to reserve those slots for Jesus and exemplary born-again Christians. Persons who will help us to grow spiritually.

Okay, it computes so far. We're to think of Jesus as our best friend, and we're well-advised to avoid becoming too close with unbelievers. But what about our Christian friends? How should we relate to them?

Our Hearts in Kindred Love

I can't help smiling to myself when hearing that contemporary Christian chorus, "Getting Used to the Family of God." We're stuck with each other. For now and for eternity. But that's not bad, for our Christian brothers and sisters are treasures of immense worth.

But this will come as no surprise: Our relationships with one another will not always be harmonious. We can truly love one another and still disagree. Paul and Barnabas did concerning whether John Mark should accompany them on their missionary journey (see Acts 15:37–40).

Our disagreements can and should eventually draw us closer together. Admittedly, this often takes time and patience.

Here's another observation. Although best friend status should be reserved for exemplary believers, all or most of our Christian friends won't be our best friends. We simply cannot accommodate that many.

7. We might refrain from doing the following with non-Christians: participate in their sinful activities, use their debase language, allow ourselves to become romantically linked with them. In attempting to reach out to sinners, often we carelessly slip into Satan's traps. Result: We become indistinguishable from those we are striving to convert.

But regardless of our degree of intimacy, as members of our Lord's family we must relate to each other in a loving and caring manner. Jesus says, "All men will know that you are my disciples, if you love one another" (John 13:35).

If we focus our attention on such love for one another, we will do two things:

Believe the best. In the Book of Titus we read, "To the pure, all things are pure" (1:15). Call it what you will— naivete, gullibility, fantasy—the fact remains that we must believe the best in our Christian brothers and sisters. That means that we'll always be willing to give one another the benefit of the doubt.

William Harley describes an invisible "love bank" that we all possess. As Christians, we continuously deposit loving actions into one another's accounts. A kind word. An earnest prayer. A needed gift. This giving occurs spontaneously as a result of Christ's presence within us.

The result is that love accumulates in our accounts. Thereafter, if we hear something that is suspicious or slanderous about one another, we draw from our stored-up reserves to cover it.[8] We say something such as, "Sorry, but I can't believe that about him. He's always been a loving and respectable person."

Of course, this does not imply that we will ignore well-documented negative evidence. It simply means that we'll be careful to not prematurely and unjustly judge.

Neglect to neglect! A few years ago a tragedy occurred along the Ohio River. The large, well-engineered bridge that links Ohio with West Virginia collapsed. Semi-trailer trucks, cars, motorcycles, and pedestrians were hurled into the deep, watery chasm below.

A thorough investigation discovered that the chief inspector had neglected to periodically examine essential parts of the structure.

---

8. See Willard Harley, *His Needs, Her Needs: How to Affair Proof Your Marriage* (Old Tappan, NJ: Fleming Revell, 1986).

No matter how strong our bridges, whether physical or relational, they will collapse if neglected.

We must never neglect the upkeep on our Christian friendship bridges. Periodic inspection tours will reveal weakness, decay, and stress points. Then we can promptly respond by making the necessary repairs. Continuous preventative maintenance is crucial.

Believe the best. Neglect to neglect. Both of these are essential ingredients in forming and building friendships. And never were they more evident than in the lives of David and Jonathan, as recorded in 1 Samuel 16–20.

From Goliath to Gilboa

Who could have predicted it? The son of a lowly sheep-herder became the best friend of the son of Israel's king.

Except for their excellent battlefield skills, they had very little in common. In fact, they might have become bitter rivals for the throne.[9]

But, instead, they became "one in spirit" (with "knit" souls, KJV). Jonathan loved David "as himself."

They made a covenant, which made them "brothers" for life. To symbolize this, Jonathan gave David some impressive gifts. His princely robe and tunic (inner garment), implying that David was now part of the royal household. Also, he offered his sword (badge of his highest honor), bow and belt (containing his purse, secrets and sacred treasures). The latter, fittingly, gave David the countenance of a respected soldier.[10]

9. "None had so much reason to dislike David as Jonathan had, because he was to put him by the crown, yet no one regards him more." *The Bethany Parallel Commentary on the Old Testament* (Minneapolis: Bethany House Publishers, 1985), p. 545. Taken from the condensed edition of *Matthew Henry's Commentary on the Whole Bible in One Volume* (1960 by Marshall, Morgan and Scott, Ltd.; 1961 by Zondervan Publishing House).

10. "Such covenants of brotherhood are frequent in the East. They are ratified by certain ceremonies, and in presence of witnesses, so that the persons covenanting will be sworn brothers for life.

"To receive any part of the dress which had been worn by a sovereign, or his eldest son and heir, is deemed, in the East, the *highest* honor which can be conferred on a subject (see Esther 6:8)." Ibid. Taken from *The Jamieson, Fausset, and Brown Commentary*.

The shepherd from Bethlehem had really cashed in. But what led to this impressive pledge of oneness? Let's set the stage.

King Saul had grievously sinned, and Samuel had denounced his sovereignty. The prophet then anointed David to become Israel's next king.

While awaiting his ascendancy to the throne, David became resident palace harpist to the tormented king. The Word declares: "Whenever the [evil] spirit from God came upon Saul, David would take his harp and play. Then relief would come to Saul; he would feel better, and the evil spirit would leave him."

Soon came threats from the Philistines and their challenge for any Israelite to fight Goliath, who was over nine feet tall. (Can you imagine his salary in the NBA, if he were alive today?)

David was delivering roasted grain and bread to his brothers on the front line when he heard Goliath's defiant shouts. Also, he saw Israel's best soldiers run away "in great fear."

This distressed him greatly. Somehow he secured permission from the king to fight this bully. His weapon was a slingshot. His ammunition was five smooth stones. In the faceoff, David yelled out his testimony: "The battle is the LORD's."

Having to use only one-fifth of his ammunition, the lad felled the giant. Then the Philistines did some running themselves. David returned a hero and had an audience with King Saul. It was just after their discussion, overheard by Jonathan, that the two boys made their friendship covenant.

"Saul's [attire] would not fit him (David), but Jonathan's did. Their bodies were of a size, a circumstance which well agreed with the suitableness of their minds. David is seen in Jonathan's clothes, that all may take notice he is a Jonathan's second self. Our Lord has thus shown his love to us, that he stripped himself to clothe us, emptied himself to enrich us; nay, he did more than Jonathan, he clothed himself with our rags, whereas Jonathan did not put on David's." Ibid. Taken from the condensed edition of *Matthew Henry's Commentary.*

So here they were. Bonded. Intimate. Totally supportive. Committed. Just as best friends are supposed to be.

We might say to ourselves, "But their covenant was
made during a time of rejoicing. They both had stars in
their eyes. Friendships flourish at such times, when
things are going well.

Good point and usually the truth. The flip side of this
statement is that when times get tough, many friendships
crumble. Did this happen in the relationship between
David and Jonathan? In a word, no.

Saul became insanely jealous of David's popularity,
especially among the women. He twice hurled his spear at
David while he was giving a harp concert. The king offered Michal, his daughter, in marriage to the young
celebrity, but for a price. He must kill one hundred Philistines. Saul's idea was to have David himself slain in the
attempt.

Neither of these attempted murders worked. The agile
boy dodged the spears and successfully completed the
military mission. He married Michal, and Saul became
even more furious. Jonathan and all court attendants were
ordered to kill David.

Hearing this, Jonathan began doing the kinds of things
that all good friends should do.

First, he warned his friend of Saul's wrath.

Second, he defended David's integrity to his father. He
"spoke well of David to Saul."

Third, after Saul calmed down and agreed to cease his
vengeant pursuance of David, Jonathan bridged between
the attackee and the attacker. He "brought him [David] to
Saul."

Unfortunately, Saul set out on another rampage upon
hearing of David's additional battlefield successes. He
attempted to "pin him [David] to the wall with his spear."

So it was back to square one. David once again fled for
his life. After stopping off to see Michal and Samuel,
David met with Jonathan. He poured out his heart. Again,
Jonathan exemplified true friendship. He listened. He

offered hope. "You are not going to die!" And he expressed a willingness to help. "Whatever you want me to do, I'll do for you."

Well, the story goes on and intensifies. Like a bloodhound, Saul continued to pursue David. Jonathan just kept on being his friend, and their friendship deepened. They "wept together" and even pledged a bonding between their descendants.

Eventually, David was forced to hide behind Philistine lines. When Saul heard this, "he no longer searched for him." The chase was over. No doubt, David was relieved. But the Scriptures tell us no more about any contacts with Jonathan. The logistics may have made it impossible for them to get together.

Nevertheless, the friendship endured. How do we know? A final battle between the house of Saul and the Philistines occurred on Mount Gilboa. Saul and Jonathan were slain. David received the news. And as expected of a good friend, he grieved deeply.

The beautiful but sad lament is recorded in 2 Samuel 1:17–27. In this moving passage, David says,

> O mountains of Gilboa,
>   may you have neither dew nor rain,
>   nor fields that yield offerings of grain.
> For there the shield of the mighty was defiled....
> I grieve for you, Jonathan my brother;
>   you were very dear to me (v. 21, 26).

Gilboa was cursed. I recently saw its rocky, barren surface. It stands there bleak and haunting.

Just as real was the intense grief that David felt for his fallen friend.

Nevertheless, he was left with many consoling memories. Memories of a friendship that was deep. And solid. And true. A friendship that stands tall as a model for our intimate relationships today.

We need friendships like David and Jonathan's. They enrich our lives as people. And as Christians.

But, we must do more than build friendship bridges. It is imperative that we establish linkage with those who do not desire us, even those who are defiant toward us. We will next explore this difficult but rewarding challenge.

I have resolved that no man shall ever lower me to the level of hatred.—Booker T. Washington

He that cannot forgive others breaks the bridge over which he must pass himself; for every man has need to be forgiven.—Lord Herbert

You know the honeymoon is over when your wife lets you lick the eggbeaters, but refuses to turn off the mixer.
        —David Davenport

6

Drawbridges to the Defiant

At San Diego's Wild Animal Park, the following sign is posted at the entrance:

Please do not!!!!!!
annoy, torment, pester, plague, molest, worry, badger, harass, heckle, persecute, irk, bullyrag, vex, disquiet, grate, beset, bother, tease, nettle, tantalize or ruffle
THE ANIMALS!

If we changed the last two words to "other people," the sign could appropriately be placed almost anywhere. On billboards. In magazines. Even in the narthexes of churches!

The simple truth is this: We're often bestial in the way we treat our fellow humans. Sometimes this is blatantly direct, but more often it is cleverly disguised.

If not the initiators of such abuse, we're likely to be the recipients of such harassment. We struggle through life. Cringing. Avoiding. Grieving.

Said another way, most of us either have interpersonal problems or we are the cause of such difficulties.

You guessed it. I'm about to suggest that we not engage in aggressive behavior, whether directly or indirectly. Paul says, "Let us therefore make every effort to do what leads to peace and to mutual edification" (Rom. 14:19).

That suggestion is probably much easier for us to comply with than my second one: We need to construct bridges to persons who defy, discourage, and even attempt to destroy us. A humorist described such people as being those who make us wish birth control could be made retroactive. Persons who serve only one useful purpose in life—to provide a terrible example. Ones who would gladly knife us in the back in order to have us arrested for concealing a weapon!

We mutter to ourselves, "Build bridges to these persons? Get serious. Who needs to be linked up with such clowns?" Answer: We do, if Jesus is our Savior.

Granted, being around such persons heightens the possibility of continual crises. But such crises need not devastate us. In the Chinese language, the word for crisis is *wei-ji*, and it has two meanings: danger and opportunity. With the Lord's help, we will focus on the second.

Excuse me, but would you help me lift this piece of steel? It's time we began building bridges to the defiant. By the way, don't expect these to be like the ornate footbridges we construct to friends. Rather, drawbridges are required, the kind the Crusaders built in the Middle Ages.

I stood on one such structure in Caesarea. It extended from the ancient castle over a deep moat. Our guide explained that it, like all drawbridges of that time, was built during an unstable, threatening period. It offered protection, for when raised, it functioned as a wall that restrained potential enemies.

A stationary bridge would have allowed invasion by providing complete access to the castle.

Again, bridges to the defiant must be drawbridges. And sometimes they must be raised. Interchange should be discontinued. Emotions are too high. Threat is too great. Things need to settle down. But, such bridges stand ready to be lowered the moment there is potential for productive and peaceful relationships.

But why must drawbridges be constructed to those in the church? How could *that* be a threatening environment?

Welcome to the Alligator Pond

As mentioned in the last chapter, even sincere and conscientious Christians can become abrasive. When they accept the new life in Christ but refuse to grow in grace, interpersonal problems can quickly develop. And when this occurs, shock waves are likely to be felt throughout the entire church body.

Unfortunately, as we all know, many church people fit this description. They're intentionally misery-makers. Human alligators. Who look threatening and behave viciously.

I prefer to term such persons "irregular people." That's better than calling them what some do: schizoids, paranoids, sickies, or weirdos.

Let's examine some of their telltale characteristics. And, perhaps, names and faces to surface in our minds.

First, irregulars usually have "selective blindness." They might be perfectly capable of seeing most people with flawless 20/20 vision. However, when peering at others, their eyesight is distorted.

One of their children might be targeted for unfair criticism, while the others are treated with great respect. Or they may unfairly criticize a Sunday school teacher, vocalist, or pastor for fictitious reasons.

When we're victims of such persons, we're at a severe disadvantage, for other people who are treated hospitably by our attacker just can't seem to empathize with our plight.

Second, in putting off and putting down certain people, irregular people make biased comparisons. They cite others who are smarter, richer, more talented or—worst of all—better. They make such comparisons in staccato regularity.

When confronted by these unfair contrasts we often panic. Some of us fight. Others of us flee. But most of us simply try harder to please.

Ironically, increased effort usually does little more than reinforce the irregular's negative stereotype of us. According to his twisted logic, our trying harder only substantiates the reality of our "problem."

I vividly recall an ordeal during my teen years. Our church youth leader seized every opportunity to make me feel badly about myself. His attempts fed into the pool of tremendous insecurities I already possessed.

In order to compensate, I began a rigorous self-improvement program. The increased effort brought results. But, my nemesis wasn't impressed in the least. In fact, he became even less receptive of me, and even refused to acknowledge my presence in public. The hurt was especially deep, because my father was the minister.

What I experienced is not unusual. Many of us have endured similar experiences. And the painful memories linger.

Third, irregular persons have a knack for possessing emotional deafness. They ebb and flow. Sometimes, they come across as open and sensitive. Then, with as much warning as a California earthquake, they become deaf to what we're saying and feeling. They pull away. Constrict. Become human walls.

It's then that we feel like screaming, "Why don't you hear me?" Also, we hear ourselves repeating messages to them over and over again. But to no avail. It isn't long before we see that we're no longer talking to living, breathing human beings. They've become stone masks.

Parent-teen conversations often take this unfortunate turn. So do discussions between persons who insist on voicing positions that they have received, warmed over, from family or friends. In both cases the result is impasse.

Fourth, irregulars almost always have serious communication problems. As someone remarked, "About the only time they open their mouths is to change feet!"

IPs love to select only the most inflammatory words from their vast arsenals. Not only that, they blurt out such verbal bullets at the most inappropriate moments.

Example. I served on a church board with someone who detested me. If I were on fire, I'm certain this person would gladly have contributed a can of gasoline.

We were interviewing a prospective senior pastor. Things were going well. The spirit was upbeat. Communication flowed. That is, until this person caught wind that I felt positive about the candidate.

Immediately, the jagged-edged questions were posed to the candidate. "Why do you have to leave the church you're from? Have you been asked to leave?" Questions that were obviously intended to put him on the defensive.

The hearts of the other board members sank in unison. The candidate stuttered a bit and then awkwardly attempted to rephrase the question. But it was futile. A tub of verbal ice water had been thrown in his face. He withdrew his name.

We've all been victimized by the misplaced, mistimed statements of aggressors. Persons who seem to have words for everything but an apology.

Fifth, irregular people are easily offended. Although they dish it out, they're unable to take it. Their oversensitivity is astounding. As someone mused, "Whenever a football team huddles, they're apt to think that the players are talking about them."

No doubt, their own aggressiveness provides irregulars with hypersensitivity. They continually fear that they might receive returns on their painful investments of ill will. Their victims are likely to retaliate.

This implies that IPs are very insecure, though most display a gruff exterior. The slightest criticisms from others cut them to the quick.

I recall knowing a church organist who was the epitome of irregularity. He demanded perfection, and targeted certain people for abuse. The latter were persons who might interfere with his Sunday performance. People shuddered in his presence.

One day our music committee met to brainstorm. A few minor improvements were suggested concerning his performance. Well, our friend came completely unglued at the hint that his area manifested any weaknesses.

Furthermore, he promptly took a walk. He wasn't about to stay around and receive such slanderous abuse. To his surprise, our church drew one big, corporate deep breath.[1]

Why are irregulars irregular? How do they arrive at that unfortunate condition?

Taxonomy of Troublemakers

Author Joyce Landorf offers a helpful classification of irregular people.

Regular Irregulars

She terms the first type "regular irregulars." These are persons who have had the misfortune of a deficient upbringing. Their parents were too restrictive or too passive, too miserly or too giving, too committed or too complacent. Somehow, there was a lack of balance.

Regular irregulars are usually not favorite children. They have sensed from earliest childhood that their parents consider them inferior. And they're reminded of this by continuous comparisons between themselves and their siblings or peers. They can shut their eyes and hear, "Why can't you be like_____?"

1. Joyce Landorf, *Irregular People* (Waco, TX: Word Books, 1982), Excerpted from Chapter 2, pp. 27–50.

This tragic form of child abuse has caused them to perpetually weep inside. And to manifest such counterproductive emotions as guilt, anger, and jealously.

Personality-defect Irregulars

The second classification is "personality-defect irregulars." These are persons who are serious misfits in society.

Such persons are everywhere, even on the campuses of universities. Students are often blunt in their assessment of such persons. Rejecting verbal subterfuge, they call them some pretty uncomplimentary names.

There are "flakes," who never follow through. Though making grandiose promises, they inevitably flake out, disappointing and infuriating all who have counted on them. Flakes do such things as stand up their dates and forget appointments with professors.

Then there are "nerds," who are awkward and absent-minded. As a result, they are unaware of others and live in their own worlds. They eat alone or with other nerds in the cafeteria, lurk around libraries or labs, and wear outdated, unpressed clothes. Their hygiene approximates that of a camel's.

Finally, my students refer to "bozos," who are known for their glaring incompetencies. When physically uncoordinated, they are called "klutzes." Bozos match their incompetence with inconsideration. They do such things as never returning library books that the rest of the class needs, and insulting their professors by closing their notebook fifteen minutes before the end of the session.

We smile at their graphic university jargon while recalling similar persons we know. These people, again, have one thing in common: They're plagued with a crippling personality defect.[2]

---

2. Seen in *The Christian Reader*, in an article entitled "Bookshorts—Condensed from the Book: Irregular People," by Joyce Landorf, p. 103.

Sociopathic Irregulars

Here is a third classification: "sociopathic irregulars." Such individuals appear to have no feeling. They are as calculating as a tax accountant. As cold as a mortician. And it doesn't seem to bother them.

They appear to need no one's assistance. They're totally self-sufficient. At least, they like to think they are.

Nevertheless, these lone rangers know how to turn on the charm. In their detached manner they're able to demonstrate great social skills in public. And the unaware are greatly impressed.

I'm reminded of Stanley the cat, who lives next door. I've tried everything I know to relate to the little iceberg. Food. "Cat talk." But nothing has worked. The feline has remained his independent self.

That is, until my sister-in-law came to visit. She brought Tiger II (Tiger I was consumed by a California coyote).

The moment she let her animal out of the car, Stanley came running. Bright eyes. Polite meows. Playful rollovers in the grass. Instant charm.

Incidentally, that was over a year ago. And since Tiger II left that day, Stanley has backslid into his former pattern. Such hypocritical behavior qualifies him to be classified as a sociopathic irregular—just like some people we all know.

Mental Irregulars

To these three types author Joyce Landorf adds a fourth: "mental irregulars." They have a form of mental illness due to genetic or stress-related causes. As a result, they are genuinely handicapped in their ability to relate in a healthy, positive manner.

Are there many of these persons in our world? Yes. It is estimated, for example, that over 60 percent of America's homeless fall into this category.

Do mental irregulars congregate in our churches? Affirmative. Why? Because there they feel most accepted. We should be honored to have them in our midst, for they provide us with an opportunity to serve Jesus. It was he who said, "...Whatever you [do] for one of the least of this brothers of mine, you [do] for me" (Matt. 25:40).

I admittedly have a soft spot in my heart for those whose mental deficiency is related to advanced aging. Problems associated with arteriosclerosis, which affects certain processes of the brain, are tragic indeed.

During the waning days of my father's life, I witnessed some of these difficulties. He began having small strokes, causing him to lose touch temporarily. He babbled. His mind wandered. He dozed off continuously. He even drove through red lights without seeing them.

But what concerned me most was his abrupt change in attitudes. He became caustic and reactive. Many things upset him greatly. I worried, and asked myself if Christians are supposed to manifest such attitudes, even in old age.

Anyone who knew Dad will tell you that he had always been upbeat and energetic. He was one to take control, to see the best in everyone and in every situation, no matter how bleak. That is why his stroke-plagued behavior was such a shock.

But after talking with a medical specialist, I understood what was occurring. It was quite normal for such a stroke syndrome to set in. The personality typically makes convulsive changes. Often for the worse.

Best of all, our Lord truly understands. So should we.

There we have four kinds of irregular people, all of whom can become very difficult for us to relate to, especially when we're close to them.

What approaches can we take? Are there any suggestions that might assist us? I believe that there are. Allow me to share a few.

The first group of tips focuses on our personal perspectives that can assist us in coping with these people. The second will zero in on specific strategies for relating to the defiant ones and irregulars.

Brushing Up Our Psyches

Difficult people are about as rare as air. They invade our jobs, shopping malls, marriages, and churches. Our particular interest is on the last of these.

But, before reflecting on irregulars that inhabit pews, let's turn our attention toward their victims. That's us. We need to be able to cope. And that has a lot to do with the perspective we choose.

Psychologist Harry Stack Sullivan refers to the need to "reframe life's" experiences, especially painful ones. The image is one of an old picture in a faded cardboard frame. It couldn't look more unappealing. But, when we place the same photograph inside a large, polished cherrywood frame, it looks like a masterpiece.

Similarly, we must take distasteful and discouraging events in our lives and put them in new "perception frames." We will then see the irregulars, who have heretofore haunted us, in a different and better light. Best of all, we'll be in control of—rather than victimized by —the perceptions of our experiences.

In creating the kinds of perceptions that will help us cope, we should keep in mind the following strategies.

First, we must put far more emphasis on the future, less on the present, and still less on the past. As Earl Lee likes to say, "It's straight ahead into life's tomorrows."

All too often we get bogged down in taking repeated "museum tours" into the past. We focus on past injustices. Past attacks. Past slights. And the longer we dwell on history's blows, the more resentful and depressed we're likely to become. Increasingly, we wish for revenge.

Again, the past must be shelved. When referring to it at all, we can rejoice in its rewards and be thankful for its valuable lessons.

In a very real sense, we should do a bit of romanticizing about past pains. I recall hearing about a lad whose father had been hung. When asked one day how his dad died, he replied, "My dad met his end when a platform on which

he was standing in the town square suddenly collapsed."
Now that's painting a rosy picture of a tragic event!

Paul encapsulates this principle in his admonition to
the church at Philippi. "Forgetting what is behind and
straining toward what is ahead, I press on toward the
goal" (Phil. 3:13b).

Church leader J. B. Chapman stated it this way: "There
are too many tomorrows for me to accept as final *any*
slight, or defeat, or failure that may come today!"[3] I say,
"Amen."

It's time to tear down the museums. To bury the
hatchets. To lay to rest past grievances.

Second, we must exchange rigidity for flexibility. The
Golden Gate Bridge was made to sway up to twenty-one
feet in either direction. If not given that latitude, it would
surely collapse when hit by the slightest ocean breeze.

Likewise, we must be willing to bend. The Apostle
from Tarsus testifies, "I have become all things to all men
so that by all possible means I might save some" (1 Cor.
9:22).

This means refusing to react in a defensive manner
when irregular people insult us. Roy Angell, author of
Holiness Alive and Well, admonishes us to "be a little
kinder, a little sweeter, a little more giving. . . than anyone has a right to expect you to be!"[4]

What should we do when receiving unfair attacks? Pass
them along to Jesus. We are only the middle persons. He
desires to receive our burdens, no matter how heavy.
Peter says, "Cast all your anxiety ["care," KJV] on him
[Jesus] because he cares for you" (1 Peter 5:7).

When irregular persons see that they're not getting to
us, they can lose their enthusiasm for launching assaults.
But, whether they do or not, flexibility will help us to
cope.

3. Bertha Munro, *Truth for Today* (Kansas City, MO: Beacon Hill Press, 1947), p. 338.
4. Roy Angell, as quoted by W. T. Purkiser in *Holiness Alive and Well* (Kansas City,
MO: Beacon Hill Press, 1973), p. 40.

Third, we must be willing to reduce our level of expectation. Often we carry around a visual image of what people should become, as well as a timetable for this to occur.

Only our Lord knows what all of us should become. We are not omniscient and should refrain from judging each other. Joaquin Miller articulates this truth.

> In men, whom men condemn as ill,
> I find so much of goodness still.
> In men whom men pronounce divine,
> I find so much of sin and blot.
> I dare not draw a line between the two,
> where God has not.[5]

We're well advised to put away our measuring instruments and chisels, and allow God to change irregular persons as he wishes when he wishes.

Furthermore, we must patiently await his time for us to construct drawbridges to the defiant. Just as no engineer would advocate building while swollen flood waters race by, so we must bide our time. The writer to the Hebrews reveals the secret. "For [we] have need of patience . . ." (10:36, KJV).

How are these three goals accomplished? Through faithful and intense prayer. When our hearts become melted and obedient, our Savior will help us to envision a glorious tomorrow. He will make us flexible and provide the gift of patient endurance. And when he does, our coping will become a cinch.

But, it's not enough to sit back and cope. We must employ Bible-based strategies for interfacing with irregular persons. What are these strategies?

---

5. Joaquin Miller, "In Men Who Condemn." Transcribed from a sermon delivered by Lamar Kincaid, at Longboat Key Chapel, Longboat Key, FL, 1973.

Warning to Irregular People: Here We Come!

Strategy number one: We must forgive.

Even though we are the innocent recipients of wrong, the first move toward healing is always ours, and it consists of total forgiveness. Ephesians 4:31–32 reads:

> Get rid of all bitterness, rage and anger, brawling and slander, along with every form of malice. Be kind and compassionate to one another, forgiving each other, just as in Christ God forgave you.

Often our forgiving will also involve asking forgiveness. First from our heavenly Father, and second from those we have wronged or thought wrongly about. Our Lord provides the procedures for the latter in Matthew's Gospel.

1. "Remember that your brother has something against you" (5:23).
2. "Leave. . . and be reconciled to your brother" (5:24).
3. "Come and offer your gift [to God]" (5.24).

The key word is "reconciled." It means "to resolve or settle." Thus, when we're at fault or share in the blame, we must do our utmost to correct the situation. For some this seems like a giant, square pill to swallow. But with the Savior's guidance, it can be a meaningful act of supreme worship.

But how about when we're completely free of fault or guilt? When irregular people have sought to mangle our psyches? To use our hearts for target practice?

Again, we must rise above the temptation to become paralytically bitter. The kind of bitterness that expresses itself in statements such as, "I've been used and abused." "Everyone's against me." "I'm being neglected, forgotten, and overlooked." "Curse it all, I'd rather be dead!"

We must break through the threatening clouds of such defeat and into the brilliant sunlight of forgiveness. David Augsberger wisely instructs us to:

1. Forgive immediately after you feel the first hurt. With time comes resentment, and it is much cheaper to pardon than to resent. Forgive before the sting begins to swell and the molehill mushrooms into a mountain. Before bitterness sets in.

2. Forgive continually. People usually mature slowly. It's often two steps forward and one step backward. Focus on their direction rather than their rate of progress. Generously forgive, as Jesus said to Peter, "not seven times, but seventy-seven times" (Matt. 18:22b).

3. Forgive finally. Forgetful forgiveness is not "a case of holy amnesia which erases the past." It is the healing which extracts the poison from the wound. So that the memory is powerless to arouse us to anger.[6]

Forgiveness restores the present, helps the future, and helps us to release the past.[7] Again, its purpose is true reconciliation. Often that occurs. But frequently it does not. At times, those involved remain apart. The drawbridge remains slightly raised, enough to disallow the flow of interchange.

6. "Does Forgiving Take Time?" in *Building Self-Esteem*, ed. Gene Van Note (Kansas City, MO: Beacon Hill, 1983), pp. 46–54. Charles Swindoll quotes Amy Carmichael's helpful statement on the need to forget: "If I say, 'Yes, I forgive, but I cannot forget,' as though the God, who twice a day washes all the sands on all the shores of all the world, could not wash such memories from my mind, then I know nothing of Calvary love." Charles R. Swindoll, *Improving Your Serve: The Art of Unselfish Living* (Waco, TX: Word Books, 1981), p. 68.

7. Author Lewis Smedes addressed Pepperdine University faculty on the subject of forgiveness. He offered these timely insights: (1) Forgiveness doesn't mean tolerating past pain, forgetting instantaneously, or excusing the offender. (2) The reasons for forgiving are: (a) The hurting of the once offended will not continue. (b) God has forgiven, and requires all offended who bear his name to forgive. (c) Forgiving releases the offended from feeling that God loves the offender less because of anything he has done or might do. (d) The principle of forgiveness makes for a better world. Ghandi: "If everyone lived by the eye-for-an-eye premise, the whole world would be blind." (3) Red Flags! (a) Don't impose forgiveness as a moral duty. Few forgive because of this reason; rather, they do so because failure to forgive causes them great misery. (b) Don't demand that people forgive too fast. It wasn't

However, when authentic reconciliation does occur, our relationships can become more intimate and valuable than we have previously experienced. Enough to permit the final strategy.[8]

Strategy number two: We will seek to "carefront."

This term was coined by Augsberger to imply "speaking the truth in love." (See Ephesians 4:15.)

Carefronting means to courageously work through our own tensions and differences while lovingly seeking the other's optimum good. It is the perfect balance of confronting and caring.

Again, carefronting is only advisable when there is a measure of reconciliation through forgiveness. But once that occurs and carefronting begins to take place, the relationship is sure to deepen. And future episodes necessitating the need for additional forgiveness become increasingly less likely. Midcourse corrections are made before any major crisis occurs. And that's the way it should be.

Carefronting involves increased doses of both honesty and love. Carefronting means saying things such as, "I love you, brother, but you're starting to get on my

---

until age seventy-three that C. S. Lewis forgave his childhood schoolmaster. God forgives in a single swoosh. We can't always expect others to do so. "God forgives wholesale, we forgive retail." (c) Don't wait for the ideal time to forgive. Some say, I'll forgive after he thoroughly repents." That is unwise. Forgive, regardless of the offender's sorrow for past wrongs or his resolutions for future improvements. (d) Don't assume that forgiveness means a "Hollywood ending." We are not required to become close friends with those we forgive. Future relationships must take care of themselves.

Professor Smedes teaches ethics at Fuller Theological Seminary. Among the books he has written is *To Forgive and Forget: Healing the Hurt We Do Not Deserve* (San Francisco; Harper & Row, 1984).

8. David Augsberger, in his book *Caring Enough to Confront*, lays down seven "before" requirements for confronting. Prior to any confrontation (or carefrontation), these foundations must be established: A context of caring must exist before confrontation; a sense of support before criticism; an experience of empathy before evaluation; a basis of trust before one risks advising; a floor of affirmation before assertiveness; a gift of understanding before disagreeing. An awareness of love sets us free to level with each other. *The Christian Reader*, op. cit., p. 105.

nerves." "I know you don't mean to hurt me, but when you refer to my past, it's like a dagger into my heart." "Your continual neglect is beginning to be a real problem for me. Can we talk and pray together?"

Augsberger stated a truth when he said "[We] grow most rapidly when supported with the arm of loving respect, than confronted with the arm of clear honesty." In other words, when we practice carefronting.[9]

From Tears to Triumph

Earlier, I referred to my visit to Caesarea. That occurred on an anthropological study trip to the Middle East and Europe. Our stated purpose was to investigate archeological sites and study existing cultures. But my unstated goal was for us to receive inspiration. We weren't disappointed in either case.

One student traveler was the daughter of a well-known television actor. In her pretrip interview, she unashamedly expressed her love for Jesus and an overwhelming desire to visit the land where he had walked. For her it would be a pilgrimage.

On the trip we seemed to enter the pages of the Bible, recounting the moving stories and allowing the Savior to speak to our hearts.

A highlight was our visit to the traditional site where Jesus delivered his Sermon on the Mount. As we sat on large rocks, gazed out on the glistening Sea of Galilee, and read the moving sermon, all of us were greatly inspired.

Shortly thereafter, the young coed felt impressed to tell me how she found the Lord. Her story vividly illustrates how Jesus can help us to transcend the most difficult situations involving defiant people.

After two decades of marriage, her famous father de-

---

9. David Augsberger, "Caring Enough to Confront," in *How to Live the Holy Life: A Down-to-Earth Look at Holiness,* ed. Stephen M. Miller, pp. 67–75.

cided to leave her mother. The children were crushed. Her mother was demolished; bitterness rushed into her being, and she became completely miserable.

This bitterness was accentuated further when the celebrity married a much younger woman, someone whose age approximated that of his own daughter. The heart of my student's mother cried out, "How could he?"

Then something wonderful occurred. Her mother accepted Christ. Instantly, everything changed for this afflicted and tormented lady.

Through him she was able to completely forgive. And when she did, all traces of resentment instantly evaporated. The joy she felt exceeded all happiness she had ever experienced. She became, quite literally, a new person.

And so, near Galilee's shores that day, this student traveler looked at me and said, "Dr. Jon, I'll bet you're wondering why I became a Christian." I replied that I would be interested to know.

She continued, "It wasn't through hearing an inspirational sermon. Nor was it because I was raised in a Christian home." Then, with a face that exuded gratitude, she declared, "It was because of what Jesus did for my mom. He picked her up off the floor and completely transformed her life!"

When defiant, irregular persons hurt us grievously, we need not throw in the towel. It's not over until it's over. The one who picked up the towel to wipe his disciples' feet can turn our horror into hope. Our torture into triumph!

Footbridges must extend to the devoted—our friends. Drawbridges must reach to the defiant—our foes.

But can there be linkages between ourselves and those who are truly different? Persons from whom we're isolated? The next chapter attempts to answer these questions.

Prejudice is the child of ignorance.—Hazlitt

Cynics build no bridges; they make no discoveries; no gaps are spanned by them . . . the onward march of Christian civilization demands an inspiration and motivation that cynicism never affords.—Paul L. McKay

Many in today's church are content to be keepers of the aquarium rather than fishers of men.

7

Causeways to the Different

Animals behave in the strangest ways!

A lioness will not hesitate to consume her own cubs if alternative food sources are not available.

Stick a knife into a horse's side, but don't expect him to make a sound. Unlike the coyote, wolf, or other predator, he does not register pain in that manner.

And how about the unique ways that male animals flirt? The bowerbird strives to build a more beautiful love nest than his competitors. The desert iguana (lizard) performs rapid, attention-getting pushups. And the stickleback fish displays his bright red chest.

Animals seem so different from us. That's why we're intrigued by their behavior.

But, we are different from one another. We Americans are repulsed by even the thought of eating horse flesh, while persons from India react similarly toward the consumption of cattle. Germans refrain from drinking water,

123

eating corn ("the food of swine"), and taking frequent baths. But, they won't hesitate to take their dogs into restaurants. We're the opposite on all counts.

As an anthropologist, I enjoy comparing cultural differences—and watching greenhorn tourists attempting to negotiate those differences. Take away pure tap water, washcloths, and toilet paper, and most American first-time travelers become extremely patriotic.

It's confession time. I must admit that I have real difficulty with international cuisine. My palate has remained embarrassingly selective. No sparrow on a stick, rat jerky, or worm burgers for me!

Case in point. On our last trip to the People's Republic of China, one of my Asian students intimidated me into eating a sea cucumber. I assumed that it must be a vegetable harvested from the ocean floor. After consuming the slithery object, Tian informed me that I had just eaten an oversized sea snail!

But, in spite of this and other equally repulsive culinary experiences, intercultural exposure has greatly enriched my life. Here are a couple reasons why.

First, it has expanded my perspective. To paraphrase anthropologist Peter Hammond, I've become increasingly "liberated from the prison of the tribal (my own people) and the intellectual tyranny of the contemporary (my own times)."[1]

I've emerged from my smug, cultural cocoon to experience God's great world.

Diverse cultures now seem like beautiful, multicolored Persian carpets. Unique. Creative. Exciting.

Second, my intercultural exposure has helped me to see myself more clearly.

1. Peter B. Hammond, *An Introduction to Cultural and Social Anthropology* (London: Macmillan Company, 1971).

Another pertinent comment by this author is, "Whatever is learned about men anywhere is ultimately relevant to understanding men everywhere" (p.25).

Different people have become mirrors that reflect who I really am.[2]

Strangers can be painfully candid. Why? Because they don't feel tied or obligated to us. When we lapse into ugly American behavior, they're likely to tell us so.

For these and many other reasons, we're encouraged to learn about others. By watching travelogues, reading anthropology books, and interacting with different persons, we can grow.

But, there is another side to this coin. Heightened awareness of cultural differences can also result in wall building. Differences are often perceived as threats. Consider what is happening in Northern Ireland, South Africa, and the Middle East.

Somehow, perceptions of our uniqueness become tangled with a powerful propensity toward prejudice. Let's see how.

Weighing Facts with Thumbs on the Scales

Theologian Martin Marty speaks of the "bigotry-brotherhood paradox." Its meaning is simple. The more intense our in-group morale, the thicker our walls. In other words, the more we like *us*, the more we detest *them*.

With this in mind, we clearly see that prejudice is like Topsy—it just grows. It is mostly unplanned, unexpected, and even unwanted. But, it doesn't hesitate to crash the party. And it usually does so in three stages:

2. Charles Horton Cooley, sociologist, coined the expression "looking-glass self." He compared other people to a mirror. We gaze into it, note how others respond to us, and as a result of their reactions we develop feelings about ourselves. That is, we gain a conception of self by reflection. The individual becomes largely what he understands his friends, acquaintances, and others with whom he interacts think he is. See Charles Horton Cooley, *Human Nature and the Social Order*, rev. ed., (New York: Schocken, 1964), chapters 5 and 6.

Stage 1   stereotyping (making a mental judgment that the different one is inferior);

Stage 2   prejudice (rejecting the different one emotionally and attitudinally;) and

Stage 3   discrimination (taking action to lash out at the different one)

Prejudice thrives in all cultures. Satan sees to that. Glynn Ross uses humor to describe prejudice. Note the underlying stereotypes.

In heaven
  the chefs are French,
  the police are English,
  the lovers are Italian,
  the mechanics are German,
  and the whole place is run by the Swiss.
In hell
  the chefs are English,
  the police are German,
  the lovers are Swiss,
  the mechanics are French,
  and the whole place is run by the Italians.[3]

Prejudice is reflected in literature. Consider these proverbs:

Italian: "The Italian is wise when he undertakes a thing; the German while he is doing it; and a Frenchman when it is over."

Arabian: "The difference between Arabs and Persians is the same as that between a date and stone."

When cultures are so prejudicial that they become obsessed with their own uniqueness, they are said to be ethnocentric. In short, they see themselves as the measur-

3. *New Times*, May 28–June 3, 1986, Glynn Ross (Artistic Director, Arizona Opera Company).

ing stick for everyone else.[4] To the degree that the others differ, they are considered to be inferior.

On the South Sea island Bali, the natives look upon American tourists with pity. Their reasoning goes something like this. We Balinese never leave our country because we love it so much. But those Americans, who wear funny looking polka dot shorts and carry big cameras, show a lot of interest in our ways. That must mean that they despise their homeland and wish that they could be us.

But that's Bali. Does ethnocentrism exist inside our churches? Yes. In fact, it flourishes.

A Divine Blunder?

Who are the widespread targets of abuse among Christians?

While eating lunch recently, someone said, "Something really concerns me. Why would a good God create

4. According to Eskimo beliefs, the first man, though made by the Great Being, was a failure, and was consequently cast aside and called *kob-lu-na*, which means "white man." But a second attempt of the Great Being resulted in the formation of a perfect man, and he was called *In-nu*, the name the Eskimo gave to themselves.

When anything foolish is done, the Chippewas use an expression which means "as stupid as a white man."

The Veddah of Ceylon have a very high opinion of themselves and regard their civilized neighbors with contempt.

When Greenlanders see a foreigner of gentle and modest manners, their usual remark is, "He is almost as well-bred as we."

Most preliterates regard their own people as "the" people, as the root of all others, and as occupying the middle of the earth. The Hottentots love to call themselves "the men of men." The Aborigines of Haiti believed that their island was the first of all things, that the sun and moon issued from one of its caverns, and men from another.

The Chinese were taught to think of themselves as being superior to all peoples. According to Japanese ideas, Nippon was the first country created and the center of the world.

The Greeks called Delphi, or rather the round stone in the Delphic temples the "navel" or the "middle point of the earth." Howard Becker and Harry Elmer Barnes, *Social Thought From Lore to Science*, Third edition, Vol. 1 (New York: Dover Publications, Incorporated, 1961), Chapter 1, pp. 3–42.

so many different kinds of people, knowing full well that our differences cause us to dislike one another?"

My immediate response was, "No way! I'm not about to allow my heavenly Father to receive the rap for our prejudice."

He created a rich variety of cultures to add beauty to his planet. His plan is for us to perceive that his creation is good, just as he confirmed that it was (Gen. 1:31).

He desires that we openly and lovingly accept all that he has created. His matchless handiwork in nature. But even more, all humanity, which is the apex of his creation.

Prejudice is Satan's invention. God's people must reject it. Emphatically. Finally.

Deep down, those of us who have accepted God's Son as our Savior understand this truth, for it is so basically biblical.

However, many of us are far from being purged of a prejudicial spirit. Even though we attend church. In a sense, we're like some of our forefathers, who "went to God's House to pray on their *knees*—but on their way home, they preyed on the *Aborigines* (Indians)!"

We sing "Holy, Holy, Holy, Lord God Almighty." At the same time, we harbor ill feelings toward those whom through his might he has created.

We send vast sums to missionaries in Africa, while neglecting to realize that there is an "Africa" on this side of the Atlantic.

When it comes to whom of our members we transgress, we're up front and consistent; We can easily pinpoint the lepers in our midst. In our minds, their spots betray them.

Lyle E. Schaller provides this list of popular undesirables. When we dispense our prejudice, they are the targets likely to receive a generous supply.

Our Targets

ethnics
(especially
blacks,
Indians,
Mexicans,
Puerto Ricans,
Koreans,
Filipinos)
people
uncomfortable
with our style
of worship or
theology
teenagers
illiterates
the very poor
drug addicts
deaf or hard-of-
hearing

mentally
retarded or ill
widows
single parents
single adults
(especially
males)
alcoholics
the extremely
shy
people who work
on Sundays
couples and
children of
interracial
marriages
visually
handicapped

persons in
wheelchairs
childless couples
divorced and
remarried
unmarried
couples living
together
non-Christians
people who dress
poorly
radical dissenters
(or extremely
creative)
lacking verbal
skills
physically
deformed[5]

To this list can be added the homeless, aged, orphans, victims of disease (e.g., AIDS), homosexuals, obese. All have one thing in common. They are different enough from the majority, who consider them to be lowly. They are the kind of people to whom Jesus offered kind and special attention.

But the question is, why do we shun the very sheep that our Lord reached out to? Let's explore two possible reasons.

First, often we fear unfamiliar persons. And our fear translates into a crippling shyness.

During the last decade, psychologist Philip Zimbardo and his Stanford University colleagues examined shyness, which they term the prisoner within.

They explain that shy persons receive continuous "in-

---

5. Lyle E. Schaller, *Assimilating New Members* (Nashville: Abingdon Press, 1978), pp. 49–50. This list is slightly modified.

ner commands from the guard self"—commands that activate inhibitions. The guard self says things such as, "If you do that (raise your hand, sing, be friendly), you'll look ridiculous. The only way to be safe is to be unseen and unheard."[6]

Result: the prisoner within meekly complies and withdraws. Hawthorne probably had shyness in mind when he penned these words:

> What other dungeon is so dark
> —as one's heart?
> What jailer so inexorable
> —as one's self?[7]

Shyness exists in epidemic proportions, and can rightfully be considered a social disease. Zimbardo found that 80 percent admit to having been shy at some point in their lives, and of these 40 percent see themselves as presently shy. Twenty-five percent disclose that for them shyness is a chronic condition.

Perhaps the best term to describe the effects of shyness is "reticence." It means an exaggerated reluctance to relate to others, especially strangers.

When forced to interact, the reticent person typically has butterflies within and blushing without. These reactions are often accompanied by painful self-consciousness, guilt, and loneliness. (If you are afflicted with shyness or are curious about it, please take the Stanford Shyness Survey in Appendix 1.)

Many of us resemble the rabbit-hole Christians whom theologian John Stott describes. Only when it's absolutely necessary do we shyly pop out of our holes, scurry to people unlike ourselves, then quickly rush back into

6. Quoted by Philip G. Zimbardo, *Shyness: What It Is, What To do About It* (New York: Jove Publications, 1977), pp. 25, 39.

7. Ibid., p. 16.

our holes again. To linger outside, we reason, is to risk great danger. We're afraid of our shadows.

Second, in addition to being fearful, we forget about the people outside our circles of security who need us. We're so caught up with our safe and familiar cronies that we wall out the others. Friends so dominate our time and energy that meaningful involvement with others is precluded.

It's so ironic. Those of us who forget about others are usually unaware of our omissions. We're basically decent people. It's not our design to hurt anyone by either intent or neglect.

But make no mistake about it, we often seem cruel to those we forget. They feel the full impact of our slights. They're emotionally broadsided when we do such things as turn our backs, refuse to have eye contact, or communicate some other you-don't-count message.

As followers of Jesus, we're to neither fear nor forget persons who differ from ourselves. Like Jesus, we must devote an inordinate amount of attention to such persons. If we in the church don't, who will?

But this requires concentration and sacrificial effort. The kind that Jesus describes in his Parable of the Good Samaritan.

Where's the "Triple A" When You Need Them?

In a very real sense, we are all expected to be Good Samaritans, and that means becoming truly neighborly to those who are not our own kind.

Let's recall Jesus' story by focusing on its principal characters.

First, there was the traveler who was obviously reckless and foolhardy. He embarked on the notoriously dangerous road from Jerusalem to Jericho.[8] Over its twenty-mile span, it drops 3,600 feet in altitude. Besides being extremely narrow and winding, it was the happy hunting ground of robbers. Nobody in their right mind would have set out on it alone. Nevertheless, this Jewish traveler did, and he was waylaid.

Enter character number two, the priest. After a quick glance at the poor man's plight, he turned into a road-runner. While streaking by, he likely remembered that anyone who touched a dead man was considered unclean for seven days (Num. 19:11). Why take the chance?

If he stopped, touched, and found the man to be dead, he must lose his turn of duty in the Temple.

Here was a man who cared more for ceremony than charity. More for liturgy than providing a loving lift!

Third, there was the Levite. The chances are that he realized that bandits often used decoys. One would act wounded; then when a good-hearted person stopped to help, the other robbers would pounce on him. Reassuring himself that his mother hadn't raised a fool, the Levite felt justified in passing by. For him, it was safety first.

Finally, down the road came the Samaritan. A hated half breed from the region of that name—a region that orthodox Jews avoided.[9]

Two important features set him apart from the other

8. William Barclay furnishes useful background on the treachery of this infamous road which still exists. It now winds around the modern highway that was constructed this century, and is hiked upon by many.

"In the fifth century Jerome tells us that it was still called 'The Red, or Bloody Way.' In the nineteenth century it was still necessary to pay safety money to the local sheiks before one could travel on it. As late as the early 1930s, H. V. Morton tells us that he was warned to get home before dark if he intended to use the road, because a certain Abu Jildah was an adept [criminal] at holding up cars and robbing travelers and tourists, and escaping to the hills before the police could arrive. When Jesus told this story, he was telling about the kind of thing that was constantly happening on this Jerusalem to Jericho road." William Barclay, *Daily Study Bible: The Gospel of Luke* (Philadelphia: The Westminster Press, 1953), p. 141.

9. Ibid., p. 143. According to Barclay, the Samaritan may have been a "racial Samaritan"—a hated half breed from the region of that name which orthodox Jews avoided. Or, he could have been someone considered ceremonially unclean. The Jews called such persons by that name. Even Jesus was so tagged. (John 8:48)

passersby. For one thing, only he was determined to assist. Notice the Luke 10:33–35 progression. He "came where the man was" (proximity), "took pity" (compassion), "bandaged his wounds, pouring on oil and wine" (crisis intervention), "took him to an inn" (donkey ambulance service), "took care of him" (nursing), gave "two silver coins...to the innkeeper" (financing short-term care), and said, "'When I return, I will reimburse you for any extra expense'" (financing long-term care).

A second noteworthy fact about the Samaritan was that his credit was good. The innkeeper placed implicit trust in his promise to pay later. He was recognized as an honest person in a day of rampant dishonesty.

Nice story. Great ending, the kind that Hollywood likes. A tale that we can hear and forget? Not quite. Scottish theologian William Barclay admonishes us to derive from it these valuable lessons:

1. People must be helped, even when they bring trouble on themselves—as the traveler did.

2. Regardless of how different from ourselves they are, people who are in need must be thought of as our closest neighbors.

3. Compassion in theory is not compassion at all. We must dispense tangible help.

After fully digesting these truths, we must vow to model our lives after the Good Samaritan. His approach to persons different from himself must become our approach. How do we know? Because our Lord said so. After concluding the parable, his words to his audience were (and are), "Go and do likewise." (v. 37)[10]

---

10. The Samaritan stopped, stooped, and stayed. Then he carried, cared for, and became committed to (leaving an open bill).

Another perspective is offered by theologian and author Ralph Earle. He contrasts the principal characters this way: *robbers*: Their approach is beat him up, and their attitude is, "What belongs to you is mine—I'll take it." *priest and Levite*: Their approach is pass him

Are there any tips for fulfilling this important mission? I think so. Allow me to suggest a few.

The World's Longest Rafts

During our last trip to Florida, some friends suggested that we all travel down to the Keys to get some key lime pie. Believe me, the pie was well worth the trip. So was the beautiful scenery. Swooping seagulls. Clear skies. Whitecaps.

Actually, the Keys resemble a string of pearls going southward off the Florida coast. They are connected by bridges called causeways. Now, these bridges are unique, for they actually float on the surface of the water. This gives them flexibility when hammered by the frequent tropical storms.

If linkages with friends are like footbridges, and linkages with foes resemble drawbridges, the bridges we build toward the persons different from us are like causeways. They are flexible, adaptive, and extend great distances.

In constructing such expansive structures toward outsiders, here are some of the things we keep in mind.

Discipling the Different

To begin, when reaching out causeway style to persons who are distinctively different from ourselves, it is important that we cease thinking hierarchically. We must reject our natural inclination to measure people and to respond to them according to our assessment of their importance.

It's time to realize that cultivating oneness necessitates our becoming unimpressed by titles, authority ladders,

---

up, and their attitude is, "What belongs to me is mine—I'll keep it." *Samaritan*: His approach is help him up, and his attitude is, "What belongs to me is yours—I'll give it."
From a lecture at Nazarene Theological Seminary, 1966.

status symbols, and awards. Listen to James' pronounce-
ment.

> My brothers, as believers in our glorious Lord Jesus Christ,
> don't show favoritism. Suppose a man comes into your
> meeting wearing a gold ring and fine clothes, and a poor
> man in shabby clothes. . . . If you show special attention to
> the man wearing fine clothes and say, "Here's a good seat
> for you," but say to the poor man, "You stand there,"
> . . . have you not discriminated among yourselves? . . . If
> you show favoritism, you sin. . . James 2:1–4, 9).

If we would only grasp how much our Lord despises all
semblances of elitism and its grotesque first cousins cro-
nyism and nepotism! To him, it matters not

how much money a person makes (i.e., giving potential);

how famous he is in the world or church;

who he is related to, that is (or once was) renowned; nor

how long he has been a Christian

Someone said it well "At the foot of the cross, all
ground is level." To Christ we are all on equal footing.
Therefore, when reaching out to different people, we
must admonish ourselves to not be respecters of persons.
Regardless of how much our church needs money, or
regardless of our craving for friends with clout.

Another suggestion. In attempting to relate to different
people, we must go beyond trying to be nice. Outsiders are
turned off by our saccharine smiles, backslaps, and glad-
handing. They don't want to be processed as persons are at
used-car lots and political rallies.

As Moishe Rosen states, "The early Christians didn't

post a slogan on a church announcement board stating, 'Come to the friendliest place in town.'"[11]

The same author assures us that God never commanded his people to be nice and congenial. He requires them to love one another, which involves "proper attitudes and unselfish acts that promote [their] best interests."[12]

Niceness isn't enough. We're to be far more than experts in public relations. Courtesy and good manners are basic requirements, but we must go beyond that. Otherwise, we're likely to only win people to ourselves and not to Jesus Christ.

Acceptance of people is more than a posture, it's a position. It's more than a smile and "an affable greeting or exchange of pleasantries." It is a commitment to be someone—something—to those who feel different and estranged. True acceptance transcends being nice to persons in an occasional social encounter; rather, it implies standing with them in the midst of their unpleasantness.

I don't know about you, but when I feel excluded, I prefer someone dour who relates to me authentically over a person who smiles and relates superficially.

My appeal is simple. We must stop trying to be merely nice, merely friendly. All such self-engineered attempts can only produce a veneer of acceptance.

Instead of *trying* to be nice, we must *be* nice—from our hearts outward. Our loving acceptance of different persons must come from the overflow of Christ's presence inside us.

Finally, when the different ones are enslaved by sin, we must help them to accept Jesus into their lives. Our primary purpose on earth, as Christians, is to make disciples for the master (see Acts 1:8). Our unprejudiced and

---

11. Moishe Rosen, "Don't Try to Be Nice," *The Jews for Jesus Newsletter*, Vol. 10:5745
12. Ibid.

complete acceptance of them is not enough. Our relationship must draw others to him.

Are there practical strategies for leading such people to the Lord? Yes. They are offered by Win and Charles Arn in their book *The Master's Plan for Making Disciples*. Here is a summary of their useful suggestions.

1. Cease being timid. Boldly venture out from behind the wall of fear and risk failure for Jesus.

2. Make God's top priority—soul winning—your own. Make this your favorite hobby, and give it generous amounts of time and energy.

3. Become increasingly reliant on and sensitive to the Holy Spirit. As your comforter and guide, he will use your words to convict others of sin.

4. Know your Bible. To spread the Word, you must thoroughly grasp what it says and means.

5. Join with others who share your burden for the lost. A support group provides needed accountability, courage, faith, and honest feedback.

6. Learn the dynamics of effectively relating in all environments to all kinds of people. No matter what your temperament is, grasp principles that will allow you and God to penetrate walls of resistance.

7. Expand your sphere of influence. Go beyond family, neighbors, and friends—though the latter must not be neglected.

8. Meet more than spiritual needs. Every non-Christian has a "handle of interest" and a "handle of need." By relating to the former, or giving support to the latter, people become more open to the good news of salvation.[13]

13. Win Arn and Charles Arn, *The Master's Plan for Making Disciples* (Kansas City, MO: Beacon Hill Press, 1982), pp. 14–30.

Forget thinking in terms of hierarchies. Accept all persons on equal footing. They have nothing to prove to Jesus, why should they to us? So, go far beyond superficial niceness. Express a congeniality that overflows from a pure, Spirit-filled heart.

But, most important, we must allow Jesus to help us to lead those who are outside of the ark of salvation to a saving assurance of sins forgiven. He can make every one of us soul winners. And he can begin to do it immediately.

It's Up and Over!

Father Damian. Does the name mean anything to you? It didn't to me until I heard his gripping story.

Many years ago, leprosy was common in the Hawaiian Islands. Victims of this dreaded, deadly contagious disease were quarantined on Hawaii's island Molokai. Isolated. Alone to suffer. Without hope.

Then, our faithful Savior tapped a lowly Catholic priest, Father Damian, to minister to his leprous sheep. Father Damian obeyed.

From outside the walls of their encampment, the loving minister called out words of encouragement and hope. The people listened intently, but they remained quite detached. Words are cheap when they come from non-sufferer to sufferer. And Father Damian, as none other, realized this fact.

His burden weighed more heavily each day. He prayed that he might somehow get through to these estranged people. Then, our Lord heard and provided him with an answer. An answer that he least expected but willingly accepted.

One Sunday morning the good priest addressed his suffering congregation. But this time it was different. No longer did a wall separate him from the lepers, for he had entered their compound.

His captivating words rang out that day. Words that have been etched on my mind since I first heard them

"My friends, before, I have always begun my sermon by addressing you as *you* lepers. This morning I say *we* lepers."

Father Damian paid the ultimate sacrifice to reach Molokai's perishing lepers. He intimately identified with their plight. As we might expect, the sufferers were profoundly moved by this identification. And they began to dramatically respond to the good news that he preached. A genuine spiritual renewal took place in that compound.

It all happened because a dedicated priest built a causeway of love to some desperate, different people. Even though eventually it cost him his life.

As with the devoted and the defiant, we must lovingly link ourselves with the different.

Challenging? Absolutely. But, with God's power fueling our energies and inspiring our hearts, we can meet the challenge.

There is still one last kind of bridge we must construct. This one is to the distant or indifferent.

For many of us, this is the most difficult of all to build. It will require our best endeavors, together with the best that God can give us.

The seven last words of the church are, "We never did it that way before."

The grave itself is but a covered bridge
Leading from light to light, through a brief darkness.
> —Henry Wadsworth Longfellow "A Covered Bridge at Lucern"

At age twenty we worry about what others think of us; at forty we don't care what others think of us; at sixty we discover that others haven't been thinking of us at all!

8

Covered Bridges to the Distant

This tongue-in-cheek notice may not strike all of us as humorous. Only those of us who have been employed at such places as I have.

Notice to All Employees

It has come to the attention of the management that employees have been dying on the job and either refusing or neglecting to keel over. This practice must stop. Any employee found dead on the job, either in an upright or prone position, will immediately be dropped from the payroll.

In the future, if a supervisor notices that any employee has made no movement for a period of two hours, it will be his duty to investigate. As it is almost impossible to distinguish between death and the natural movement of some employees, supervisors are cautioned to make a careful investigation.

140

Holding a paycheck in front of the suspected employee is generally considered an authentic test,
but there have been cases reported where the natural instinct has been so deeply embedded that the
hand of the employee has made a spasmodic clutch
even after rigor mortis has set in.

The Management.[1]

We have all sorts of names for this malady: apathy,
listlessness, halfheartedness, detachment, turned off.

When the malady is job-related, our work becomes
sheer duty. Someone defined "duty" as "what we look
forward to with distaste, do with reluctance, and boast
about forever after." Duty implies boredom. A grind. A
slow burn. An absence of enthusiasm.

When the same spirit of detachment characterizes relationships with other persons, it is even more tragic. We
then feel alienated. Alone. Distant. And this feeling can
be even more prevalent when we're in a crowd. Every
person who pushes or bumps into us only reinforces our
dispirited attitudes.

Distancing ourselves from others can occur in two
ways. First, we can push off and become isolated. This
implies physically separating ourselves from others. We,
quite literally, become "islands" surrounded by tall, thick
walls.

Such is the plight of American Indians who reside on
reservations. When first placed there, they made awkward attempts to escape and recapture what they had lost,
only to face impenetrable walls of rejection.

Now, scores of them have rediscovered the value of
their uniqueness. An about-face has occurred. They've
built some formidable walls of their own. Recently, one
chief vividly expressed this strong sentiment: "White

---

1. Seen on a plaque produced by Ogunquit Corporation, Costa Mesa, California.

man, the fences that you built to *keep us in* are now intended to *keep you out!*"[2] (ital. mine)

A second way that we unplug ourselves from the electrical current of social involvement is by becoming insulated. By becoming immune and oblivious. Numbed and desensitized.

This usually occurs gradually. We scarcely recognize that we're pulling away, for we may very well remain physically close.

A classic experiment in biology class comes to mind. The professor places a twisting, wiggling frog into a glass container filled with water. The amphibious creature glides through the water with ease and obvious delight.

Then, a Bunsen burner is placed under the small tank. The fire is lit, but only the smallest possible flame is exposed. The cold water ever-so-gradually gets warmer. But our little green friend never notices that this is taking place.

A few hours later the experiment is all over. The frog has been cooked. No struggle. No splashing. No attempts to escape.

When we gradually insulate ourselves from others we, likewise, can become desensitized. We're decreasingly aware of the slow death that is beginning to paralyze our relationships.

Wives, children, and church friends may become alarmed and warn us.

We assure them that we haven't noticed anything, saying, "Relax. Don't worry. Things are fine." Meanwhile, our circulation continues to ebb as we cook.

2. The term revitalization, coined by A. F. C. Wallace, is frequently applied to such radical responses. Such brash reactions are a means of coping with tension experienced by members of simple, small-scale cultures when contacts with technologically more advanced ones threaten their traditional way of life. It's a way of saying, "We have value." Such responses or movements, which are intended to achieve an ideologically effective response to rapidly shifting or discouraging circumstances, are also described as "nativistic," "messianic," or "millenarian." Examples are the ghost dance of the Plains Indians; Cargo Cults of the South Pacific.

See Peter B. Hammond, *An Introduction to Cultural and Social Anthropology* (New York: Macmillan Company, 1971), p. 272.

The point is clear: Isolation and insulation are real killers.

Therefore we Christian bridge builders first of all must consciously avoid cutting ourselves off from others. God made us all to be social persons—regardless of our temperaments or natural inclinations. Without meaningful relationships, everyone's psyches would shrivel.

Second, with desire and skill we must build bridges to persons who have pushed away from us. And we must do it even if they resist.

It is important to remember that distant persons are usually unaware of their pitiful and terminal conditions. Like the frog, they're becoming desensitized by degrees. Thus, even if they rebuff us, we must continue to reach out to them in love. Edwin Markham captures this perspective in his poem entitled "Outwitted."

> He drew a circle that shut me out—
> Heretic, rebel, a thing to flout;
> But Love and I had the wit to win:
> We drew a circle that took him in![3]

Bridge Beauty-Contest Winner

As you've probably guessed, the imagery of another bridge invades my consciousness. Allow me to share it.

Line them up. All the bridges we've described, plus any others we can think of. In my view, none is more picturesque or romantic than the classic covered bridge. But don't take only my word for it. Ask anyone in New England, where such structures dot the landscape.

Ask the air force pilots who flew in World War II. In addition to locating and bombing the elusive enemy, they were commanded to avoid dropping explosives on the centuries-old covered bridges of Europe.

3. *An Anthology of American Poetry*, ed. Alfred Kreymborg (New York: Tudor Publishing Company, 1930), p. 214.

Case in point. The famous Ponte Vecchio Bridge of Florence, Italy, majestically spans the Arno River. It is lined with quaint, old-world shops—and is a camera buff's delight. All other bridges in the area were hit, but this piece of history was declared off limits. In the midst of the fire and rubble, it remained completely unscathed.[4]

Then there is my favorite covered bridge. It is the rustic Chapel Bridge, located in Lucerne, Switzerland. Constructed in 1333 over the Reuss River, it was meant to fortify the city. Gables overhead feature paintings by the seventeenth-century artist Heinrich Wagmann depicting the city's history. A multitude of swans glide through the waters below.[5]

We say to ourselves, "Granted, covered bridges are beautiful. But what is their connection with the kind of relationships that link us with people who are distant?"

Well, to most of us, covered bridges suggest a feeling of warmth and friendliness. When we enter them, in our cars or on foot, we seem to be drawn together in a snug environment of intimacy. The darkness and close quarters seem to enwrap us together in a place of concealment and protection. Covered bridges are like proverbial tunnels of love.[6]

4. The Ponte Vecchio's history extends back to the era that preceded Christ's birth. When Emperor Hadrian repaired the Via Cassia (Road to Rome) in A.D. 1200, the bridge was given a masonry and wood edifice. From that time on, it witnessed the steps of legionnaires and the roll of farmers' and merchants' carts as they brought goods to the city.

In 1333 there was a great flood that destroyed the bridge. It was again intact by 1345. In its rebuilt state, it was conceived as a street with two rows of houses along its sides. (This was never thought of before nor seen afterwards.) Then, the bridge turned into a meat market during the sixteenth century. The shopkeepers built rooms that extended over the river. Finally, the goldsmiths moved in offering some of the finest jewelry in the world. Today it still has shops on both sides of a walkway.

The world-famous structure was studiously avoided during the bombing raids of the Allied Forces in World War II. Piero Bargellini, *This is Florence* (Florence: G. C. Sansoni Editore Nuovo S. P. A., 1977).

5. At the bridge's midpoint is a stone, octagonal-shaped water tower. This has served as a defense post, dungeon, and a place to store archives throughout the centuries.

6. But not all covered bridges connote such positive feelings. North of Rome is Venice, the "City of Canals" and home of the famous covered Bridge of Sighs. It is an ornate, concrete transept that connects two ancient buildings, Doge's Palace and the State Prison. Built by Antoni Contoni in the 1500s and described in Lord Byron's "Childe Harold's

In reaching out to isolated and insulated persons, these are the very feelings that we must communicate so that they sense our warmth, closeness, and desire for intimacy. From us they must pick up definite cues that we consider them to be very special.

Furthermore, in communicating this private "care bear" message, we must in a very real sense shut out the noise of the outside world. It must be just us and them. Alone. Together. Intimate.

Such intense feelings and focused attention can do wonders for even the most emotionally immobilized persons. Their numbness can begin to vanish, their spirits start to kindle. Just as they gradually became emotional zombies, they can gradually become real, live, pulsating persons again. In short, they can be liberated from the lonely prison walls that they have constructed.

But, before we attempt such noble and empathetic ventures, it is crucial that we understand how such persons became victims. Allow me to suggest some possible answers.

The Desensitizers

The kind of emotional numbness that overtakes those of us who become distant and indifferent usually begins with our perceived threat of pain.

We protect ourselves by withdrawing. It's the old if-you-can't-fight-it-flee-it syndrome. And our constricture leads to desensitization.

Pilgrimage," this structure contains two passages. Through one, the accused went to trial. Through the other, the condemned went to their execution.

How did the bridge get its unusual name? It is said that prisoners en route to their deaths would pause on it, have one last look at their beloved city, take a deep sigh, and then move on to the inevitable.

So venerated is this bridge that replicas of it exist at Cambridge University in England, as well as in New York City. In the latter location, it connects Tombs Prison and what was formerly the criminal courts. Prisoners once used this passageway "in order to avoid [the gazes and comments of] street pedestrians." See "Bridge of Sighs," *The World Book Encyclopedia*, Wm. Nault, ed. (Chicago: World Books, Inc., 1987).

Modern society pushes us to retreat. How? By overloading us with stressful experiences.

Many of us receive more stimulation than we can adequately process. Our minds and emotions can't keep up. We buzz-out. Social psychologists term this phenomenon "psychic overload."

Our constitutions can only take so much stress. Beyond that point, a deterioration of emotional and/or physical health is likely to occur.

Furthermore, our relationships are apt to suffer. This is why persons contracting debilitating illnesses often get divorces. Why parents who lose a child frequently turn on each other. Inordinate amounts of stress cause us to search for scapegoats.

T. H. Holmes and R. H. Rahe have rated stress events according to their impact on our well-being. Their assessment of the impact of the top ten (of forty-three) stressful life events looks like this:

Rank	Life Event	Life Change Unit Value (note: maximum stress = 100)
1	Death of a spouse	100
2	Divorce	73
3	Marital separation	65
4	Jail term	63
5	Death of a close family member	63
6	Personal injury or illness	53
7	Marriage	50
8	Fired from job	47
9	Marital reconciliation	45
10	Retirement	45[7]

7. Irving Wallace, *The Book of Lists #2* (New York: Bantam Books, 1980), pp. 362–363.

(For the complete list of forty-three "Life Events" see Appendix 2, and for lists of "Highest and Lowest Pressure Jobs in the U.S.A." see Appendix 3.)

Again, when our coping mechanism malfunctions because of such stress-related overload, we're likely to give up. At such times, the words of Jesus become the grand oasis in our bleak desert. "Come to me, all you who are weary and burdened, and I will give you rest" (Matt. 11:28).

In addition to overwhelming stress, we're desensitized by two activities that consume much of our time. What are they?

First, watching our televisions. The desensitizing effects of television overdose are undeniable.

Television has the advantage of being edited. Therefore, it is nearly flawless in its production. If we are not careful, its quality can prompt us to expect near perfection from persons we encounter.

Also, television can engender impatience. Its programming is rapid fire. Its delivery is immediate. We're conditioned to expect to be constantly entertained. Result: We begin to expect instant everything. The word *wait* is deleted from our vocabulary.

But, most important of all, television has had a hardening effect on our minds and emotions. We have come to fear little and grieve even less.

When movies were first made, some persons would faint at the sight of an oncoming train. By contrast, today's children clamor for monster-thrillers, and parents barely wince at the tragic events shown on the evening news.

Television desensitizes. Thus, it lessens our compassion and dulls our willingness to reach out in love.

Another modern desensitizing activity is driving our cars.

Jesus walked. Even at his steady gait he could only hope to travel thirty miles per day. By contrast, we blitz down the highway, unless we enter the halo zone of a police car.

When Jesus walked, people could and did have meaningful encounters with him. He was approachable.

People can't possibly approach us when we are strapped
in our multihorsepowered chariots of fire. We rush by
them—even those who are beside the road in distress—
like the priest and Levite of old.

Here's something else. Our automobiles have allowed
us to live in suburbia, away from the decadent inner city
with its masses of undesirables. To us, those other persons don't really exist.

Stress overload. Television. Cars. They combine to
numb us, so that we no longer truly feel for our distant
fellow man.

We must break through these walls. There must be an
encounter—so that our lives interface with the indifferent.

This must take place in the world, but even more so in
our churches. There, it should be impossible for us to
remain distant. Circles must be drawn "to take us in."

But who are we talking about? To which of us should
our churches devote special, concentrated attention?
Let's focus on two distant-prone groups. The first is insulated, and the second is isolated.

Singles: Going It Alone

One fifth of all families in America have single parents,
and that's an 80 percent increase in the past ten years.
One-half of all children born today can expect to live with
only one parent.

Stereotypes of singles are that they typically manifest
these undesirable characteristics: hostility toward marriage and the opposite sex, homosexual tendencies, unat-
tractiveness, fixation on parents, physical disability,
inability to attract a mate, extreme loneliness. The con-

clusion: To think that singlehood leads to happiness is to be deluded.[8]

Unfortunately, our churches have accepted this negative stereotype as much as anyone. While businesses see singles as goldmines, our religious enclaves picture them as pariahs or victimized unfortunates.[9] In addition, we Christians characteristically consider the nuclear family (dad, mom, and the children) as God-ordained and sacrosanct.

To compensate for this glaring and blatant intimidation of singles, some Christians have attempted to minister to them. Creative programs and sensitive materials have emerged. We should applaud and support such efforts.[10] Not only that, we must support them.

8. Considering their rapidly growing numbers, it is surprising that sociology and psychology has not produced a plethora of books on singles. Most likely, the reason is this: They are perceived as being in transition—on their way to being remarried or (if aged) deceased. As Carolyn Koons states, "Sociology and psychology must wake up and do serious research on the singles phenomenon, for it is here to stay!" See Robert White, *Going It Alone: The Family Life and Social Situations* (New York: Basic, 1981)

9. The world of business realizes that singles are responsible for its largest single pool of sales. In short, singles make or break products. For this reason, business does all it can to relate to this booming market. Commercials depict young, attractive, free-spirited, athletic persons. Appliances are geared to singles: single burners for weiners ("The Hot Dogger") and coffee ("Mr. Coffee"); one-person refrigerators, washers and dryers. Automobiles are made much smaller, with youthful styling. Footwear is made to appeal to the recreationally-minded singles. Real estate favors condo living, which is best suited for this affluent group. (Information extracted from a recent lecture by Carolyn Koons.)

10. Author Harold Ivan Smith leads an organization called Tear Catchers, which ministers to persons who have experienced divorce. Multitudes of similar programs exist, especially in large churches, for those who never married, who possess homosexual tendencies, whose spouses are deceased, etc.

Most of these programs, like Tear Catchers, are commendable. But I have some real problems with others. First, some cultivate a hedonistic world view. Enjoyment is their only purpose. There is more to Christian singledom than ski trips and swimming parties. Singles must have fun, but more important, they must become involved in helping-hand ministries. They must become givers far more than takers.

Secondly, singles' programs often over emphasize the value of being single. This is unfortunate. Granted, singles must rid themselves of inferiority complexes, but *not* by becoming egotistical. Elton Trueblood spoke the truth when he once said to me, "There is a real danger in giving undue emphasis to our own uniqueness."

Finally, some programs engender isolation and insulation from the church body. Separateness breeds loneliness, defeating idiosyncrasies, and inability to relate in an effective manner. Christian singles must refuse to become "groupies." To do so is to be considered odd by others, who draw conclusions with the only information accessible to them.

Singles specialist Carolyn Koons offers people in local churches ten outstanding suggestions for ministering to these persons whose natural inclination is to become distant and uninvolved.

1. No more band-aid ministry to singles. They are broken, and we must freely and generously offer hope.

2. This isn't just another specialized ministry like caring for the handicapped. Singles must be perceived as and incorporated into the church body.

3. We must redefine our concept of family. In addition to nuclear, there are extended, expanded, blended, single, etc. We must accept all types equally.

4. Barriers that separate marrieds from singles must be smashed. Don't separate them physically or programmatically.

5. Forget about overseeing singles. There's no need for insulting chaperones, or a chaperone mentality.

6. Encourage singles to become leaders in our churches. This sends the right signals to the congregation, and affirms other singles.

7. Let's make our churches places of refuge for singles. For their tough times, we must offer them a loving support group.

8. Emphasize the New Testament concept of community. Play down differences and uniqueness—accentuate our oneness in Christ.

9. We must become equippers rather than directors. Singles chafe under the direction of benevolent dic-

---

It is imperative that singles work into the mainstream of the church. This implies involvement with everyone. Forget about homogeneous enclaves, regardless of what church growth theorists say. The New Testament model is one of heterogeneity, different kinds of people forming a loving community, where authentic fellowship exists, all because they have the most binding thing in common—their oneness in Christ!

tators. They need to be taught to minister to one another as leaders (responsible for themselves) and healers (ministering to mutual hurts).

10. Most important, our singles programs must have spiritual power and depth. To go on a binge of fun-type activities is to encourage shallowness. Prayer retreats and compassionate projects, by contrast, build spiritual muscle.[11]

It's tough to go it alone. No singles in our churches should have to do so if the rest of us are being the kind of disciples that Jesus expects us to be.

There is a second distant group which is likewise commonly overlooked. Unlike the first, however, they have physically removed themselves from the church premises. They've checked out completely. And often for understandable reasons.

Dropouts: When Love Webs Tear Apart

The Narrows Bridge in Tacoma, Washington, looked as sturdy as any in the country. Its handsome beams glistened in the sunshine. Its strong cables were the picture of security.

But one day something amazing occurred. A powerful crosswind did a number on this structure. It swayed left and right, then suddenly, another crosswind gave it a terrific up and down movement. In a matter of seconds it completely disintegrated—before the lens of a tourist's movie camera.[12]

This scene reminds me of another bridge falling that is equally tragic, namely, the disintegration of relationships between persons and their churches.

11. Taken from the previously referred-to lecture by Carolyn Koons.

12. The often-shown movie of this spectacular collapse, taken by a tourist, reveals what occurred that day. A single automobile started to cross. The rumble began. The man immediately stopped his car, grabbed his dog, and began running to safety. He barely made it before the collapse.

Such persons, whom I term dropouts, are found all over. I've spoken with more than a few. Many delight in describing former days of close communion. But their eyes become downcast as they cite circumstances that led to the dissolution of that communion. They say things such as, "It happened so fast. If only I could recapture relationships that I once enjoyed."

Some of us resent dropouts for having left the church, for it seems they are betrayers. Others of us are unwilling to provide the time, patience, and effort that is required to rebuild the bridges.

But our Savior would urge us to minister to dropouts. This is clear in his parable of the lost sheep. Without contemplation, the good shepherd left ninety-nine to locate the one that was lost. And in so doing, he risked his life. When the errant animal was found, there was great rejoicing.[13]

William Barclay makes two important observations concerning this parable that is recorded in Luke 15:

1. There was more rejoicing for the lost that was found than for the never lost (v. 7).

13. According to William Barclay, Judea's shepherd had a very arduous task. Pasture was scarce. The narrow central plateau extended for only a few miles, then plunged down to the jagged cliffs and parched desert. No restraining walls existed, and the sheep could wander.

George Adam Smith wrote of the shepherd: "On some high moor across which at night the hyenas howl, when you meet him, sleepless, far-sighted, weather-beaten, armed, leaning on his staff and looking out over his scattered sheep, every one of them on his heart, you understand why the shepherd of Judea sprang to the front in his people's history; why they gave his name to the kind, and made him the symbol of providence; why Christ took him as the type of self-sacrifice."

The shepherd was personally responsible for his animals. If one was lost, he was required to return the fleece to the owner to reveal how the sheep perished. He was adept at tracking, and could trace a stray's footprints for miles.

Many of the flocks were communal, belonging to entire villages. There would be two or three shepherds in charge. When a sheep was lost, the entire village would be very concerned. Then, when from a distance, they saw the shepherd coming home with the lost sheep across his shoulders, there would be a great shout of thanksgiving. This is the picture that Jesus drew of God, as he responds to one lost sinner returning to the fold.

William Barclay, *Daily Study Bible Series: The Gospel of Luke* (Philadelphia: The Westminster Press, 1953), pp. 206–207.

2. The sheep was lost because of his own foolishness and thoughtlessness, but that didn't cause the shepherd to resent him (v. 5).[14]

The application of these principles to dropouts is clear. But how can we best minister to these wandering sheep?

Researcher and minister John Savage sought answers to this question in the 125 "dropout studies" that he conducted. He discovered these stages that people typically go through when they go from active membership to dropout:

Dropout Stages

1. Faith in spasm

2. Cry for help

3. Anger

4. Limbo

5. Skunk or turtle

6. Sealing off

Ceasing active membership,[15] the potential dropout enters faith in spasm, in which there is a decreased involvement in attendance, commitment, financial contribution, positive attitude, and willingness to articulate his faith. Ninety-five percent of those entering this stage do so because of an anxiety-provoking event.[16]

---

14. Ibid.

15. In this study, active membership refers to the person who: (1) participates in worship at least 75 percent of the time, excluding summers; (2) has one (or more) commitments such as choir, usher, teacher; (3) makes a financial pledge and pays at least 80 percent of it; (4) has a positive attitude regarding the church; and (5) can articulate the faith that he holds, though perhaps not in an orthodox manner.

16. These four types of anxiety were discovered among the faith-in-spasm people: (1) reality-provoked anxiety: Something happened that created a crisis, and it was witnessed by the person and (or) others. For example, a church leader says, "We must replace you because your Sunday school teaching is inferior." (2) morality-provoked anxiety: An ethical crisis occurred that produces consternation. For example, the choir leader is known

Faith in spasm triggers the doubt mechanism, which pushes the person into stage two: cry for help. This cry is often faint, indirect, impersonal—simply an expression of dislike, such as "Keep treating me this way and I'm leaving."

Ironically, when such cries are heard by persons in the congregation, the response is often critical and defensive. The grapevine goes to work constructing informal systems to screen out such malcontents before they ruin others.

Savage says that between six and ten cries for help are heard each Sunday in the typical church of one hundred. If responded to promptly and appropriately, 98 percent of these members can be salvaged.[17]

The third stage is anger, which the person arrives at when he has reached two conclusions:

1. Nobody *does* hear or help.

2. Nobody *will* hear or help.

At first, such anger is disguised and engulfed in ambivalent language. But before long, it regresses into outright hostility. A rapid change in behavior then occurs: less attendance, less committee work, less involvement in the choir. Finally, the person writes a letter of resignation and stops church affiliation altogether.

---

to be having an affair. (3) neurotically provoked anxiety: Psychic pain is produced through the imagination. For example, due to an overload of responsibilities, the pastor seems to be ignoring the person. He assumes that the pastor no longer likes him. (4) existentially provoked anxiety: This develops when what Tillich terms "awareness of nonbeing" has taken place. There has been a loss of meaning for living. For example, a godly friend dies tragically, and the person concludes that God no longer cares, nor is he fair.

17. These kinds of responses should be given to persons who cry for help: (1) Caring, sensitive persons should be a *perception check*. The crier should be asked a question such as, "Is there something that is making you uncomfortable?" (2) *Listening* to the person's words, but even more to the "throb" of his pain. (3) *Doing something immediately* to assist—even if it is very little. Goal: To communicate that somebody cares. (4) *Revealing your own humanity*, so that the hurting person has somebody to identify with. As one social psychologist suggested, "Misery likes miserable company!"

As a dropout, the individual enters stage four: limbo. He waits, and even hopes, for a visit. He gives the church one last opportunity before closing the door. If no visit occurs, he has a complete change in perspective. That's why this stage is so critical.

During stage five, the dropout becomes either a "skunk" or a "turtle." The former blames external items such as the minister's preaching, and exhibits open criticism. The turtle, by contrast, blames himself, which results in guilt feelings. Skunks feel helpless; turtles sense that they are hopeless.[18]

Stage six involves a sealing-off of emotion from the church, a pervasive feeling of indifference. This is accompanied by a reinvestment of time and energy into other commitments. Once a person becomes entrenched in this new perspective for four months, Savage says, the task of getting him to return is exceedingly difficult.

But all hope is not vanished. Rescue is yet possible if the right approach is used. Over 63 percent of the dropouts visited by persons trained by the researcher *did* return—and after just *one* visit.

What specific skills and attitudes did they use? The same ones we must employ if we expect to reach these isolated persons. They are as follows:

1. Recognize that dropouts often have serious family problems. Be prepared for shocking revelations, as well as hidden messages.

2. Do not go to tell but to listen. Dropouts have waited long to pour out their ideas and feelings to persons who truly care enough to listen.

3. Be very patient. There will be no quick fix. Rebuilding confidence is a gradual, time-and-energy-

18. As an addendum, the researcher explains that "skunks" tend to marry "turtles." And sometimes "turtles" marry "turtles." But rarely do "skunks" marry "skunks."

Also, it is a fact that most ministers tend to be turtlelike. That is why they often hesitate to make calls on dropouts. It makes them feel guilty and responsible.

consuming process. In the words of Savage, "Sheep get lost blade-by-blade. They nibble themselves lost, and they must return the same way."

4. The church body must be prepared to welcome these persons once they return. Total forgiveness. Quickly reknit friendships. Immediate involvement in responsibilities. And most crucial of all, a complete absence of screening systems that demand penance, open confession, and a demonstration of worth.

It must not be assumed that all dropouts have turned their backs on God. Some have been unjustly treated by laymen or pastors in the church. In such cases, apologies are essential, followed by complete acceptance.[19]

No ministry lies closer to the heart of the good shepherd than that to lost sheep. It's time that we his followers adopt the same priority.

Singles and dropouts. Persons who, for whatever reason, have become distant from the church. We must go to them with open, sensitive, and compassionate hearts. It is what our Lord does and what he expects of us.

The End of Two Romances

I wish that you could have known her when she was young, vibrant, very much in love with her new husband —as well as with her growing, caring church. She spoke freely of spiritual things. Of God's goodness. Of her closeness with Christian brothers and sisters.

Then came a multiplicity of explosions in rapid succession. The news that she had an incurable disease. The discovery that her husband was seeing another woman. The suspicions from church members she had trusted very much. The pastor who somehow became too uncon-

19. The John Savage material was extracted from a videotape presentation, "The Dropout Track." For more information about these study materials, or the John Savage seminars, please contact: L. E. A. D. Consultants, Incorporated, Post Office Box 664, Reynoldsburg, Ohio 43068. Telephone (614) 864–0156.

cerned to respond to her. Like the Tacoma bridge, all the crosswinds converged to result in her sudden collapse.

Her response, like Job's, was predictable: "Why me, Lord? What have I possibly done to deserve this?"

Then came the formal split of her marriage, followed by her husband's unwillingness to provide for her care as the court had ordered. Have you heard the expression "hung out to dry?"

It was then that this broken young lady turned off completely. She decided to break all ties with church people. After all, they had forsaken her when she needed them most. Instead of compassion, all they could give her was a suspicious look and unfair judgment. Why should she subject herself to such punishment?

Cherry and I have continued to befriend her since she dropped out. Little by little she has begun to melt. She has even attended a few church services on special occasions.

Nevertheless, our friend remains distant. From the church. And far worse, from Jesus Christ.

We'll continue to try. Miracles are possible. We hope for one to soon occur.

But, while reaching out in love, our minds continue to focus on the lack of loving response that put her in this sad state. Loyal, regularly attending church persons failed to reach out. To them she was an expendable casualty.

It is crucial that we clearly see that, in the eyes of Jesus, there is no such person!

Neglecting One, We Neglect All

Section Two of this book focuses on four distinct kinds of people. People to whom we as followers of the master must build bridges.

As we have seen, different approaches are required for each bridge type. Our preparation for these varied challenges will require learning in our heads as well as in our hearts. Few of us have mastered the necessary skills and attitudes.

Many of us are quite content to reach out to our favorite kind of people. We're intent on being relationship specialists. Somehow, we feel that this is sufficient.

The Savior sees it differently. He says that it is his will that *all* should come to repentance (2 Peter 3:9). When it comes to his loving acceptance of mankind, he is certainly no specialist. His grace is so abundant and indiscriminate. He knows that by slighting one, he would be neglecting all. Likewise, we as his followers dare not be selective.

Section One admonishes us to construct our bridges in skillful, correct ways so that they are sound and reliable. Section Two appeals to us to build a variety of bridges that extend to a diversity of people.

Section Three, to which we now turn, focuses on what our bridges should transport once they are in place. To make them reliable and extend them to worthy destinations is not enough. The purpose of our bridges is to allow necessary goods to be delivered. Spiritual commerce must take place.

What goods are we referring to? The life-giving fruit of the Spirit. Let's taste and see that they are good.

Part **3**

Bridges/Delivery
Holy Relationships

Today you will meet all kinds of unpleasant people; they will hurt you, injure you and insult you; but you cannot live like that; you know better, for you are a man in whom the (S)pirit of God dwells.—Roman Emperor, Marcus Aurelius, to his son

Society is the walls of our imprisonment in history
—Peter Berger

Just because you're not paranoid doesn't mean the world is not out to get you.

9

Fruit Cluster #1:
Love, Joy, Peace

Cultivating healthy and holistic relationships prepares us for the main event—creating ones that are holy. Ones that free us to become delivery systems of Christ's love.

Construction is complete. Our tall, stalwart bridges are custom designed for the four kinds of persons we will (or should) encounter.

Now it's time to begin transporting our spiritual fruit across the bridges, all nine varieties itemized in Galatians 5:22–23: "love, joy, peace, patience, kindness, goodness, faithfulness, gentleness and self-control."[1]

1. The "prince of expositors," Alexander Maclaren, notes that Paul refers to fruit, not fruits. Thus, "all this rich variety of graces, of conduct and character, is [to be] thought of as one." He continues by saying, "The individual members are not isolated graces, but all connected, springing from one root and constituting an organic whole."

The works of the flesh have no such unity (i.e., not worthy to be termed fruit). Alexander Maclaren, *Expositions of Holy Scripture: Second Corinthians, Galatians and*

Here are some basic principles related to these life-giving fruit.

First, love should be perceived as the super fruit. Some suggest that the other eight are hybrids, or derivatives, of love. Others see love as the life sap that rises through the tree, giving sustenance and form to the other fruit. Both viewpoints have merit.

The fruit of the Spirit increase and decrease together, just like the water levels in the battery cells of my car. Thus, when we mature in patience, we also grow in joy and peace.

Second, the fruit of the Spirit always comes in a package that includes all nine. When we purchase ice cream bars at the grocery store, we can't usually buy just one or two. We're required to take the whole box. Similarly, as Christians we must buy into all nine fruit. It's a simple case of all or nothing, feast or famine, abundance or destitute poverty.

Finally, the fruit is not optional for those of us who love the Lord. Jesus made this clear in his farewell message on the eve of his crucifixion.

> I am the vine; you are the branches. If a man remains in me and I in him, he will bear much fruit. . . . You did not choose me, but I chose you . . . to go and bear fruit—fruit that will last (John 15:5, 16).

If this is all true, why do we not hear more about the fruit of the Spirit? Because we hear so much about the gifts of the Spirit.

Philippians (New York: Hodder and Stoughton—George H. Doran Company, n.d.) pp. 162–163.

Another interesting perspective is presented by Jim Elliot "Rot will encourage rot, but one ripe piece of fruit will not allay rottenness in another." Implication: Fruit exist in unity. One piece that goes bad can make others distasteful. However, the reverse is not true. A good piece cannot make one that's gone bad better. "The Journals of Jim Elliot," *Christianity Today*, November 21, 1986, page titled "Classic and Contemporary Excerpts," p. 25.

To Be or to Do?

Author Donald Cole is right. Christians today seem obsessed with the gifts of the Holy Spirit. Perhaps it's because they are more observable. More closely related to our insatiable craving to perform. To do wonders and be seen while doing them. Having a bunch of gifts allows us to be ostentatious.

Or, it could be that compared with the fruit of the Spirit, spiritual gifts are more spectacular. The latter are more like the ocean's rip-tide, while the former resemble the sea's hidden, silent current. We gravitate to the spectacular. The sensational. Just as did those who harassed Jesus to perform nonstop miracles.

Certainly, the gifts get an inordinate amount of press— compared with the fruit.

Admittedly, Paul mentions such gifts (Rom. 12:3–8; 1 Cor. 12—14; Eph. 4:7–16).[2] Yet, they pale in significance when contrasted with the fruit.

Everything that Paul says about spiritual gifts centers on one thing: holy living. On bearing fruit of the Spirit in our lives.

2. Kenneth Kinghorn has summarized the gifts of the Spirit on this helpful chart. From *Gifts of the Spirit* (Abingdon Press, 1976).

Romans 12:6–8	1 Corinthians 12:4–11	1 Corinthians 12:28	Ephesians 4:11
Prophecy	Prophecy	Prophecy	Prophecy
Teaching		Teaching	Teaching
Serving			
Exhortation			
Leadership			
Giving Aid			
Compassion			
	Healing	Healing	
	Working miracles	Working miracles	
	Tongues and their interpretation	Tongues and their interpretation	
	Wisdom		
	Knowledge		
	Faith		
	Discernment		
		Apostleship	Apostleship
		Helps	
		Administration	
			Evangelism
			Shepherding

His conclusion must be the same as our own. Our gifts profit nil if we lack the Son-ripened fruit of holiness in our lives (1 Cor. 13).

Gifts can be faked. Phonies can learn to preach like prophets—TV evangelists notwithstanding. As Cole says, "Convincing pretenses can counterfeit giftedness."

Not so with Christian fruit. They cannot be feigned. The quality of their harvest gives them away. James says so.

> But the wisdom that comes from heaven is . . . pure; then peaceloving, considerate, submissive, full of mercy and good fruit, impartial and sincere. Peacemakers who sow in peace raise a harvest of righteousness (3:17–18).

For any of us who might be tempted to become spiritual fruit impostors, Jesus says,

> By [your] fruit [I] will recognize [you]. Do people pick grapes from thornbushes, or figs from thistles? Likewise every good tree bears good fruit, but a bad tree bears bad fruit. A good tree cannot bear bad fruit, and a bad tree cannot bear good fruit (Matt. 7:16–18).

Here is a final, essential contrast between gifts and fruit. The former diminish in effectiveness through time. The curve ball of poor health, as well as the church's moth-ball mentality regarding its aged, take their toll.

By contrast, the older we get, the more fruit should be expected in our lives. Cole reflects the sentiments of many of us when he says, "Nothing is sweeter than Christlike character in aging people." Why? Because it gives all of us hope for our own future. Someday, we can be that way, too. And in the meantime, we can work, toward that idea.

In summary, there's no contest. Fruit is more important than gifts, in spite of what we're likely to hear.[3]

---

3. "Opinion: To Be or to Do?" *Moody Monthly*, September, 1983, p. 17.

But if fruit outshine gifts, they don't even deserve to be compared with sins. Paul does so anyway, just to tell us how good we have it.

Beware of the Briar Patch!

In Galatians 5:19–21 Paul writes,

The acts of the sinful nature are obvious: sexual immorality, impurity and debauchery; idolatry and witchcraft; hatred, discord, jealousy, fits of rage, selfish ambition, dissensions, factions and envy; drunkenness, orgies, and the like. I warn you. . . those who live like this will not inherit the kingdom of God.

The list of losers has been called the misery index. As with the fruit, all of these come—and go—in a package. They are inseparable.

By making this contrast, Paul provides a classic statement concerning the inner strife between spirit and flesh.[4] The first causes us to bear fruit; the second produces thorns of sin.

That strife is ended when our sinful nature is crucified[5] (Gal. 2:20; 5:24;[6] Rom. 6:6). As Lamar Kincaid vividly

4. W. T. Purkiser declares that the Galatians 5 contains a classic statement related to "flesh-Spirit" inner strife. Along with Romans 7, it has been taken as normative for the highest Christian life. "For the sinful nature (Gr., *sarx*; flesh, KJV, RSV) desires what is contrary to the Spirit, and the Spirit what is contrary to the sinful nature." The *sarx*, or "sinful nature" here doesn't imply bodily or physical as do the acts of sin that are listed. W. T. Purkiser, *Exploring Christian Holiness: The Biblical Foundation*, Volume I (Beacon Hill Press of Kansas City, 1983), p. 166.

5. Raymond T. Stamm writes: "Crucifixion with Christ means three things. a) Participation in the benefits of Christ's death, including freedom from law, forgiveness for past sins, and a passionate urge never to sin again (Rom. 4:24–25; 2 Cor. 5:14–15, 20; Col. 3:1–4). b) A moral, spiritual fellowship with Christ in his death and resurrection, which takes the Christian's "I will" captive to "the mind of Christ," replacing the law as a design for living (2 Cor. 10:3–6; Phil. 3:10; Rom. 6:1–11). c) A partnership with Christ in his creative suffering, which requires the Christian to "complete what remains of Christ's afflictions" for the sake of his body the church (Col. 1:24–25; 3:5; Rom. 8:17)." *The Interpreter's Bible*, Volume 10 (Abingdon Press), p. 489.

6. In Galatians 5:24, the crucifixion is "the sinful nature with its passions and desires." Such a crucifixion relates to "those who belong to Christ Jesus." Belonging to Jesus in its

declared, we must "ruthlessly nail our sinful nature to the hard wood [of the cross] with resolute, unrelenting blows; and like the crucifixion squad [that slew our Lord], we must sit and watch it with hard eyes, wither and plead how it may, until it dies."[7]

It is as simple as this. When our sinful nature dies with Jesus on the cross, he becomes resurrected in us through his abiding Spirit. And what evidence do we possess that this miracle has occurred? His fruit exhibited in our lives. We become spiritual fruit vendors!

With this background in mind, we're now ready to examine the nine fruit. We will be focusing on them in groups of three.[8] The first group—love, joy, and peace—have to do with our relationship with our heavenly Father and the resulting renewal of our inner life.
Let's begin with love.

The World's Best Four-letter Word

Aldous Huxley stated that the word *love* is bankrupt. "Of all the worn, smudged, dog-eared words in our vocabulary, *love* is the grubbiest." Yet most people prefer thinking about this term more than all others.

---

full scope involves these three states. 1) *We are Christ's by creation—he made us;* 2) *We are Christ's by the cross, by redemption—he purchased us;* 3) *We are Christ's by consecration—the self-yielding of those already "alive from the dead"* (Rom. 6:13 KJV). Purkiser, op. cit., p. 167.

7. Lamar Kincaid, in a sermon preached at Longboat Key Chapel, Longboat Key, Florida, 1973.

Just as Romans 7:14–25 must be interpreted in harmony with its context in Romans 6 and 8, so Galatians 5:17 must be interpreted in harmony with verse 24. The inner strife—so far as "sinful nature" is concerned—is concluded when it is crucified. To see crucifixion as a gradual, continual dying that never results in death is to miss the biblical and natural meaning of the term. Thus, our death to self comes at one point in time. Ibid.

8. It is probable that Paul did not have well-tailored triads in mind when he listed the fruit of the Spirit. But, for purposes of conceptualizing, we follow Alexander Maclaren's lead in doing so. Admittedly, this categorization seems to be more forced than those traditional ones that have grouped the Beatitudes and Ten Commandments. Nevertheless, we shall do so anyhow.

Maclaren, in making his classification, states, "It is perhaps not too artificial to point out that we have three triads, of which the first describes the life of the Spirit in its deepest secret; the second, the same life in its manifestations to men; and the third, that life in relation to the difficulties of the world, and of ourselves." Maclaren, *op. cit.*, p. 163.

In a secular sense, the word *love* is used a million different ways,[9] the first meaning that comes to mind for most people is love between the sexes. In contrast to infatuation, love is often more realistic, as reflected in this viewpoint:

> Infatuation is when you think he's as handsome as Robert Redford, as smart as Henry Kissinger, as noble as Ralph Nader, as funny as Woody Allen, and as athletic as Jimmy Connors. Love is when you realize that he's as handsome as Woody Allen, as smart as Jimmy Connors, as funny as Ralph Nader, as athletic as Henry Kissinger, and nothing like Robert Redford—but you'll take him anyway![10]

Is there more to love than infatuation from a secular perspective? Psychologist Robert Trotter states that love has three sides, like a triangle.

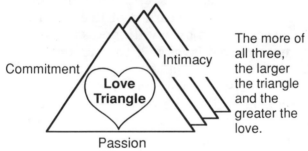

The more of all three, the larger the triangle and the greater the love.

Commitment / Love Triangle / Intimacy / Passion

9. According to J. A. M. Meerloo, the phrase "I love you" can be: (1) a stage song, repeated daily without any meaning; (2) a barely audible murmur, full of surrender; (3) a statement that means "I desire you," "I want you sexually," "I hope you love me," or "I hope that I will be able to love you"; (4) a phrase that often means "It may be that a love relationship can be developed between us"; (5) a wish for emotional exchange: "I want your admiration in exchange for mine," or "I give my love in exchange for some passion," or "I want to feel cozy and at home with you," or "I admire some of your qualities"; (6) a deep, intimate request: "I desire you," or "I want you to gratify me," or "I want your protection," or "I want to be intimate with you," or "I want to exploit your loveliness"; (7) a need for security and tenderness—for parental treatment; (8) an expression of submissiveness: "Please take me as I am," or "I feel guilty about you"; (9) a self-sacrifice and masochistic wish for dependency—or a full affirmation of the other, taking the responsibility for mutual exchange of feelings; (10) a weak feeling of friendliness—or the scarcely-whispered expression of ecstasy.

"I love you"—wish, desire, submission, conquest. It is never the word itself that tells the real meaning." *Conversation and Communication*

10. *Redbook*, February, 1975.

Commitment is the mental component of love. It's what some couples have left after intimacy is lost and passion has subsided.

Intimacy, says Trotter, is the emotional side of love. Some can bare their souls to one another, but have little commitment or passion. Theirs is a high-grade friendship.

Passion is the motivational aspect of love. When it alone rules, there may be an affair in which there is little intimacy and even less commitment. This is the infatuation described above.[11]

Christian love, indeed, includes commitment, intimacy, and passion. Nevertheless, Christian love goes beyond the world's ideas of love: the brotherly, erotic, and other kinds that the ancient Greeks described.[12]

Christian love is agape, the love we extend to all people, the God-breathed love that permeates our being when his Spirit inhabits our hearts. It is unconditional (given without its recipient having to earn it or live down the past); unselfish (accompanied by a willingness to suffer for the beloved); unrestricted (available to everyone, especially the unlovely and unlovable).

How does Christian love penetrate our lives? By our relinquishing our will to the will of Jesus. To quote Paul Ramsey, it has "nothing to do with feelings, emotions, taste, preferences, temperament, or any of the qualities in

11. Robert J. Trotter, "The Three Faces of Love," *Psychology Today* (September, 1986), pp. 46–54.

12. In Greek there are four different words for "love." (1) *Storge*, which implies family love, the love of a parent for a child and vice versa. "Sweet is a father to his children if he has *storge*." (2) *Eros*, which describes the love of a man for a woman—passionate and sexual love. Nothing immoral is necessarily implied, but through time it has taken on the implication of lust. (3) *Philia*, which describes warm, tender affection—the kind that exists between close friends. Hence, the name "Philadelphia," the city of brotherly love." (4) *Agape*, which means "unconquerable benevolence, invincible good will." It does not mean a feeling of the heart, which we cannot help; it means a "determination of the mind" and will toward those who are unlovely. We can only have *agape* when Jesus helps us to conquer our natural tendency to anger and bitterness.

William Barclay, *The Daily Study Bible: The Gospel of Matthew*, Volume 1 (Philadelphia: The Westminster Press, 1956), pp. 172–173. Most Christians call John the Apostle of love, but Paul used the term *agape* seventy-five times. John's Gospel only employs it seven, while his First Epistle uses it another eighteen times.

other people that arouse feelings of revulsion or attraction, negative or positive preferences. Christian love depends on the direction of the will...not on stirring emotion.[13]

The Bible is replete with words about the love that characterizes us as Christians. It is

a prize to be won. 1 Corinthians 14:1 instructs us to "follow the way of love." The Greek word for "follow" implies a strenuous activity. Paul translates the same word "press," in Philippians 3:14 KJV: "I press toward the mark...of the high calling of God in Christ Jesus."

an object of prayer. Paul says, "And this I pray, that your love may abound yet more and more."(Phil. 1:9, KJV). The term *abound* comes from the Latin word that means "overflowing like the breaking waves of the sea."

a model to be followed. 1 John 4:19 declares, "We love because he first loved us." As Reuben Welch likes to say, "When we think of love, color it Jesus."

The great symphony of love is located in the thirteenth chapter of 1 Corinthians. Fifteen beautiful refrains blend perfectly into a rhapsody of splendor.

Love is patient	Love is not self-seeking	Love protects
Love is kind	Love is not easily	Love trusts
Love does not envy	angered	Love hopes
	Love keeps no record of	Love endures
Love does not boast or is not proud	wrongs	Love never fails
	Love does not delight in evil	(verses 4–8a)
Love is not rude	Love rejoices with the truth	

Charles Swindoll summarized these spectacular char-

13. Quoted by J. Glenn Gould in "Neighborly Love in the Christian Life," Herald of Holiness, April 1, 1987, p. 7.

acteristics of Christian love into five statements. He terms them the *ABCs of love.*

> I *A*ccept you as you are.
> I *B*elieve you are valuable.
> I *C*are when you hurt.
> I *D*esire only what is best for you.
> I *E*rase all offenses.[14]

This kind of loving spirit is bound to penetrate the lives of all we encounter, as does salt, light, and leaven. I can't help thinking of a custom of an African tribe. Whenever someone does something vile and unlawful, he is required to stand in the center of a circle that is formed by all members of the group. While there, he must listen to and look into the eyes of each person, who in turn explains why he still loves him.

The effect is amazing. He leaves, that day, determined to rise to the level of the others' expectation. To never disappoint those who love him so deeply, again. To begin loving with the same kind of love that he has generously received.

No matter what we do, Jesus loves us without limit or reservation. As Karl Barth once said, the greatest truth in God's Word is this: "Jesus loves me, this I know, for the Bible tells me so."

Whenever we falter and stumble, whether by wickedness or by weariness, he looks straight into our eyes and says, "I love you." That should be enough to make us, like the Africans, love everyone with the same kind of love that Jesus gives us.

Color It Orange

Orange is my favorite color. So alive. So vibrant. So pulsating with energy.

But not just any shade of orange will do. It must be

---

14. Charles R. Swindoll, *Dropping Your Guard: The Value of Open Relationships* (Waco, TX: Word Books, 1983), p. 122.

bright like a Popsicle, a freshly peeled carrot, or the swing set in the city park.

If joy is a spiritual fruit, I like to think of it as orange— bright orange. Like the Golden Gate on a sunny day, gleaming on San Francisco's skyline, guarding the sparkling, azure waters below.

Don't expect to read about joy in a psychology textbook or a philosophy treatise. It's purely a Christian attitude. And that is why it appears nearly two hundred times in God's Word.

We read that angels brought "good tidings of great joy" when they announced our Savior's birth (Luke 2:10 KJV). Later, Jesus declared the purpose of his teaching to be "my joy . . . in you, and . . . your joy . . . full" (John 15:11 KJV).

Our only source of authentic joy is Christ. With comforting assurance we sing

> If you want joy,
>   real joy,
>   wonderful joy.
> Let Jesus come into
> you heart.[15]

We must not get confused. Joy is not the same as fun. The kind purchased at Disneyland or a World Series game.

Nor is it like happiness, which depends on favorable outward circumstances.

Rather, joy is strictly an inside job! It is generated from the wellsprings of our souls when our souls have been touched by God.

For this reason we Christians can be joyful even when things appear dark, dismal, destitute, and depressing. When fun and happiness make their exit, joy can linger.

Joy causes us to be a blessing to those in need. We encourage others by being joyful. Also, it grounds us in

15. "If You Want Joy," author unknown.

the will of God. He is pleased when our cups are full and running over. Finally, joy yields plenty of personal satisfaction and fulfillment. It adds zest to our lives. As Charles Swindoll said, too many go around looking like their rich aunt just willed her millions to her pregnant hamster!

Once Christ's joy floods our hearts, how should we best use it to his glory? The Bible clearly instructs us.

1. Do something for and in the Name of our Lord. His disciples did so, and "returned again with joy" (Luke 10:17 KJV).

2. Freely ask and generously receive from the hands of Christ. He instructed: "Ask and ye shall receive, that your joy may be full" (John 16:24 KJV).

3. Close the book on devastating memories and crippling resentments. After enduring great persecution, Paul and Barnabas were "filled with joy" (Acts 13:52).

4. With divine guidance, learn to cope with life's constant stresses. James admonished: "Reckon it nothing but joy whenever you find yourselves surrounded by various temptations" (James 1:2, Weymouth).

Like love, joy is God's free gift to us, although it cost him plenty. It is a fruit that we can possess that will make our lives fulfilling. With it, we are soaring eagles. Without it, we are little more than worms on a hangglider.

Prior to becoming a minister, my dad, like his father, worked in the coal mines of southern Illinois. One day I heard him recall how black soot would blanket everything nearby.

But it always used to intrigue him how lilies never had a speck of coal dust on their petals. They could be located right next to the cave entrance. Still they remain unblemished.

Out of curiosity, one day my father investigated how this occurred. What he discovered taught him an interesting thing about nature, but an even more valuable lesson about the Christian life.

He learned that lilies continuously excrete a cleansing solution. The petals are thus bathed so that the irritating and unpleasant-looking soot rolls right off.

Joy is like lilies. Because of the presence of Jesus within, our spirit is continually vitalized and encouraged. Although Satan's "coal dust" of disappointment, evil, and confusion may come our way, it cannot attach itself to our inner spirits. Joy is like having perpetual windshield wipers on our hearts.

Again, joy keeps us spiritually upbeat regardless of anything this world can throw in our direction, or, for that matter, anything other Christians can lob our way. Christians? You bet. They can be pain inflicting. One bumper sticker captured this sentiment: "The more Christians I know, the more I like my dog!"

Granted. It shouldn't be that way. Our brothers and sisters in Christ should soothe our spirits. To paraphrase Tom Dooley, they should be "comforting the afflicted" not "afflicting the comforted."

But having said that, it is just as certain that we should still remain joyful. Just as the early Christians did in the midst of intense persecution. In describing their jubilant spirits, the Bible employs a term from which we derive our word *hilarious*.

Rather than succumbing to depression or fear, they delighted in being together with hilarity and celebration. Their churches exuded joy.

We should be doing the same. So here's my challenge: Let's begin immediately to wash off the coal dust!

No More Inner Rumble

If joy is orange, peace must be white. Again, lilies come to mind, the kind that fill cemeteries. Then there is the white dove. With the traditional olive branch in his mouth, he becomes the international symbol of peace. Finally, there is the white flag, signifying that hostilities have ceased and a truce has begun.

This statement will not surprise you: Our world lacks peace. Throughout recorded history, there have only been two hundred years when fighting had altogether ceased. And most of the war years have featured multiple conflicts going on simultaneously.

But conflict, certainly, is not limited to battlefields "over there." We have plenty right here at home. Married couples do battle with words, withdrawal, and physical weapons. I heard about one fellow who went to a restaurant, called the waitress over, and said, "Serve me cold eggs and burnt toast. Then, while I eat it, stand here and nag me. I'm homesick!"

Our children aren't exempt from conflict. Cartoons feature a blow a minute. I think the Roadrunner deserves the Congressional Medal of Honor. The poor fellow gets pulverized every five seconds.

We encourage our children to think in this direction. Not only do we model warfare in our marriages, but we purchase them the latest toy weapons of aggression. I had to smile when I saw this account of a request made to Santa last Christmas:

> **Santa:** Ho, ho, ho. Hello there, young fellow. Isn't this a wonderful time of the year? We're celebrating peace on earth, goodwill to men! Now, what would you like for Christmas?
>
> **Boy:** A death-ray laser zap gun, a toy electric chair, and a chainsaw murderer doll.

Nevertheless, deep down, we all see the value of peace. As in the days of Jeremiah, we cry out. "Peace, peace . . . [but] there is no peace" (6:14). Overt, as well as covert, conflict continues. Between nations. Between individuals. At work. On highways. In our homes. Even in our churches—where we're supposed to be honoring the Prince of Peace.

But we must focus on the Bible's view of peace, which contrasts sharply with the world's limited understanding of the concept.

According to William Barclay, the Greek term for *peace* (*eirene*) corresponds with the Hebrew word *shalom* that we're more familiar with. Rather than simply implying a freedom from trouble, it means a serene heart which results from the all-pervading consciousness that our lives are in God's hands.[16]

Paul used the term *peace* forty-three times. He treasured the concept, and rarely omitted it from his salutations. Repeatedly, we read "Grace to you and peace" (Rom. 1:7).

But what did he and other Bible writers declare about peace? Three main things.

First, Jesus is its source. In Ephesians, we're told that Christ's atonement brings us peace. "For he himself is our peace" (2:14). Just before ascending into heaven, he testified to the same reality. "Peace I leave with you; my peace I give you" (John 14:27).

We're tempted to set our minds on other sources as we grope for peace. On ourselves—which yields conceit or depression. On circumstances—which results in false security or broken dreams. On things—which invite slavery or total frustration. On people—which encourages idol worship or causes shattered spirits.

Again, we must look to Jesus. For, in him, we are guaranteed a deep, authentic peace. A peace which "transcends all understanding" of this world (Phil. 4:7).

Second, having the peace of Jesus within, we're at peace with his heavenly Father, others, and ourselves.

The Greek word for *peace* includes a root that means "to join or set at one." Christ's peace results in our being in harmony with God. And, as one person rightly de-

16. William Barclay, op. cit., *The Letters to the Galatians and Ephesians*, p. 55.

clared, "We can't possibly experience the peace *of* God until we're at peace *with* God."

Jesus makes it possible to be just that. Romans 5:1 says so. "Therefore, since we have been justified through faith, we have peace with God through our Lord Jesus Christ."

His peace also helps us to be at peace with others. As the chorus says, "He is our peace, who has broken down every wall."[17] The Bible, similarly, says, For he himself is our peace, who has made the two [Jew and Gentile] one and has destroyed the barrier, the dividing wall of hostility (Eph. 2:14).

Because he has made the gift of peace possible, his Word commands us to activate it in our lives and to become peacemakers.[18]

Finally, the peace of God provided by his Son our Savior makes us at peace within ourselves. Peace like a river floods our hearts and lives, just as Isaiah the prophet predicted. "Thou wilt keep him in perfect peace, *whose mind is* stayed *on thee*: because he trusteth in thee" (26:3 KJV).

Many of us have an acute case of the jitters. We nail bite our way through life, fearing everything that moves. We're so paranoid that our fears have fears.

J. L. Glass has written a humorous article, titled "Five Ways to Have a Nervous Breakdown." He lists them as follows:

1. Try to figure out the answer before the problem arises. "Most of the bridges we cross are never built, because they are unnecessary." We carry tomorrow's load along with today's. Matthew 6:34 says: "Do not worry about tomorrow, for tomorrow will worry about itself."

---

17. "He Has Broken Down Every Wall," Kandela Groves, Maranatha Music, 1975.
18. See Matthew 5:9, 10:34; Mark 9:50; Romans 12:18, 14:19; 2 Corinthians 13:11; 1 Thessalonians 5:13.

2. Try to relive the past. As we trust him for the future, we must trust him with the past. And he can use the most checkered past imaginable for his good. See Romans 8:28.

3. Try to avoid making decisions. Doing this is like deciding whether to allow weeds to grow in our gardens. While we're deciding, they're growing. Decisions will be made in our delay. We must come to grips with the realities of life. Choice "is man's most godlike characteristic."

4. Demand more of yourself than you can produce. Unrealistic demands result in "beating our heads against stone walls. We don't change the walls. We just damage ourselves." Romans 12:3 says, "Do not think of yourself more highly than you ought, but rather think of yourself with sober judgment."

5. Believe everything Satan tells you. The New Testament speaks of the "devices of the devil" (Eph. 6:11, NEB). Jesus described Satan as the "father of lies" (John 8:44). He's a master of disguise, masquerading as an angel of light. But our Lord declared *that his* sheep follow him because they "know His voice" (John 10:4). Why? They have listened to it in his Word.[19]

We need to replace these foolish prescriptions with Christ's abiding peace placed in our hearts by his Spirit, so that we can sing, "It is well with my soul" and really mean it.

His peace does wonderful things for us. It causes us to love his law (Ps. 119:165), be protected (Luke 19:41–42), quiet, and assured (Isa. 32:17). As a result, we need not be anxious over anything (Phil. 4:6–7)—even death.

---

19. Quoted by W. T. Purkiser in "Five Ways to Have a Nervous Breakdown," *Herald of Holiness*, October 9, 1974.

General Booth, godly founder of the Salvation Army, lay dying. He seemed to glow with God's presence. All of a sudden he seemed to grimace with pain.

One of his dear friends, standing by his bedside, leaned down and whispered, "Tell me how you feel, my brother." With a very weak voice, the saint said, "The waters are rising."

But then, in a voice almost too weak to be heard, he muttered, "But, praise Jesus, I am rising with the waters."

Inner peace does that, you know. With it filling our hearts, we will rise with the waters of life, no matter how cold, how high, how rapid.

To reiterate, Paul is absolutely right in telling us:

> Do not be anxious about anything, but in everything, by prayer and petition, with thanksgiving, present your requests to God. And the peace of God, which transcends all understanding, will guard your hearts and your minds in Christ Jesus (Phil 4:6–7).

Love. Joy. Peace. All are intimately involved in our Christian walk. And all are possible only because of our relationship with Christ.

Let's turn our attention to the next three fruit. They follow the first three in logical order. Because of love, joy, and peace within, we are now prepared for patience, kindness, and goodness.

To live above with those we love,
   oh that will be glory;
But to live below with those we know,
   that's another story.

The best relations are built up, like fine lacquer finish, with accumulated layers of acts of kindness.—Alan McGinnis

The shortest possible fragment of time: between the time when the traffic light changes and the person behind you honks.

10

Fruit Cluster #2: Patience, Kindness, Goodness

In addition to our first cart of fruit—love, joy, and peace—there is a second that contains patience, kindness, and goodness. Let's load it for immediate delivery over our bridges.

As we have stated, the first triad primarily involves our intimacy with God. The second concerns our relationships with others, particularly those who are close up. Those we frequently interact with eyeball-to-eyeball. Family members. Work colleagues. Fellow parishioners.

We know the kind. They are persons we feel an emotional attachment to, but, they are also ones who have the potential of really getting on our nerves. Why? Because we're so close to them that their bad days become our bad days.

From our vantage point, these are the persons whom we tend to take for granted. We expect them to come

179

through for us, just as they always have. When they do, we offer them few, if any, thank yous or strokes. They only hear from us when they fail to meet our level of expectations.

What does this cluster of fruit have to do with the one that we loaded onto the first cart? More than we can possibly realize. Closeness with God implies a sense of oneness with others.

Theologian Martin Buber put it succinctly. He said that when our relationship with God changes from "I-It" (impersonal) to "I-Thou" (intimate)—as evidenced by his Spirit's love, joy, and peace in our lives—our associations with others take on a new and fulfilling dimension.[1]

My good friend David Best stated the same fact in a recent sermon. He said when we become dependent upon God, we'll find ourselves becoming increasingly independent of the past (guilt, painful memories) and interdependent with others.

It's fruit inspection time. Let's begin investigating this cluster by focusing on the fruit of patience.

And I Want It Right Now!

Here are some things that drive me right up the wall:

Putting a complicated gadget together—especially when the instructions don't make sense.

Getting through to someone who is carrying on a telephone marathon—especially when, after finally getting through, I get a recording.

Investing loyalty in a team (e.g., Dodgers) whose percentage of losses matches southern California's July temperature—especially when I hear reports of dissension among players.

1. Martin Buber, *I and Thou* (New York: Scribner, 1958).

Missing the green light because the driver in the car ahead of me is distracted—especially when *that* bozo makes the light.

We can all envision similar scenes that make our blood pressures rise, our heads ache, and our teeth grind. Who needs that kind of hassle, especially those of us who have type A (antsy) personalities?

What makes it particularly difficult is the fact that so many *others* are impatient, too. As Howard White once remarked, "I'm not sure whether the rat race is speeding up, or if they're just bringing on faster rats." Both seem to be true. And, the rats appear to be increasingly impatient.

Some of us might be saying to ourselves, "But our inner feeling of impatience motivates us to perform." Marchant King concurs by saying, "Impatience is the spur that motivates progress in modern business. The corporation that 'can't wait until tomorrow' is likely to become the most successful in its field."[2]

To procrastinate is indeed to fail. Like the old blacksmith, we must strike while the iron's hot. And impatience may help us to do just that.

Nevertheless, being prompt need not be the result of such a negative motivation. We can be patient and prompt, too, and as a result have the best of both worlds. We must not think of patience as synonymous with procrastination.

Our Bible is replete with references concerning patience. The Greek term *makrothumia* (translated "long-suffering," KJV), means "not being quickly or easily provoked by the unsatisfactory conduct of others." Or, as nineteenth-century Anglican Bishop J. B. Lightfoot said, it is the "self-restraint that does not hastily retaliate a wrong."[3]

2. Marchant A. King, "Patience," *Moody Monthly*, September, 1983, p. 23.
3. Ibid. Also, William Barclay, *The Daily Study Bible: The Letters to the Galatians and Ephesians* (Philadelphia, PA: The Westminster Press, 1954.)

But, what is considered a wrong tends to differ between non-Christians and those of us who love the Lord.

The unregenerated are more quickly set off by persons who sorely inconvenience them. Persons who block their personal needs and ambitions. In effect, they say, "I'll be nice, provided others don't cross me. If they do, they've got problems." It's the old don't-rattle-my-cage syndrome.

Unfortunately, some of us who have been born again react similarly. But we know better and usually feel guilty when we stoop to such attitudes and behavior.

We're more likely to become impatient with persons who fail Jesus. Persons whose lives don't match their testimonies. Persons who hurt Christ's kingdom (intentionally or not) by acting stupidly, stubbornly, or sinfully.

Also, we tend to chafe when others don't move with dispatch, especially when they're sluggardly and slothful and the needs are intense but "the workers are few" (Matt. 9:37). Those of us who want to see miraculous things happen, because God has given us this vision, tend to lose our cool around sleepy-eyed saints.

But, as the writer to the Hebrews declares, "[We] have need of patience" (10:36, KJV). And we have it for two important reasons.

First, patience will help us to persevere. To persevere means to put up with a lot of stuff that we don't deserve. Taking our licks because of our mistakes is not especially commendable, but our enduring blows that are unfairly given us is meritorious with God. 1 Peter 2:20, KJV, says so.

> For what glory *is it*, if, when ye be buffeted for your faults, ye shall take it patiently? but if, when ye do well, and suffer *for it*, ye take it patiently, this *is* acceptable with God.

James speaks of the perseverance of the prophets. "Brothers, as an example of patience in the face of suffering, take the prophets who spoke in the name of the Lord" (5:10). The most prominent of these were Isaiah and Jeremiah.

For over sixty years, Isaiah proclaimed God's message to Judah and saw only superficial response. In fact, the nation backslid into idolatry. But, to the end of his days he pleaded for a return to the Lord, while he reassured the people of the Messiah's imminent coming and the establishment of his new and glorious kingdom.

Talking about getting beat up, Jeremiah suffered intense and continuous persecution, rejection, and imprisonment. Once he sank shoulder high in mud at the bottom of a pit. But he persevered. His days on earth ended when he was ministering to a remnant of poor Jewish immigrants in Egypt.

But our supreme example of patience is Jesus. After Israel rejected his claims, overlooked his healing ministry, spurned him personally, and even planned to kill him, he wept with deep compassion over their plight. Then unflinchingly, he offered himself as their Messiah.

And though his disciples misunderstood his lessons, showed little faith, and viewed much of what he said in terms of their personal gain, Christ patiently nurtured them. He knew that Pentecost was coming.[4]

Perseverance always seems to suggest the running of a race, the kind that millions observe every four years in the Olympics. Hebrews 12 acknowledges a roll call of persevering saints: the patriarchs, the prophets, the Lord. But then the spotlight turns on us. We, too, can possess enduring patience. "Therefore, since we are surrounded by such a great cloud of witnesses, let us throw off everything that hinders and the sin that so easily entangles, and let us run with perseverance the race marked out for us" (v. 1).

---

4. In presenting himself as their Messiah, Jesus accepted the lowliness that Zechariah had said would mark Israel's promised king (Zech. 9:9).

Most remarkable was our Lord's relationship with Judas at the last supper. He took bread, dipped it in meat juice, and offered it to the errant disciple. This identified him as the betrayer (John 13:21, 26). But, it did much more; "it demonstrated the ultimate in gracious patience." Jesus gave Judas the "morsel of honor, designating a highly esteemed guest." It was the "climatic appeal of His heart, beckoning the betrayer to turn from treachery to faith." Marchant, op. cit., pp. 23–24.

Second, in addition to perseverance, we must have the kind of patience that helps us to persist.

Receiving persecution with a Christian attitude is important, but no more crucial than hanging in there until our tasks are completed. Perseverance seems to imply an endurance against extreme trial. Persistence, on the other hand, suggests a bulldozer-type tenacity that helps us to carry out God's assignment.

My mind gravitates to the Japanese army officer who was stranded on an island after the war. Although he knew that the war was over and that his side had lost, he faithfully held out. Never would he be disloyal to his great emperor. He had received a sacred trust and would never go back on his word. Well, after decades they finally located the fellow and talked him into surrendering his sword. He returned to Tokyo as a hero, and as an amazing example of persistence.

Colossians instructs us to have this kind of devotion to God's agenda:

> And we pray. . . that you may live a life worthy of the Lord and may please him in every way: bearing fruit in every good work, growing in the knowledge of God, being strengthened with all power according to his glorious might so that you may have great. . . patience (1:10–11).

James tells us that our persistent patience should resemble that of a farmer who waits for his crops to grow. The harvest we anticipate is the glorious coming of our Lord (5:7–8). Until that day we are to drive forward with diligence.

Perseverance and persistence are two sides of the coin of patience that are extremely needed in our day of multiple pressures.

This was illustrated recently in the life of my friend Andy. He is far from lethargic and phlegmatic. Neither is he plagued with indolence or indifference. Andy is a go-getter—enthusiastic, energetic, exciting to be around. He demands much of himself.

Andy and his daughter Kari were stranded in Reno Airport. It was a hot summer afternoon. En route from Salem their plane had developed mechanical difficulties. Unfortunately, no other vehicles were available to land them at their Los Angeles destination.

The tempers of the other passengers were flaring. They screamed at the airlines personnel with vehemence. Their words were cutting and extremely insulting. Having to spend an unplanned night in Reno was considered the height of CAUP (cruel and unusual punishment).

How about Andy and Kari? Well, to be honest, they experienced many of the same emotions. Andy was scheduled to preach at our church the next morning.

But in the midst of this madhouse of confusion, the still, small voice whispered calmness to his heart. The one who said, "Peace be still" to the angry waves long ago, spoke the same words to my friend. And that peace saturated his inner spirit.

He immediately began to speak to his twelve-year-old daughter. "Kari, this is our opportunity to show these people that Christians are different. We're not going to react the way they are. Jesus is going to help us to stay calm." His daughter smiled and gave an affirming nod.

Guess what? Andy and Kari did make the flight home that night. Here is what occurred. After the noise subsided, my minister friend slipped up to the ticket counter and said to the employee, "Ma'am, I appreciate what you've had to go through. It hasn't been easy. I understand completely."

The lady looked very shocked. With trembling lips she replied, "You mean that you're not here to complain like the others?" He assured her that he was not, although he would like to get home to fulfill his preaching assignment.

She immediately went to work. His patience simply must be rewarded. She located another airlines flight that was leaving that evening. He and his daughter were offered two of the twelve seats that were left.

They had persevered and persisted patiently. And answering their prayer, our Lord chose to reward them. He often does that for his disciples who manifest his fruit. As James puts it, the "trying of [their] faith [worked] patience" (1:3, KJV). May we manifest this kind of patience when we encounter a similar situation of stress.

But, in addition to being patient, we must exhibit the fruit of kindness.

Passing Out the Milk

Of all the fruit of the Spirit, kindness is among those that is most universally understood. The "milk of human kindness" is quickly recognized and widely admired.

Perhaps that is why the Golden Rule exists in varying forms among the major religions of the world.[5] Doing unto others as we wish to be done unto is basic and appreciated wherever it occurs.

5. Throughout the centuries, people of all faiths have acknowledged the Golden Rule as a vital, intrinsic part of their faith. They have expressed it in the following ways.

Bahaiism: "If thou lookest toward justice, choose then for others what thou choosest for thyself. Blessed is he who prefers his brother before himself."

Brahmanism: "This is the sum of duty: Do naught unto others which would cause you pain if done to you."

Buddhism: "In five ways should a clansman minister to his friends and familiars: by generosity, courtesy and benevolence, treating them as he treats himself and by being as good as his word."

Christianity: "All things whatsoever you would that men should do to you, do you even to them, for this is the law and prophets."

Confucianism: "Is there one word which may serve as a rule to practice for all one's life? The master said, 'Is not reciprocity (sympathy, consideration) such a word? What you do not want done to yourself, do not unto others.'"

Hinduism: "The lifegiving breaths of other creatures are as dear to them as the breaths of one's own self. Men gifted with intelligence and purified souls should always treat others as they themselves wish to be treated."

Jainism: "Indifferent to worldly objects, a man should wander about, treating all creatures in the world as he himself would be treated."

Judaism: "Thou shalt love thy neighbor as thyself."

Mohammedanism: "No one of you is a believer until he loves for his brother what he loves for himself."

Sikhism: "As thou deemest thyself, do seem others; then shalt thou become a partner in heaven."

Shintoism: "Irrespective of their nationality, language, manners and culture, men should give mutual aid, and enjoy reciprocal, peaceful pleasure by showing in their conduct that they are brethren."

Likewise, we're quick to pick up on its opposite, unkindness.

Not long ago, Cherry and I visited a friend. Only a handful of families live in her condominium complex. Among them is at least one Christian. I know this, because he attends the same church as my friend. His father, greatly respected by my father, was one of the highest executives in our denomination.

On this particular visit, I chose to park behind my friend's garage. Inadvertently, I failed to pull the car in as far as I should have. Nevertheless, I was certainly not prepared for this curt note on my windshield upon my return:

> **Please** *do not* park like this.
> It took me 15 minutes, and one
> bump of the garage to get out.

Ironically, on the back side of the note was engraved lettering that referred to his church!

Now, I'm certainly not defending how I parked. Nor am I happy about the difficulty he encountered. My focus is on his response. Inherent in his words seemed to be a spirit of unkindness. Of resentment.

How easy it is for us to react in a knee-jerk, unkind fashion when we've been inconvenienced!

But, again, how greatly appreciated is the kindness that we bestow. One of the nicest statements that is ever made at a funeral is, "He was a kind man," or, "She was a kind lady." In the final essence, that means more to people than how much wealth we accumulate, how many degrees we earn, or how many lofty positions we hold. Kindness is highly valued.

Taoism: "Regard your neighbor's gain as your own gain, and regard your neighbor's loss as your own loss."

Zoroastrianism: "That nature alone is good which refrains from doing unto another whatsoever is not good for itself."

The biblical word for kindness if *chrestotes*, meaning "a gentle or tender action, a spirit of compassion and concern."[6] It reflects a nonoffensive disposition that causes us to go out of our way to help and encourage.

Kindness is an attribute that is rooted in the very fiber of God's character.

And God raised us up with Christ and seated us with him in the heavenly realms in Christ Jesus, in order that in the coming ages he might show the incomparable riches of his grace, expressed in his kindness to us in Christ Jesus (Eph. 2:6–7).

Kindness also is synonymous with the grace of Jesus, whereby we have eternal salvation. Titus says so.

But when the kindness and love of God our Savior appeared, he saved us, not because of righteous things we had done, but because of his mercy (3:4–5a).

But, kindness is even more than a godly attribute, and more than a fruit of the Spirit. It is a command.

Therefore, as God's chosen people, holy and dearly loved, clothe yourselves with compassion, kindness, humility, gentleness and patience (Col. 3:12).

It is important to realize that this fruit is usually evidenced in behind-the-scenes service. Kindness

offers a cup of cold water in the name of Christ (Matt. 10:42).

visits widows and orphans in their distress (James 1:27).

stops to help the injured traveler on the road (Luke 10:29–37).

considers others as more important than ourselves (Phil. 2:3–4).

---

6. John Moore, "Kindness," *Moody Monthly*, op. cit., pp. 24–25.

Much in our culture mitigates kindness. Books instruct us to be on guard to protect ourselves. It's a jungle out there, every person for himself, and we're foolish to put ourselves out for another.

So, rather than seeking ways to exhibit this fruit, we're intent on maximizing our own interests. We knife into parking spaces that others are waiting on, take cuts in lines, refrain from telling salesclerks that they have mistakenly charged us too little. In short, we're out for number one, and some of us haven't even assigned numbers to others.

Sure, we warm up around Christmas or special occasions. By turning up our kindness mechanism full blast during such times, we assuage our consciences concerning the rest of the year.

Also, we're kind to persons whom, we perceive can do us good. This is called "pump-priming." Or ones who are especially kind to us. This is termed "back-scratching."

But, as Christ's redeemed and Spirit-filled followers, we must offer our milk of kindness to others. People who seem cold and unreceptive. People who are too proud (or ashamed) to ask for help. People who don't deserve our overtures—in short, people who were like us before our kind Lord reached down to us to make all things new.

Of course, it costs to be kind. Inconvenience. Overwork. Monetary sacrifice. The list goes on. And we can think of a million reasons to detour this task. As Phillip Keller states,

> Kindness is more than running a bluff on beleaguered people. It is more than pretending to be concerned by their condition. True kindness goes beyond the play acting of simulated sighs and crocodile tears. It is getting involved with the personal sorrows and strains of other lives to the point where it may well cost me pain—real pain—and some inconvenience.[7]

7. W. Phillip Keller, *A Gardener Looks at the Fruits of the Spirit* (Waco, TX: Word Books, 1979), pp. 126–127.

But, when we consider how Christ inconvenienced himself for us, our cost seems minimal. Even nonexistent.

We must be kind out of gratitude for his kindness to us, out of respect for other people, the apex of his creation. And even more than these reasons, our kindness will be generated from a heart saturated with his Holy Spirit.

Keller illustrates kindness by referring to the well-known missionary of yesteryear, David Livingstone.

His foot safaris took him thousands of miles through uncharted lands and among strange and savage tribes. Yet, wherever his footprints were left behind, there "remained the legacy of the love of Christ expressed in his simple, humble kindness to the natives." Long after his earthly journey was finished, he was remembered in Africa as the kind doctor. "What greater accolade could any man earn?"[8]

Having spoken of kindness, we now turn our attention to a fruit of the Spirit that is closely related. Let's explore the rich dimensions of goodness.

"If I've Told You Once, I've Told You a Thousand Times!"

Whenever our mothers say this oft-repeated line, invariably they want us to be good.

The French mother typically says to her child, "Be wise!" The German mother commands. "Do your duty!" And the Wintu Indian mother declares, "Obey the tribal rules."

But, the American mother's usual admonition is, "Be good!" Like little Jack Horner, of nursery rhyme fame, she wants her son to legitimately declare, "Oh, what a good boy am I."

Not only do mothers value goodness, it is considered

8. Ibid., p. 133.

a prized commodity throughout society. We usually attribute it to things. My wife's cherry cheesecake is "Uuuummm good!" Also, we attach it to activities. When our sports hero makes the winning shot, home run, or touchdown, we often say, "Good going!"

Usually, what isn't good is considered bad or, at best, mediocre. And most of us strive for the good.[9] By this, we mostly mean what seems right, comfortable, or ideal, based on the emotional and mental judgments that we (or those we respect) make.[10]

That's our broad and ambiguous connotation of the term good or goodness. How does the Bible define this important concept?

Paul uses his Greek word *agathosune*, which is defined as "virtue equipped at every point."[11] Uprightness and generosity are implied.

How does this word differ from kindness (*chrestos*)? Let's chart the two essential contrasts.

Kindness (*chrestos*)	Goodness (*agathosune*)
inward disposition of the heart	habitual actions in which the inward disposition reveals itself[12]
restricted to a focus on helping	includes helping, but also rebuking, correcting, and disciplining[13]

9. On the other hand, there is a substantial element in our society that attempts to depreciate moral goodness. Those so identified are commonly termed "dogooders," "goody-goodies" or "goody-two-shoes." Such jargon implies that moral goodness is synonymous with being weak, insipid, and even laughable. Ibid., p. 140.

10. Webster's *New World Dictionary* lists seventeen categories of definitions for "good." And each one has three or four meanings.

11. The Greek root word for "good" (*agathos*) appears 102 times in the New Testament, and fills two columns in Arndt and Gingrich's *Greek/English Lexicon of the New Testament*. The definitions include such words as genuine, uncontaminated, honorable, healthy, generous, desirable, pleasant, dependable, honest, loyal.

12. Alexander Maclaren, *Expositions of Holy Scripture: Second Corinthians, Galatians and Philippians* (New York: Hodder and Stoughton, no date), p. 165.

13. William Barclay, op. cit., p. 56.

We enjoy singing the chorus "God Is So Good." And we couldn't be more theologically on target. Our heavenly Father is the very essence of goodness.[14]

When Moses asked to see God's glory, he responded, "I Myself will make all My goodness pass before you . . . and I will be gracious to whom I will be gracious, and will show compassion on whom I will show compassion" (Exod. 33:19, NASB).

Following the dedication of the newly completed Temple, the Israelites "went to their tents joyful and glad of heart for all the goodness that the LORD had shown to David His servant and to Israel His people" (1 Kings 8:66, NASB; cf. Neh. 9:25, 35).

The psalmists declared God's goodness in providing for physical and spiritual needs. "Do not remember the sins of my youth or my transgressions; according to Thy loving kindness remember Thou me, for Thy goodness' sake, O LORD" (25:7, NASB). "I would have despaired unless I had believed that I would see the goodness of the LORD in the land of the living" (27:13, NASB; cf. 68:10; 107:9). Also, they spoke of God's goodness in protection. "How great is Thy goodness, which Thou has stored up for those who fear Thee, which Thou has wrought for those who take refuge in Thee, before the sons of men" (31:19, NASB).

And in the triumphant climax of most everyone's favorite Psalm, David declares, "Surely goodness and mercy shall follow me all the days of my life: and I will dwell in the house of the LORD for ever" (23:6, KJV).

---

14. In the original Anglo-Saxon, the very word *good* carried the same connotation as "God." God was considered good, and good was regarded as belonging essentially to God. The goodness of God isn't some "soft, spineless, sentimental indulgence of sensuality," as W. Phillip Keller declares: "Not some passing mood of the moment that makes one feel so good. It is not an emotional high in which reality fades away into some rosy glow of mystical magic.

"[His] goodness is the rugged reality of [His] coming to grips with the awfulness of sin . . . that invincible power . . . overcoming evil . . . the greatness of His love that dispels our despair and brings life out of our death . . . His generosity and graciousness in giving us Himself by His own Gracious Spirit. It is the enormous energy of His light and life extinguishing the evil in and around [us]. This goodness is the pulsating, powerful performance of right in the midst of wrong all around us." W. Phillip Keller, op. cit., pp. 141–42.

Because God is "the Source and Giver of every good and perfect gift" (James 1:17) we have an abiding hope. Why? His goodness translates into grace through his Son, whereby we might have fulfilling life on earth (John 10:10) and eternal life in heaven.

W. Phillip Keller, in his book entitled *A Gardener Looks at the Fruits of the Spirit*, offers this insight:

> Because God is good we have hope. Like the prodigal son back from the pigsty, there is a gold ring for our soil-stained hand—a white robe to clothe our sweatstained body—fresh sandals for our dung-stained feet—kisses for our tear-stained cheeks.[15]

As his goodness is bridged to our lives by Jesus, we will be certain to manifest it. Second Corinthians 5:23 (Phillips) says, "For God caused Christ. . .to be sin for our sakes, so that in Christ we might be made good with the goodness of God."

Therefore, we will first of all be good. To the very core of our being, goodness will prevail. And the result is a deep, abiding peace that this world can never know.

As Christians, we know that the truly great person is a good person, and the really good person is always great. He has lofty ideals, strong character, noble purposes, reliable conduct, trustworthy integrity.[16]

But, when we are good with God's goodness, we can expect some discomforts to occur. How do we know? Because they happened to our Lord during his earthly sojourn. Others will polarize in reacting to us. Either we'll strongly attract them, or they'll be decidedly repelled by our presence. Since fewer will be attracted to us, because most are traveling in the opposite direction of goodness, we're likely to feel pretty isolated and lonely.

Without a doubt these two realities are true concerning

15. Ibid., p. 143.
16. Ibid., p. 142.

the secular world. But, unfortunately, they can stalk us in the church. Even in that environment, persons fail to relentlessly pursue God's goodness—which puts them at odds with good people. Paul puts it plainly. "For what fellowship hath righteousness with unrighteousness? and what communion hath light with darkness?" (2 Cor. 6:14b, KJV).

Nevertheless, in being good we have nothing to fear, hide or protect. Nor do we have any need to apologize. God's goodness makes us simple, open, and uncomplicated persons who live with open hearts and hands. He supplies our every need. And as for our loneliness, he becomes our intimate friend. As the writer of Proverbs declares, "There is a friend who sticks closer than a brother" (18:24b).

But, in addition to being good we will also do good. We will sacrificially share what we are and have. This will include generosity with our time, talents, interests, strengths, energies, and capacities.

What we own we gladly place in Christ's hands. And like the loaves and fishes of old, it is blessed and multiplied a thousand times to enrich others' lives.

In a very real sense, we must think of ourselves as only the middlemen, giving to others what God has given to us. Colossians speaks of "bearing fruit in every good work" (1:10). Titus says, "Our people must learn to devote themselves to doing what is good" (3:14). Here's one of my favorites, Galatians 6:10: "Therefore, as we have opportunity, let us do good to all people, especially to those who belong to the family of believers."

The word used for goodness is translated "generous" in the story of the rich landowner (Matt. 20:1–15). His goodness is expressed in a generous act that did not rest on the recipient's performance. The latter did not deserve payment. Rather, the landowner gave because he desired the worker's well-being, just as Jesus does for us.

Likewise, we must generously give without considering the issue of fairness or deservability of those we give to. Granted. Saturated with our free enterprise mentality, such generosity is difficult for us. We say things such as, "Let them earn it like I had to do." "I'm not about to perpetuate their laziness by giving them a handout." "They've got their problems, I've got mine."

Nevertheless, we must continuously consider how undeserving we are, and how our good Lord and Savior gave to us with a generosity unparalleled. The very least we can do is return the favor to his needy children.

He expects all of us who claim to have his goodness in our hearts to

help the downtrodden	bring "oil of joy" to those
bind up broken hearts	who mourn
set prisoners free	spread light and cheer where
lift the fallen	there is darkness
feed the hungry	share the good news of God's
comfort the confused	gracious love to the lost[17]

Now, of course, being and doing good in the biblical sense is light years away from doing good works to gain merit. The first is a natural response to the indwelling Holy Spirit; the second is based on the selfish desire to be seen and praised.

Question: How can we become good persons and start growing in that goodness? Again, W. Phillip Keller makes four excellent practical suggestions.

1. Contemplate the cross. Prayerfully read the accounts of the crucifixion. Meditate over the tremendous cost to God, to Christ—who was made sin so that we might be good with his goodness. Accept his offer. Thank him. Allow him to implant goodness in the stony soil of your heart.

2. Ask Jesus to totally invade the territory of your life. Having asked him to establish a beachhead, now

17. Ibid., p. 146.

invite him to occupy. Give him liberty to love and change you, so that you become readied to exude his goodness to others.

3. As he lives in you, and you in him, keep the ground of your life clear, clean, and uncluttered. Be repentant of sins and penitent of unintentional faults, with genuine sorrow. Obey promptly, joyfully, simply (cf. Phil. 2:12–15).

4. Remind yourself always that you are the recipient, not the originator of every gift, possession and attribute that you own. All come from Jesus. Be deeply grateful for his inestimable generosity.[18]

A simple, four-step prescription for his goodness within—as well as without. We're well advised to follow it closely.

Patience. Kindness. Goodness. Christian qualities of character that we all need. Qualities that will serve us well as we relate to other people. Particularly those with whom we interface in close proximity.

These qualities can extract tension, lessen stress, provide a new, upbeat perspective that will make our worlds better. They are fruit that we in the Christian community need to produce and reveal.

But one more cluster of spiritual fruit remains. They likewise greatly help us in our relationships with others. Let's see how.

18. Ibid., pp. 148–149.

Not every slight requires a rejoinder; every fool need not be reminded that he is one.—Buckminster Fuller

God breaks up the private life of His saints, and makes it into a thorofare for the world—and for Himself.
—Oswald Chambers

Here am I, Lord; send my brother.—Prayer overheard

11

Fruit Cluster #3: Faithfulness, Gentleness, Self-control

One more cluster of Son-ripened fruit remains. This one includes three other important varieties that we must transport: faithfulness, gentleness, and self-control.

They help us relate with and respond to society in general. The system that confronts us daily. The secular culture that impinges upon us with never ceasing pressure. The Satan-dominated world that continually tempts us to dump the fruit that the Holy Spirit has given us.[1]

1. Watchman Nee, in his thought-provoking book *Love Not the World*, discusses Satan's control of the world order. He terms it "the mind behind the system." The prince of our world (Satan) governs an ordered system of unseen powers which have one main purpose: to deceive those who seek to follow God, who is the Spirit of truth. Satan seeks to enmesh men in his system. In Nee's words: "Salvation is not so much a personal question of sins forgiven or hell avoided (although it is that): (but, in addition) . . . it is a system from which we come out. When I am saved, I make my exodus out of one whole world and my entry into another. I am saved now out of that whole organized realm which Satan has constructed in defiance of the purpose of God." Watchman Nee, *Love Not the World* (Wheaton, IL: Tyndale, 1968), p. 38.

Alexander Maclaren puts it succinctly. "[These three fruit]...point to the world in which the Christian life is to be lived, a scene of difficulties and oppositions."[2] To employ the well-known phrase of J.B. Phillips, this triad keeps our alien world from "squeezing us into its mold."[3]

We can think of them in many ways, as protective clauses in our spiritual insurance policy, or shock absorbers that cushion us from society's bumpy roads. But, there is another image that really explains their extreme value more than any other.

Sometime ago I visited a marine life park. There were playful porpoises and dolphins, intelligent whales and sea lions, and many other captivating specimens of sea life. All the displays and performances were interesting.

I must say, however, that none compared to the deep sea diver's time of hand-feeding the fish. As we gazed into the glass tank from a lower lever, I saw all species of fish rapidly swim to her. Some were so small that they could hardly be seen. Others were gigantic. Most looked colorful and tame. But, then there were the sharks that looked very threatening.

The diver must have fed them for over an hour, then she glided to the surface.

Suddenly, an inspiring thought struck me. This lady had entered an alien environment. Without her oxygen tank, she would not have survived more than three minutes. If she had drunk ocean water, even in a small quantity, she would have perished.

Yet, our fish-feeding friend survived. Not only that, she seemed to thoroughly enjoy her task. Why was life so comfortable down there? Because her life-giving oxygen was supplied from an external source. She wasn't forced to rely on her immediate environment.

In a very real sense, this world is an alien environment

---

2. Alexander Maclaren, *Expositions of Holy Scripture: Second Corinthians, Galatians and Philippians* (New York: Hodder and Stoughton, no date), p. 166.

3. Romans 12:2

for us. No wonder we sing, "This world is not my home, I'm just a' travelin' through. My treasure is laid up somewhere beyond the blue."

Nevertheless, we're able to survive. More than that, we're able to enjoy life to its fullest—cultivating loving relationships, manifesting patience, exuding kindness and goodness—because of one reason: Jesus supplies us with a spiritual oxygen supply. As a result, he creates for us a new internal environment, and we can become "more than conquerors through him who loved us" (Rom. 8:37).

Bring out the microscope. We're about to take a scrutinizing look at the fruit of faithfulness. Unlocking its valuable secrets can add a remarkable dimension to our lives.

If It's Broke, Don't Fix It!

Most of us have heard the oft-repeated adage, "If it ain't broke, don't fix it!" Fully aware of my mechanical limitations, my wife tells me, "Even if it's broke, don't attempt to fix it. Call the repairman." Past attempts on my part have resulted in emotional and financial disaster.

Unfortunately for all of us, things continually break. Garbage disposals freeze. Cars won't start. Locks jam. Water heaters give out. In spite of our technological advancements, our gadgets and toys are unreliable.

Also, people are unreliable. A famous long-distance runner, in commenting on American athletes, said, "They're sensational in spirit, but get fagged out in the stretch."[4] Likewise, employers ulcerate because of absenteeism and tardiness. Christian education directors in churches cringe when the telephone rings on Sunday morning. Usually it's someone bailing out of a responsibility. As one said recently, "It's amazing what a sore hangnail can do to the Kingdom of God!"

4. Voiced by track star Herb Elliot.

Our world values reliability, trustworthiness, and fidelity. To be consistent is to be admired and appreciated. To be a flake is to be resented.

To paraphrase a quote I recently saw, nothing in the world will take the place of faithfulness.

Talent will not. Nothing is more common than unsuccessful people with talent.

Genius will not. Unrewarded genius is almost a proverb.

Education will not. The world is full of educated derelicts.

Faithfulness and determination alone will![5]

I couldn't help but laugh. In a recent major league allstar game, one player proved to be completely unreliable. Here was a fellow who had been selected by the fans. A coveted honor. Yet, he somehow couldn't bring himself to get ready for the big game.

Amazing! There he was on camera before tens of millions of television viewers wearing a ragtag outfit. It began when he forgot—yes *forgot*—to bring his uniform. Still desiring to play, he went to work putting together a makeshift arrangement. He bought a shirt from a replica shop. Wrote his number on the back with a felt-tip marker. Borrowed socks from a player on another team. And purchased his cap at the airport. What a sight!

We laugh, but how many of those we know are content to just get by? To expend the absolute minimum amount of effort? To refuse to be motivated except by crisis?

Faithfulness is a highly prized spiritual fruit. It means getting our act together. Having a self-starter that works. Making it known that people can count on us. We won't let them down. We won't flake out in the stretch.

---

5. Larry Richards and Norm Wakefield, *Fruit of the Spirit* (Grand Rapids, MI: Zondervan Publishing House, 1981), p. 108.

The Greek word for faithfulness, *pistos*, is translated many ways throughout Scripture: reliability, good faith, dependability, loyalty, assurance, and trustworthiness.

A recent Dennis the Menace cartoon has the little character holding up a handful of flowers to Mr. Wilson, and asking, "How can anything so pretty and clean come out of dirt?"[6]

We can legitimately ask the same question about ourselves as Christians. Galatians chapter five describes all the ugliness of the flesh. People so enslaved are doing little more than groveling in sin's dirt.

Yet, because of God's faithfulness, we are transformed into a bouquet of Christian graces. The point is this: Because of our heavenly Father's gift of faithfulness to us, we can exude faithfulness. In Paul's words, this can make us "a fragrant offering. . . pleasing to God" (Phil. 4:18).

Indeed, our God is faithful. 1 Thessalonians 5:24 declares, "The one who calls you is faithful." God is trustworthy. Available. Dependable. Never too busy, distracted, or tired. That's why, with assurance, we sing,

> Great is Thy faithfulness, O God my Father.
> There is no shadow of turning with Thee;
> Thou changest not, Thy compassions they fail not;
> As Thou hast been Thou forever wilt be. . .
> Great is Thy faithfulness, Lord, unto me![7]

What God says, he means. What he promises, he fulfills. What he offers, he gives. It's his nature to come through in the pinch, in the nick of time. He is totally faithful.

Likewise, Jesus our Lord is faithful. In fact, "Faithful" is one of his names (cf. Rev. 19:11). The term also describes

---

6. Donald Baker, "Faithfulness," *Moody Monthly*, September, 1983, p. 26.

7. *Worship in Song Hymnal* (Kansas City, MO: Lillenas Publishing Company, 1972), p. 86.

his witness (cf. Rev. 1:5) and his priesthood (cf. Heb. 2:17). We can fully depend on him to bring us into the presence of God.

He does more than commit; he covenants with us. Commitments are made and broken, depending on changes in circumstances. Covenants remain eternally. His are as good as his Word. And we can't imagine anything more reliable than that!

With this in mind, it is obvious that he expects us who have received the fruit of his Spirit to manifest faithfulness. This in spite of our perpetual propensity toward fickleness and flakiness.

One Corinthians 4:1–2 spells this out. "So then, men ought to regard us as servants of Christ and as those entrusted with the secret things of God. Now it is required that those who have been given a trust must prove faithful."

In his own parable of the talents, our Lord exalted the servant who demonstrated dependability. "His master replied, 'Well done, good and faithful servant! You have been faithful with a few things; I will put you in charge of many things. Come and share your master's happiness!'" (Matt. 25:21).

The emphasis here is on being diligent in the small and seemingly insignificant tasks. They are but precursors to momentous assignments, and gateways to our eternal reward.

Could this mean eventual martyrdom? Yes. That has certainly occurred in the lives of believers throughout the centuries—and even today it happens frequently. But the Christian martyr is triumphant. As Walt Emerson said,

> The martyr cannot be dishonored. Every lash inflicted is a tongue of fame; every prison a more illustrious abode; every burned book or house enlightens the world; every suppressed word reverberates through the earth from side to side.[8]

8. Walt Emerson, source unknown.

Church father Tertullian spoke the truth when he said, "The blood of the martyr is the seed of the church." Those faithful ones who have paid this supreme price are our heroes.[9] The very thought of what they went through should inspire our hearts.

Nevertheless, the likelihood is that we'll never be martyrs. Our faithfulness will be shown in other, less dramatic, manners. Things like completing assignments, keeping promises, paying bills, keeping appointments, doing work on time, honoring commitments, maintaining priorities—God's priorities.

When his Spirit within causes these to occur, we transcend the making of resolutions, which we're habitually doing at New Years. Rather, we'll experience inner revolution (2 Cor. 5:17). The latter, in contrast to the former, is generated from the core of our being.

Unlike so many today, let's vow to not sputter out in the stretch. Drawing upon God's power, let's remain faithful to the end. After all, we aren't hanging in there alone. In the very last verse of Matthew's Gospel, Jesus encourages us with these words: "And surely I am with you always, to the very end of the age" (Matt. 28:20).

Faithfulness is important. But so is the next fruit that we will now turn to, namely gentleness.

Speak Softly, and Carry No Stick!

Theodore Roosevelt (1858–1919) was our twenty-sixth President. Historians tell us that he was a feisty character, whose slogan was, "Speak softly, and carry a big stick." The idea was this: Don't threaten with words; strike at the enemy with promptness and might. To underscore his

9. "Be of good comfort," said Latimer to Ridley as they died at the stake together—at the time of Queen Mary in the 1500s. "We shall this day light a candle by God's grace, in England, and it shall never be put out."

Chrysostom advised Christians to give the name of a saint to their children, then to tell them constantly about the saint's life throughout their childhood. Hopefully, they would then grow up to model the saint's behavior.

belief in this philosophy, he sent America's "white fleet" around the world. The message went out loud and clear: "Don't mess with the U.S.A., or you'll be sorry!"

Stick theology is *not* biblical theology, regardless of what some super-patriots would have us believe. Our Lord carried a simple staff, not a threatening club.

Truly gentle persons are as rare as southern California snowstorms. Most of us react with a vengeance when experiencing the slightest provocation.

The other day, however, I found an exception to this rule. Here's a fellow who may have had a legitimate right to be less gentle than he was. I'll allow him to relate his unbelievable account, which is contained in this letter to his supervisor.

> When I arrived at the construction site I found that a hurricane had knocked some bricks off the top of the building. So, I rigged up a beam, with a pulley on the highest level. Then, I hoisted up a couple barrels full of bricks. After fixing the damaged area at the top, I noticed that a lot of bricks were left over. So, I went down to the bottom and began releasing the line. That's when the problems began.

> Unfortunately, the barrel of bricks was heavier that I was—and before I realized what was happening, the barrel started coming down—jerking me up. I decided to hang on, since I was now too far off the ground to let go. Halfway up, I met the barrel of bricks coming down fast. I received a hard blow on my shoulder. Then, I continued to the top—banging my head against the beam, and finding my fingers jammed in the pulley.

> When the barrel hit the ground hard, it burst its bottom, spilling out the bricks. Well, I was now heavier than the barrel, so I started going down again. With high speed, halfway down, I met the barrel coming up fast—and received severe injuries to my shins. When I landed on the ground, I hit the pile of bricks—getting several deep and painful bruises.

At this point, I must have lost presence of mind, because I let go of the grip of the line, and the barrel came down fast—giving me another blow on my shoulder and head. And putting me in the hospital.

I respectfully request sick leave.[10]

I surmise that most of us would have come out of that situation swinging, crying, threatening to sue, or all three! Ours would not have been a polite and gentle request for sick leave.

Why aren't we Americans more gentle? For one thing, we feel that being gentle makes us vulnerable. People may take advantage of us, mistake us for being a pawn. A chump. An easy mark.

For another, we who are macho-oriented males shy away from gentleness because it may make us appear wimpish. Real he-men, we feel, need to be aggressive and competitive. Gentleness is for women, children, and gentlemen.

Question: What does the term *gentle* mean when listed as one of the spiritual fruit?

The Greek word is *praotes*, which William Barclay says is the "most untranslatable of words." It has no less than three meanings in the New Testament

1. submissive to the will of God (cf. Matt. 5:5; 11:29; 21:5)

2. teachable in all good things—not too proud to learn (cf. James 1:21)

3. considerate toward our fellow humans (1 Cor. 4:21; 2 Cor. 10:1; Eph. 4:2)[11]

The third of these meanings is used most often.

10. Source unknown. Presented in a sermon.
11. William Barclay, *The Daily Study Bible: The Letters to the Galatians and Ephesians* (Philadelphia, PA: The Westminster Press, 1954), pp. 56–57.

Through the centuries, gentleness has referred to being tame—what a wild horse must become if he is to be of any use.

For the Christian, gentleness means being tamed by God's Holy Spirit. When we're gentle, we're tame toward others. In difficult circumstances. When others are inconsiderate. We're tender when others are abrasive, quiet when others are aloud and coarse.[12]

There's really nothing wimpish or cowardly about that. In fact, the opposite is true. When we are truly gentle, we demonstrate strength, God's strength.

For our Lord, gentleness was a life experience. It was his natural, spiritual reflex. Even while suffering on the cross, he was considerate of his mother's need for care and safety (cf. John 19:26–27).

In Matthew's Gospel, Jesus says,

> Take my yoke upon you and learn from me, for I am gentle and humble in heart, and you will find rest for your souls. For my yoke is easy and my burden is light" (11:29–30).

When approaching Jerusalem for the last time, Jesus chose to ride on a donkey. Why? To reveal his gentle spirit.

> This took place to fulfill what was spoken through the prophet: "Say to the Daughter of Zion, 'See, your king comes to you, gentle and riding on a donkey, on a colt, the foal of a donkey'" (Matt. 21:4–5; cf. Zech. 9:9).

In the nineteenth century, history records that Chancellor Bismarck of Prussia chose to make his grand entrance into Jerusalem on a white horse. And he was accompanied by such a large army of officials that a section of the wall had to be removed.

Not so with our Lord. He chose a donkey. Why? Unlike the ostentatious Chancellor, he was gentle of heart.

And if he was gentle and lowly—being the very Son of

---

12. Arthur Evans Gay, Jr., "Gentleness," *Moody Monthly*, September, 1983, p. 27.

God—we can assure ourselves that we're expected to be the same. Especially since he has provided this fruit through the blessed Holy Spirit. Like the lemons that hung on our backyard tree, his fruit of gentleness is ours for the plucking.

His Beatitudes declare, "Blessed are the poor in spirit. . . . Blessed are the meek" (Matt. 5:3, 5). Another way of saying the same truth is that we need to manifest gentleness and thereby reveal our humility.

When writing to the Colossians, Paul said, "Therefore, as God's chosen people, holy and dearly loved, clothe yourselves with compassion, kindness, humility, gentleness and patience" (3:12).

Any time we clothe ourselves with garments, they are displayed for everyone to see. We're making a fashion statement. We're wearing a costume that says something significant about who we are. Let's be certain to include gentleness in our wardrobe!

The disciple called Rock instructs us to be gentle when presenting the gospel to others—not harsh, condemning, insulting, not with a distasteful air of self-righteousness. Rather, we are to do so with gentleness.

> Always be prepared to give an answer to everyone who asks you to give the reason for the hope that you have. But do this with gentleness and respect (1 Peter 3:15b).

How about when we're being unfairly confronted, or when people come at us with slanderous remarks? When Timothy encountered such situations, Paul instructed him to

> [not] have anything to do with foolish and stupid arguments, because. . . they produce quarrels. And the Lord's servant must not quarrel; instead he must be kind to everyone, able to teach, not resentful. Those who oppose him he must gently instruct, in the hope that God will grant them repentance leading them to a knowledge of the truth (2 Tim. 2:23–25).

The point is crystal clear. We are to display and transport the fruit of gentleness.

In our *conversation*. Gentle words are comforting and edifying. They reflect a heart filled with God's presence.

In our *conduct*. Proverbs 16:7 tells us: "When a man's ways are pleasing to the *Lord*, he makes even his enemies live at peace with him." Concerning fellow Christians, Paul exhorts, "If someone is caught in a sin, you who are spiritual should restore him gently" (Gal. 6:1).

Finally, in our conflict. As Timothy was told above, quarreling gets us nowhere!

Norman Wakefield summarizes gentleness in this manner:

> When I am indwelt by the spirit of gentleness my own life is enriched. I enjoy more harmonious relationships with others. God's indwelling peace allows me to approach uncertain and stressful situations without anxiety.
>
> In the strength of meekness I can act with gentleness. I am able to be a better steward of my energy because I do not dissipate it with anxiety, strife or frustration.[13]

May gentleness reign in our hearts. In spite of this world's sea of beckoning fingers that lure us to react with abruptness and hostility.

We can become truly gentle. We can possess this Christlike strength.

There is one more fruit that God's Spirit produces in us. Like gentleness, self-control can provide enrichment and fulfillment in the midst of a morally bankrupt world. Let's examine it closely.

Leashes and Lashes

In describing the kind of restraint persons should exhibit, one writer appealed for willpower that is both a leash and a lash.

13. Richards and Wakefield, op. cit., pp. 120–121.

As any poodle in my neighborhood can tell you, a leash restricts his behavior. He isn't able to wander off.

A lash is used on a racehorse to make him change his behavior. Either he's made to go faster or to get back in his lane.

In essence, this is exactly how we should be able to control ourselves. *Leashing* or restricting ourselves from doing impulsive, self-defeating things. *Lashing* or motivating ourselves to excel, together with chiding ourselves when we fail.[14]

Self-control is a remarkable, greatly admired quality in our society. But the Chinese do more than admire this virtue, they put it into practice. Perhaps rooted in their eastern religion heritage, the orientals are adept at conditioning themselves to be passive, respectful, reserved.[15]

I had to smile recently when I came upon the rejection letter that was sent from a Chinese publisher to an aspiring author. Talk about polite ways to say no, this one takes the cake.

Dear respected sir:

We have read your manuscript with boundless delight. But if we were to publish your book, it would be impossible for us to publish work of lower standard. And as it is unthinkable that, in the next 3,000 years, we shall see its

14. Plato antedated Sigmund Freud's tripartite explanation of the self by declaring that every person has a horse named Passion, and another one called Reason. These two animals run hitched-up in the same team. Furthermore, they continually battle for supremacy. The charioteer is the core self that must unsparingly use the whip on these animals when either attempts to dominate the other. [Note: The horse Passion is roughly equated to Freud's id; Reason is a near approximation of the super ego; and the charioteer might be construed as the ego.]

15. Buddhism, Taoism and the other eastern religions emphasize the importance of being passive, of allowing reality to flow into us by noninvolvement and noneffort (*wo-wei*). The idea is to empty oneself of sensual concerns, through meditation and other means. Only then can "cosmic consciousness" (a vague, God-like, universal spirit) take over our beings. Whereas western religions accentuate doing, eastern ones emphasize being—or even nonbeing. [See Ernest Benz. "On Understanding Non-Christian Religions," in *Religion, Culture and Society: A Reader in the Sociology of Religion*, ed. Louis Schneider, (New York: John Wiley and Sons, Incorporated, 1964), pp. 3–9.]

equal, we are regretfully compelled to return your divine composition. We beg you a thousand times to overlook our short sight and timidity.

Your humble servants[16]

Now *that's* a controlled response, compared with the kind that I have received—the don't-call-us-we'll-call-you variety.

Whether related to how we communicate, act, or think, self-control is a great virtue. Rather than leading to rigidity, it more often results in freedom. Just as the tightness of the violin string allows the musician to freely engender beautiful sounds, so the control we exercise gives us latitude to experience more of life. Persons who can concentrate come up with creative ideas. Individuals who can focus attention on their jobs—be they in offices or on athletic fields—are freed to excel!

When we lack self-control, we invariably feel the need to fake, fudge (misrepresent facts and figures), or finagle by making excuses.

On her syndicated radio program, Psychologist Dr. Joyce Brothers states that we customarily make three kinds of excuses to cover our ineptitude.

1. not me ("This is a clear case of mistaken identity. I'm not the culprit!")

2. not so bad ("Sure, I'm guilty, but the results aren't nearly as tragic as you think!")

3. not all the picture ("You bet, I did it, and the effects are pretty devastating. But, there are mitigating circumstances that should make you excuse my behavior.")[17]

Here's the irony of lacking self-control: It often requires

16. Source unknown. Read at a conference on leadership.
17. Joyce Brothers, heard on KABC radio in Los Angeles, July 29, 1987.

more time, money, and energy to cover up the shabby results of our incompetence than does simple TCB (taking care of business).

This principle may figure into why Paul includes self-control in his list of spiritual fruit. The Greek word is *egkrateia*, which implies "the kind of self-mastery that makes us into true servants." According to William Barclay, the term was used to describe an emperor who never allowed his private interests to influence his role in government. He had the willpower to separate the two.

Paul employed the word to describe an athlete's discipline of his body. "And every man that striveth for the mastery is temperate in all things. Now they *do it* to obtain a corruptible crown; but we an incorruptible" (1 Cor. 9:25, KJV).

In the same Letter, he relates self-control to sexual temptations. "But if they [unmarried and widows] cannot control themselves, they should marry, for it is better to marry than to burn with passion" (7:9).

Peter instructs us to "make every effort to add to [our] faith...self-control" (2 Peter 1:5, 6). It's in his list of essentials—and it must be in ours.

And as Norman Wakefield states, life for many of us is much like an ocean. "The mire of failure is constantly being stirred up. Instability controls [us] like unseen currents. Crashing waves break up the little order [we] have. For [us] the hope of self-control [seems like] a vanishing dream."[18]

But, when the love of Jesus floods into our hearts and saturates us completely, when God's Spirit reigns supreme, then self-control will be the natural expression of our lives. It will somehow fit with what we are and what we aspire to be. This is in contrast to the bite-the-bullet, radical denial kind of self-control that the world speaks about.

18. Richards and Wakefield, op. cit., p. 132.

This contrast is vividly revealed in a story I recently heard. A Christian lady was married to an ogre. A cruel taskmaster who was impossible to please. When she served him perfectly, he ignored mentioning it. When she failed concerning some minute task, she was quick to hear his fear-inducing roar.

Her husband went so far as to make a long list of his demands. They filled an entire page with small print. Just glancing at it gave her a headache and depression.

Well, in the providence of God, the man suddenly died. She was released from her torturous imprisonment.

After a few years she met a truly Christian gentleman—the polar opposite of her previous husband. They fell in love and married, and their love continued to accelerate for one another because of their oneness in Christ.

One particular day she found herself cleaning the house. She opened a drawer, looked down, and froze. There it was. *That* note. That list of cruel, impossible demands. How could he have possibly expected so much?

Then something very enlightening occurred. Upon closer scrutiny, the woman realized that she was doing *everything listed* for her second husband. Everything. And she hadn't even realized it.

Why had the duties been a drudgery before, when they were so easy and even enjoyable now? Because now her labor was the fruit of mutual love and respect. Same work. Same Tasks. But now they were a natural response from her heart.

Self-control that emerges from our love for Christ is far from being a slow burn. It is enlivening. A privilege. Something we accept willingly—no matter how long the list!

Faithfulness, or reliability. Gentleness, or consideration of others. Self-control, or self-mastery that makes us into his servants. All are so essential. We need to transport them all over the bridges that he has helped us to build.

Added to the other spiritual fruit that we have described, these are destined to satiate the appetites of our spiritually famished world.

But it all starts with bridge building. We must construct bridges that are strong, that extend to a wide variety of persons, and that transport life-giving fruit of the Spirit.

Jesus cares deeply about bridge building. He demonstrated this countless times throughout history, and in his Word he admonished us to do the same.

Saints of the past accepted his challenge. His disciples. Saint Francis, Martin Luther, John Wesley, some of our own ancestors. These, and so many more, have linked us with the God they faithfully served in spite of dungeon, fire, or sword.

And there are scores of present-day bridge builders. We have heard of their dedicated lives: Billy Graham, who courageously ventured behind the Iron Curtain to preach Christ; Chuck Colson, whose prison ministry has touched the lives of thousands of destitute inmates; Anthony Campolo, whose convicting message has effectively linked the world's impoverished with the vast resources of Christians.

Who could possibly forget Mother Teresa! This tireless, remarkable woman cares for India's poor and dying. Even when on a trip to be honored by our President, this angel of mercy visited Washington, D.C.'s suffering. We would have expected that.

Coming closer to home, most of us realize that we owe much to certain persons who have built bridges to us. They're in our families, friendships, places of employment, churches. Toward them we feel a tremendous sense of gratitude as well as an eternal love-bond.

Furthermore, it inspires our hearts to hear about others who have built Christian bridges.

In the final chapter, allow me to tell three brief stories that will encourage your heart. Perhaps they will motivate you to reach out in love as never before.

You can tell the character of a man by the way he treats those who can do nothing for him.—Dan Reeves

If only all the hands that reach could touch.—Loberg

My wife and I sleep in separate bedrooms, take separate vacations and eat separately at mealtimes. We're doing all we can to keep this marriage together.
—Rodney Dangerfield

12

He Makes the Pieces Fit!

The writer of Proverbs sounds much like a jeweler: "A word aptly spoken is like apples of gold in settings of silver" (25:11).

He is right. Words can conjure up beautiful mindscapes that yield intense pleasure. Also, words can engender great energy, so that perspectives are enlarged and actions motivated.

Nevertheless, as we've all heard, one picture is worth a thousand words.

Vision transcends verbiage. While an absence of words can bring relief (cf. 1 Thess. 4:11), a lack of vision can cause us to perish (cf. Prov. 29:18, KJV).

With this in mind, allow me to show you not one but three pictures. They're not like the photographs we have in our scrapbooks. Rather, they more closely resemble action-filled moving pictures. One scene follows another with eye-blink rapidity. And the providential events combine to yield intense Christian drama.

Not only that. Each story provides a valuable lesson for those of us who commit ourselves to excellent Christian bridge building.

Cranberries, Anyone?

In Ted Engstrom's insightful book, *The Fine Art of Friendship*, he relates a story about his wife Dorothy.

It was the day before Thanksgiving. She rushed to the market to pick up one item, a jar of cranberries.

There was only one jar left on the shelf. As she reached for it, another lady's hand reached out to grasp the same jar. Apparently, she also needed this item to make her Thanksgiving dinner complete.

Each of the ladies insisted that the other take the jar. Finally, the store manager intervened and assured them that there were more jars of cranberries in the stock room.

Was this a happenstance? A chance encounter? A fluke? Not really. Instead, it was the beginning of a friendship that had eternal significance.

Here are the events that quickly transpired. Dorothy offered Bette a favorite recipe, a pink and fluffy cranberry sherbet.

Then, soon after the holidays, the two women began meeting socially. Before long, Bette's husband Ned began stopping by the Engstroms' home to visit.

One day Ned and Bette requested assistance in meeting people in the community, for they had just moved there.

The master bridge-building architect gave his servant Dorothy a plan. She invited Bette to her Christian women's Bible study. This led to an invitation to an afternoon prayer meeting.

Dorothy didn't wish to appear pushy, but the Holy Spirit seemed to be urging her to link Bette to positive, spiritual influences.

At the first afternoon prayer session something marvelous occurred. Bette quietly slipped to her knees, and brushing back tears that ran down her cheeks, asked Jesus to come into her life.

Our Lord only had to be asked once. His presence flooded Bette's heart.

Well, this event occurred over twenty years ago. Today, Bette, Ned and their five children are some of the Engstroms' closest friends. More important, the entire Vessey family has invited Jesus into their lives.

And it all began when two women providentially reached for a lone jar of cranberries![1]

What useful lesson can we learn from this inspiring account? *Bridges can be built just about anywhere and at any time. Therefore, we must be continually perceptive of people's situations, open to them, and prepared to start building.*

Don't Charge *Me* for Your Prayers!

This story did not begin on such a positive, cordial note. I know, because I was there.

The setting was a university classroom. I had been invited to guest lecture to three hundred students.

After being introduced, I did something that is my usual practice. I invited the class to join me in a brief word of prayer. This is perfectly in order at our Christian university.

The prayer couldn't have lasted over thirty seconds. Then my lecture on "Culture" began.

When the class was dismissed, I lingered in front to answer questions of individual students. Several approached me, mainly to clarify certain issues for their notes.

But one student stalked toward me with something else on his mind. It was evident in his eyes and demeanor. He did not wish to ask anything. Instead, he wanted to tell

1. Ted W. Engstrom (with Robert C. Larson), *The Fine Art of Friendship* (Nashville, TN: Thomas Nelson Publishers, 1985), pp. 25–26.

me something. Something that made him very upset. His voice was very audible.

This student deeply resented the fact that I had chosen to pray in class. I'll never forget his words. "You used class time to pray, time that I paid money for. I feel robbed!"

Being as nondefensive as I knew how, I invited the young man to my office. He showed up within minutes.

To begin, I asked him to tell me about himself. He seemed to relax a bit as he spoke.

I learned that his family originated in India but currently resided in Hong Kong. They were wealthy. Like him, they did not believe in the views of Christianity, for they were Hindu.

As he spoke, I realized that there were thick layers of walls between us: professor versus student, Indian versus American, wealthy versus not wealthy, Christian versus Hindu. We were continents apart.

I must confess I was too unprepared to say much of anything. I just listened. But that seemed to calm him considerably. When he departed that day, I simply invited him back to talk some more. He seemed shocked, but said that he would come.

And he did. The next time he carried with him a book that he wanted me to read. It was about love from an Eastern religions perspective. Because the book had meant so much to him, I decided to take the time to read it.

In a couple weeks he returned. This time to discuss the book he had given me to read. I assured him that I had found certain parts of the book informative. He seemed very pleased.

Then I asked him if he had ever read the Bible. He assured me that he had not. But more important, he did not assure that he would not. Since I had read his favorite book, he agreed to read mine.

Following this, we met a number of times. I was amazed to see how the young man began to change. The antagonism vanished. He relaxed, and we communicated. At times we would have a hearty laugh together.

My nemesis actually became my friend. Sure, the walls remained, but they became shorter and thinner. We were able to transcend them easily because of Jesus.

Well, our relationship continued, and deepened, for two years. My friend was now a senior. He still was not a Christian, and it seemed that he would not become one. His attention gravitated toward the lucrative family business that he would be heading after his graduation.

As I recall, he had not stopped by my office for several weeks. I assumed that he was in the throes of a hectic year and might not return at all. Nevertheless, I prayed for his spiritual welfare.

At the close of a typical school day, I grabbed my briefcase and began walking toward the car. My thoughts were homeward as I saw the Malibu sun chinning itself on the horizon.

Suddenly, I heard a loud voice calling out from the opposite end of the parking lot. "Dr. Jon, wait a minute!" I looked up, and running toward me with a beaming smile was my Indian friend.

After catching his breath he said the words I wanted to hear "I have accepted Jesus Christ into my heart, and I never knew that it could be so wonderful!"

My heart leaped within me. I could hardly believe what I was hearing. All of the walls collapsed at once. We were now more than friends, we were Christian brothers!

Some Christian students had invited him to a weekend retreat. He had responded to their love and teaching, putting it together with what we had discussed. The Lord had faithfully dealt with his open heart. Praise his name!

Words cannot express the joy I felt that day, greater than if the young man had offered me a million dollars.

A love bridge had been constructed. One that would last forever.

As I drove home, I could only pray that this scene would be repeated over and over again.

Is there a helpful lesson that can be learned from this experience? Yes. *We must relentlessly work at building a bridge, regardless of the other person's reaction and in spite of how long the construction process requires.*

The Undelivered Christmas Present

This story seems as though it could be a best-selling novel. Certainly, all the necessary drama is present.

But unfortunately it isn't fiction. It really occurred. And one of my best friends felt the full, tragic impact.

At the time, Tom was a small boy living in southern California. His father had a severe drinking problem, and the whole family endured the pain.

One evening just before Christmas, Tom's father clutched a present for his son. He was on his way home to deliver it. Anyone seeing him walk could see that he had had too much to drink. He stumbled into the path of an oncoming car, which struck him with terrific force. He lay there motionless. Tom's father was dead.

At this critical time, a kind minister and loving lay-persons reached out. Tom crossed their bridge to the Savior. Jesus became his missing father and changed his life forever.

We attended church youth camps together. He spoke of a divine call to become a minister.

Before long, we found ourselves at the same Christian college. I recall his disciplined study habits and spiritual growth. That pattern continued when we attended seminary.

His mother, still not a Christian, voiced no uncertain objection to the pathway he had chosen. She had greater aspirations for her son, and felt the pain of this denouncement. Nevertheless, he continued his ministerial preparation with an unwavering faith.

After graduating from seminary, he accepted a prestigious ecclesiastical position. This involved traveling throughout the country, speaking, and planning, which he did with expertise and innovation.

His successes, however, led to his demise. Certain superiors felt that he was overzealous, and this seemed to make their jobs more difficult.

In response, my friend was released from his position for being too excellent in his dispatch of duty.

Refusing to give up, he accepted a pastorate. His dreams were big. Unfortunately, so were his failures. In spite of some church growth, the people were not very responsive to him. So the young minister resigned from that church with a heavy heart. He began to seriously wonder about his future.

Eventually, this tenacious servant of God accepted another church. But this time, as never before, he tirelessly labored to build bridges to his members and even more to the needy in the city.

For example, he started a "happy hour" for reformed alcoholics. He and his wife taught a divorce recovery workshop, along with a seminar for single parents. Scores of people attended.

My friend rode night patrol with policemen in order to minister to victims of tragedy.

Many crossed the bridges he had constructed, and began attending the church. The pastor with all the members of the choir would meet them in the parking lot with a heartfelt welcome.

What had been a very small church grew to become the largest in the city.

Why? Because my friend had demonstrated and taught the importance of bridge building. Of getting beyond the church's four walls in order to truly minister.

Concerning the church walls, they had to be greatly expanded. Growth occurred in geometric proportions. Everyone seemed to come to hear "that minister who welcomes you in the parking lot."

Many other churches heard about my friend's success and invited him to be their pastor. He politely withdrew his name. He wasn't interested in climbing any ecclesiastical success ladder. He was content to continue carrying out a fruitful ministry in a needy city.

But, as we might expect, this faithful servant was sensitive to the voice of God. And one day an invitation came that his heavenly Father would not permit him to ignore. A shocked congregation heard him say that he was leaving.

This time he went to a strong church, with the intention of making it stronger. At the time of this writing, my friend has served this church for just over two years. The growth has been remarkable—nearly thirty percent.

What is the precipitant? Again, it is the bridge-building efforts of a minister and his people. They are offering the life-giving fruit of the Spirit to multitudes of needy people. They comb hospital wards. Visit prisoners and shut-ins. And operate nearly two dozen recovery groups that are extended to such persons as substance abusers, divorcees, and the poor.

My friend is now preaching three sermons on Sunday mornings. His church building, again, cannot contain the large crowds.

In spite of this, he continues to greet visitors in the parking lot, cordially welcoming them to the house of God.

And when they enter the doors, church members warmly receive them with a "Where-have-you-been-all-my-life?" look in their eyes.

That's only the beginning. On the following Monday, newcomers receive a plate of warm cookies along with materials that explain the church's programs and ministries.

Soon after, Sunday school teachers, youth leaders, and other laypersons begin to visit. As a body, the entire church extends tender loving care. Could any of us resist this for long?

Well, my friend never received his earthly father's Christmas present that traumatic day. But, on another day—this one triumphant—his heavenly Father will make up for it. For then, he shall receive an eternal reward.

What essential lesson does this minister's story teach us? *Regardless of the pain and resistance we endure, we must refuse to build walls of protection. Instead, our divine imperative is to continue building bridges.*

Three stories. Three lessons. All point to both the possibility and necessity of building bridges to those who need us. And to those we need to serve.

A Parting Word

Jesus built bridges. So *durable* they've lasted for two thousand years. So *diverse* that they connect all human beings with his heavenly Father.

Likewise, he expects us his faithful followers to join the spiritual bridge builder's union. He promises to show and tell us about this important enterprise each step of the way. He shows by his example. He tells by his revealed Word.

Most of us cannot expect to construct bridges as impressive as the ones built by Mother Teresa, Chuck Colson, or Billy Graham. Their "Golden Gates" are beyond our capabilities.

Nevertheless, we can all begin constructing bridges that are commensurate with our God-given capabilities, bridges that

link others with *Jesus*;

connect them with dynamic *ministers*;

bond outsiders with consecrated, Christian *laymen*; and

fuse lonely isolates with *ourselves*.

In so doing, we must constantly remind ourselves that Christian bridge building involves three essential steps: design (construction), destination (connection), delivery (commerce). We have attempted to explain each of these in the three sections of this book.

William Barclay speaks the truth when he emphasizes the importance of relationships for the Christian.

> It is very significant that Christianity began with a group. The Christian faith is something which, from the beginning, had to be discovered and lived out in relationship.[1]

While the ancient Pharisees, whose very name means "separated ones," sought isolation and insulation, Christians have always lived in communion. In oneness. In unity. When we build walls rather than bridges, we are, without a doubt, acting in an un-Christian manner.

Ninety-nine out of one hundred believers will agree with this biblical conclusion. However, becoming dedicated bridge builders is another issue.

Some of us have earnestly, conscientiously attempted to build bridges, but have failed. We've not been adequately trained. When it comes to relationships skills, we're klutzes. Or, we know how to construct only one type of bridge and think that it will suffice for all kinds of people. Or, we build self-designed structures according to our mistake-prone specifications. We refuse to construct them God's way.

Others of us have constructed some pretty decent-looking structures, but have neglected to use them for spiritual commerce. Instead of transporting authentic fruit of the Spirit, we've used our linkages for secular purposes—just to be sociable. To have fun. To avoid being lonely.

Still others of us have been far too selective. We've divided humanity into two categories: designers and ge-

1. *The Daily Study Bible: Gospel of Mark* (Philadelphia: The Westminster Press, 1954), pp. 68–69.

nerics. The first we respond to warmly; the second we avoid like the plague, or we do un-Christlike things such as putting them down ("You are beneath me and my kind"), putting them on ("I'll only let you see what I choose to let you see"), putting them off ("I'll do anything to avoid having an authentic relationship with you").[2]

We must begin today to build bridges. And as we do, grotesque walls in our lives will crumble and collapse.

We have no time to waste, for life is so short. John Wesley's comment is pointed:

> I am a creature of a day, passing through life, as an arrow through the air. I am a spirit come from God, and returning to God; just hovering over the great gulf; until a few months hence, I am no more seen! I will drop into an unchangeable eternity.
>
> I want to know *one* thing, the way to heaven; how to land safely on that happy shore.[3]

What we do we must do quickly. For the time that knows us now will soon know us no more. Bridge building on the double!

But while we're deeply absorbed in our important task, we are well-advised to keep this fact in mind: While we are building bridges *for* God, we are building bridges *to* him.

In short, the linkages we construct to others will become our bridges to heaven's blissful shores. For, by joining God in doing his will, we assure ourselves of the fact that we will someday receive the fullness of his will.

We've talked enough. Excuse me. Will you please hand me that plank?

---

2. Jon Johnston, *Will Evangelicalism Survive Its Own Popularity?* (Grand Rapids, MI: Zondervan Publishing House, 1980), p. 44.

3. John Wesley, Preface to his two volumes of sermons.

Appendix **1**

Stanford Shyness Survey

T his is a version of the survey that we gave to over 5,000 people around the world. Fill it out quickly, then go back over it more carefully to see how exactly shyness affects your life. This is not a scored test, rather it is intended to stimulate self-appraisal and group discussion.

_____ 1. Do you consider yourself to be a shy person?
   1 = yes
   2 = no

_____ 2. If yes, have you always been shy (were shy previously and still are)?
   1 = yes
   2 = no

_____ 3. If no to question 1, was there *ever* a prior time in your life when you were shy?
   1 = yes
   2 = no

   If no, then you are finished with this survey. Thank you.
   If yes to any of the above, please continue.

_____ 4. How shy are you when you feel shy?
   1 = extremely shy
   2 = very shy

226

        3 = quite shy
        4 = moderately shy
        5 = somewhat shy
        6 = only slightly shy

_____ 5. How often do you experience (have you experienced) these feelings of shyness?
        1 = every day
        2 = almost every day
        3 = often, nearly every other day
        4 = one or two times a week
        5 = occasionally, less than once a week
        6 = rarely, once a month or less

_____ 6. Compared with your peers (of similar age, sex, and background), how shy are you?
        1 = much more shy
        2 = more shy
        3 = about as shy
        4 = less shy
        5 = much less shy

_____ 7. How desirable is it for you to be shy?
        1 = very undesirable
        2 = undesirable
        3 = neither desirable nor undesirable
        4 = desirable
        5 = very desirable

_____ 8. Is (or was) your shyness ever a personal problem for you?
        1 = yes, often
        2 = yes, sometimes
        3 = yes, occasionally
        4 = rarely
        5 = never

_____ 9. When you are feeling shy, can you conceal it and have others believe you are not feeling shy?
        1 = yes, always

2 = sometimes I can, sometimes not
3 = no, I usually can't hide it

_____ 10. Do you consider yourself more of an introvert or an extrovert?
1 = strongly introverted
2 = moderately introverted
3 = slightly introverted
4 = neither
5 = slightly extroverted
6 = moderately extroverted
7 = strongly extroverted

(11–19) Which of the following do you believe may be among the causes of your shyness? Check all that are applicable to you.

_____ 11. Concern for negative evaluation

_____ 12. Fear of being rejected

_____ 13. Lack of self-confidence

_____ 14. Lack of specific skills (specify): _____
_____

_____ 15. Fear of being intimate with others

_____ 16. Preference for being alone

_____ 17. Value placed on nonsocial interests, hobbies, etc.

_____ 18. Personal inadequacy, handicap (specify): _____
_____
_____

_____ 19. Others (specify): _____
_____
_____

(20–27) Perceptions of your shyness
Do the following people consider you to be shy? How shy do you think they judge you to be? Answer using this scale.

1 = extremely shy
2 = very shy
3 = quite shy
4 = moderately shy
5 = somewhat shy
6 = only slightly shy
7 = not shy
8 = don't know
9 = not applicable

_____ 20. your mother

_____ 21. your father

_____ 22. your siblings (brothers and/or sisters)

_____ 23. close friends

_____ 24. your steady boy/girlfriend or spouse

_____ 25. your high-school classmates

_____ 26. your current roommate

_____ 27. teachers, employers, or fellow workers who know you well

_____ 28. In deciding whether or not to call yourself a shy person, was your decision based on the fact that:
1 = you are (were) shy all of the time in all situations
2 = you are (were) shy at least 50 percent of the time, in more situations than not
3 = you are (were) shy only occasionally, but those occasions are (were) of enough importance to justify calling yourself a shy person

_____ 29. Have people ever misinterpreted your shyness as being a different trait such as indifference, aloofness, poise?
1 = yes

Specify: _____

_____

2 = no

_____ 30. Do you ever feel shy when you are alone?
1 = yes
2 = no

_____ 31. Do you ever feel embarrassed when you are alone?
1 = yes
2 = no

_____ 32. If yes, describe when, how, or why:

_____

_____

(33–36)   What makes you shy?

_____ 33. If you now experience or have ever experienced feelings of shyness, indicate which of the following situations, activities, and types of people make you feel shy. Place a check mark next to all of the appropriate choices.

Situations and activities that make me feel shy:

_____ social situations in general
_____ large groups
_____ small, task-oriented groups (e.g., seminars at school, work groups on the job)
_____ small social groups (e.g., parties, dances)
_____ one-to-one interactions with a person of the same sex
_____ one-to-one interactions with a person of the opposite sex
_____ situations where I am vulnerable (e.g., when asking for help)

_____ situations where I am of lower status than others (e.g., when speaking to superiors, authorities)

_____ situations requiring assertiveness (e.g., when complaining about faulty service in a restaurant or the poor quality of a product)

_____ situations where I am the focus of attention before a large group (e.g., when giving a speech)

_____ situations where I am the focus of attention before a small group (e.g., when being introduced, when being asked directly for my opinion)

_____ situations where I am being evaluated or compared with others (e.g., when being interviewed, when being criticized)

_____ new interpersonal situations in general

_____ where sexual intimacy is possible

34. Now go back and indicate next to each item you checked whether your shyness has been elicited in the past month by this situation or activity:

   0 = not in the past month, but prior
   1 = yes, very strongly
   2 = yes, strongly so
   3 = moderately so
   4 = only mildly
   5 = not at all

35. Types of people who make me feel shy:

   _____ my parents
   _____ my siblings (brothers and/or sisters)
   _____ other relatives
   _____ friends
   _____ strangers

_____ foreigners
_____ authorities (by virtue of their role—
police, teachers, superior at work)
_____ authorities (by virtue of their knowledge—intellectual superiors, experts)
_____ elderly people (much older than I)
_____ children (much younger than I)
_____ persons of the opposite sex, in a
group
_____ persons of the same sex, in a group
_____ a person of the opposite sex, one-to-
one
_____ a person of the same sex, one-to-one

36. Now go back and indicate next to each one
you checked under 35 whether your shyness
has been elicited in the past month by this
person (or type of person):
0 = not in the past month but prior
1 = yes, very strongly
2 = yes, strongly so
3 = moderately so
4 = only mildly

(37–40) Shyness reactions

_____ 37. How do you know you are shy; that is, what
cues do you use?
1 = my internal feelings, thoughts, symp-
toms only (private)
2 = my overt behavior in a given situation
only (public)
3 = I use a mix of internal responses and
overt behavior

Physical reactions

38. If you do experience or have ever experienced
feelings of shyness, which of the following
physical reactions are associated with such

feelings? Put 0 next to those that are not
relevant, then order the rest from 1 (most
typical, usual, severe) to 2 (next most), and so
on, or: –be more specific.

_____ blushing
_____ increased pulse
_____ butterflies in stomach
_____ tingling sensations
_____ heart pounding
_____ dry mouth
_____ tremors
_____ perspiration
_____ fatigue
_____ others (specify): _____

Thoughts, feelings

39. What are the specific thoughts and sensations
associated with your shyness? Put 0 next to
those that are not relevant, then order the rest
from 1 (most typical, usual, severe) to 2 (next
most), and so on. More than one item can be
given the same rank.

_____ positive thoughts (e.g., feeling content with myself)
_____ no specific thoughts (e.g., daydream-
ing, thinking about nothing in particular)
_____ self-conciousness (e.g., an extreme
awareness of myself, of my every action)
_____ thoughts that focus on the unpleasantness of the situation (e.g., thinking that the situation is terrible,
thinking that I'd like to be out of the
situation)

_____ thoughts that provide distractions (e.g., thinking of other things that I could be doing, thinking that the experience will be over in a short while)

_____ negative thoughts about myself (e.g., feeling inadequate, insecure, inferior, stupid)

_____ thoughts about the evaluation of me that others are making (e.g., wondering what the people around me are thinking of me)

_____ thoughts about the way in which I am handling myself (e.g., wondering what kind of impression I am creating and how I might control it)

_____ thoughts about shyness in general (e.g., thinking about the extent of my shyness and its consequences, wishing that I weren't shy)

_____ others (specify): _____

Actions

40. If you do experience or have ever experienced feelings of shyness, what are the obvious behaviors which might indicate to others that you are feeling shy? Put 0 next to those that are not relevant, then rank order the rest from 1 (most typical, usual, severe) to 2 (next most), and so on. More than one item can be given the same rank.

_____ low speaking voice

_____ avoidance of other people

_____ inability to make eye contact

_____ silence (a reluctance to talk)

_____ stuttering

_____ rambling, incoherent talk

_____ posture

_____ avoidance of taking action
_____ escape from the situation
_____ others (specify): _____
_____
_____

(41–42) Shyness consequences

41. What are the negative consequences of being shy? Check all those that apply to you.

_____ none, no negative consequences

_____ creates social problems; makes it difficult to meet new people, make new friends, enjoy potentially good experiences

_____ has negative emotional consequences; creates feeling of loneliness, isolation, depression

_____ prevents positive evaluations by others (e.g., my personal assets never become apparent because of my shyness)

_____ makes it difficult to be appropriately assertive, to express opinions, to take advantage of opportunities

_____ allows incorrect negative evaluations by others (e.g., I may unjustly be seen as unfriendly or snobbish or weak)

_____ creates cognitive and expressive difficulties; inhibits the capacity to think clearly while with others and to communicate effectively with them

_____ encourages excessive self-consciousness, preoccupation with myself

42. What are the positive consequences of being shy? Check all those that apply to you.

_____ none, no positive consequences

_____ creates a modest, appealing impression; makes one appear discrete, introspective

_____ helps avoid interpersonal conflicts

_____ provides a convenient form of anonymity and protection

_____ provides an opportunity to stand back, observe others, act carefully and intelligently

_____ avoids negative evaluations by others (e.g., a shy person is not considered obnoxious, overaggressive, or pretentious)

_____ provides a way to be selective about the people with whom one interacts

_____ enhances personal privacy and the pleasure that solitude offers

_____ creates positive interpersonal consequences by not putting others off, intimidating them, or hurting them

_____ 43. Do you think your shyness can be overcome?
   1 = yes
   2 = no
   3 = uncertain

_____ 44. Are you willing to seriously work at overcoming it?
   1 = yes, definitely
   2 = yes, perhaps
   3 = not sure yet
   4 = no

Appendix **2**

Stress Rating the Effects of Forty-Three Personal Crises

Background

In the 1920's, Dr. Walter Cannon began recording connections between stressful periods in a person's life and the appearance of physical ailments. A decade later, Dr. Adolf Meyer compiled a life chart which specifically correlated health problems with a person's particular life circumstances at the time. This process was refined during the 1950s and 1960s, and resulted in the creation of the Social Readjustment Rating Scale (SRRS), which ranks 43 life crises on a scale of Life Change Units (LCUs). The ratings were arrived at by researchers who used in-depth interviewing techniques on an international sample of 5,000 people from Europe, the U.S., Central America, Oceania, and Japan. Because of the consistency with which marriage was rated as one of the most significant life changes, it was given a value of 50 on the scale, and 42 other life crises were judged in relation to it. Some cultural differences surfaced (for example, the Japanese ranked minor law violations near the middle of the list and jail terms second from the top), but on the whole there was a remarkable uniformity of results, cutting across all national and socioeconomic levels. SRRS sup-

237

porters contend that there is a direct correlation between annual LCUs and stress-related diseases. One of their studies found that with a mild stress level (150–199 LCUs in a single year), health problems increased 37% above the average; with a moderate level (200–299 LCUs), the increase was 51%; and with major crisis level (300 LCUs and above), 79% more health problems occurred. The researchers noted that what counted was the cumulative total, not whether the life changes in themselves were positive or negative.

Rank	Life Event	LCU Value
1.	Death of a spouse	100
2.	Divorce	73
3.	Marital separation	65
4.	Jail term	63
4.	Death of a close family member	63
6.	Personal injury or illness	53
7.	Marriage	50
8.	Fired from job	47
9.	Marital reconciliation	45
9.	Retirement	45
11.	Change in health of family member	44
12.	Pregnancy	40
13.	Sex difficulties	39
13.	Gain of a new family member	39
13.	Business readjustment	39
16.	Change in financial state	38
17.	Death of a close friend	37
18.	Change to a different line of work	36
19.	Change in number of arguments with spouse	35
20.	Mortgage over $10,000	31
21.	Foreclosure on mortgage or loan	30
22.	Change in responsibilities at work	29
22.	Son or daughter leaving home	29
22.	Trouble with in-laws	29
25.	Outstanding personal achievement	28

28

26.	Wife begins or stops working	26
26.	Beginning or end of school	26
28.	Change in living conditions	25
29.	Revision of personal habits	24
30.	Trouble with boss	23
31.	Change in work hours or conditions	20
31.	Change in residence	20
31.	Change in schools	20
34.	Change in recreation	19
34.	Change in church activities	19
36.	Change in social activities	18
37.	Mortgage or loan less than $10,000	17
38.	Change in sleeping habits	16
39.	Change in number of family get-togethers	15
39.	Change in eating habits	15
41.	Vacation	13
42.	Christmas	12
43.	Minor violations of the law	11

Source: T.H. Holmes and R.H. Rahe, "The Social Readjustment Rating Scale," *Journal of Psychosomatic Research*, Vol. 11. Copyright 1967, Pergamon Press, Ltd.

Highest and Lowest Pressure Jobs in the U.S.A.

I n the two-year study conducted by NIOSH (National Institute for Occupational Safety and Health) in cooperation with the Tennessee Department of Mental Health and Mental Retardation, over 22,000 health records of workers in 130 occupations were analyzed with respect to stress-related diseases. The frequency with which these diseases occurred in the various occupations resulted in the following determination of the highest- and lowest-stress jobs.

Highest-pressure Jobs

1. Manual laborer
2. Secretary
3. Inspector
4. Waitress-waiter
5. Clinical lab technician
6. Farm owner
7. Miner
8. Office manager
9. House painter

10. Manager-administrator
11. Foreman
12. Machine operator

Lowest-pressure Jobs

1. Clothing sewer
2. Checker, examiner of products
3. Stockroom worker
4. Craftsman
5. Maid
6. Heavy-equipment operator
7. Farm laborer
8. Freight handler
9. Child care worker
10. Packer, wrapper in shipping
11. College or university professor
12. Personnel, labor relations
13. Auctioneer-huckster

Source: *Occupational Stress*, U.S. Department of Health, Education, and Welfare, National Institute for Occupational Safety and Health, 1978.

Subject Index

Aaron, 44, 45
abundant life, 97
acceptance; as bridge builder, 80–83;
    of Jesus, 136; of people, 136
accepting spirit, 80
agape love, 94, 168
aggressive behavior, 107
Allen, Woody, 65
American Indians, 141–42
Angell, Roy, 116
anger. *See* dropouts, stages of
Arn, Charles, 137
Arn, Win, 70, 137
arteriosclerosis, 114
associate friends, 90
Augsberger, David, 119–21
Aurelius, Marcus, 161

Bahaiism, 186
Bali, 127
bantam rooster, 91–92
Barclay, William, 133, 175, 205,
    211, 224
Barnabas, 64, 99, 172
Barth, Karl, 170
behavior, aggressive, 107
believers, as priests, 44–46
Bellah, Robert, 57
Berger, Peter, 161
Berkan, Lisa, 30
Best, David, 180
biased comparisons, 109

Bible, 50, 137; impact on building,
    41–53; message of compassion, 51
Bible-based strategies, 117–21;
    carefronting, 120–21; forgiveness,
    118–19; reconciled, 118
bigotry-brotherhood, paradox, 125
Bismarck, Chancellor, 206
blueprints for building, 41–43;
    compassion, 46–48; involve
    fellow Christians, 48–52
bonding, 58, 102
Booth, General, 177–78
Brahmanism, 186
bridge building, 30–33, 134–35;
    acceptance as, 81; causeway style,
    134–35; Christian, 215; dedicated,
    224; divine imperative, 222;
    effective, 75–77; efforts of, 221;
    for God, 225; importance of, 220;
    Jesus on, 213; letting go, 81;
    present-day, 213; results of work,
    225; steps of, 224; to God, 225; to
    the defiant, 106–22
bridges; Christian, 215; Chapel, 144;
    characteristics of, 31; Christian,
    213; covered, 143–57; collapse of,
    55; construction, 55; diverse, 223;
    durable, 223; functions of, 30,
    223; Golden Gate, 116, 171; Jesus
    built, 223; love, 218; Narrows,
    151, 157; neglect of, 77–78; Ponte
    Vecchio, 142; relationship, 83;

selecting materials, 55–56; to the distant or indifferent, 139–58; type of, different approaches to, 157–58

Brothers, Dr. Joyce, 210

Buber, Martin, 180

Buddhism, 186

building; Christian, 215; friendships, 101; relationships, 41–53; structures, 72–77

Butler, Samuel, 87

Caesarea, 107, 121

Campolo, Anthony, 75, 213

Cannon, Walter, 237

casualty, expendable, 157

causeways, 123–39

Chambers, Oswald, 197

Chapman, J. B., 116

child abuse, 112

China, 124

Christian community, 196

Christianity, 186

Churchill, Winston, 59

cliques, 61–62

Cole, Donald, 163

Colson, Chuck, 213, 223

commitment, 56–57, 58, 136; in relationships, 58; of time, 59–61; to affirmation, 63–65; to flexibility, 65–68; to Jesus, 202; to love, 167, 168; to risk, 61–63

communicate, 145

communication; positive patterns, 63; problems, 110

compassion, 188, 207

complete friendship with Jesus, 97–98

Confucianism, 186

congeniality, 138

consideration of others, 212

contacts; as bridge builder, 78–79; caring, 79–80

covenants, 202

Crusaders, 107

cry for help. *See* dropouts, stages of

Dangerfield, Rodney, 214

Davenport, David, 106

David, 101–02, 104, 192

demotion party, 64

desensitizers, 145–48

destination of bridge, 82–83

detachment; from unbelievers, 98–99; spirit of, 141

determination, 200

devil, devices of, 177

difficult people, 115

diligence, 202

discrimination, 126

distancing, 141

distant persons, 143

Donne, John, 30

Dooley, Tom, 173

dove, 91–92

drawbridges, 107, 108, 117, 122, 134

dropouts, 151–60; application of principles to, 153; ministry to, 152; skills and attitudes to reach, 155–56; stages of, 153–56

duty, 141

dynamics of effective relating, 135

Eastern religions, 217

Eliot, George, 87

Emerson, Walt, 202

emotional deafness, 109

emotional numbness, 145–48

Emperor Frederick II, 87

Engstrom, Dorothy, 215–16

Engstrom, Ted W., 12, 215–16

ethnocentrism, 126–27

Evans, Gloria, 14, 28

exchange rigidity for flexibility, 116

excuses to cover ineptitude, 210

expendable casualty, 157

faithfulness, 212; as spiritual fruit, 200; God's gift of, 201; nothing can take place of, 200; results of, 197–213

faith in spasm. *See* dropouts, stages of

Father Damian, 138

fear, 129, 131

Fields, W. C., 95

Fine Art of Friendship, The, 215
footbridges, 88, 122, 134
forgetfulness, 131
friends; as bridge builders, 89;
    associate, 90; building, 100;
    committed, 102; manual, 95;
    mentor, 90; personal, 90; pseudo,
    98; upkeep, 101
friendships, building, 101
Frost, Robert, 22, 54
fruit of the Spirit, 15, 158, 161–66,
    221, 224; Christian, 164;
    kindness, 186 ; spiritual, 164, 166
Fuller, Buckmaster, 197

*Gardner Looks at the Fruits of the
    Spirit, A,* 193
Garfunkel, Arthur, 39
gentleness, 212; as vulnerability,
    205; in conduct, 208; in
    conversation, 208; meaning of,
    205; Paul writing about, 207;
    results of, 197–213
gifts of the Spirit, 162–66
give-me generation, 58
Glass, J. L., 176
Golden Gate Bridge, 116, 171
Golden Rule, 186
Goliath, 102
God, the Father; as source of
    goodness, 193; bridge builder, 32;
    closeness with, 180; goodness of,
    194; priorities of, 203
good; being, 194–95; doing, 194–95;
    will to be, 193
Good Samaritan, parable of, 131–33
goodness, 179–96; actions of, 195; as
    generosity, uprightness, 191;
    differs from kindness, 191;
    dimensions of, 190; exuding, 199;
    principles for growth in, 195–96;
    result of, 193
Graham, Billy, 213, 223
Gray, John, 94

Hammond, Peter, 124
Harley, William, 100
harassment, 106

Hawaiian Islands, 138
Hawthorne, Nathaniel, 130
Hazlitt, 123
Hindu, 217
Hinduism, 186
holiness, 164
Holmes, T. H., 146, 239
Holy Spirit, 15, 137, 207, 211
Homans, George, 79
Homans thesis, 78
Hughes, Howard, 60
Humphrey, Hubert, 46
Huxley, Aldous, 166
hypersensitivity, 110

impatience, 181–82
ineptitude, excuses to cover, 210
inflammatory words, 110
inflexibility, 65, 66
influence, sphere of, 79
insulation, 142–43, 145, 224
intimacy, levels of, 89, 167
interpersonal problems, 107, 108
irregular people, 108–22; acceptance
    of, 136; biased comparisons, 109;
    classification of, 111; emotional
    deafness, 109; four kinds, 114;
    mental, 113–14; personality-
    defect, 112; regular irregulars, 111;
    selective blindness, 108;
    sociopathic irregulars, 113; unfair
    contrasts 109
Isaiah, 176, 182–83
isolation, 143, 145, 224

James, 182, 184, 186
Jainism, 186
Jeremiah, 174, 182–83
Jesus Christ; acceptance of, 136; as
    faithful, 201–02; as friend, 96,
    98–99; bridge builder, 33, 34–37,
    213; Christ-centered fellowship,
    91; crucifixion, 166; describing
    the devil, 177; destroying walls,
    27; distance from, 157; farewell
    message, 162; followers of, 129;
    friend of, 96; fruit of his Spirit,
    202; generosity of, 196;

instruction, 76; love of, 170, 211; making disciples, 137; master link, 32; miracles, 163; newness in, 95; opportunity to serve, 114; our bridge to, 80, 193; patience, example of, 183; peace of, 176–77; Savior, 107, 122, 138, 219; source of peace, 175; Spirit-filled followers, 189; spiritual kin, 91; spiritual oxygen supply, 199; transcends walls, 218; walked, 147–48; will of, 168; words of, 147, 203, 206

Job, 157

jobs; highest-pressure, 240; lowest-pressure, 241

Jonathan, 101, 103, 104

Johnson, Barbara, 81

joy; as color, 173; as free gift, 172; authentic, 171; Christ's, 172

Judaism, 186

Keller, Phillip, 189–90, 193

Kincaid, Lamar, 165–66

kindness, 179, 187–89; evidences of, 188; exuding, 199; Paul writing about, 207

King, Marchant, 181

King Saul, 100, 102–04

Kinghorn, Kenneth, 163

Koons, Carolyn, 150

Landorf, Joyce, 111, 113

law; new, 94; of right, 94

Lee, Earl, 13, 95, 115

leprosy, 138

levels of intimacy, 89

Lewis, C. S., 63

Lightfoot, J. B., 181

lilies, 172–73

limbo. it.See dropouts, stages of

Lincoln, Abraham, 88, 98

linkages, 105, 122, 134

Livingstone, David, 190

Long, Jim, 49

Longfellow, Henry Wadsworth, 140

longsuffering, 181

Lord Herbert, 106

love; ABCs of, 170; agape, 92, 168; as a prize, 169; as model to be followed, 169; as object of prayer, 169; between sexes, 167; Christian, 169; described by Greeks, 168; emotional side of, 168; fruit of, 162, 179; kindred, 99; meaning of, 166–67; motivational aspect of, 168; new, 94; of Jesus, 170; passion, 168; spirit of, 170; triangle, 167

Lovelace, Richard, 69

Luther, Martin, 44–45, 213

Maclaren, Alexander, 198

Mark, John, 99

Markham, Edwin, 143

Martin, Dean, 80

Marty, Martin, 125

martyrdom, 202–03

McGinnis, Alan, 179

McKay, Paul L., 123

McNeill, Daniel, 48

meaningful relationships, 143

me generation, 58

mentor friends, 90

Meyer, Adolf, 237

Michal, 103

Middle Ages, 107

Miller, Joaquin, 117

misery index, 165

Mohammedanism, 186

Moody, D. L., 98

Moses, 98, 192

Mother Teresa, 60, 213, 223

Munro, Bertha, 59

neglect, 100, 101

nervous breakdown, 176–77

new aim, 93

new kinship, 93

new rights, 93

Newton, Joseph Fort, 19

nice, niceness, 136, 138

numbness, emotional, 145–48

numbness factor, 148

Occupational Stress, 241

omissions, acts, 93, 131
oneness; cultivating, 134; with
    others, 180
orange, color of, 170–71
Overstreet, Bonaro, 76

Paul, 64, 98–99, 107, 116, 163, 172,
    175, 201, 207, 208, 211
Parker, Andrew, the human bridge,
    52–53
passion, 167–68
patience, 162, 179–96; enduring, 183;
    manifesting, 199; Paul writing
    about, 207; persistent, 184, 186
peace; color of, 173; definition of,
    175; fruit of, 179; inner, 178; of
    Jesus, 175–76; Prince of, 174;
    result of, 175–76; source of, 175
peacemakers, 176
Pentecost, 183
perception frames, 115
perseverance, 183
persevere, as result of patience, 182
personal friends, 90
personality, 73–75; oblivious, 73–74;
    obnoxious, 74; ostentatious, 74
Peter, 98, 116, 207, 211
Philippi, 116
Phillips, J. B., 42, 198
positive communication
    patterns, 63
prejudice, 125–26, 128
priests, as bridge-builders, 44–46
principle of rightness, 94
prodigal son, 81
Prudden, Bonnie, 61
psychic overload, 146

Rahe, R. H., 239
Ramsey, Paul, 168
Reeves, Dan, 214
relationship(s); bridges, 83; building
    of, 41–53; construction of, 76–77;
    cultivating loving, 199; dynamics
    of effective, 135; essential items
    in, 56–68; holistic, 161; rightness
    principle of, 94; specialists, 158;
    value of, 58

reliability, 212
reticence, 130
revolution, inner, 203
Roosevelt, Theodore, 203
Rosen, Moishe, 135–36
Ross, Glynn, 126

saints of the past, 213
Samaritan woman, 34–37, 43
Sandburg, Carl, 39
San Diego's Wild Animal Park, 106
Satan, 26; described by Jesus, 177;
    New Testament, 177
Savage, John, 153–56
Schaller, Lyle E., 128
Schuller, Robert, 63
sealing off emotion. See dropouts,
    stages of
selective blindness, 108
self-control; as virtue, 210; Chinese
    practice of, 209–10; Holy Spirit
    and, 211; Paul on, 211; Peter on,
    211; results of, 197–213
senior citizens, 65
shelving the past, 115–16
Shintoism, 186
shyness, 63, 129–30, 225–36
Sikhism, 186
Simon, Paul, 39
singles, 148–51; ministering to, 150;
    singlehood, 149; single parents,
    148
skunk. See dropouts, stages of
Social Readjustment Rating Scale,
    238–39
sphere of influence, 79
Spirit-filled followers, 189
St. Francis, 213
St. Julian of Norwich, 69–70
Stanford Shyness Survey, 130,
    225–36
statistics, 70–71
steadfastness, 57
Stott, John, 130
stereotyping, 126
stress; events, table of, 146; Social
    Readjustment Rating Scale,
    238–39

stroke syndrome, 114
structures, maintaining, 77–83
Sullivan, Harry Stack, 115
support; as bridge builder, 88; of friends, 102
Swindoll, Charles, 26, 169–70, 172

Taoism, 186
Task Number One, 72–77
Task Number Two, 77–83
television, desensitizing effects of, 147
Tertullian, 203
Thoreau, Henry David, 54, 71
Timothy, 207
Tower Bridge, London, 80
Trotter, Robert, 167, 168
turtle. *See* dropouts, stages of

undesirables, 128–29
unfair comparisons, 109
unkindness, 187
upkeep, 101

Vessey, Bette, 215–16
Vessey, Ned, 215–16
vision, 214

Wagmann, Heinrich, 144
Wakefield, Norman, 208, 211
Wall, The: A Parable, 14, 28
walls; ancient, 23; as barriers, 43–44; barricade from one another, 28; Berlin, 24; caring for, 43–44; destroying those that block, 43–44; functions of, 24; isolate, 28; of sin, 43, 44; physical, 24; self-preservation, 47; separate from God, 25; short, 23; thick, 23, 25–26; thin, 23; turn in on us, 29; Western, 23
Washington, Booker T., 106
Welch, Reuben, 30, 71, 80, 169
Wesley, John, 29, 87, 225
white; dove, 173; flag, 174; lilies, 172–73; peace, color of, 173
White, Jerry, 89
willpower, as leash and lash, 208–09
withdrawing, 145
Wolfe, David, 58
world as alien environment, 198

Zimbardo, Philip, 129–30
Zoroastrianism, 186

Scripture Index

Genesis

1:31—128
9:8–14—32
12:3—79 n. 5
32:22—29 n. 15

Exodus

33:19—192

Numbers

19:11—132

Joshua

2—25 n. 8
2:7—29 n. 15

Judges

3:28—29 n. 15

1 Samuel

16–20—101

2 Samuel

1:17–27—104
1:21—104
1:26—104
19:18—29 n. 15
22:30—39

1 Kings

8:66—192

2 Kings

17:24—34

Nehemiah

8—40, 42 n. 2
9:25—192
9:35—192

Esther

6:8—101 n. 10

Psalms

23:6—192
25:7—192
27:13—192
31:19—192
51:5—26
68:10—192
107:9—192
119:105—42 n. 2
119:165—177

Proverbs

16:7—208
17:17—91 n. 3
18:11—19

18:24b—96, 194
25:11—214
27:6—91 n. 3, 92
27:9—91 n. 3
27:17—91 n. 3
28:1—61
29:18—214

Isaiah

26:3—176
32:17—177
60:18—69

Jeremiah

6:14—174
23:29—42 n. 2

Ezekiel

13:14—54

Zechariah

9:9—183 n. 4, 206

Matthew

5:3—207
5:5—205, 207
5:9—176
5:23—118
5:24—118
6:34—176

7:16–18—164
9:36—46
9:37—182
10:34—176
10:42—76, 188
11:28—64, 145
11:29—38, 205
11:29–30—206
18:4—74
18:22b—119
20:1–15—194
21:4–5—206
21:5—205
25:21—202
25:40—114
28:20—203

Mark

9:50—176

Luke

2:10—171
6:36—46
10:17—172
10:29–37—188
10:33–35—133
10:37—133
15:4—153
15:7—152
19:41–42—177

John

3:16—26, 71
4—34
8:44—177
8:48—132 n. 9
10:4—177
10:10—97, 193
13:21—183 n. 4
13:26—183 n. 4
13:34—51 n. 6
13:35—51 n. 6, 100
14:21—97
14:27—175
15:5—162
15:10—97
15:11—171

15:13—97
15:14—97
15:15—97
15:16—162
16:24—172
17:11b—52
19:26–27—206

Acts

1:8—136
2:42—51
4:36—64
11:23—64
13:52—172
15:37–40—99
17:30—26 n. 10
20:32—42 n. 2
21:28–29—33 n. 18

Romans

1:7—175
3:23—26
4:24–25—165 n. 5
5:1—176
6:1–11—165 n. 5
6—166 n. 7
6:6—27, 43, 165
6:13—166 n. 6
7—165 n. 4
7:14–25—166 n. 7
7:15b—26
7:18b—26
8—166 n. 7
8:1–2—27
8:16–17—26 n. 10
8:17—165 n. 5
8:28—177
8:37—199
10:9–10—26 n. 10
12:1–2—26 n. 10
12:2—27, 198 n. 3
12:3—177
12:3–8—163
12:5—51 n. 6
12:6–8—163 n. 2
12:10—51 n. 6
12:16—51 n. 6
12:18—176

14:19—51 n. 6, 107, 176
15:14—51 n. 6

1 Corinthians

4:1–2—202
4:21—205
7:9—211
9:22—116
9:25—211
12–14—163
12:4–11—163 n. 2
12:25—51 n. 6
12:28—163 n. 2
13—164, 169
13:4–8a—169
14:1—169
15:58—57, 82

2 Corinthians

3:1–4—165 n. 5
5:14–15—165 n. 5
5:17—26 n. 10, 92, 203
5:20—165 n. 5
5:23—193
6:14—98
6:14b—194
6:17–18—98
7:10—26 n. 10
10:1—205
10:3–5—24
10:3–6—165 n. 5
10:4–5—27
10:5—27
13:11—176

Galatians

2:1—64
2:9—64
2:20—165
3:26–28—52
5—165 n. 4, 201
5:13—51 n. 6
5:17—166 n. 7
5:19–21—165
5:22–23—161
5:24—165, 165 n. 6
5:26—51 n. 6

6:1—208
6:2—51 n. 6
6:10—194

Ephesians

2:6–7—188
2:14—33 n. 18, 175, 176
4:2—51 n. 6, 205
4:7–16—163
4:11—163 n. 2
4:15—120
4:22–24—26 n. 10
4:25—51 n. 6
4:29—65
4:31–32—118
4:32—51 n. 6
5:19—51 n. 6
5:21—51 n. 6
6:11—177
6:17—42 n. 2

Philippians

1:9—169
2:3–4—50, 188
2:6–8—32, 48
2:12–15—196
3:10—165 n. 5
3:13b—116
3:14—169
4:6–7—177, 178
4:7—175
4:18—201

Colossians

1:10—194
1:10–11—184
1:24–25—165 n. 5
3:5—165 n. 5
3:9–13—51 n. 6
3:12—188, 207
3:13—51 n. 6
3:16—51 n. 6

1 Thessalonians

1:3—26 n. 10
1:4—26 n. 10
1:6—26 n. 10
1:7—26 n. 10
2:13—26 n. 10, 42 n. 2
4:11—214
4:18—51 n. 6
5:13—176
5:15—51 n. 6
5:23—26 n. 10
5:24—201

1 Timothy

2:4—71

2 Timothy

2:23–25—207
3:16—41

Titus

1:15—100
3:4–5a—188
3:14—194

Hebrews

2:17—202
3:13—51 n. 6
4:12—42 n. 2
4:14—44
4:16—32, 80
5:8—62
5:13–14—42 n. 2
6:10—82
7:26–28—44
10:24—51 n. 6
10:36—117, 182
12:1—183
12:14—93

James

1:2—172
1:3—186

1:17—193
1:21—205
1:23–25—42 n. 2
1:27—188
2:1–4—135
2:9—135
3:17–18—164
4:6—74
4:11—51 n. 6
4:14—59
5:7–8—184
5:10—182
5:16—51 n. 6

1 Peter

1:22—51 n. 6
2:2—42 n. 2
2:4–5—45
2:20—182
3:15b—207
4:9—51 n. 6
5:5—51 n. 6, 75
5:7—116

2 Peter

1:5—211
1:6—211
3:9—158

1 John

1:3—51
1:9—26 n. 10
4:7—51 n. 6
4:12—51 n. 6
4:19—169

Revelation

1:5—202
1:5b–6—45
5:10—45
19:11—201
20:6—45